CASANOVA
GULA

MATT FRACTION
FÁBIO MOON

colors by Cris Peter
letters by Dustin Harbin

book design

Drew Gill & Gabriel Bá

IMAGE COMICS, INC.
Robert Kirkman – Chief Operating Officer
Erik Larsen – Chief Financial Officer
Todd McFarlane – President
Marc Silvestri – Chief Executive Officer
Jim Valentino – Vice-President

Eric Stephenson – Publisher
Ron Richards – Director of Business Development
Jennifer de Guzman – Director of Trade Book Sales
Kat Salazar – Director of PR & Marketing
Corey Murphy – Director of Retail Sales
Jeremy Sullivan – Director of Digital Sales
Emilio Bautista – Sales Assistant
Branwyn Bigglestone – Senior Accounts Manager
Emily Miller – Accounts Manager
Jessica Ambriz – Administrative Assistant
Tyler Shainline – Events Coordinator
David Brothers – Content Manager
Jonathan Chan – Production Manager
Drew Gill – Art Director
Meredith Wallace – Print Manager
Monica Garcia – Senior Production Artist
Addison Duke – Production Artist
Tricia Ramos – Production Assistant
IMAGECOMICS.COM

Matt Fraction:

For Kel
Who heard it first
Who held it longest
Who kept it like a secret and never flinched.
Sorry about dinner.

Fábio Moon:

Dedicated to Gabriel Bá, who drew this bad-ass comic in the first place, setting such high standards, and it made me jealous to the point that I had to go and draw it as well.

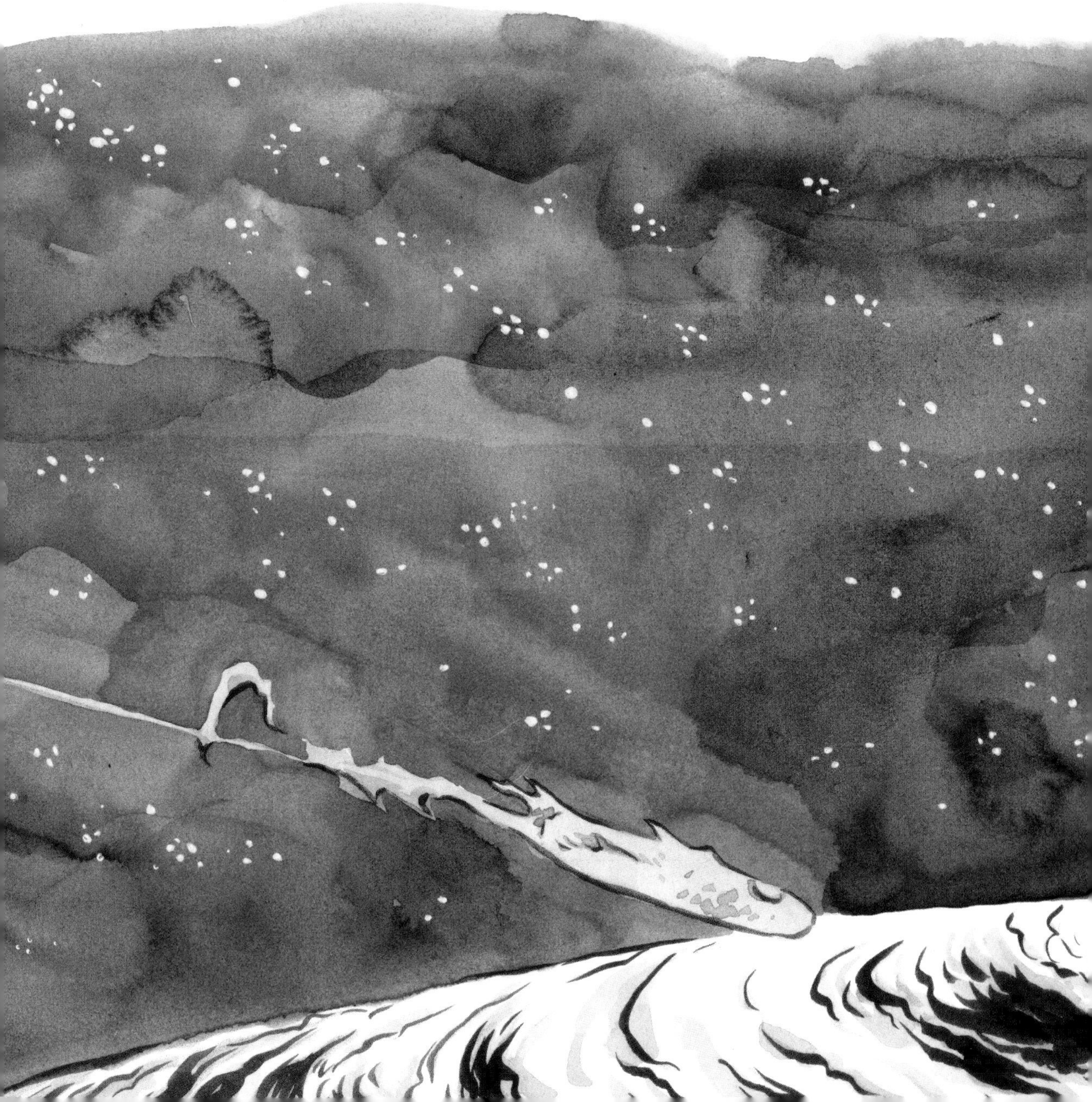

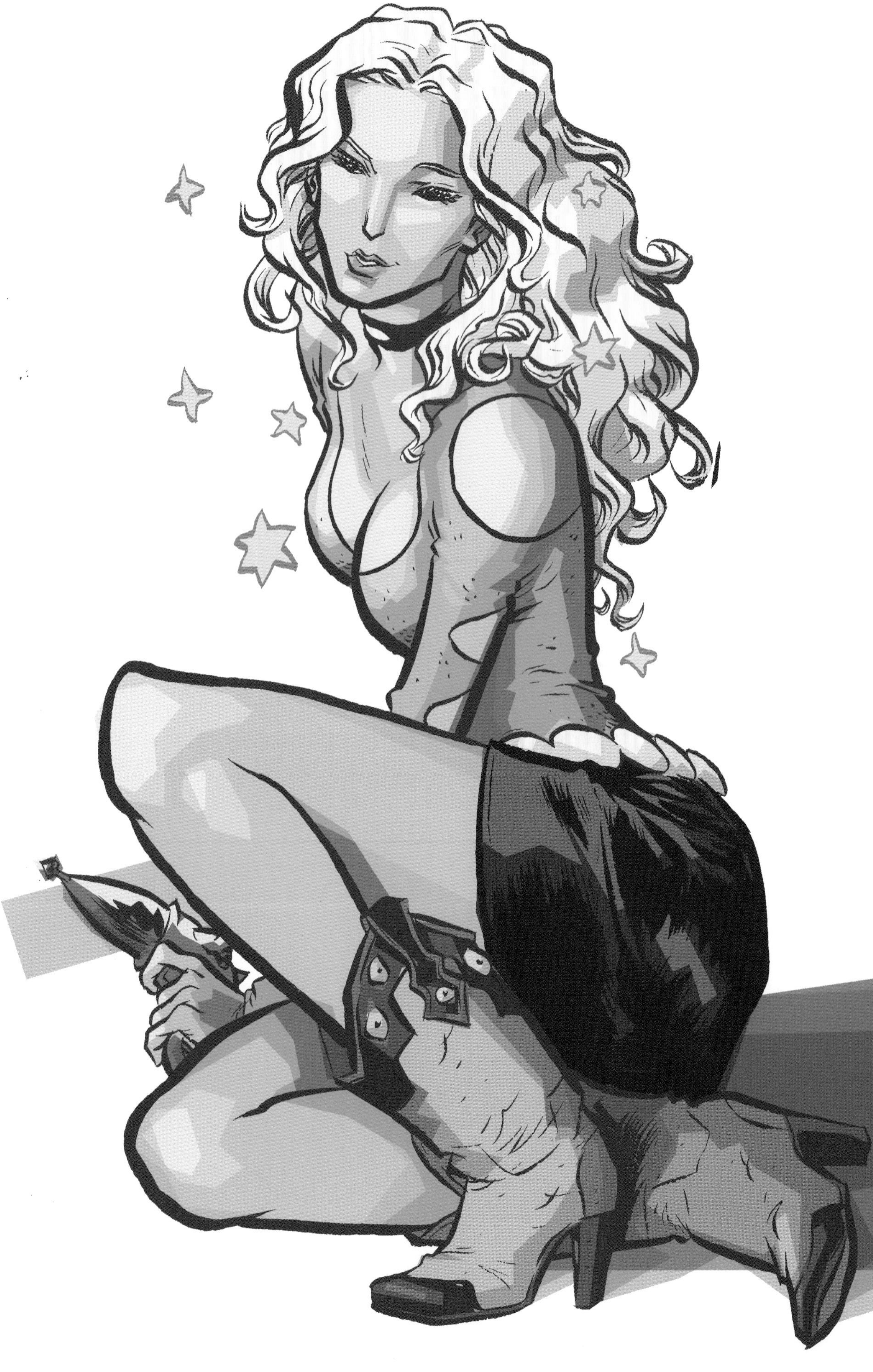

"Only a traitor undresses his
metaphors as if they
were whores."

John Darnielle, 2005

"There was the distinct feeling that
'nothing was true' anymore and that
the future was not as clear-cut as it
had seemed. Nor, for that matter, was
the past. Therefore, everything was up
for grabs. If we needed any truths, we
could construct them ourselves. The main
platform would be, other than our shoes,
'We are the future now.'"

David Bowie, 2002

"You'll stay on the fucking label.
Hare Krishna."

George Harrison,
in a letter to Paul McCartney, 1970

IN MEDIAS RES

WHEN THE WOLF COMES HOME

SEVENTEEN

NAOMI I MOAN

FUCK SHIT UP

SOME OF THE THINGS THAT
HAPPENED TO THE MURDERERS
AND MURDERED AMONG US

HALLO SPACEBOY

DIT DIT DIT
DAH DAH DAH
DIT DIT

BACKMATTER

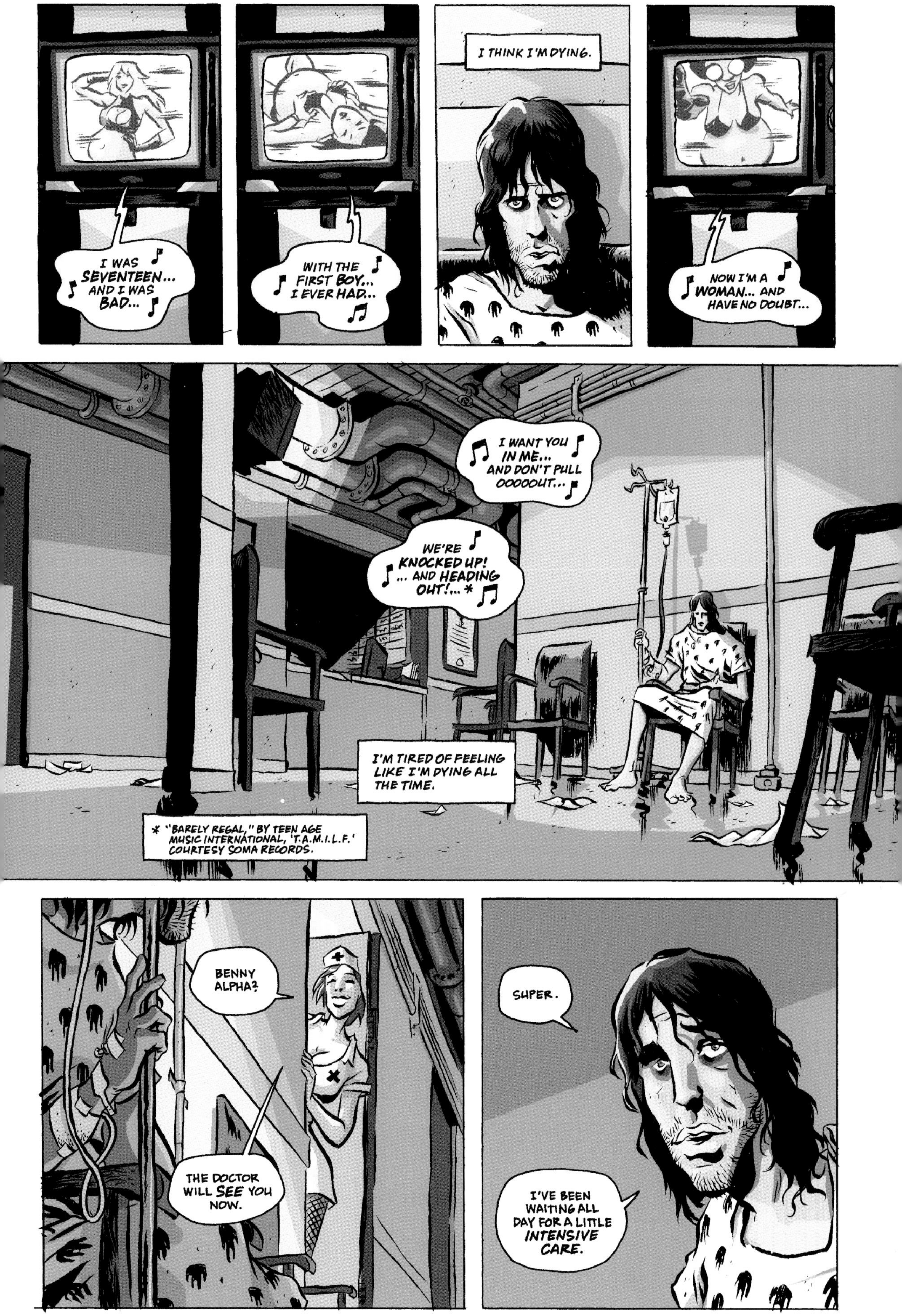
I WAS SEVENTEEN... AND I WAS BAD...
WITH THE FIRST BOY... I EVER HAD...
I THINK I'M DYING.
NOW I'M A WOMAN... AND HAVE NO DOUBT...
I WANT YOU IN ME... AND DON'T PULL OOOOOUT...
WE'RE KNOCKED UP! ... AND HEADING OUT!... *
I'M TIRED OF FEELING LIKE I'M DYING ALL THE TIME.
* "BARELY REGAL," BY TEEN AGE MUSIC INTERNATIONAL, 'T.A.M.I.L.F.' COURTESY SOMA RECORDS.
BENNY ALPHA?
THE DOCTOR WILL SEE YOU NOW.
SUPER.
I'VE BEEN WAITING ALL DAY FOR A LITTLE INTENSIVE CARE.

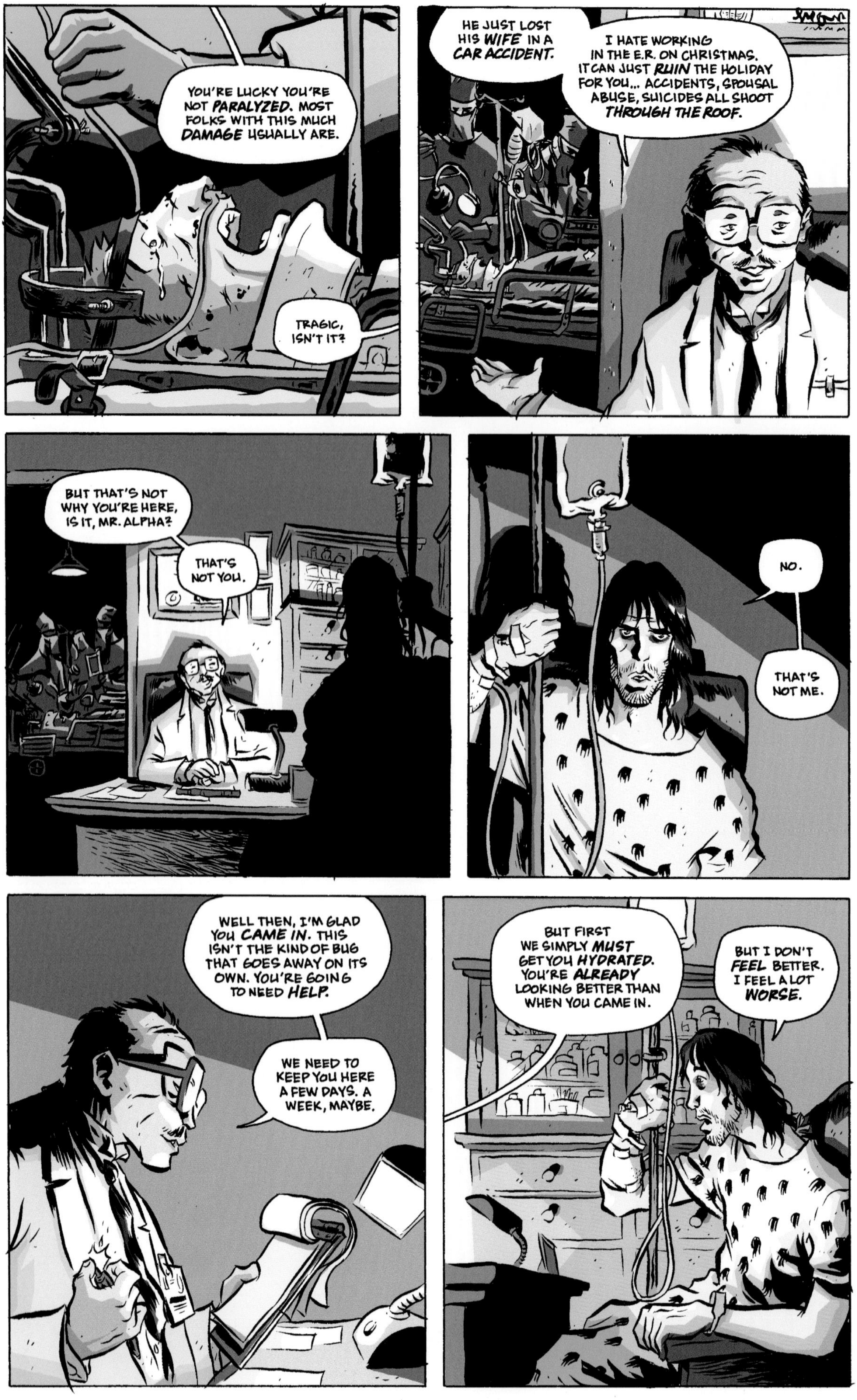
YOU'RE LUCKY YOU'RE NOT PARALYZED. MOST FOLKS WITH THIS MUCH DAMAGE USUALLY ARE.
TRAGIC, ISN'T IT?
HE JUST LOST HIS WIFE IN A CAR ACCIDENT.
I HATE WORKING IN THE E.R. ON CHRISTMAS. IT CAN JUST RUIN THE HOLIDAY FOR YOU... ACCIDENTS, SPOUSAL ABUSE, SUICIDES ALL SHOOT THROUGH THE ROOF.
BUT THAT'S NOT WHY YOU'RE HERE, IS IT, MR. ALPHA?
THAT'S NOT YOU.
NO.
THAT'S NOT ME.
WELL THEN, I'M GLAD YOU CAME IN. THIS ISN'T THE KIND OF BUG THAT GOES AWAY ON ITS OWN. YOU'RE GOING TO NEED HELP.
WE NEED TO KEEP YOU HERE A FEW DAYS. A WEEK, MAYBE.
BUT FIRST WE SIMPLY MUST GET YOU HYDRATED. YOU'RE ALREADY LOOKING BETTER THAN WHEN YOU CAME IN.
BUT I DON'T FEEL BETTER. I FEEL A LOT WORSE.

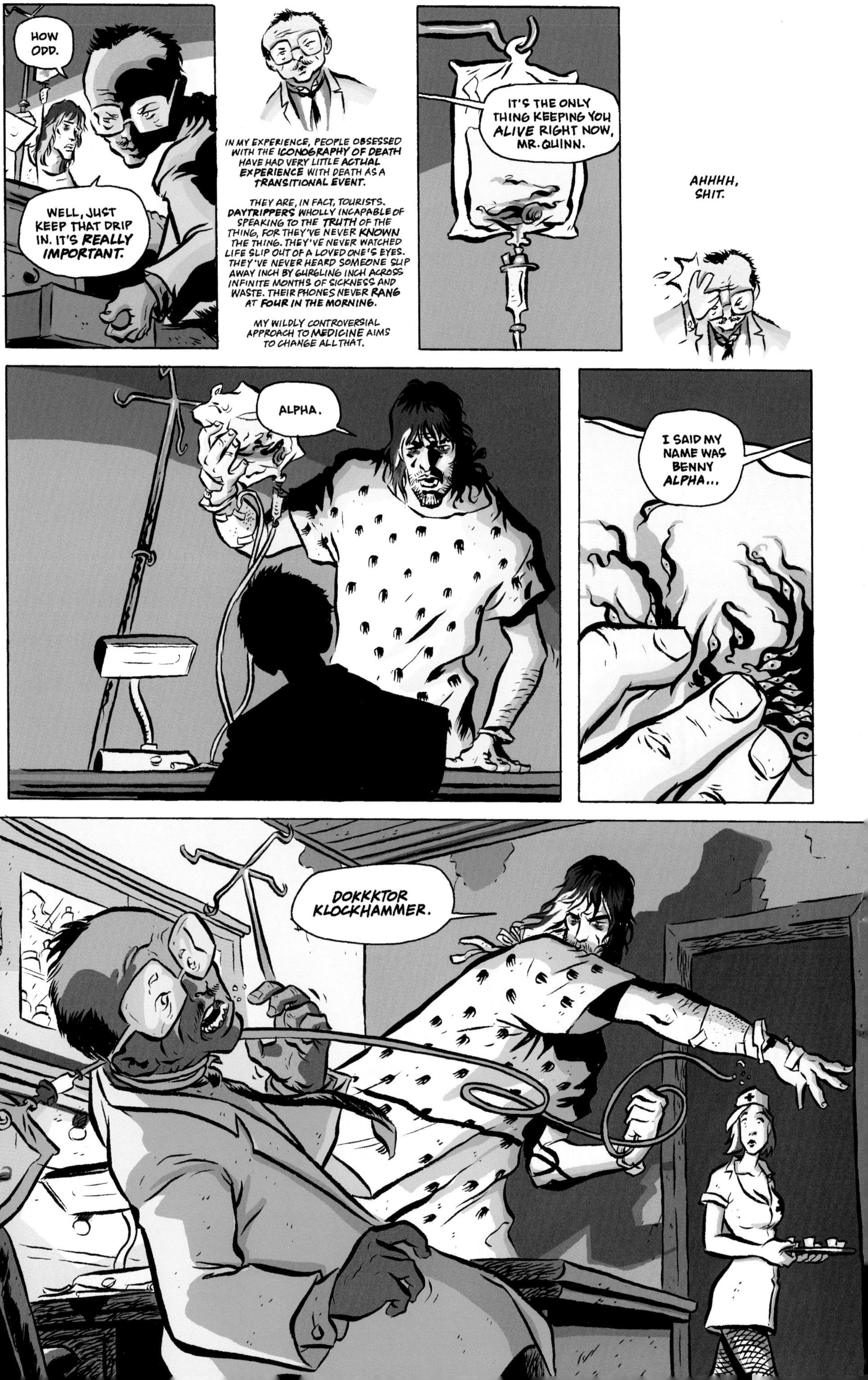
HOW ODD.
WELL, JUST KEEP THAT DRIP IN. IT'S REALLY IMPORTANT.
IN MY EXPERIENCE, PEOPLE OBSESSED WITH THE ICONOGRAPHY OF DEATH HAVE HAD VERY LITTLE ACTUAL EXPERIENCE WITH DEATH AS A TRANSITIONAL EVENT.
THEY ARE, IN FACT, TOURISTS. DAYTRIPPERS WHOLLY INCAPABLE OF SPEAKING TO THE TRUTH OF THE THING, FOR THEY'VE NEVER KNOWN THE THING. THEY'VE NEVER WATCHED LIFE SLIP OUT OF A LOVED ONE'S EYES. THEY'VE NEVER HEARD SOMEONE SLIP AWAY INCH BY GURGLING INCH ACROSS INFINITE MONTHS OF SICKNESS AND WASTE. THEIR PHONES NEVER RANG AT FOUR IN THE MORNING.
MY WILDLY CONTROVERSIAL APPROACH TO MEDICINE AIMS TO CHANGE ALL THAT.
IT'S THE ONLY THING KEEPING YOU ALIVE RIGHT NOW, MR. QUINN.
AHHHH, SHIT.
ALPHA.
I SAID MY NAME WAS BENNY ALPHA...
DOKKKTOR KLOCKHAMMER.

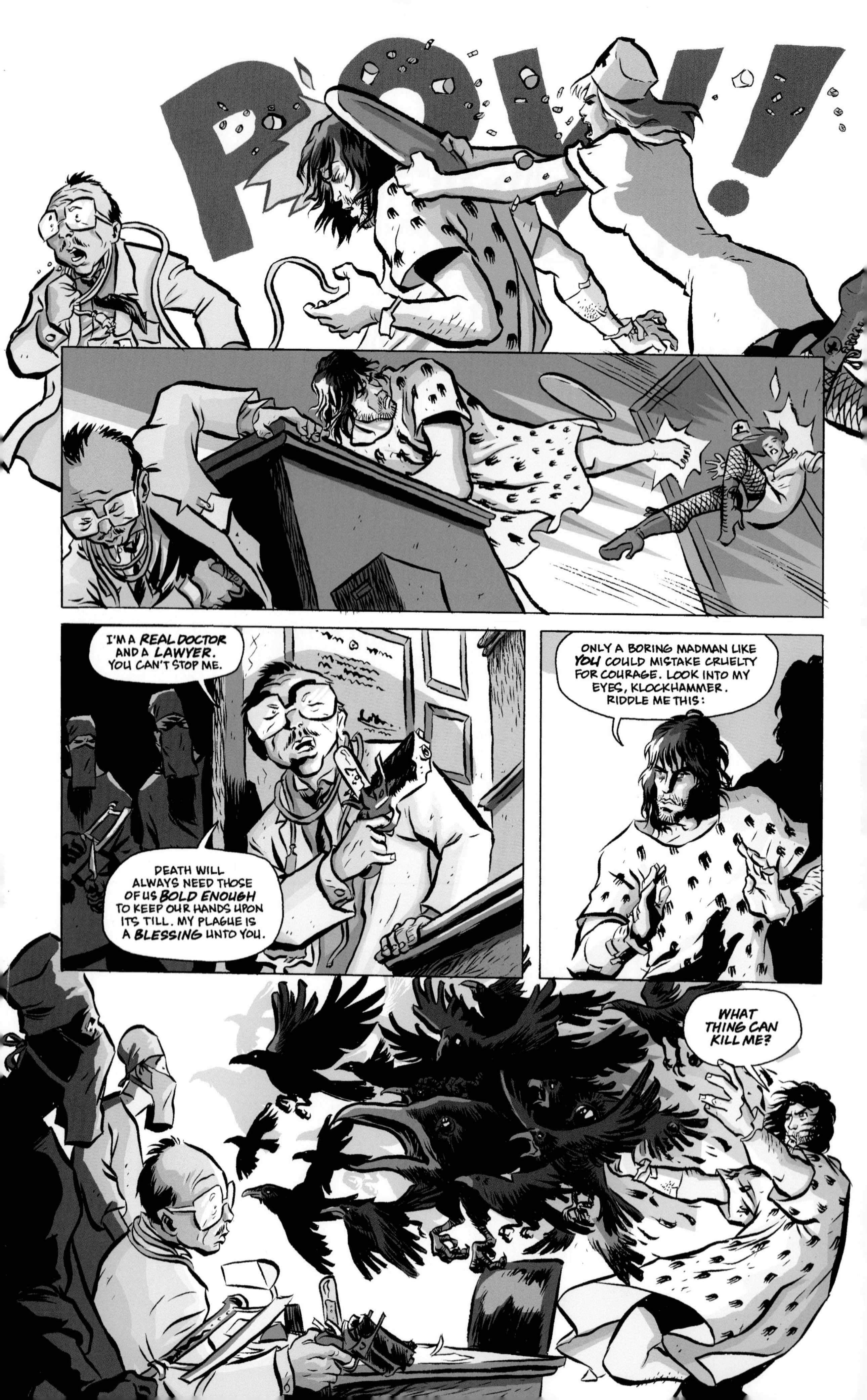
POW!!
I'M A REAL DOCTOR AND A LAWYER. YOU CAN'T STOP ME.
DEATH WILL ALWAYS NEED THOSE OF US BOLD ENOUGH TO KEEP OUR HANDS UPON ITS TILL. MY PLAGUE IS A BLESSING UNTO YOU.
ONLY A BORING MADMAN LIKE YOU COULD MISTAKE CRUELTY FOR COURAGE. LOOK INTO MY EYES, KLOCKHAMMER. RIDDLE ME THIS:
WHAT THING CAN KILL ME?

AAAAAAAAAAAAA--

I -- I'M NOT--

I'M NOT DEAD?

NO ONE EVER REALLY DIES.

WE'RE ALL JUST BECOMING FREE.

CAN YOU FEEL IT, DOC?

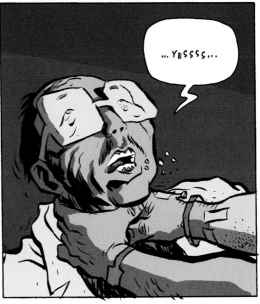
...YESSSS...

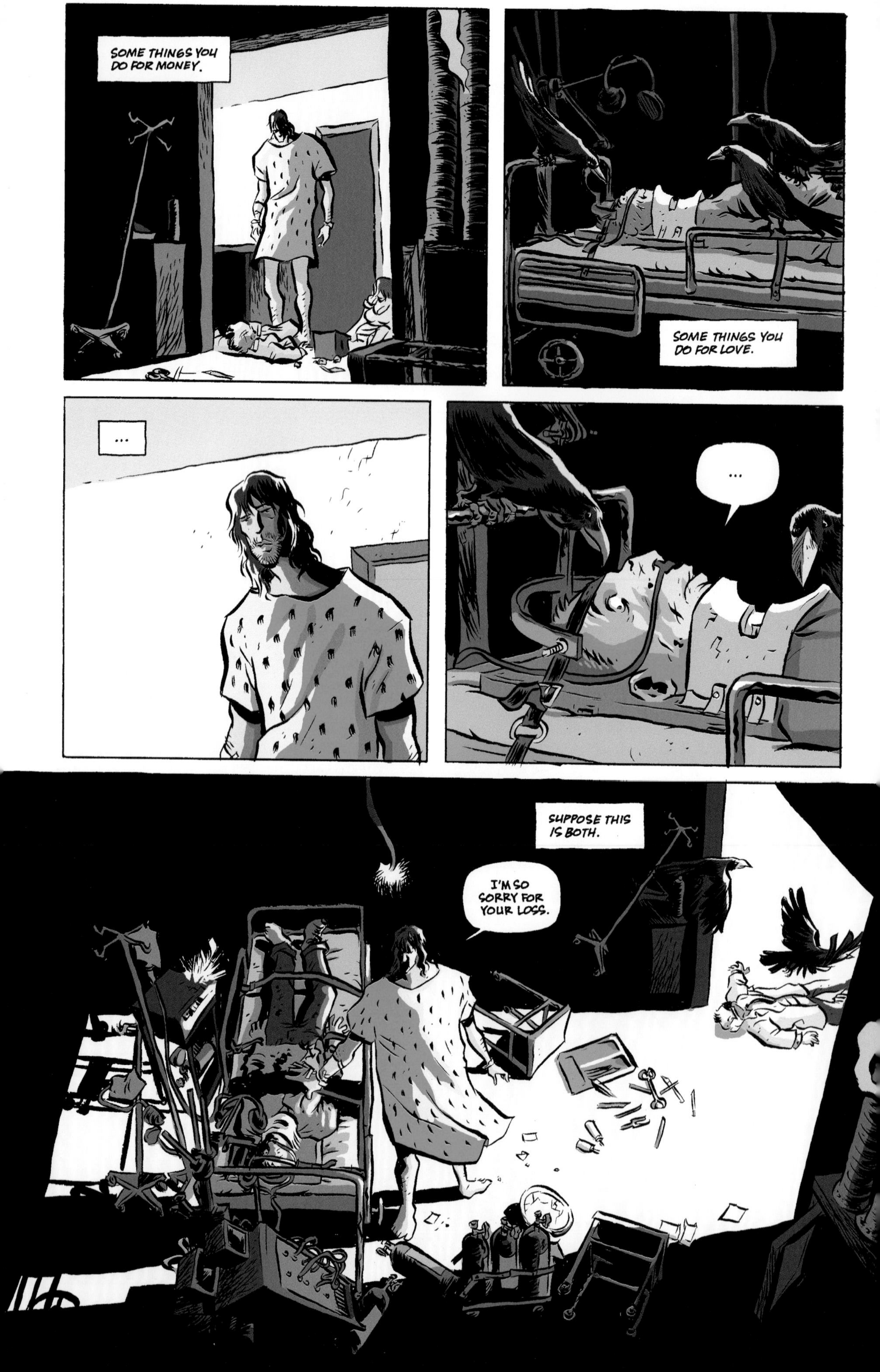
SOME THINGS YOU DO FOR MONEY.
SOME THINGS YOU DO FOR LOVE.
...
...
SUPPOSE THIS IS BOTH.
I'M SO SORRY FOR YOUR LOSS.

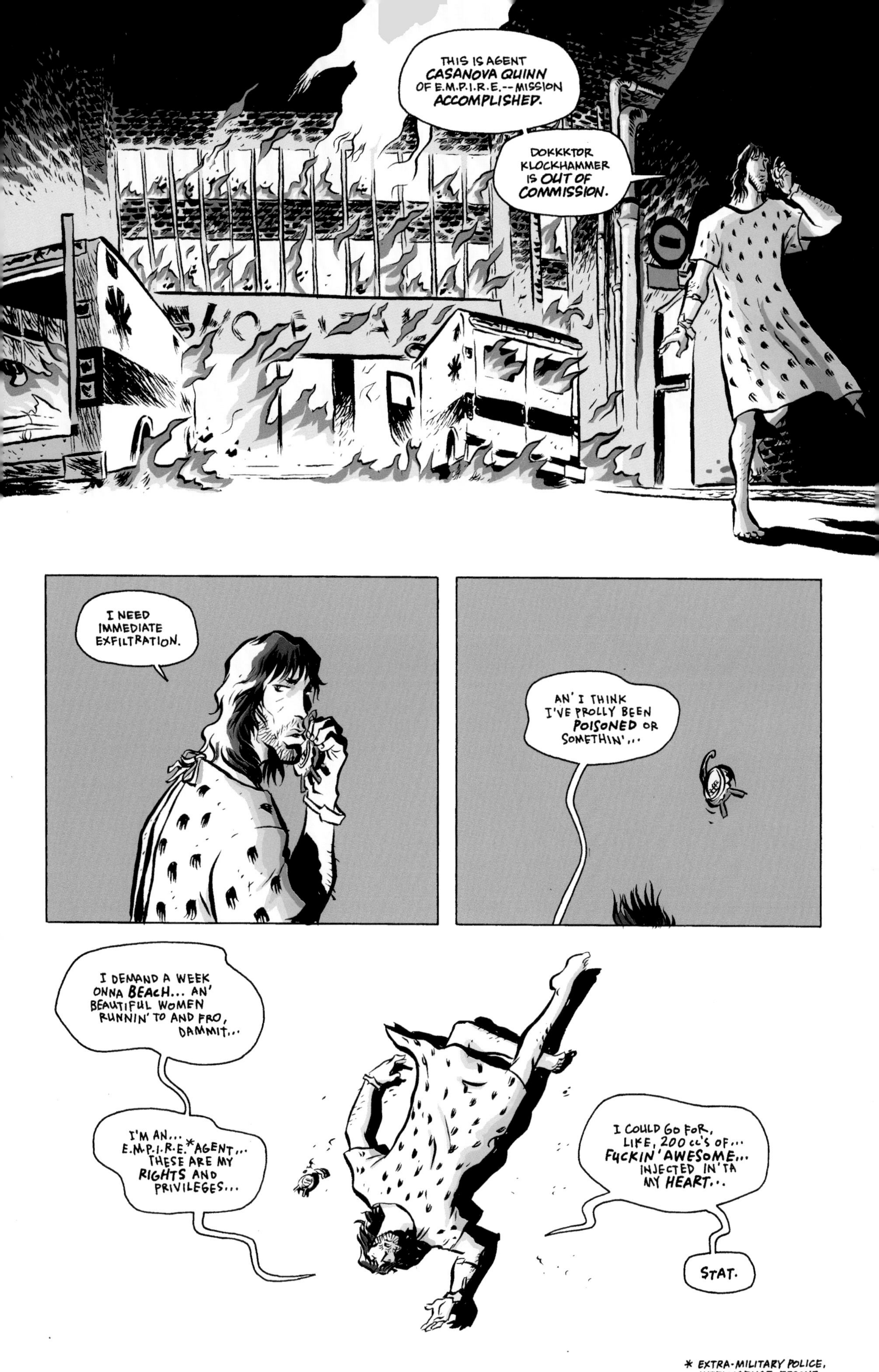
THIS IS AGENT CASANOVA QUINN OF E.M.P.I.R.E.--MISSION ACCOMPLISHED.
DOKKKTOR KLOCKHAMMER IS OUT OF COMMISSION.
I NEED IMMEDIATE EXFILTRATION.
AN' I THINK I'VE PROLLY BEEN POISONED OR SOMETHIN'...
I DEMAND A WEEK ONNA BEACH... AN' BEAUTIFUL WOMEN RUNNIN' TO AND FRO, DAMMIT...
I'M AN... E.M.P.I.R.E.* AGENT... THESE ARE MY RIGHTS AND PRIVILEGES...
I COULD GO FOR, LIKE, 200 cc's OF... FUCKIN' AWESOME... INJECTED IN'TA MY HEART...
STAT.

* EXTRA-MILITARY POLICE, INTELLIGENCE, RESCUE, AND ESPIONAGE!

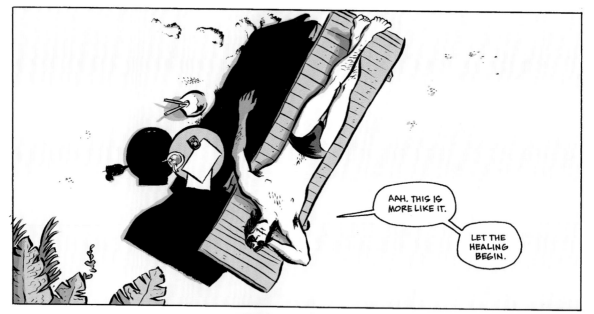

AAH. THIS IS MORE LIKE IT.

LET THE HEALING BEGIN.

RUBY, BABE, YOU MAKE A BETTER *DOOR* THAN A *WINDOW*.

AND IF YOU WERE TO OPEN ME, CASANOVA QUINN, WHAT DO YOU THINK YOU'D FIND?

RUBY BERSERKO, CASANOVA'S MISTRESS OF INTEL AND OPS PLANNING.

INSIDE OF YOU SURELY HIDES ALL OF THE STARS IN THE SKY AND THE ANGELS IN HEAVEN.

I BET YOU SAY THAT TO ALL THE GIRLS.

AS EARLY AND AS OFTEN AS I CAN.

I GOTTA TAKE THIS.

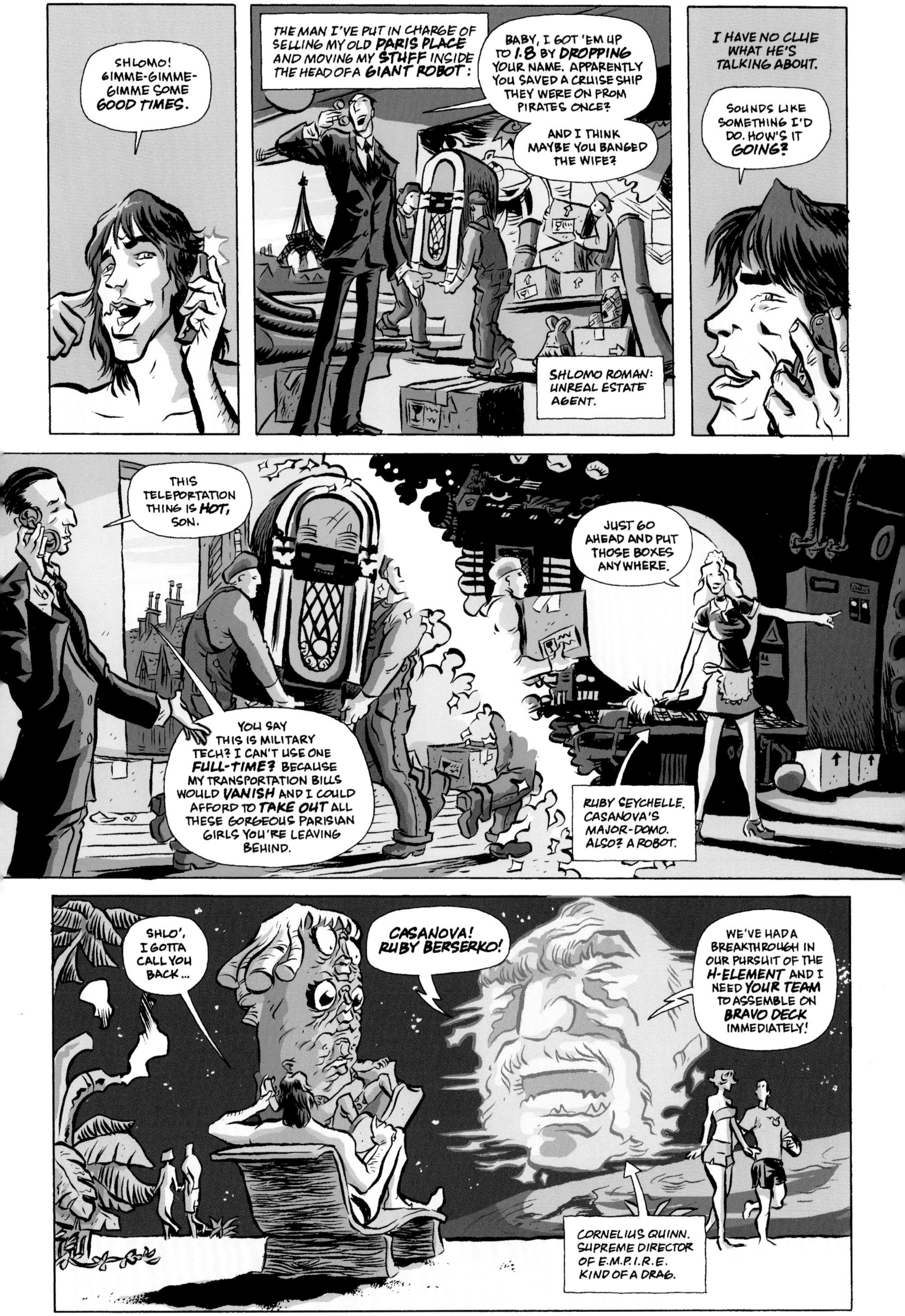
SHLOMO! GIMME-GIMME-GIMME SOME GOOD TIMES.
THE MAN I'VE PUT IN CHARGE OF SELLING MY OLD PARIS PLACE AND MOVING MY STUFF INSIDE THE HEAD OF A GIANT ROBOT:
BABY, I GOT 'EM UP TO 1.8 BY DROPPING YOUR NAME. APPARENTLY YOU SAVED A CRUISE SHIP THEY WERE ON FROM PIRATES ONCE?
AND I THINK MAYBE YOU BANGED THE WIFE?
SHLOMO ROMAN: UNREAL ESTATE AGENT.
I HAVE NO CLUE WHAT HE'S TALKING ABOUT.
SOUNDS LIKE SOMETHING I'D DO. HOW'S IT GOING?
THIS TELEPORTATION THING IS HOT, SON.
YOU SAY THIS IS MILITARY TECH? I CAN'T USE ONE FULL-TIME? BECAUSE MY TRANSPORTATION BILLS WOULD VANISH AND I COULD AFFORD TO TAKE OUT ALL THESE GORGEOUS PARISIAN GIRLS YOU'RE LEAVING BEHIND.
JUST GO AHEAD AND PUT THOSE BOXES ANYWHERE.
RUBY SEYCHELLE. CASANOVA'S MAJOR-DOMO. ALSO? A ROBOT.
SHLO', I GOTTA CALL YOU BACK...
CASANOVA! RUBY BERSERKO!
WE'VE HAD A BREAKTHROUGH IN OUR PURSUIT OF THE H-ELEMENT AND I NEED YOUR TEAM TO ASSEMBLE ON BRAVO DECK IMMEDIATELY!
CORNELIUS QUINN. SUPREME DIRECTOR OF E.M.P.I.R.E. KIND OF A DRAG.

IT WAS WORSE THAN WE THOUGHT-- KLOCKHAMMER WAS USING THE **ELECTROMAGNETIC SUPERCHARGE** RELEASED UPON **DYING** TO POWER AN EXPERIMENTAL **H-ELEMENT GENERATOR.**

AND THE ONLY REASON HE'D BE DEVELOPING AN **EXPERIMENTAL** GENERATOR WOULD BE THAT A **PRACTICAL** ONE ALREADY **EXISTS.**

SABINE SEYCHELLE. ROBOT MANUFACTURER TURNED E.M.P.I.R.E. TECH AND STRATEGY DESIGNER. CHAOTIC-GOOD.

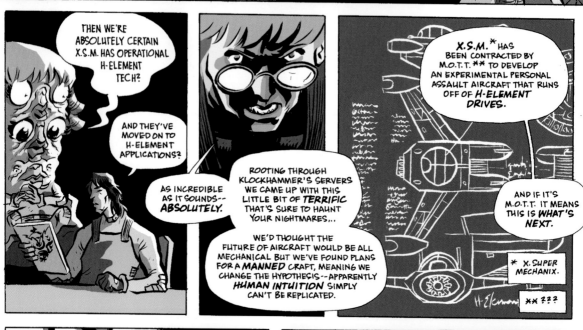

THEN WE'RE ABSOLUTELY CERTAIN X.S.M. HAS OPERATIONAL H-ELEMENT TECH?

AND THEY'VE MOVED ON TO H-ELEMENT APPLICATIONS?

AS INCREDIBLE AS IT SOUNDS-- **ABSOLUTELY.**

ROOTING THROUGH KLOCKHAMMER'S SERVERS WE CAME UP WITH THIS LITTLE BIT OF **TERRIFIC** THAT'S SURE TO HAUNT YOUR NIGHTMARES...

WE'D THOUGHT THE FUTURE OF AIRCRAFT WOULD BE ALL MECHANICAL BUT WE'VE FOUND PLANS FOR A **MANNED** CRAFT, MEANING WE CHANGE THE HYPOTHESIS--APPARENTLY **HUMAN INTUITION** SIMPLY CAN'T BE REPLICATED.

X.S.M. * HAS BEEN CONTRACTED BY M.O.T.T. ** TO DEVELOP AN EXPERIMENTAL PERSONAL ASSAULT AIRCRAFT THAT RUNS OFF OF H-ELEMENT DRIVES.

AND IF IT'S M.O.T.T. IT MEANS THIS IS **WHAT'S NEXT.**

* X. SUPER MECHANIX.

** ???

THIS AIRCRAFT **MUST NOT** BE BUILT.

RUBY, YOU'LL WORK **OPS** WITH US; CASS AND KAITO, YOU'RE THE GROUND TEAM. YOU THINK YOU CAN HANDLE IT?

I LOVE MY JOB.

KAITO BEST. JUNIOR AGENT, CASANOVA'S SIDEKICK. CRAZY KUNG-FU.

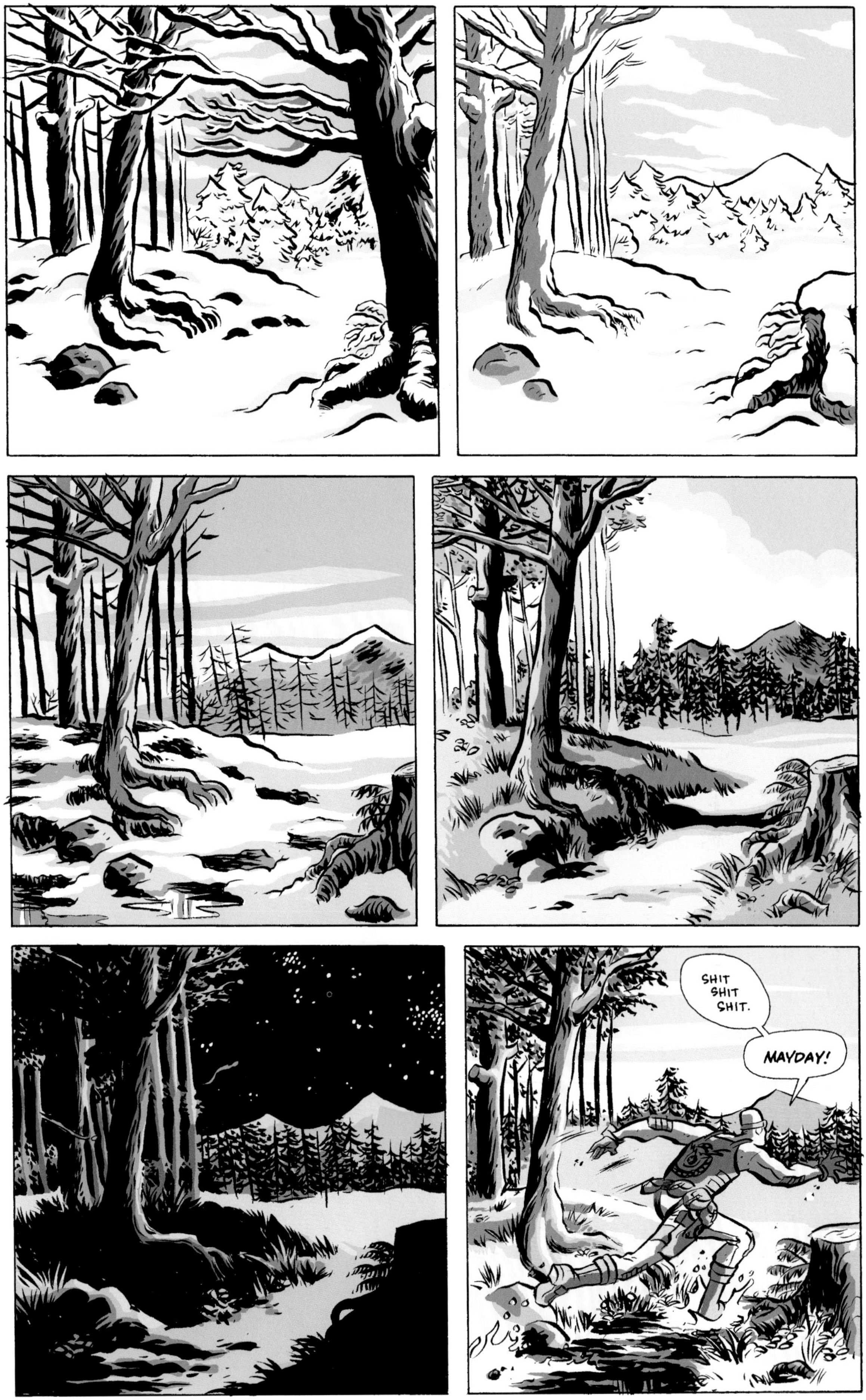
SHIT SHIT SHIT.
MAYDAY!

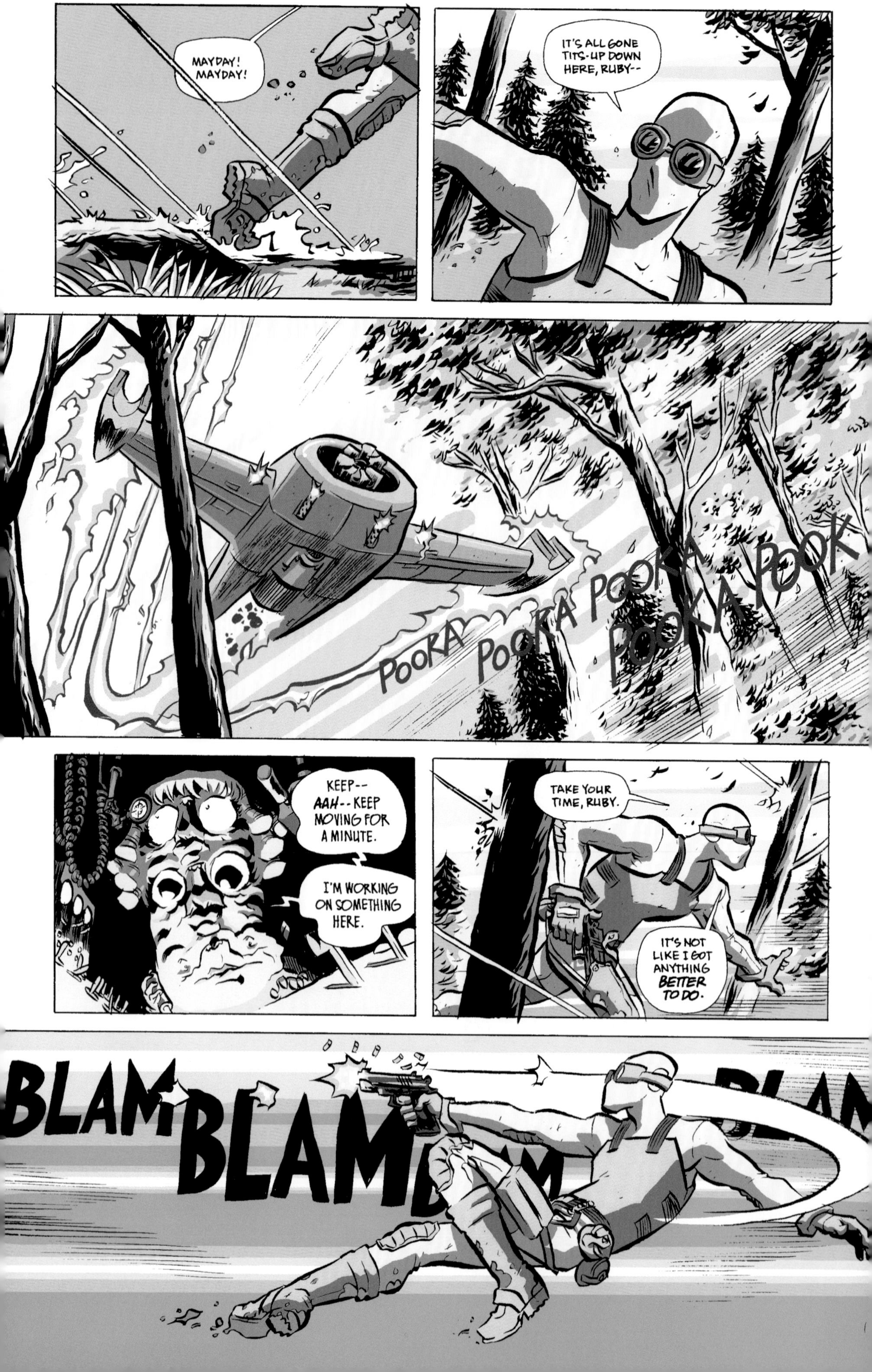
MAYDAY!
MAYDAY!
IT'S ALL GONE TITS-UP DOWN HERE, RUBY--
POOKA
POOKA POOKA
POOKA POOK
KEEP-- AAH--KEEP MOVING FOR A MINUTE.
I'M WORKING ON SOMETHING HERE.
TAKE YOUR TIME, RUBY.
IT'S NOT LIKE I GOT ANYTHING BETTER TO DO.
BLAM
BLAM

WELLLLLLL...

THAT DIDN'T REALLY WORK.

RUBY!

GODDAMMIT!

WE'RE ALL SET DOWN BELOW.

OKAY--WELL--WELL, THIS IS THE FIRST TIME I'VE EVER *DONE* THIS.

HOLD *ON*, OKAY?

I ALWAYS BELIEVED IN YOU.

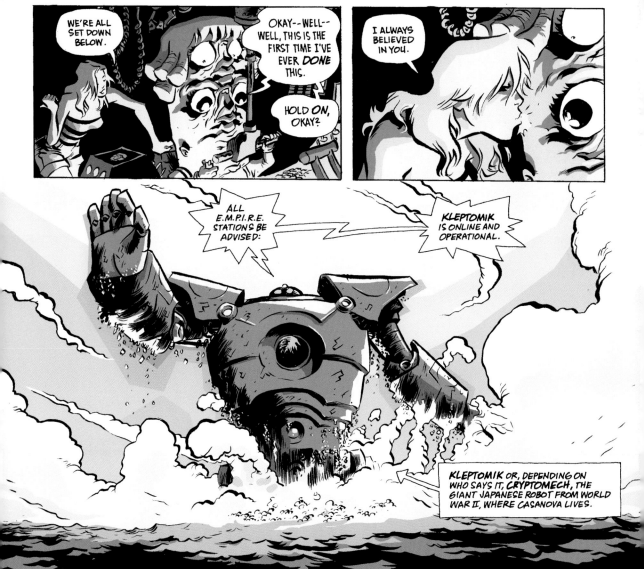

ALL E.M.P.I.R.E. STATIONS BE ADVISED:

KLEPTOMIK IS ONLINE AND OPERATIONAL.

KLEPTOMIK OR, DEPENDING ON WHO SAYS IT, *CRYPTOMECH*, THE GIANT JAPANESE ROBOT FROM WORLD WAR II, WHERE CASANOVA LIVES.

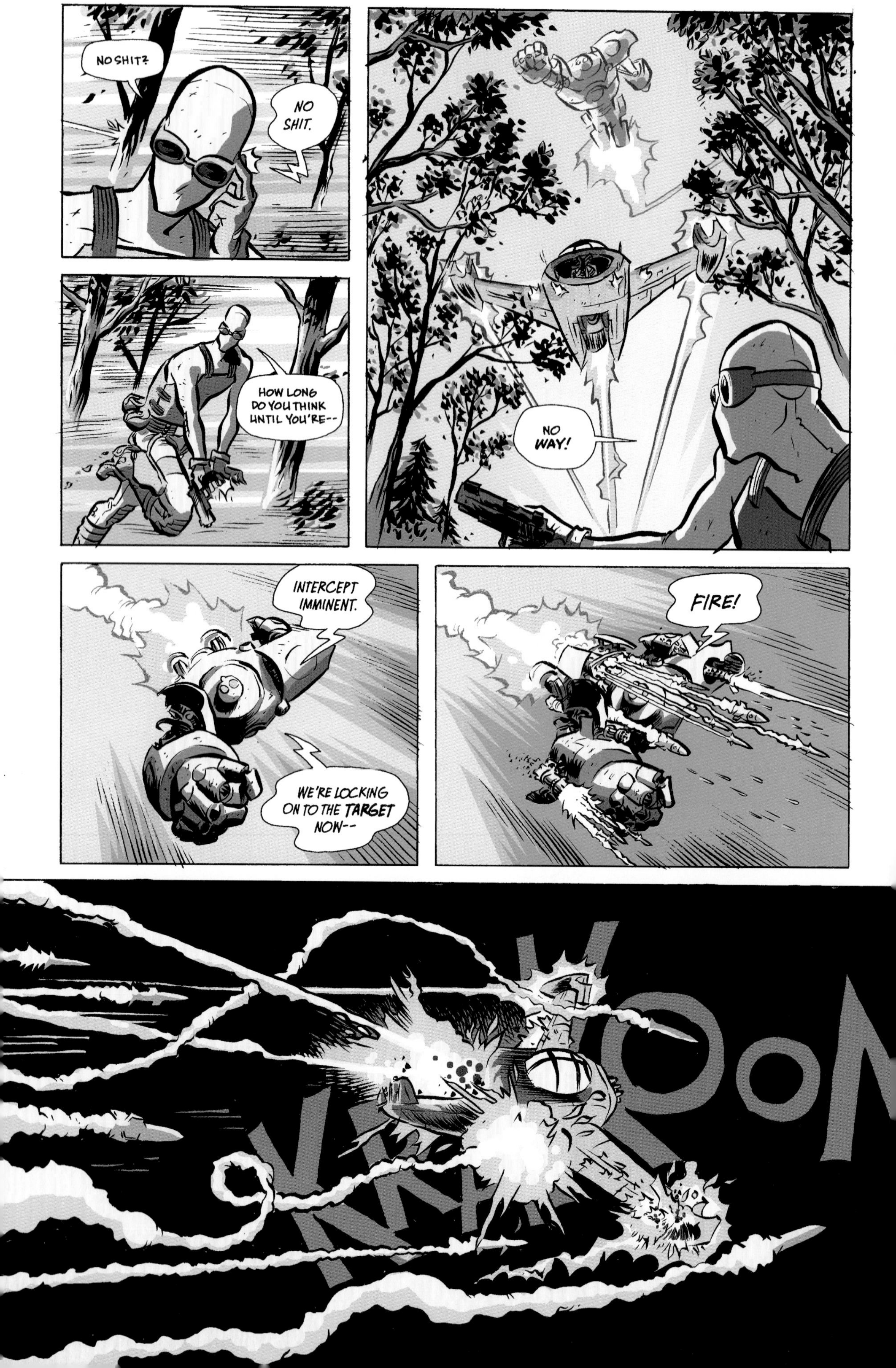
NO SHIT?
NO SHIT.
HOW LONG DO YOU THINK UNTIL YOU'RE--
NO WAY!
INTERCEPT IMMINENT.
WE'RE LOCKING ON TO THE TARGET NOW--
FIRE!
VVVVOOOM

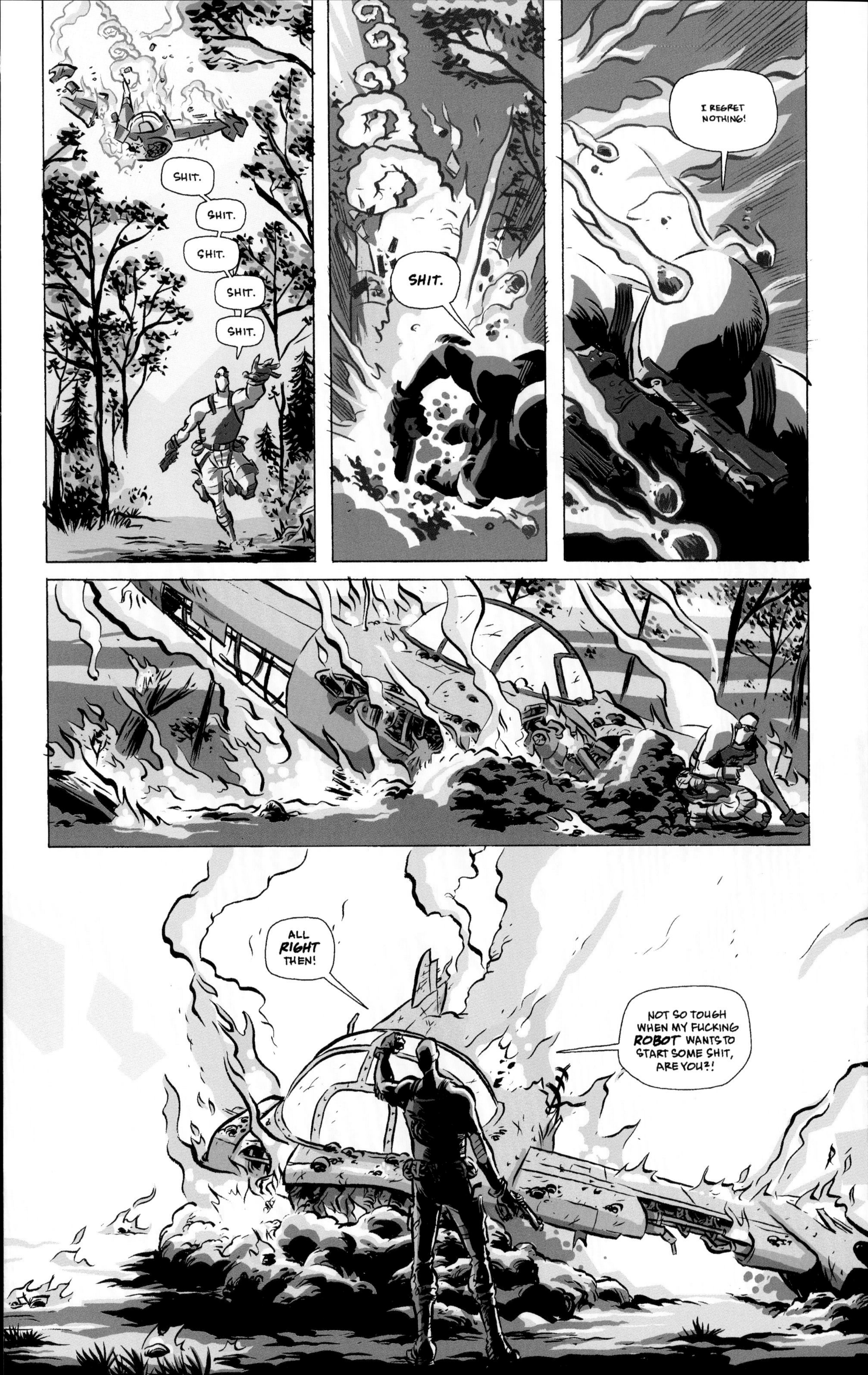
SHIT.
SHIT.
SHIT.
SHIT.
SHIT.
SHIT.
I REGRET NOTHING!
ALL RIGHT THEN!
NOT SO TOUGH WHEN MY FUCKING ROBOT WANTS TO START SOME SHIT, ARE YOU?!

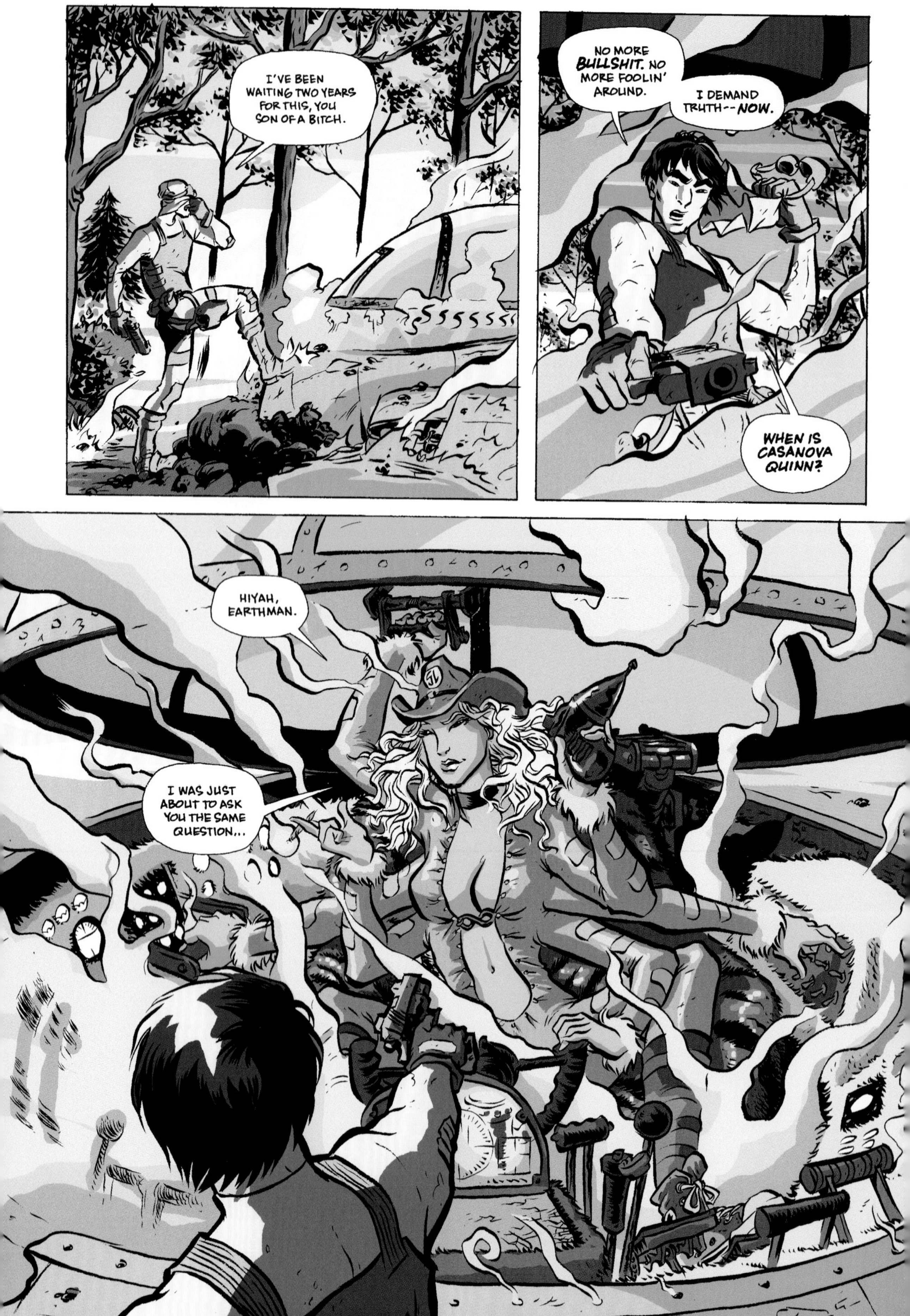
I'VE BEEN WAITING TWO YEARS FOR THIS, YOU SON OF A BITCH.
NO MORE BULLSHIT. NO MORE FOOLIN' AROUND.
I DEMAND TRUTH--NOW.
WHEN IS CASANOVA QUINN?
HIYAH, EARTHMAN.
I WAS JUST ABOUT TO ASK YOU THE SAME QUESTION...
FÁBIO 2007

IN MEDIAS RES

WHEN THE WOLF COMES HOME

SEVENTEEN

NAOMI I MOAN

FUCK SHIT UP

SOME OF THE THINGS THAT
HAPPENED TO THE MURDERERS
AND MURDERED AMONG US

HALLO SPACEBOY

DIT DIT DIT
DAH DAH DAH
DIT DIT

BACKMATTER

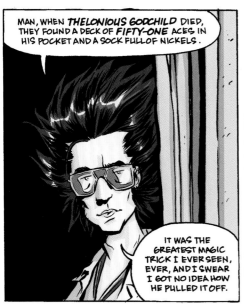

MAN, WHEN *THELONIOUS GODCHILD* DIED, THEY FOUND A DECK OF *FIFTY-ONE* ACES IN HIS POCKET AND A SOCK FULL OF NICKELS.

IT WAS THE GREATEST MAGIC TRICK I EVER SEEN, EVER, AND I SWEAR I GOT NO IDEA HOW HE PULLED IT OFF.

KUBARK BENDAY:

TERRORIST. INTERNATIONAL ART THIEF. POTENTIAL LOVE INTEREST.

OF COURSE, WHEN NOBODY SAYS HE CAME *BACK* THEY FOUND THE MISSING CARD AND A CHIT-TON OF ACELESS DECKS, BUT WHATEVER, MAN.

NOTHING NOBODY SAYS CAN TAKE THAT GAG AWAY FROM HIM, YOU KNOW?

THAT WAS A MAGIC TRICK.

THIS... I DUNNO *WHAT* THIS IS.

...WHAT ARE YOU TALKING ABOUT?

RAZZLE-DAZZLE, GIRL, YOU KNOW? SHOWMANSHIP. THE OLD PA-ZOW.

ZEPHYR QUINN.

TOTALLY NOT CASANOVA QUINN.

YEAH--WAIT. PA-ZOW? NO. SORRY-- NO.

...WITNESSING ORGIES OF *SUPER-VIOLENCE* ALWAYS MAKES ME A LITTLE TETCHY.

YOU SHOULD'A JOINED ME FOR SOME. WOULD'A TOOK THAT EDGE OFF.

YOU HUNGRY?

"SIFERS VALOMILK, THE *ORIGINAL* 'FLOWING CENTER' *CANDY CUPS*," RUSSELL SIFERS CANDY CO., MERRIAM, KANSAS.

MERRIAM, *KANSAS!* THEY SHOULD CALL THAT PLACE *DELICIOUS CITY*.

DAVID? YOU STILL IN THERE, DAVID?

I'M THE GREATEST ESCAPE ARTIST IN THE WORLD. I'M THE--

DAVID?

--GREATEST ESCAPE ARTIST IN THE WORLD, I'M THE GREATEST--

IT'S A *LOCKED ROOM*, DAVID, AN *ACTUAL* LOCKED ROOM. THERE'S LITERALLY NO WAY OUT.

WE'RE GOING TO GET *THE LIST* FROM YOU ONE WAY OR THE OTHER. AND THAT WAY IS UP TO YOU.

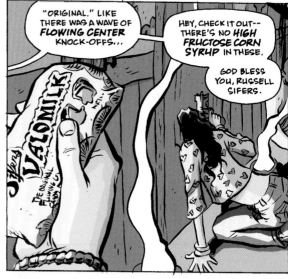

"ORIGINAL." LIKE THERE WAS A WAVE OF *FLOWING CENTER* KNOCK-OFFS...

HEY, CHECK IT OUT-- THERE'S NO *HIGH FRUCTOSE CORN SYRUP* IN THESE.

GOD BLESS YOU, RUSSELL SIFERS.

DAVID. QUIT--

TAP

WASTING--

TAP

MY--

TAP TAP

TIME.

TOK

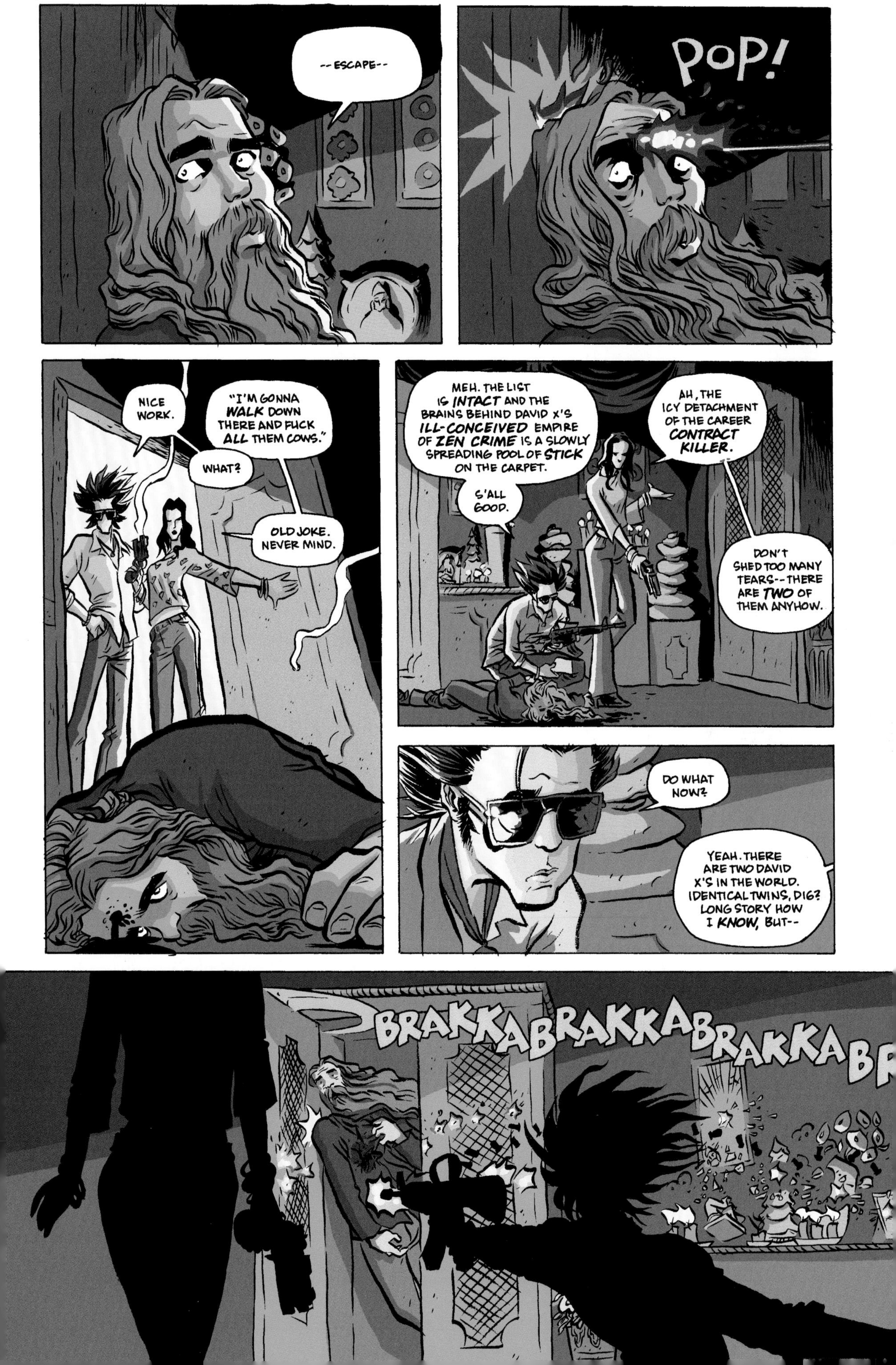
--ESCAPE--
POP!
NICE WORK.
"I'M GONNA WALK DOWN THERE AND FUCK ALL THEM COWS."
WHAT?
OLD JOKE. NEVER MIND.
MEH. THE LIST IS INTACT AND THE BRAINS BEHIND DAVID X'S ILL-CONCEIVED EMPIRE OF ZEN CRIME IS A SLOWLY SPREADING POOL OF STICK ON THE CARPET.
S'ALL GOOD.
AH, THE ICY DETACHMENT OF THE CAREER CONTRACT KILLER.
DON'T SHED TOO MANY TEARS--THERE ARE TWO OF THEM ANYHOW.
DO WHAT NOW?
YEAH. THERE ARE TWO DAVID X'S IN THE WORLD. IDENTICAL TWINS, DIG? LONG STORY HOW I KNOW, BUT--
BRAKKABRAKKABRAKKABR

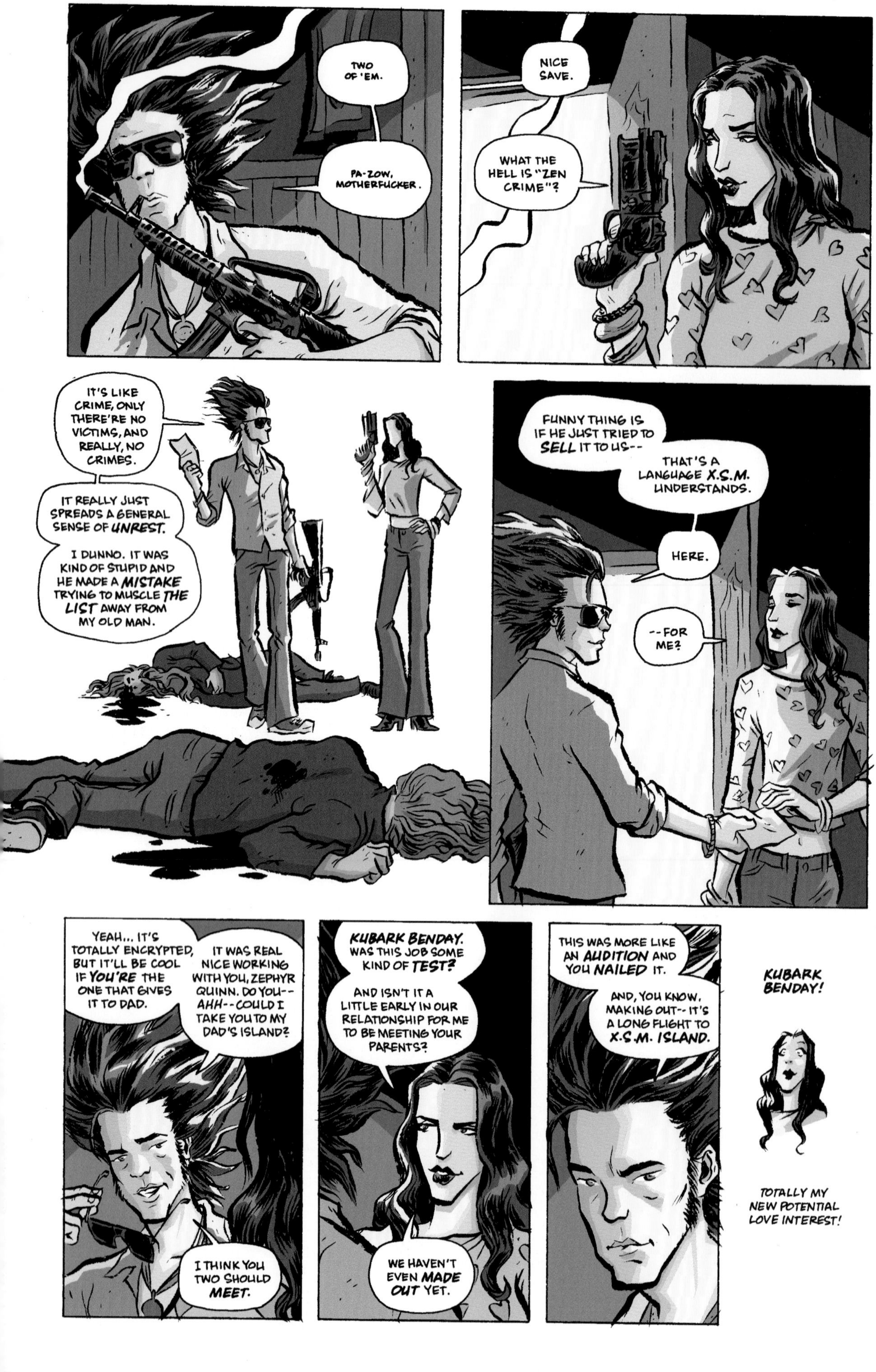
TWO OF 'EM.
PA-ZOW, MOTHERFUCKER.
NICE SAVE.
WHAT THE HELL IS "ZEN CRIME"?
IT'S LIKE CRIME, ONLY THERE'RE NO VICTIMS, AND REALLY, NO CRIMES.
IT REALLY JUST SPREADS A GENERAL SENSE OF UNREST.
I DUNNO. IT WAS KIND OF STUPID AND HE MADE A MISTAKE TRYING TO MUSCLE THE LIST AWAY FROM MY OLD MAN.
FUNNY THING IS IF HE JUST TRIED TO SELL IT TO US--
THAT'S A LANGUAGE X.S.M. UNDERSTANDS.
HERE.
--FOR ME?
YEAH... IT'S TOTALLY ENCRYPTED, BUT IT'LL BE COOL IF YOU'RE THE ONE THAT GIVES IT TO DAD.
IT WAS REAL NICE WORKING WITH YOU, ZEPHYR QUINN. DO YOU-- AHH--COULD I TAKE YOU TO MY DAD'S ISLAND?
I THINK YOU TWO SHOULD MEET.
KUBARK BENDAY. WAS THIS JOB SOME KIND OF TEST?
AND ISN'T IT A LITTLE EARLY IN OUR RELATIONSHIP FOR ME TO BE MEETING YOUR PARENTS?
WE HAVEN'T EVEN MADE OUT YET.
THIS WAS MORE LIKE AN AUDITION AND YOU NAILED IT.
AND, YOU KNOW, MAKING OUT-- IT'S A LONG FLIGHT TO X.S.M. ISLAND.
KUBARK BENDAY!
TOTALLY MY NEW POTENTIAL LOVE INTEREST!

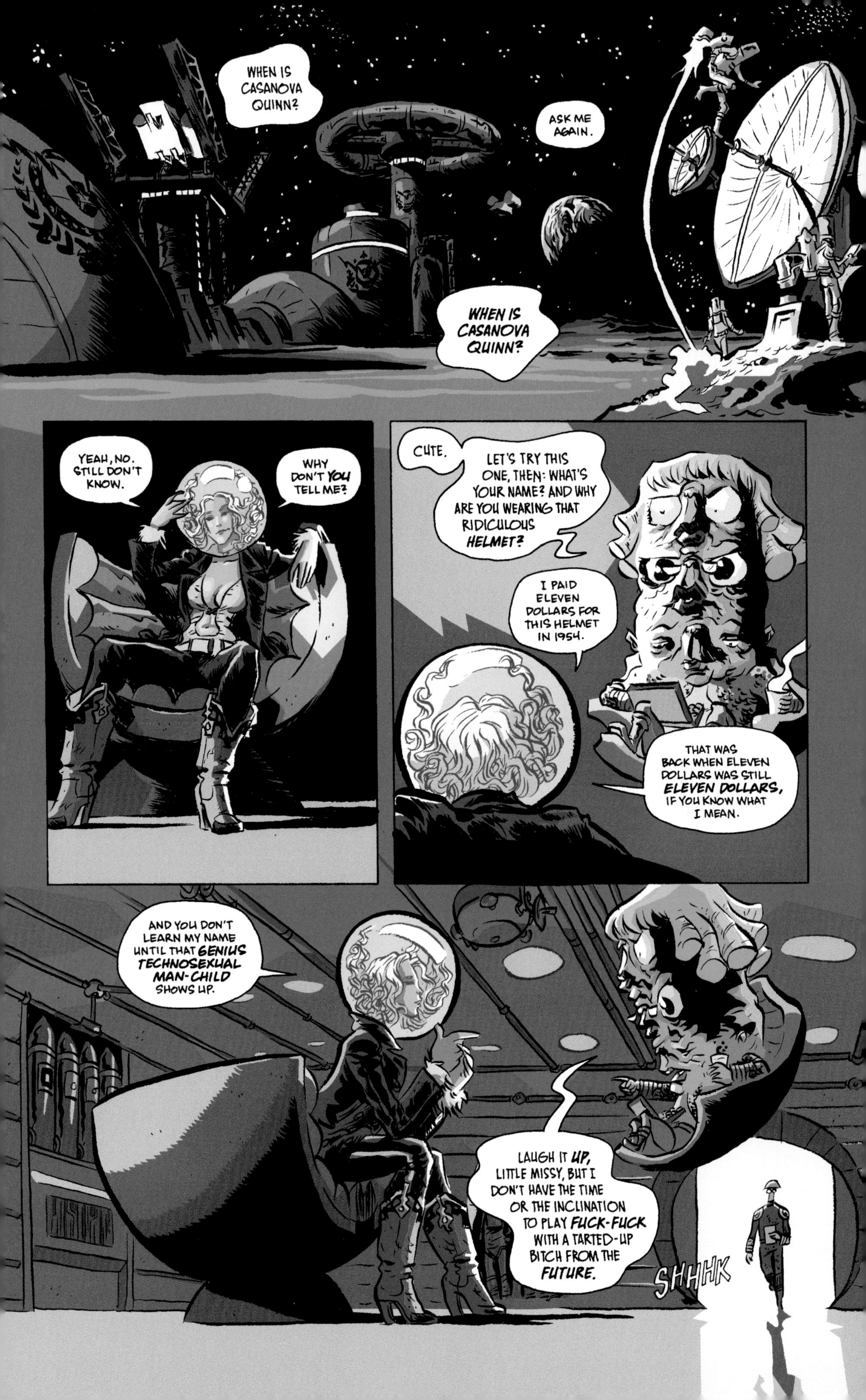
WHEN IS CASANOVA QUINN?
ASK ME AGAIN.
WHEN IS CASANOVA QUINN?
YEAH, NO. STILL DON'T KNOW.
WHY DON'T YOU TELL ME?
CUTE.
LET'S TRY THIS ONE, THEN: WHAT'S YOUR NAME? AND WHY ARE YOU WEARING THAT RIDICULOUS HELMET?
I PAID ELEVEN DOLLARS FOR THIS HELMET IN 1954.
THAT WAS BACK WHEN ELEVEN DOLLARS WAS STILL ELEVEN DOLLARS, IF YOU KNOW WHAT I MEAN.
AND YOU DON'T LEARN MY NAME UNTIL THAT GENIUS TECHNOSEXUAL MAN-CHILD SHOWS UP.
LAUGH IT UP, LITTLE MISSY, BUT I DON'T HAVE THE TIME OR THE INCLINATION TO PLAY FUCK-FUCK WITH A TARTED-UP BITCH FROM THE FUTURE.
SHHHK

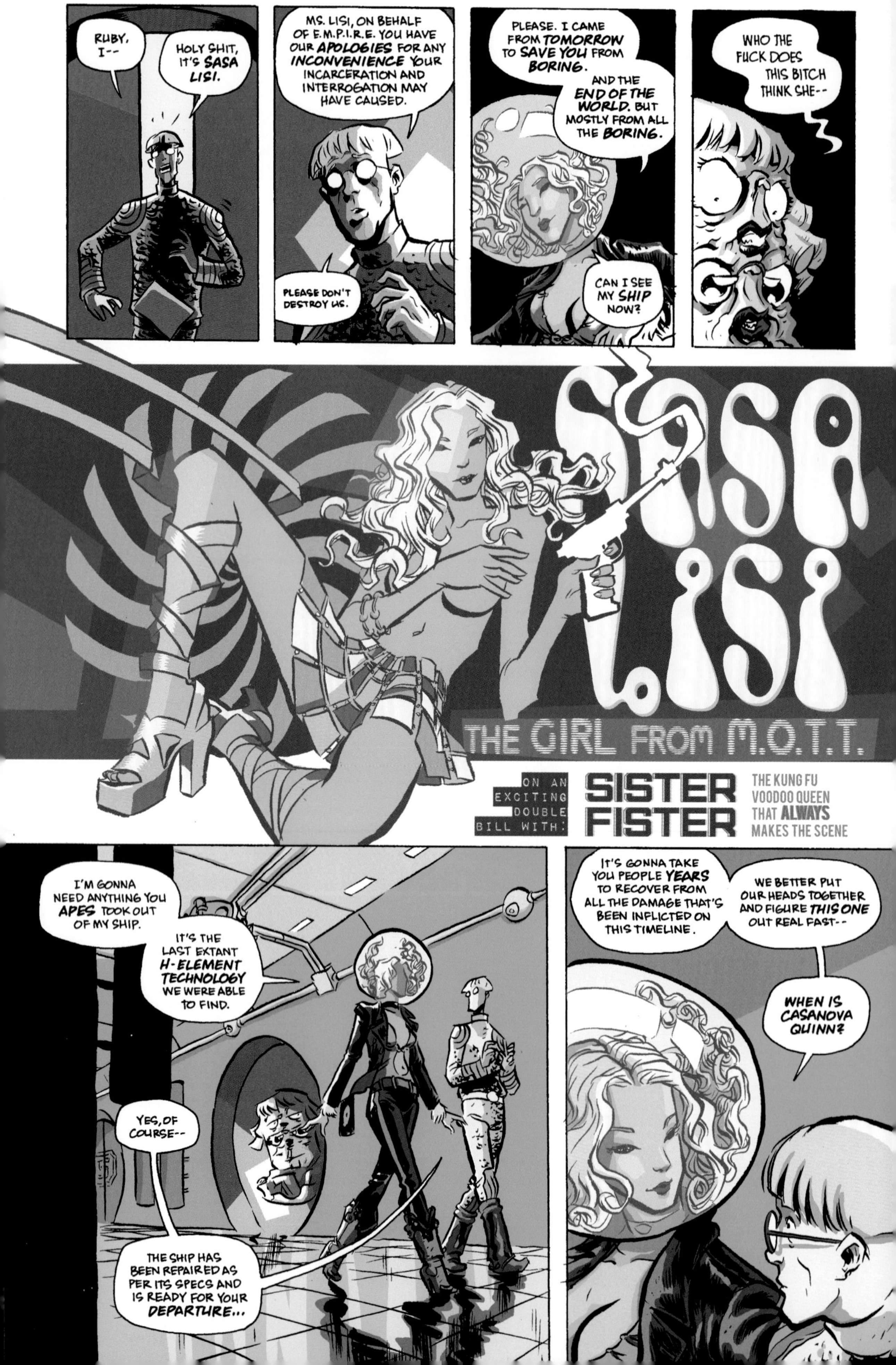
RUBY, I--
HOLY SHIT, IT'S SASA LISI.
MS. LISI, ON BEHALF OF E.M.P.I.R.E. YOU HAVE OUR APOLOGIES FOR ANY INCONVENIENCE YOUR INCARCERATION AND INTERROGATION MAY HAVE CAUSED.
PLEASE DON'T DESTROY US.
PLEASE. I CAME FROM TOMORROW TO SAVE YOU FROM BORING.
AND THE END OF THE WORLD. BUT MOSTLY FROM ALL THE BORING.
CAN I SEE MY SHIP NOW?
WHO THE FUCK DOES THIS BITCH THINK SHE--
SASA LISI
THE GIRL FROM M.O.T.T.
ON AN EXCITING DOUBLE BILL WITH:
SISTER FISTER
THE KUNG FU VOODOO QUEEN THAT ALWAYS MAKES THE SCENE
I'M GONNA NEED ANYTHING YOU APES TOOK OUT OF MY SHIP.
IT'S THE LAST EXTANT H-ELEMENT TECHNOLOGY WE WERE ABLE TO FIND.
YES, OF COURSE--
THE SHIP HAS BEEN REPAIRED AS PER ITS SPECS AND IS READY FOR YOUR DEPARTURE...
IT'S GONNA TAKE YOU PEOPLE YEARS TO RECOVER FROM ALL THE DAMAGE THAT'S BEEN INFLICTED ON THIS TIMELINE.
WE BETTER PUT OUR HEADS TOGETHER AND FIGURE THIS ONE OUT REAL FAST--
WHEN IS CASANOVA QUINN?

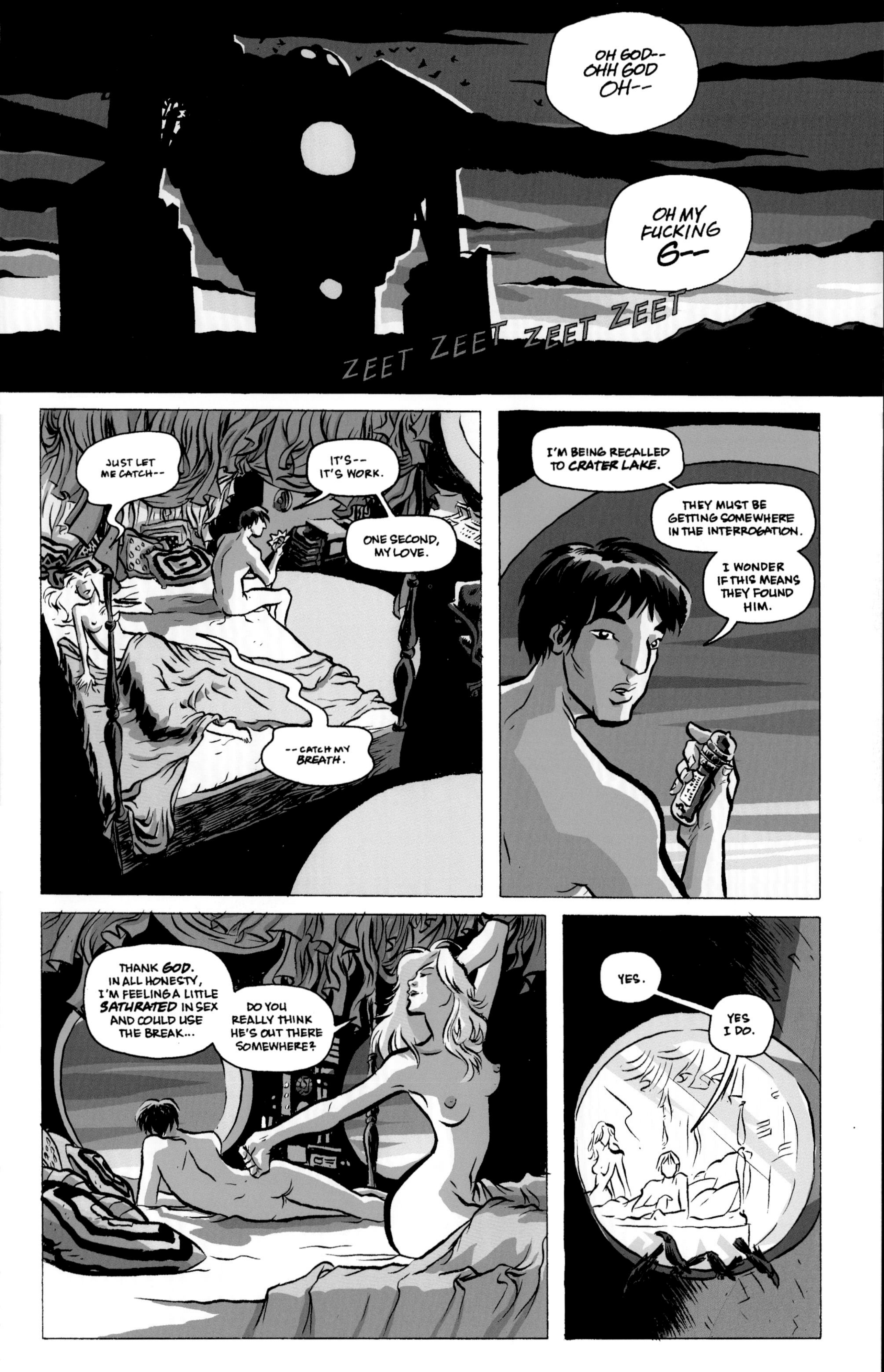
OH GOD-- OHH GOD OH--
OH MY FUCKING G--
ZEET ZEET ZEET ZEET
JUST LET ME CATCH--
IT'S-- IT'S WORK.
ONE SECOND, MY LOVE.
--CATCH MY BREATH.
I'M BEING RECALLED TO CRATER LAKE.
THEY MUST BE GETTING SOMEWHERE IN THE INTERROGATION.
I WONDER IF THIS MEANS THEY FOUND HIM.
THANK GOD. IN ALL HONESTY, I'M FEELING A LITTLE SATURATED IN SEX AND COULD USE THE BREAK...
DO YOU REALLY THINK HE'S OUT THERE SOMEWHERE?
YES.
YES I DO.

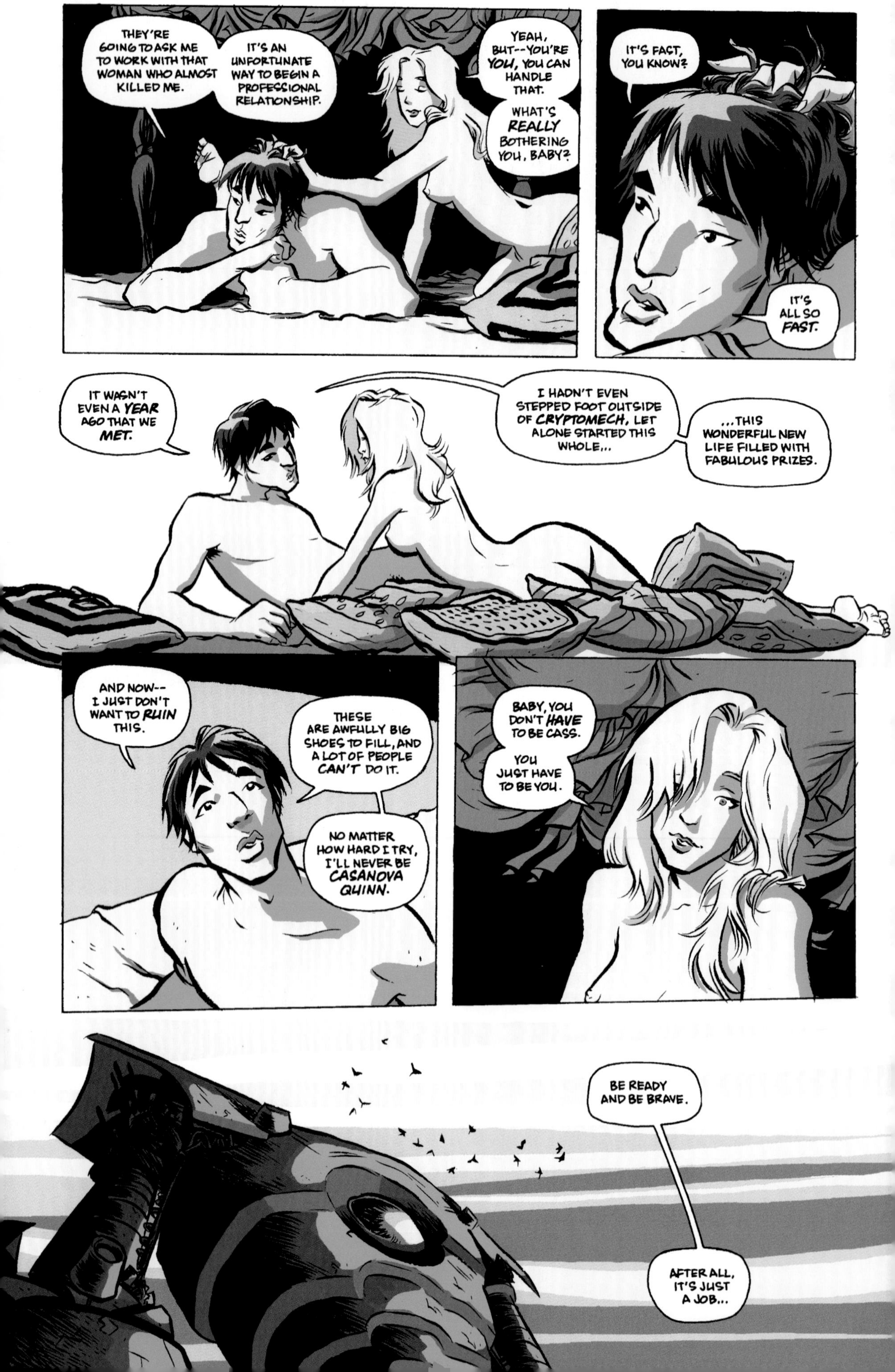

THEY'RE GOING TO ASK ME TO WORK WITH THAT WOMAN WHO ALMOST KILLED ME.
IT'S AN UNFORTUNATE WAY TO BEGIN A PROFESSIONAL RELATIONSHIP.
YEAH, BUT--YOU'RE YOU, YOU CAN HANDLE THAT.
WHAT'S REALLY BOTHERING YOU, BABY?
IT'S FAST, YOU KNOW?
IT'S ALL SO FAST.
IT WASN'T EVEN A YEAR AGO THAT WE MET.
I HADN'T EVEN STEPPED FOOT OUTSIDE OF CRYPTOMECH, LET ALONE STARTED THIS WHOLE...
...THIS WONDERFUL NEW LIFE FILLED WITH FABULOUS PRIZES.
AND NOW-- I JUST DON'T WANT TO RUIN THIS.
THESE ARE AWFULLY BIG SHOES TO FILL, AND A LOT OF PEOPLE CAN'T DO IT.
NO MATTER HOW HARD I TRY, I'LL NEVER BE CASANOVA QUINN.
BABY, YOU DON'T HAVE TO BE CASS.
YOU JUST HAVE TO BE YOU.
BE READY AND BE BRAVE.
AFTER ALL, IT'S JUST A JOB...

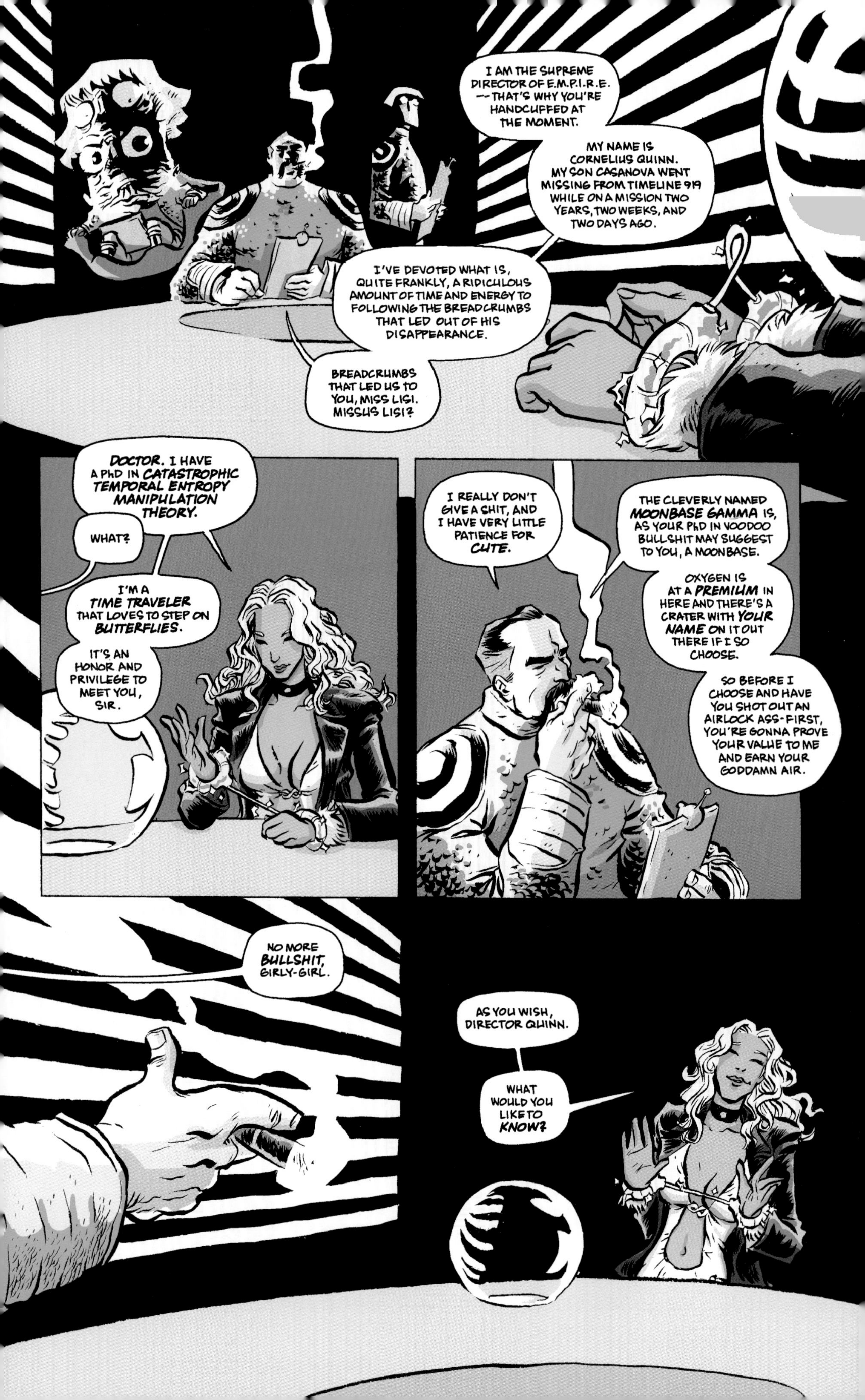
I AM THE SUPREME DIRECTOR OF E.M.P.I.R.E. -- THAT'S WHY YOU'RE HANDCUFFED AT THE MOMENT.
MY NAME IS CORNELIUS QUINN. MY SON CASANOVA WENT MISSING FROM TIMELINE 919 WHILE ON A MISSION TWO YEARS, TWO WEEKS, AND TWO DAYS AGO.
I'VE DEVOTED WHAT IS, QUITE FRANKLY, A RIDICULOUS AMOUNT OF TIME AND ENERGY TO FOLLOWING THE BREADCRUMBS THAT LED OUT OF HIS DISAPPEARANCE.
BREADCRUMBS THAT LED US TO YOU, MISS LISI. MISSUS LISI?
DOCTOR. I HAVE A PhD IN CATASTROPHIC TEMPORAL ENTROPY MANIPULATION THEORY.
WHAT?
I'M A TIME TRAVELER THAT LOVES TO STEP ON BUTTERFLIES.
IT'S AN HONOR AND PRIVILEGE TO MEET YOU, SIR.
I REALLY DON'T GIVE A SHIT, AND I HAVE VERY LITTLE PATIENCE FOR CUTE.
THE CLEVERLY NAMED MOONBASE GAMMA IS, AS YOUR PhD IN VOODOO BULLSHIT MAY SUGGEST TO YOU, A MOONBASE.
OXYGEN IS AT A PREMIUM IN HERE AND THERE'S A CRATER WITH YOUR NAME ON IT OUT THERE IF I SO CHOOSE.
SO BEFORE I CHOOSE AND HAVE YOU SHOT OUT AN AIRLOCK ASS-FIRST, YOU'RE GONNA PROVE YOUR VALUE TO ME AND EARN YOUR GODDAMN AIR.
NO MORE BULLSHIT, GIRLY-GIRL.
AS YOU WISH, DIRECTOR QUINN.
WHAT WOULD YOU LIKE TO KNOW?

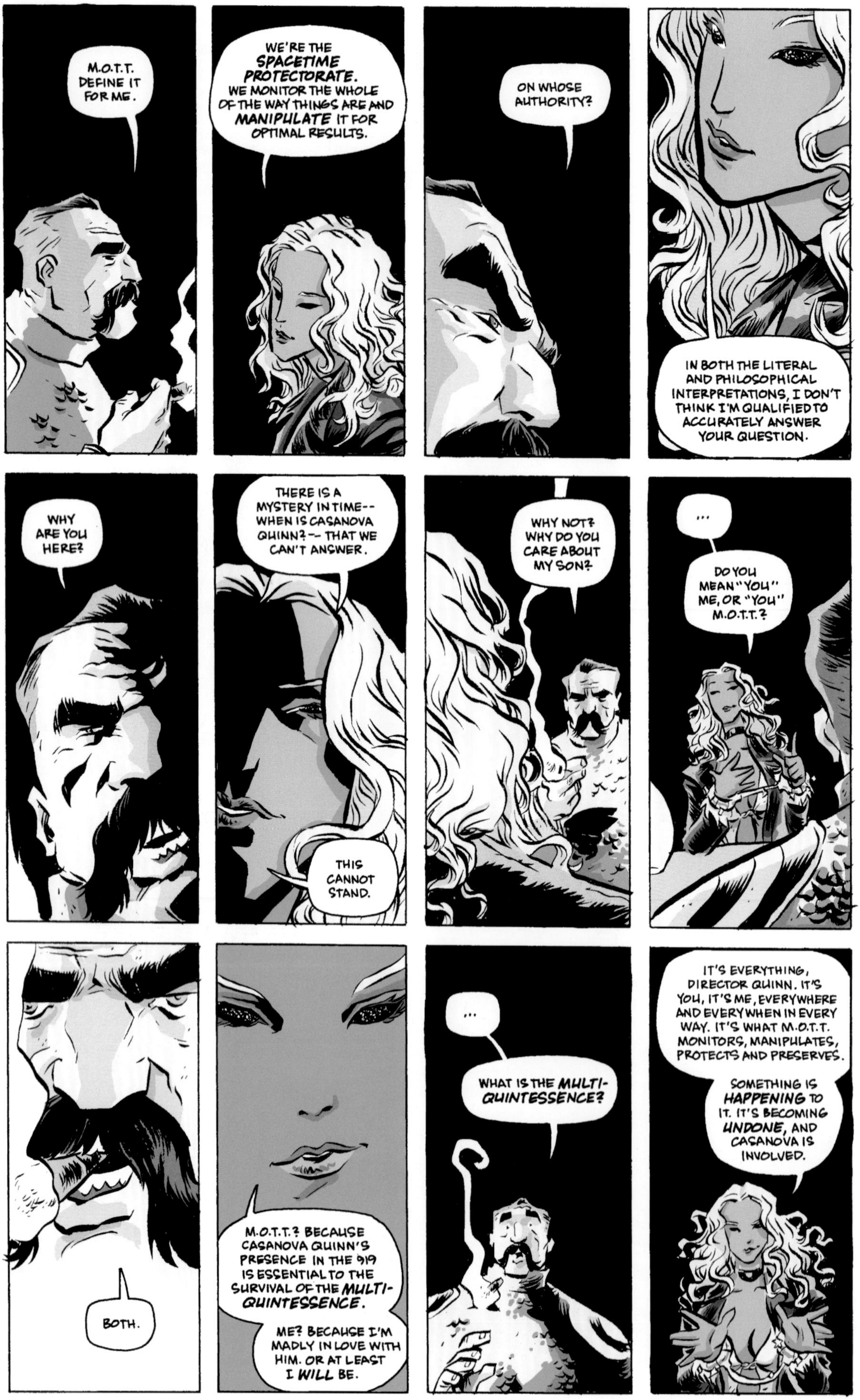
M.O.T.T. DEFINE IT FOR ME.
WE'RE THE SPACETIME PROTECTORATE. WE MONITOR THE WHOLE OF THE WAY THINGS ARE AND MANIPULATE IT FOR OPTIMAL RESULTS.
ON WHOSE AUTHORITY?
IN BOTH THE LITERAL AND PHILOSOPHICAL INTERPRETATIONS, I DON'T THINK I'M QUALIFIED TO ACCURATELY ANSWER YOUR QUESTION.
WHY ARE YOU HERE?
THERE IS A MYSTERY IN TIME-- WHEN IS CASANOVA QUINN? -- THAT WE CAN'T ANSWER.
THIS CANNOT STAND.
WHY NOT? WHY DO YOU CARE ABOUT MY SON?
...
DO YOU MEAN "YOU" ME, OR "YOU" M.O.T.T.?
BOTH.
M.O.T.T.? BECAUSE CASANOVA QUINN'S PRESENCE IN THE 919 IS ESSENTIAL TO THE SURVIVAL OF THE MULTI-QUINTESSENCE.
ME? BECAUSE I'M MADLY IN LOVE WITH HIM. OR AT LEAST I WILL BE.
...
WHAT IS THE MULTI-QUINTESSENCE?
IT'S EVERYTHING, DIRECTOR QUINN. IT'S YOU, IT'S ME, EVERYWHERE AND EVERYWHEN IN EVERY WAY. IT'S WHAT M.O.T.T. MONITORS, MANIPULATES, PROTECTS AND PRESERVES.
SOMETHING IS HAPPENING TO IT. IT'S BECOMING UNDONE, AND CASANOVA IS INVOLVED.

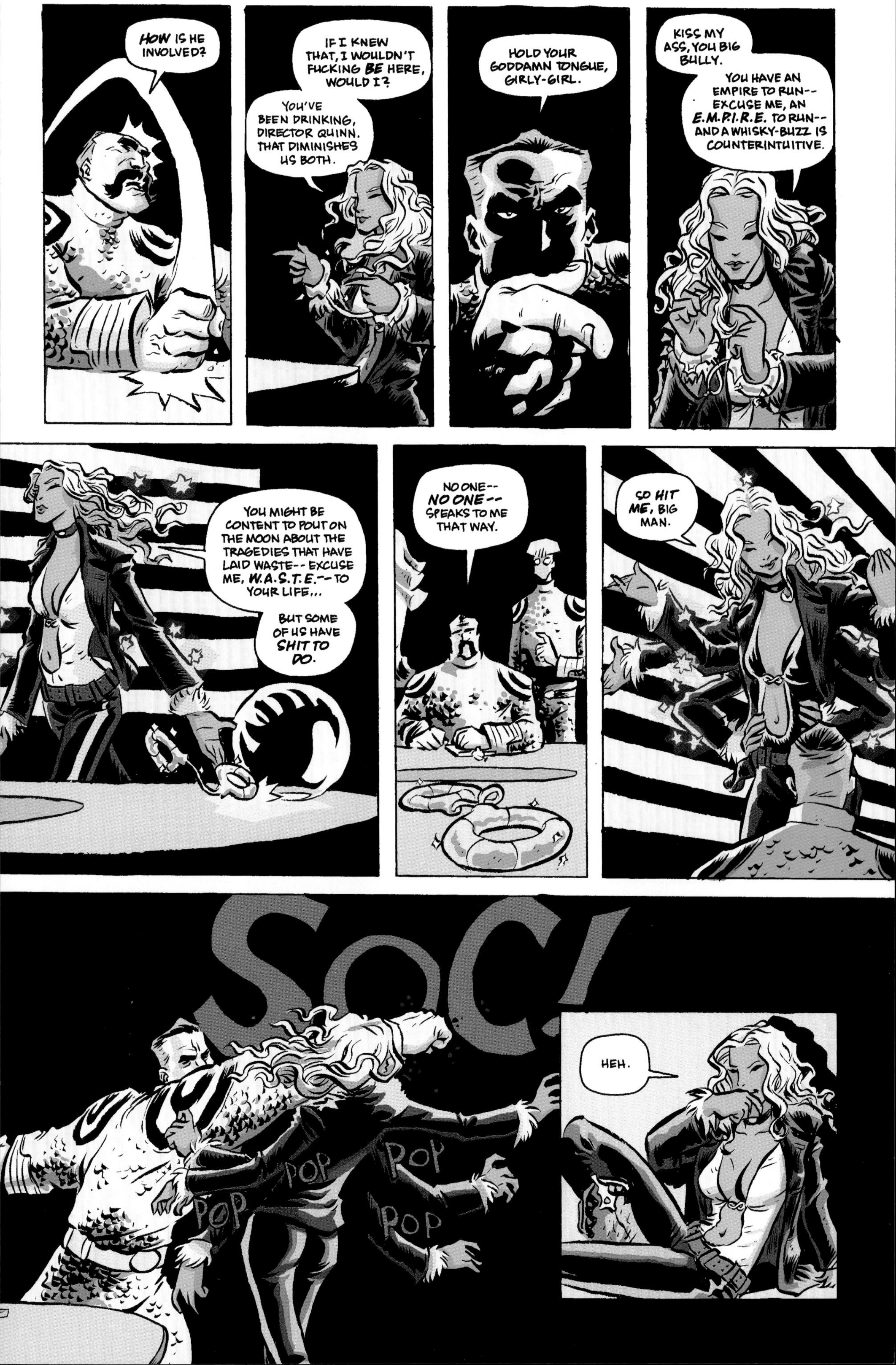
HOW IS HE INVOLVED?
IF I KNEW THAT, I WOULDN'T FUCKING BE HERE, WOULD I?
YOU'VE BEEN DRINKING, DIRECTOR QUINN. THAT DIMINISHES US BOTH.
HOLD YOUR GODDAMN TONGUE, GIRLY-GIRL.
KISS MY ASS, YOU BIG BULLY.
YOU HAVE AN EMPIRE TO RUN-- EXCUSE ME, AN E.M.P.I.R.E. TO RUN-- AND A WHISKY-BUZZ IS COUNTERINTUITIVE.
YOU MIGHT BE CONTENT TO POUT ON THE MOON ABOUT THE TRAGEDIES THAT HAVE LAID WASTE-- EXCUSE ME, W.A.S.T.E.-- TO YOUR LIFE...
BUT SOME OF US HAVE SHIT TO DO.
NO ONE-- NO ONE-- SPEAKS TO ME THAT WAY.
SO HIT ME, BIG MAN.
SOC!
POP
POP
POP
POP
HEH.

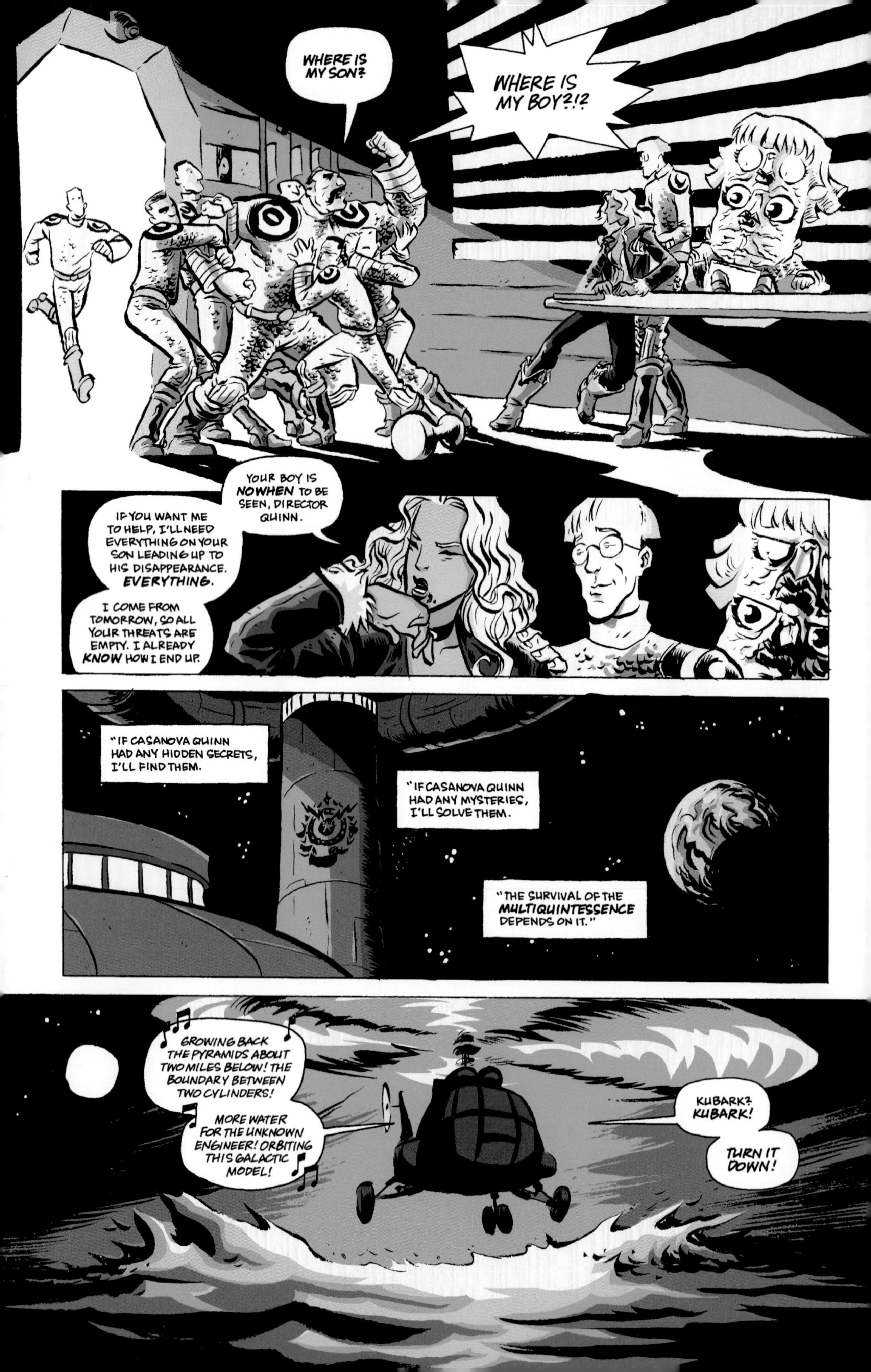
WHERE IS MY SON?
WHERE IS MY BOY?!?
YOUR BOY IS NOWHEN TO BE SEEN, DIRECTOR QUINN.
IF YOU WANT ME TO HELP, I'LL NEED EVERYTHING ON YOUR SON LEADING UP TO HIS DISAPPEARANCE. EVERYTHING.
I COME FROM TOMORROW, SO ALL YOUR THREATS ARE EMPTY. I ALREADY KNOW HOW I END UP.
"IF CASANOVA QUINN HAD ANY HIDDEN SECRETS, I'LL FIND THEM.
"IF CASANOVA QUINN HAD ANY MYSTERIES, I'LL SOLVE THEM.
"THE SURVIVAL OF THE MULTIQUINTESSENCE DEPENDS ON IT."
GROWING BACK THE PYRAMIDS ABOUT TWO MILES BELOW! THE BOUNDARY BETWEEN TWO CYLINDERS!
MORE WATER FOR THE UNKNOWN ENGINEER! ORBITING THIS GALACTIC MODEL!
KUBARK? KUBARK!
TURN IT DOWN!

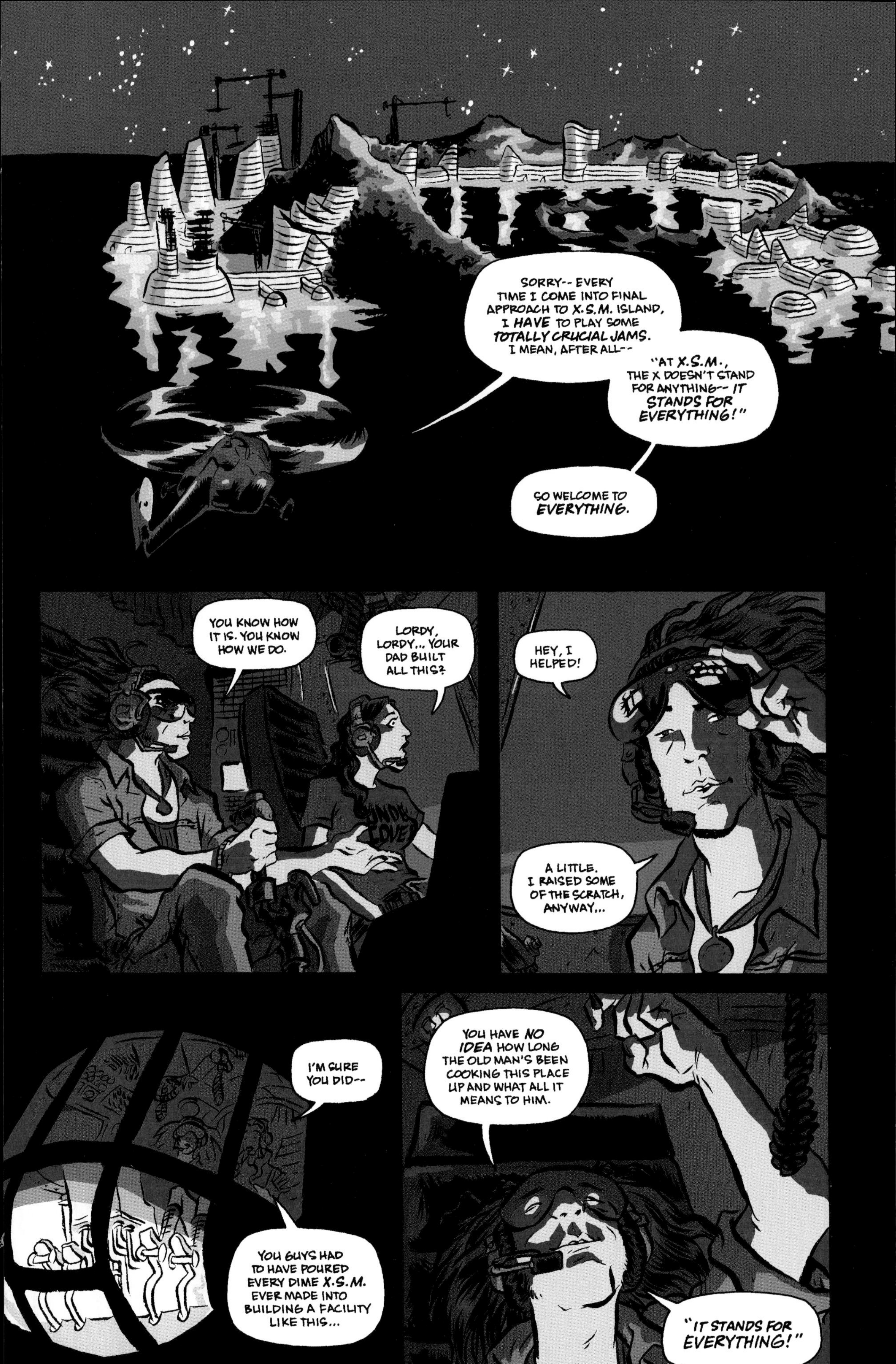
SORRY-- EVERY TIME I COME INTO FINAL APPROACH TO X.S.M. ISLAND, I HAVE TO PLAY SOME TOTALLY CRUCIAL JAMS. I MEAN, AFTER ALL--
"AT X.S.M., THE X DOESN'T STAND FOR ANYTHING-- IT STANDS FOR EVERYTHING!"
SO WELCOME TO EVERYTHING.
LORDY, LORDY... YOUR DAD BUILT ALL THIS?
YOU KNOW HOW IT IS. YOU KNOW HOW WE DO.
HEY, I HELPED!
A LITTLE. I RAISED SOME OF THE SCRATCH, ANYWAY...
I'M SURE YOU DID--
YOU GUYS HAD TO HAVE POURED EVERY DIME X.S.M. EVER MADE INTO BUILDING A FACILITY LIKE THIS...
YOU HAVE NO IDEA HOW LONG THE OLD MAN'S BEEN COOKING THIS PLACE UP AND WHAT ALL IT MEANS TO HIM.
"IT STANDS FOR EVERYTHING!"

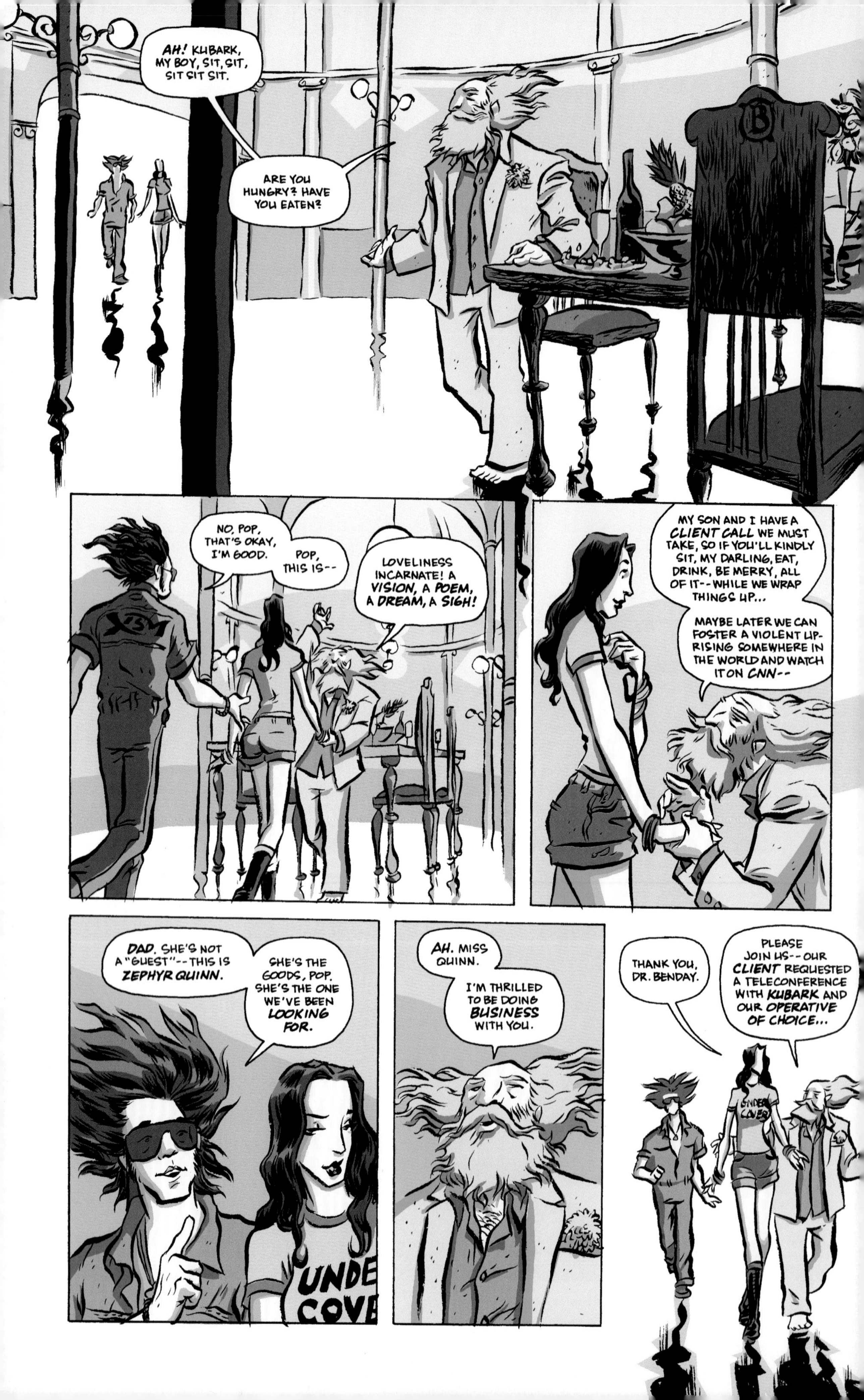
AH! KUBARK, MY BOY, SIT, SIT, SIT SIT SIT.
ARE YOU HUNGRY? HAVE YOU EATEN?
NO, POP, THAT'S OKAY, I'M GOOD.
POP, THIS IS--
LOVELINESS INCARNATE! A VISION, A POEM, A DREAM, A SIGH!
MY SON AND I HAVE A CLIENT CALL WE MUST TAKE, SO IF YOU'LL KINDLY SIT, MY DARLING, EAT, DRINK, BE MERRY, ALL OF IT--WHILE WE WRAP THINGS UP...
MAYBE LATER WE CAN FOSTER A VIOLENT UPRISING SOMEWHERE IN THE WORLD AND WATCH IT ON CNN--
DAD. SHE'S NOT A "GUEST"--THIS IS ZEPHYR QUINN.
SHE'S THE GOODS, POP. SHE'S THE ONE WE'VE BEEN LOOKING FOR.
AH. MISS QUINN.
I'M THRILLED TO BE DOING BUSINESS WITH YOU.
THANK YOU, DR. BENDAY.
PLEASE JOIN US--OUR CLIENT REQUESTED A TELECONFERENCE WITH KUBARK AND OUR OPERATIVE OF CHOICE...

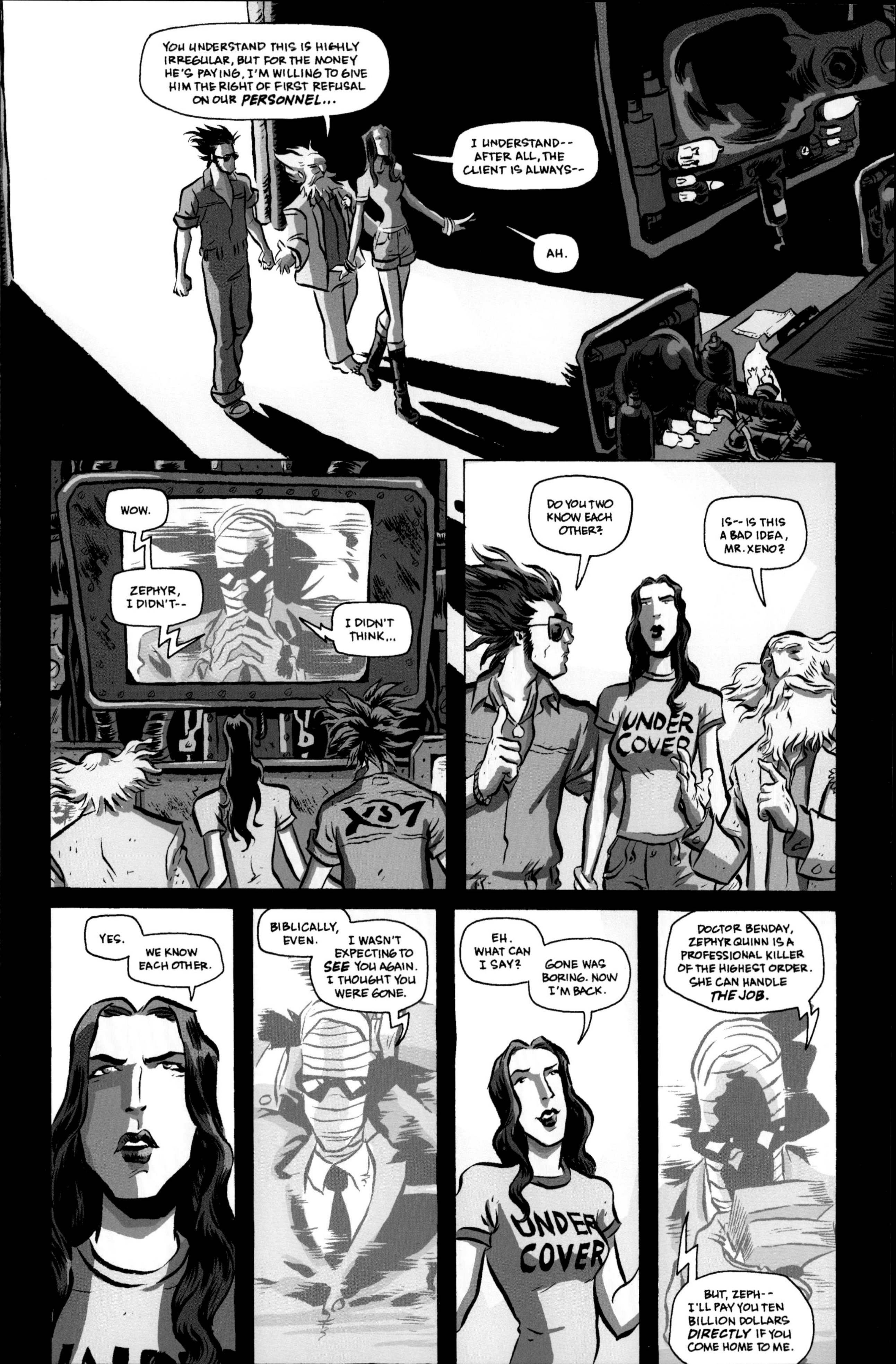

YOU UNDERSTAND THIS IS HIGHLY IRREGULAR, BUT FOR THE MONEY HE'S PAYING, I'M WILLING TO GIVE HIM THE RIGHT OF FIRST REFUSAL ON OUR PERSONNEL...
I UNDERSTAND-- AFTER ALL, THE CLIENT IS ALWAYS--
AH.
WOW.
ZEPHYR, I DIDN'T--
I DIDN'T THINK...
DO YOU TWO KNOW EACH OTHER?
IS-- IS THIS A BAD IDEA, MR. XENO?
UNDER COVER
YES.
WE KNOW EACH OTHER.
BIBLICALLY, EVEN.
I WASN'T EXPECTING TO SEE YOU AGAIN. I THOUGHT YOU WERE GONE.
EH. WHAT CAN I SAY?
GONE WAS BORING. NOW I'M BACK.
UNDER COVER
DOCTOR BENDAY, ZEPHYR QUINN IS A PROFESSIONAL KILLER OF THE HIGHEST ORDER. SHE CAN HANDLE THE JOB.
BUT, ZEPH-- I'LL PAY YOU TEN BILLION DOLLARS DIRECTLY IF YOU COME HOME TO ME.

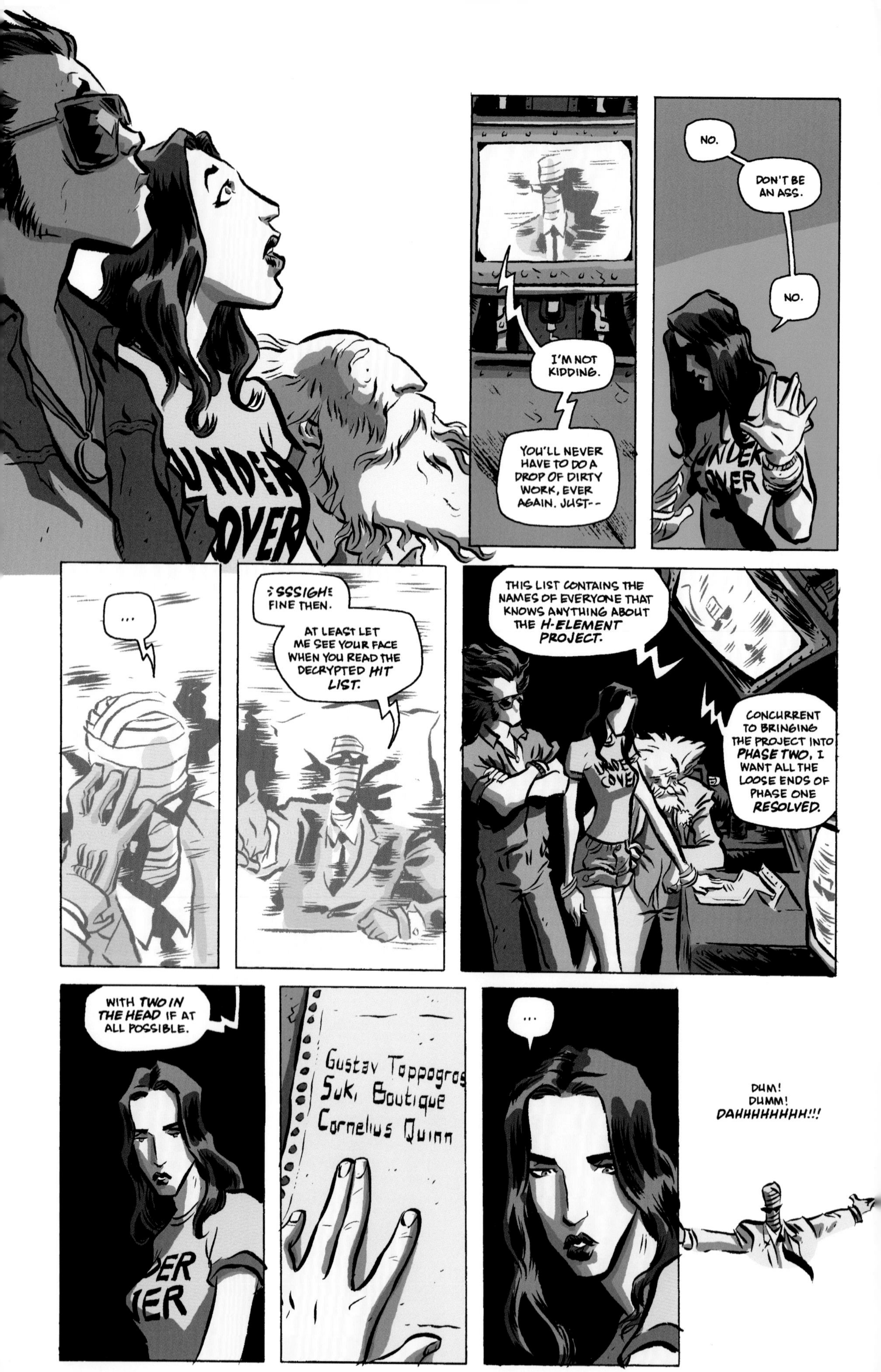
I'M NOT KIDDING.
YOU'LL NEVER HAVE TO DO A DROP OF DIRTY WORK, EVER AGAIN. JUST--
NO.
DON'T BE AN ASS.
NO.
...
SSSIGH FINE THEN.
AT LEAST LET ME SEE YOUR FACE WHEN YOU READ THE DECRYPTED HIT LIST.
THIS LIST CONTAINS THE NAMES OF EVERYONE THAT KNOWS ANYTHING ABOUT THE H-ELEMENT PROJECT.
CONCURRENT TO BRINGING THE PROJECT INTO PHASE TWO, I WANT ALL THE LOOSE ENDS OF PHASE ONE RESOLVED.
WITH TWO IN THE HEAD IF AT ALL POSSIBLE.
Gustav Toppogros
Suki Boutique
Cornelius Quinn
...
DUM!
DUMM!
DAHHHHHHHH!!!

IN MEDIAS RES

WHEN THE WOLF COMES HOME

SEVENTEEN

NAOMI I MOAN

FUCK SHIT UP

SOME OF THE THINGS THAT
HAPPENED TO THE MURDERERS
AND MURDERED AMONG US

HALLO SPACEBOY

DIT DIT DIT
DAH DAH DAH
DIT DIT

BACKMATTER

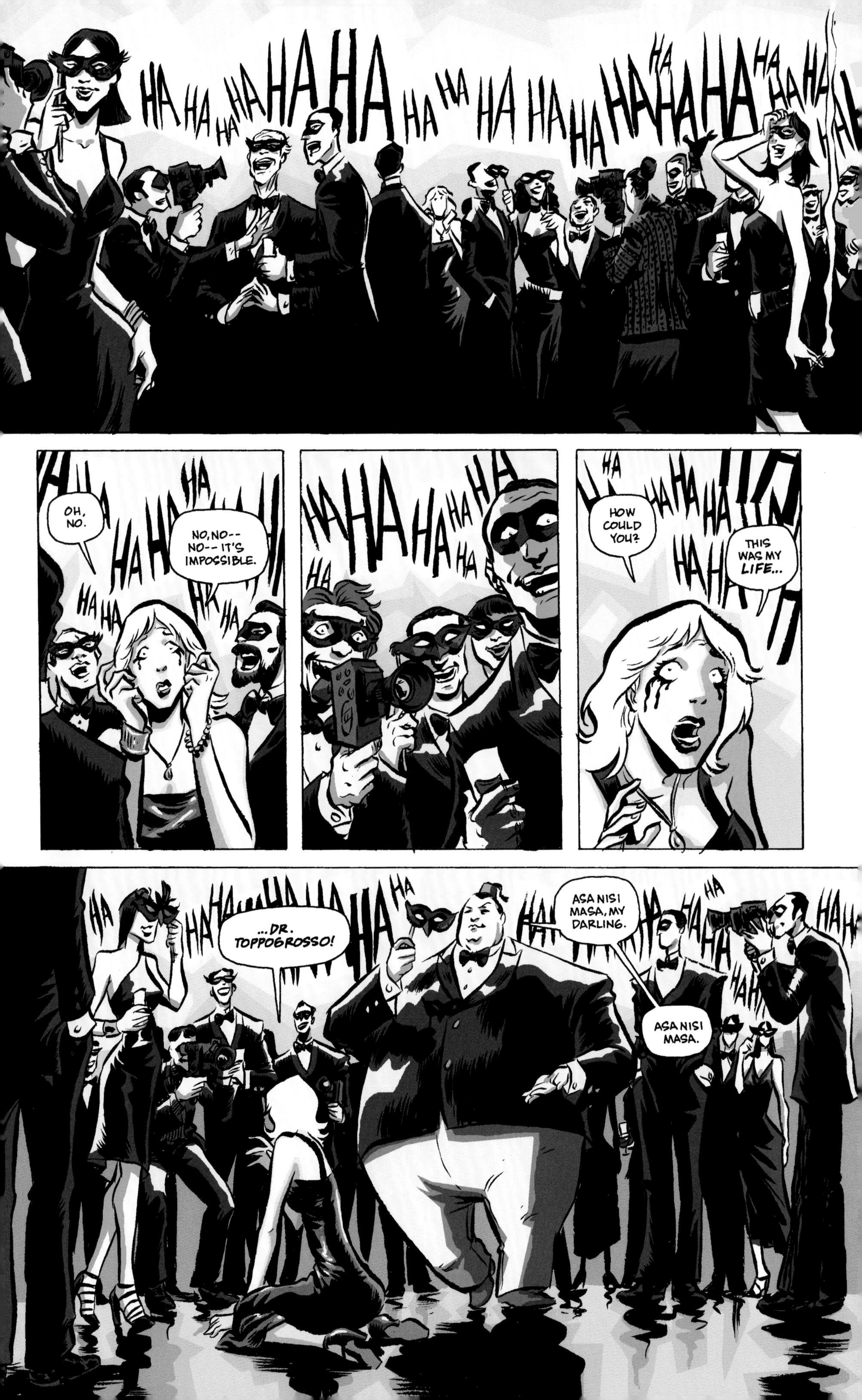

HA HA HA HA HA HA HA HA HA HA HA HA HA HA HA HA HA HA
OH, NO.
NO, NO-- NO-- IT'S IMPOSSIBLE.
HA HA HA HA HA HA HA
HA HA HA HA HA HA
HOW COULD YOU?
THIS WAS MY *LIFE*...
HA HA HA HA HA
...DR. TOPPOGROSSO!
ASA NISI MASA, MY DARLING.
ASA NISI MASA.
HA HA HA HA

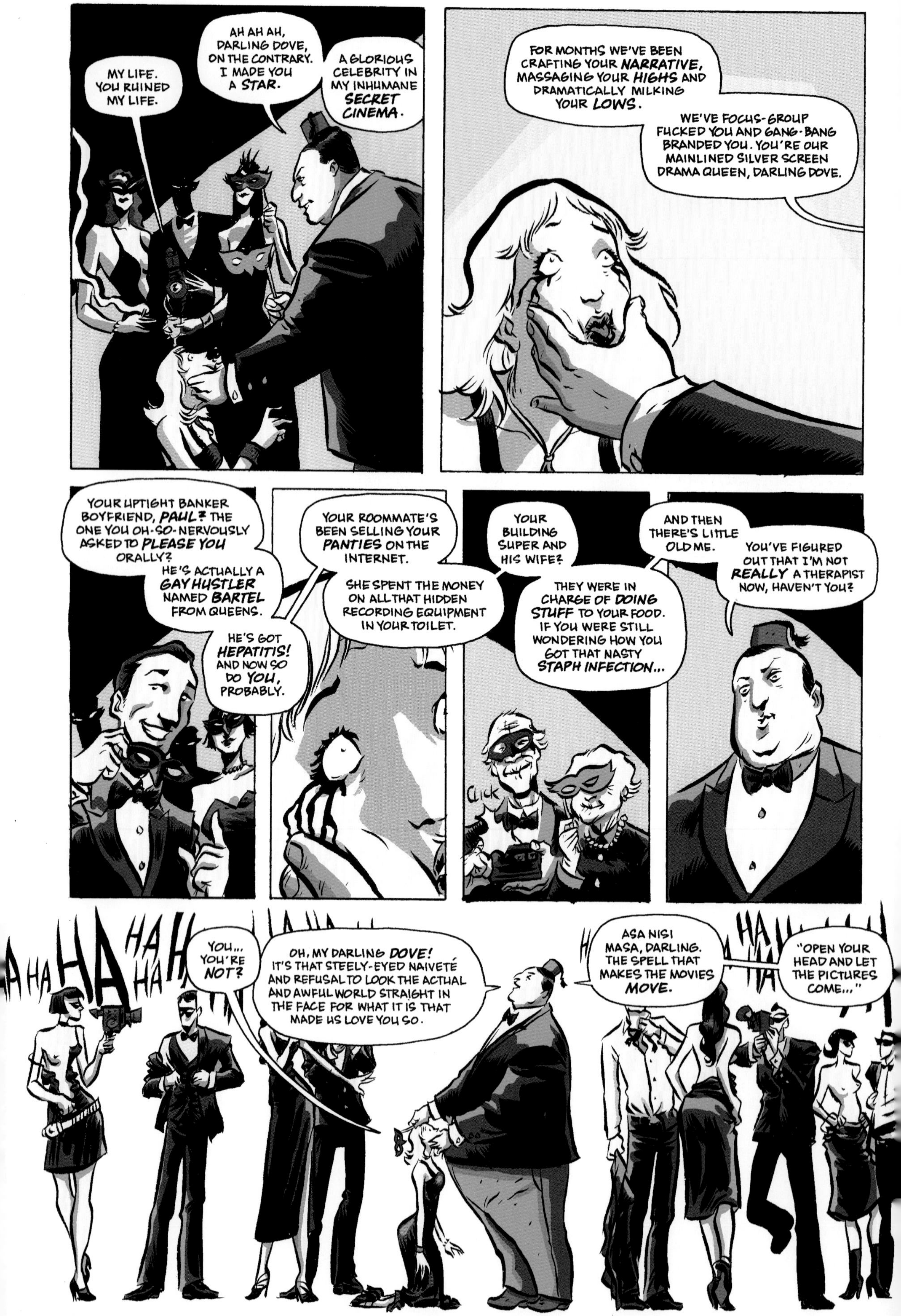
MY LIFE. YOU RUINED MY LIFE.
AH AH AH, DARLING DOVE, ON THE CONTRARY. I MADE YOU A STAR.
A GLORIOUS CELEBRITY IN MY INHUMANE SECRET CINEMA.
FOR MONTHS WE'VE BEEN CRAFTING YOUR NARRATIVE, MASSAGING YOUR HIGHS AND DRAMATICALLY MILKING YOUR LOWS.
WE'VE FOCUS-GROUP FUCKED YOU AND GANG-BANG BRANDED YOU. YOU'RE OUR MAINLINED SILVER SCREEN DRAMA QUEEN, DARLING DOVE.
YOUR UPTIGHT BANKER BOYFRIEND, PAUL? THE ONE YOU OH-SO-NERVOUSLY ASKED TO PLEASE YOU ORALLY?
HE'S ACTUALLY A GAY HUSTLER NAMED BARTEL FROM QUEENS.
HE'S GOT HEPATITIS! AND NOW SO DO YOU, PROBABLY.
YOUR ROOMMATE'S BEEN SELLING YOUR PANTIES ON THE INTERNET.
SHE SPENT THE MONEY ON ALL THAT HIDDEN RECORDING EQUIPMENT IN YOUR TOILET.
YOUR BUILDING SUPER AND HIS WIFE?
THEY WERE IN CHARGE OF DOING STUFF TO YOUR FOOD. IF YOU WERE STILL WONDERING HOW YOU GOT THAT NASTY STAPH INFECTION...
CLICK
AND THEN THERE'S LITTLE OLD ME.
YOU'VE FIGURED OUT THAT I'M NOT REALLY A THERAPIST NOW, HAVEN'T YOU?
HA HA HA HA HA HA HA
YOU... YOU'RE NOT?
OH, MY DARLING DOVE! IT'S THAT STEELY-EYED NAIVETÉ AND REFUSAL TO LOOK THE ACTUAL AND AWFUL WORLD STRAIGHT IN THE FACE FOR WHAT IT IS THAT MADE US LOVE YOU SO.
ASA NISI MASA, DARLING. THE SPELL THAT MAKES THE MOVIES MOVE.
"OPEN YOUR HEAD AND LET THE PICTURES COME..."

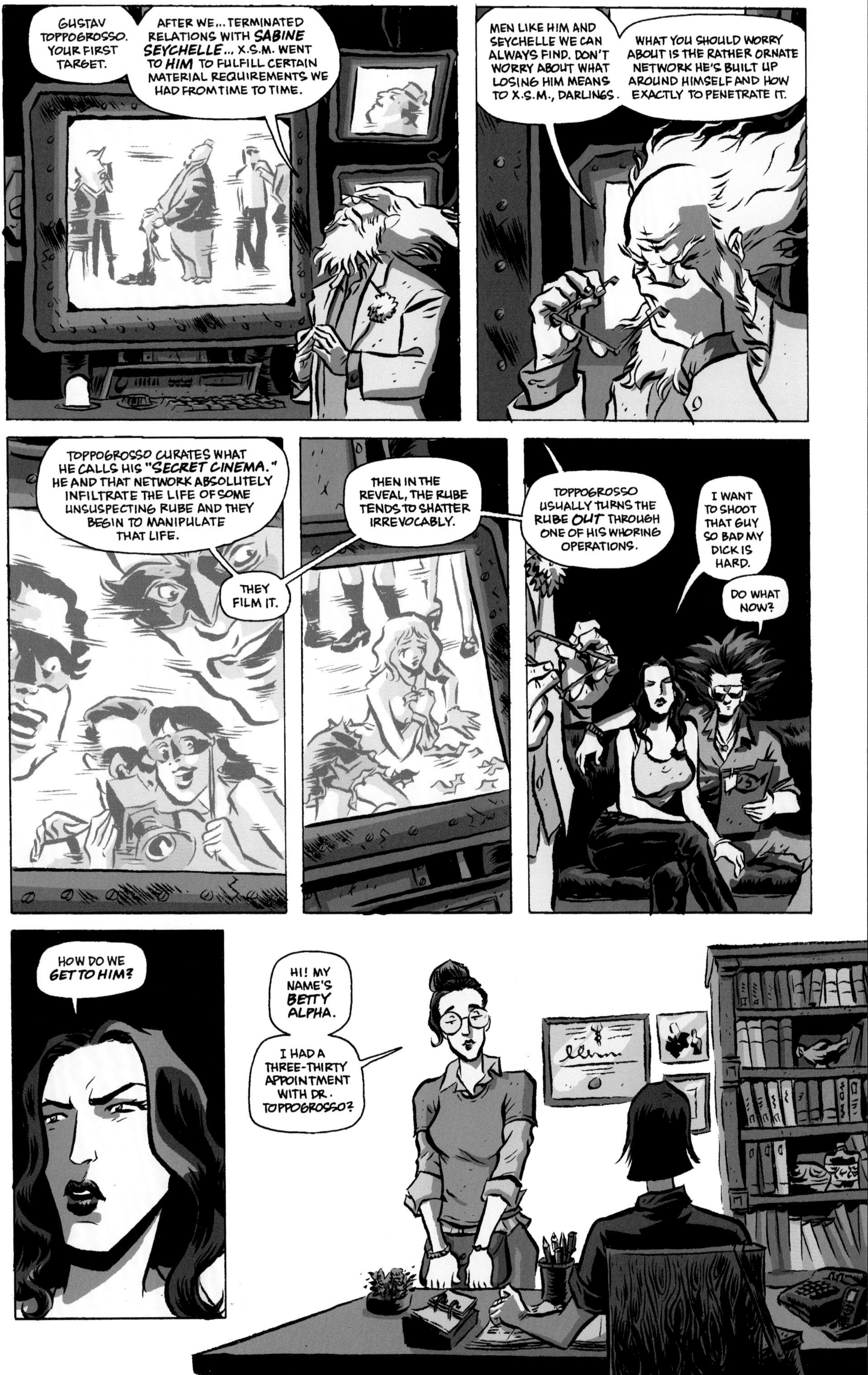
GUSTAV TOPPOGROSSO. YOUR FIRST TARGET.
AFTER WE... TERMINATED RELATIONS WITH SABINE SEYCHELLE... X.S.M. WENT TO HIM TO FULFILL CERTAIN MATERIAL REQUIREMENTS WE HAD FROM TIME TO TIME.
MEN LIKE HIM AND SEYCHELLE WE CAN ALWAYS FIND. DON'T WORRY ABOUT WHAT LOSING HIM MEANS TO X.S.M., DARLINGS.
WHAT YOU SHOULD WORRY ABOUT IS THE RATHER ORNATE NETWORK HE'S BUILT UP AROUND HIMSELF AND HOW EXACTLY TO PENETRATE IT.
TOPPOGROSSO CURATES WHAT HE CALLS HIS "SECRET CINEMA." HE AND THAT NETWORK ABSOLUTELY INFILTRATE THE LIFE OF SOME UNSUSPECTING RUBE AND THEY BEGIN TO MANIPULATE THAT LIFE.
THEY FILM IT.
THEN IN THE REVEAL, THE RUBE TENDS TO SHATTER IRREVOCABLY.
TOPPOGROSSO USUALLY TURNS THE RUBE OUT THROUGH ONE OF HIS WHORING OPERATIONS.
I WANT TO SHOOT THAT GUY SO BAD MY DICK IS HARD.
DO WHAT NOW?
HOW DO WE GET TO HIM?
HI! MY NAME'S BETTY ALPHA.
I HAD A THREE-THIRTY APPOINTMENT WITH DR. TOPPOGROSSO?

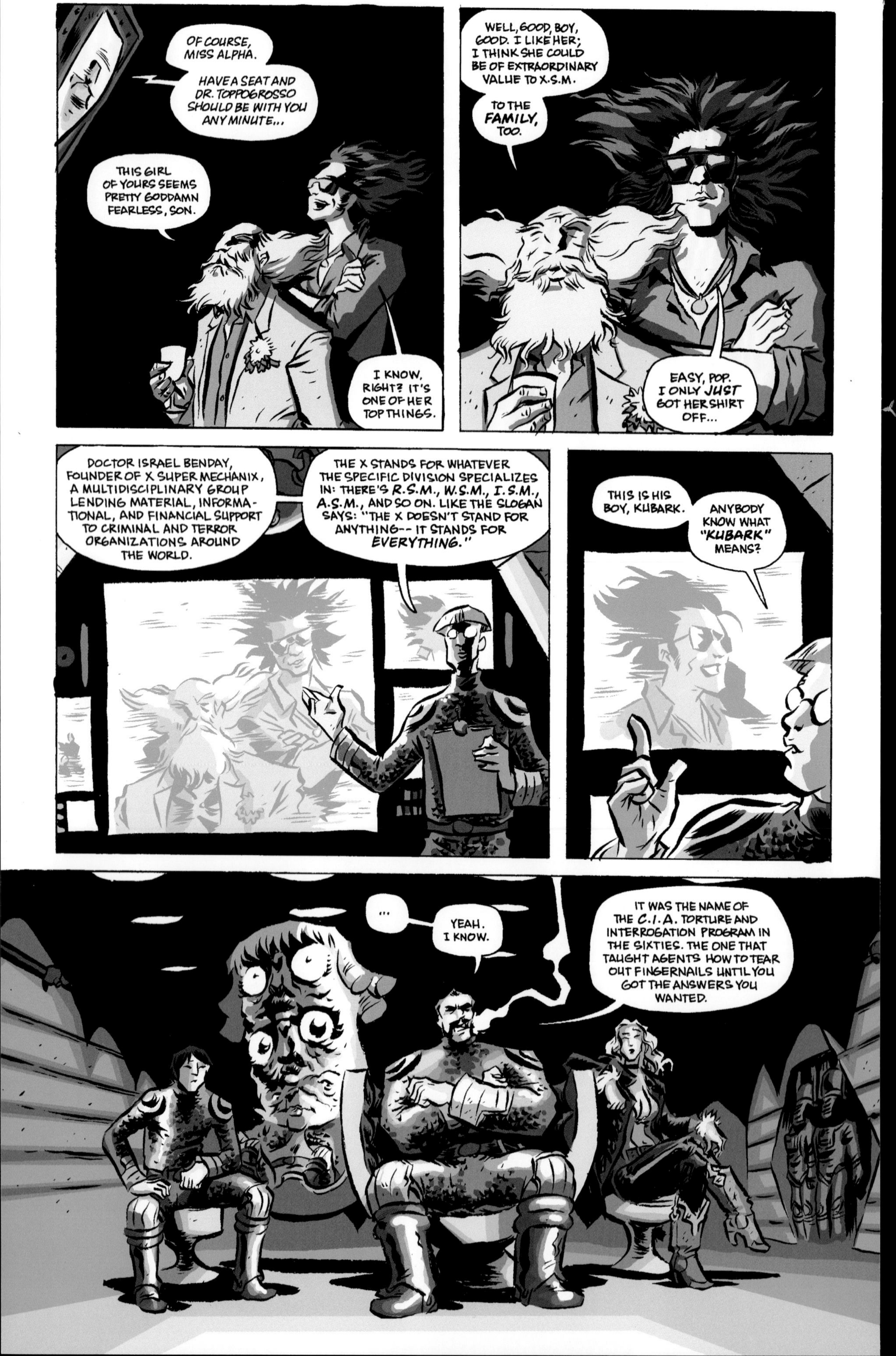
OF COURSE, MISS ALPHA.
HAVE A SEAT AND DR. TOPPOGROSSO SHOULD BE WITH YOU ANY MINUTE...
THIS GIRL OF YOURS SEEMS PRETTY GODDAMN FEARLESS, SON.
I KNOW, RIGHT? IT'S ONE OF HER TOP THINGS.
WELL, GOOD, BOY, GOOD. I LIKE HER; I THINK SHE COULD BE OF EXTRAORDINARY VALUE TO X.S.M.
TO THE *FAMILY*, TOO.
EASY, POP. I ONLY *JUST* GOT HER SHIRT OFF...
DOCTOR ISRAEL BENDAY, FOUNDER OF X SUPER MECHANIX, A MULTIDISCIPLINARY GROUP LENDING MATERIAL, INFORMATIONAL, AND FINANCIAL SUPPORT TO CRIMINAL AND TERROR ORGANIZATIONS AROUND THE WORLD.
THE X STANDS FOR WHATEVER THE SPECIFIC DIVISION SPECIALIZES IN: THERE'S *R.S.M.*, *W.S.M.*, *I.S.M.*, *A.S.M.*, AND SO ON. LIKE THE SLOGAN SAYS: "THE X DOESN'T STAND FOR ANYTHING-- IT STANDS FOR *EVERYTHING*."
THIS IS HIS BOY, KUBARK.
ANYBODY KNOW WHAT *"KUBARK"* MEANS?
...
YEAH. I KNOW.
IT WAS THE NAME OF THE *C.I.A.* TORTURE AND INTERROGATION PROGRAM IN THE SIXTIES. THE ONE THAT TAUGHT AGENTS HOW TO TEAR OUT FINGERNAILS UNTIL YOU GOT THE ANSWERS YOU WANTED.

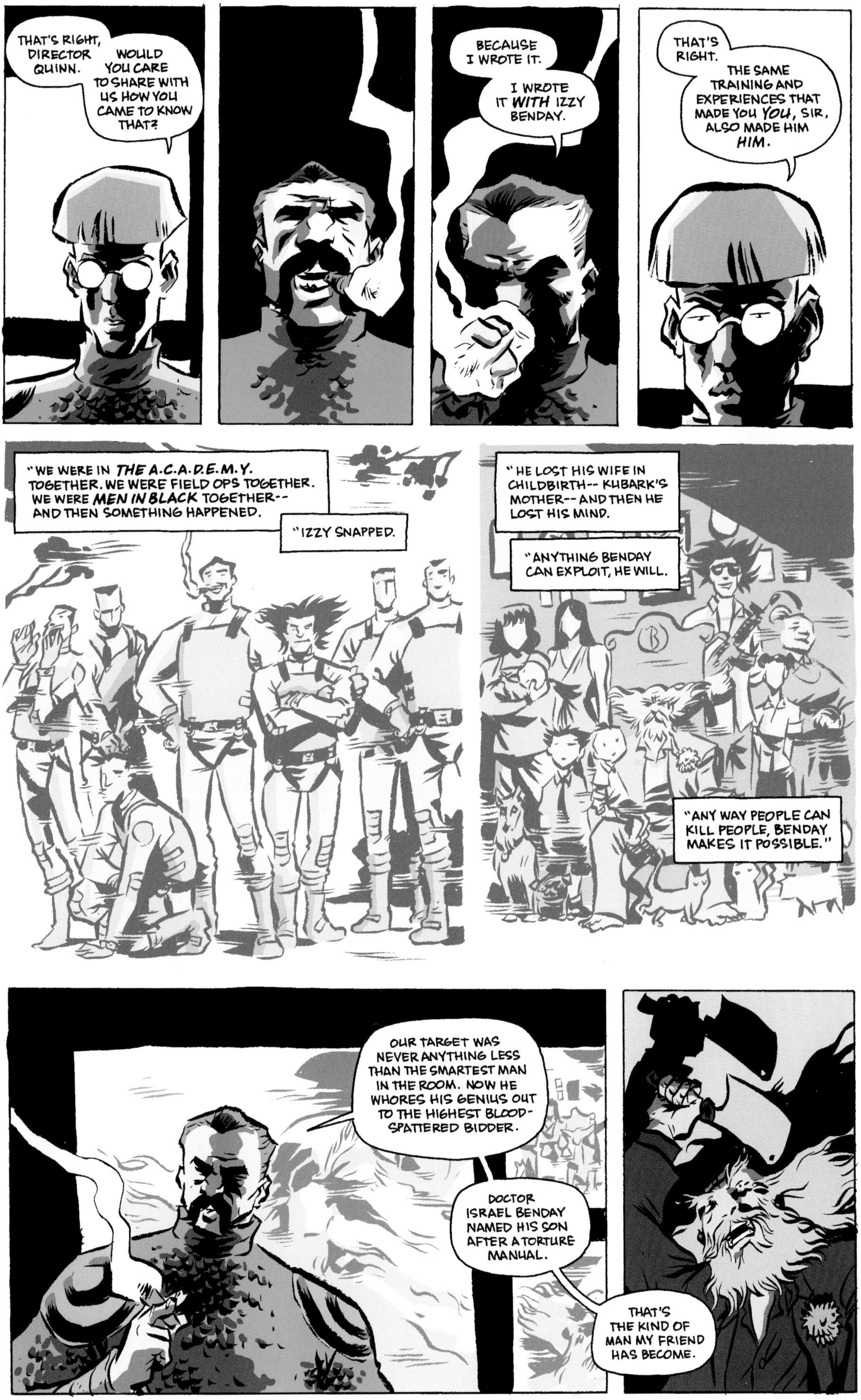
THAT'S RIGHT, DIRECTOR QUINN.
WOULD YOU CARE TO SHARE WITH US HOW YOU CAME TO KNOW THAT?
BECAUSE I WROTE IT.
I WROTE IT WITH IZZY BENDAY.
THAT'S RIGHT.
THE SAME TRAINING AND EXPERIENCES THAT MADE YOU YOU, SIR, ALSO MADE HIM HIM.
"WE WERE IN THE A.C.A.D.E.M.Y. TOGETHER. WE WERE FIELD OPS TOGETHER. WE WERE MEN IN BLACK TOGETHER-- AND THEN SOMETHING HAPPENED.
"IZZY SNAPPED.
"HE LOST HIS WIFE IN CHILDBIRTH-- KUBARK'S MOTHER-- AND THEN HE LOST HIS MIND.
"ANYTHING BENDAY CAN EXPLOIT, HE WILL.
"ANY WAY PEOPLE CAN KILL PEOPLE, BENDAY MAKES IT POSSIBLE."
OUR TARGET WAS NEVER ANYTHING LESS THAN THE SMARTEST MAN IN THE ROOM. NOW HE WHORES HIS GENIUS OUT TO THE HIGHEST BLOOD-SPATTERED BIDDER.
DOCTOR ISRAEL BENDAY NAMED HIS SON AFTER A TORTURE MANUAL.
THAT'S THE KIND OF MAN MY FRIEND HAS BECOME.

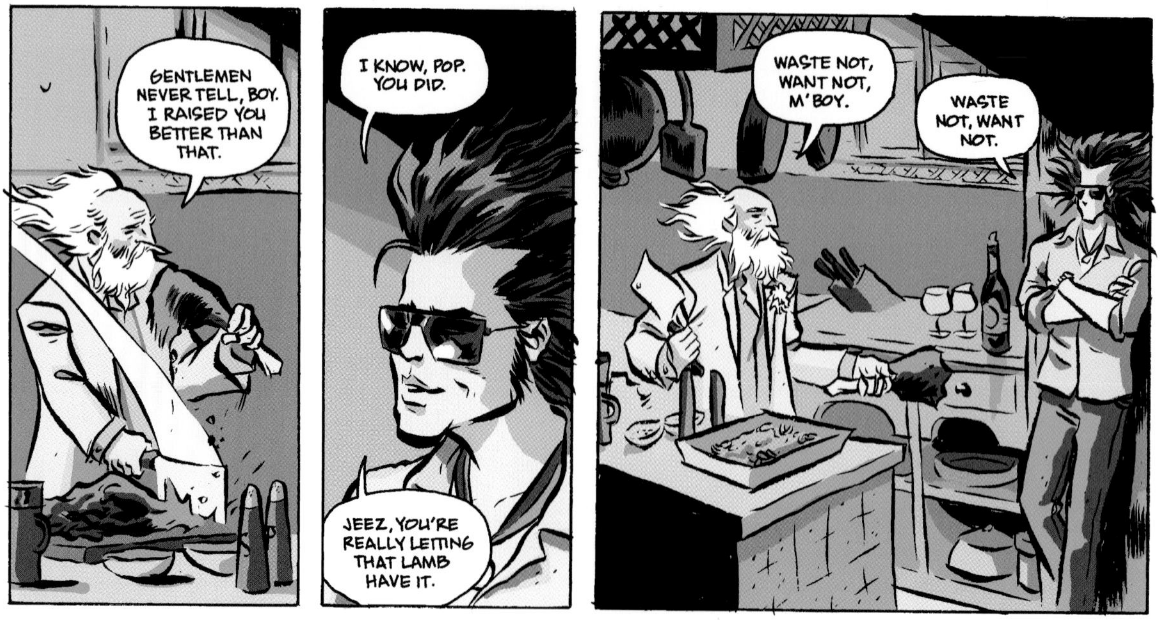
GENTLEMEN NEVER TELL, BOY. I RAISED YOU BETTER THAN THAT.
I KNOW, POP. YOU DID.
JEEZ, YOU'RE REALLY LETTING THAT LAMB HAVE IT.
WASTE NOT, WANT NOT, M'BOY.
WASTE NOT, WANT NOT.

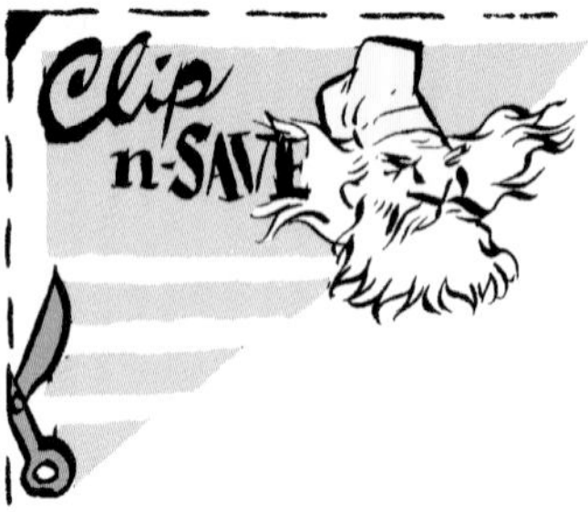
Clip n-SAVE

Epaule d'Agneau Confite de Benday

One shoulder of Lamb, bone in (3 lbs, no more than 3 1/2)
Extra-virgin Olive Oil
1 tbsp. Thyme
1 tbsp. Basil
1 tbsp. Marjoram
2-3 tbsp. Rosemary (fresh)
1 head of Garlic
1/2 cup Dry White Wine
Sea Salt
Fresh Cracked Pepper

Rub the lamb with olive oil, then rub herbs across the meat, adding the rosemary last. Wrap in butcher's paper and refrigerate overnight. Let meat sit out as oven preheats to 250°F. Clove the garlic. Put the garlic cloves in the bottom of a heavy iron pot with a good lid. Put the lamb in the pot and sprinkle it with the salt and pepper. Pour the wine into the pot. Close the pot and put it in the oven for 4 hours. Flip the lamb every half-hour, basting it each time. If the juice runs low--and it will if your lid doesn't fit properly--add more wine.

The lamb is ready when tender, dark, and fragrant. Serve at moonrise near an open window above night-blooming jasmine.

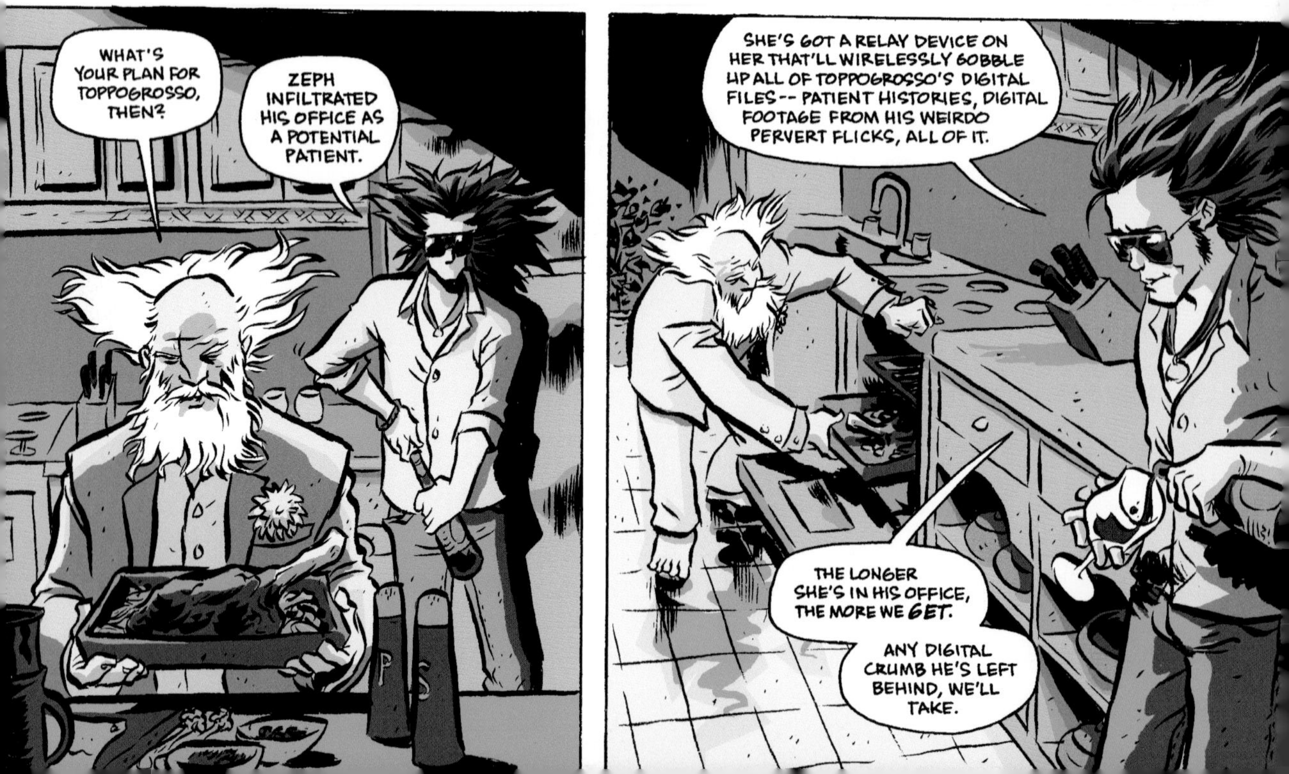
WHAT'S YOUR PLAN FOR TOPPOGROSSO, THEN?
ZEPH INFILTRATED HIS OFFICE AS A POTENTIAL PATIENT.
SHE'S GOT A RELAY DEVICE ON HER THAT'LL WIRELESSLY GOBBLE UP ALL OF TOPPOGROSSO'S DIGITAL FILES-- PATIENT HISTORIES, DIGITAL FOOTAGE FROM HIS WEIRDO PERVERT FLICKS, ALL OF IT.
THE LONGER SHE'S IN HIS OFFICE, THE MORE WE GET.
ANY DIGITAL CRUMB HE'S LEFT BEHIND, WE'LL TAKE.

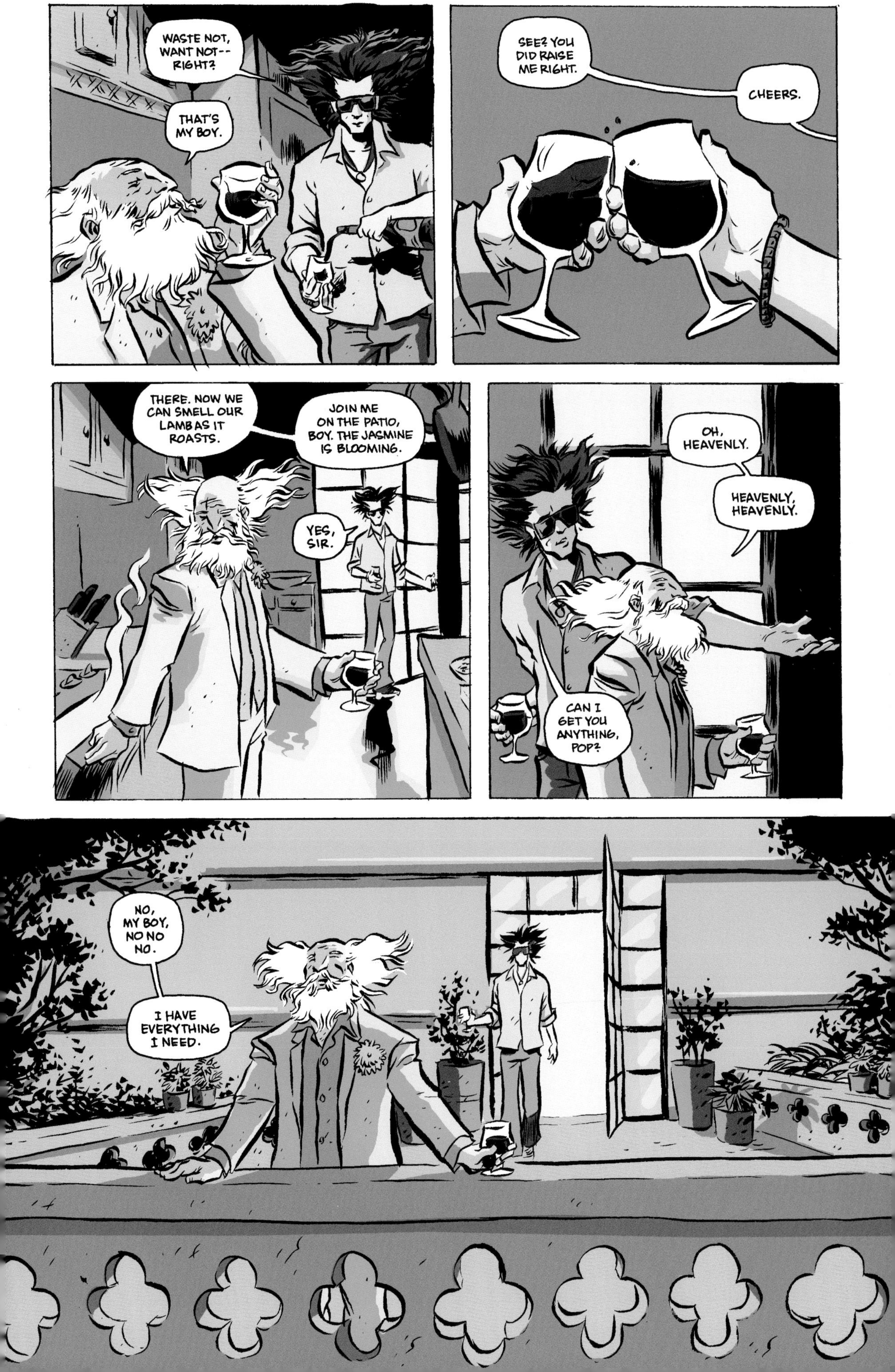
WASTE NOT, WANT NOT-- RIGHT?
THAT'S MY BOY.
SEE? YOU DID RAISE ME RIGHT.
CHEERS.
THERE. NOW WE CAN SMELL OUR LAMB AS IT ROASTS.
JOIN ME ON THE PATIO, BOY. THE JASMINE IS BLOOMING.
YES, SIR.
OH, HEAVENLY.
HEAVENLY, HEAVENLY.
CAN I GET YOU ANYTHING, POP?
NO, MY BOY, NO NO NO.
I HAVE EVERYTHING I NEED.

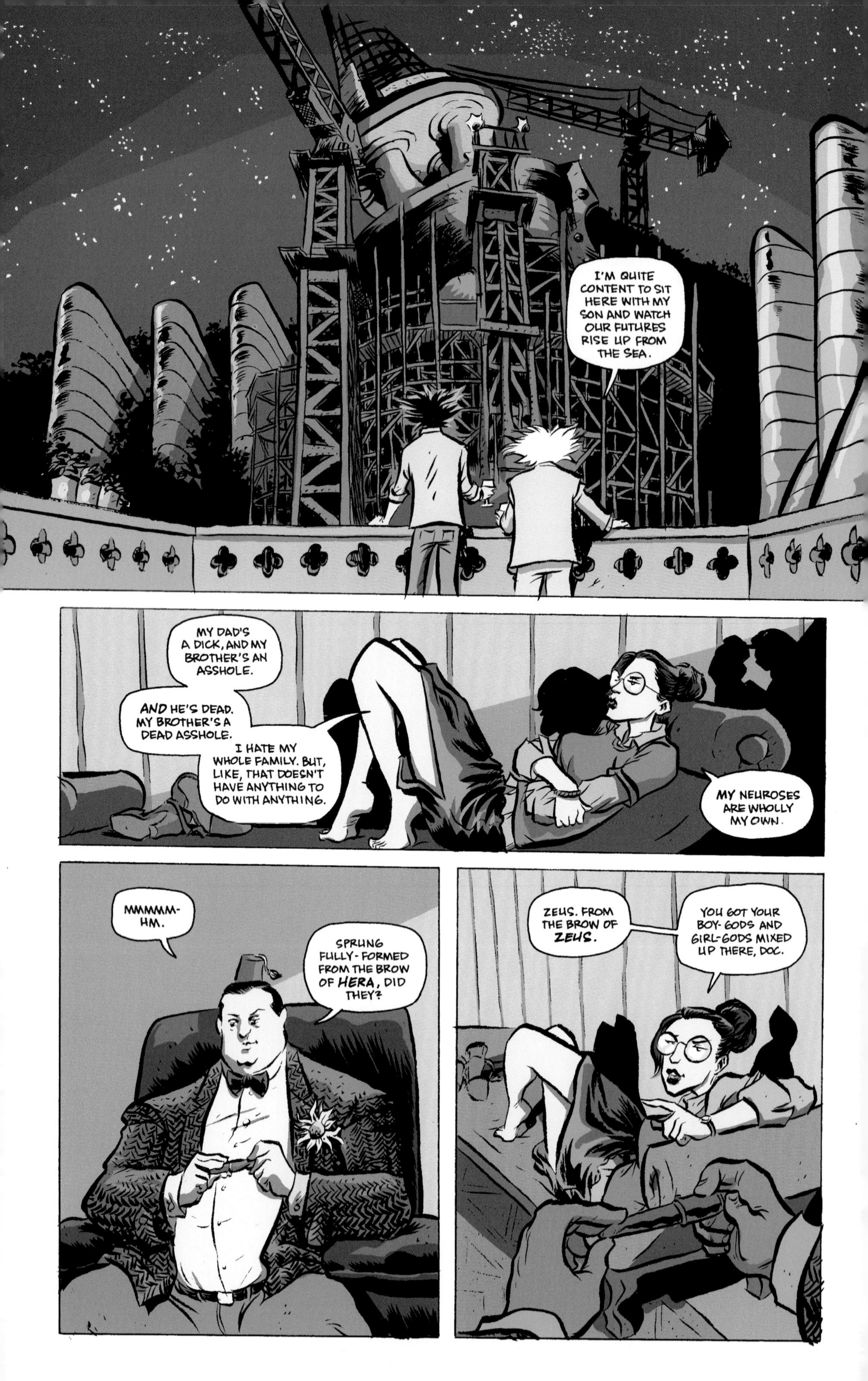
I'M QUITE CONTENT TO SIT HERE WITH MY SON AND WATCH OUR FUTURES RISE UP FROM THE SEA.
MY DAD'S A DICK, AND MY BROTHER'S AN ASSHOLE.
AND HE'S DEAD. MY BROTHER'S A DEAD ASSHOLE.
I HATE MY WHOLE FAMILY. BUT, LIKE, THAT DOESN'T HAVE ANYTHING TO DO WITH ANYTHING.
MY NEUROSES ARE WHOLLY MY OWN.
MMMMM-HM.
SPRUNG FULLY-FORMED FROM THE BROW OF **HERA**, DID THEY?
ZEUS. FROM THE BROW OF **ZEUS**.
YOU GOT YOUR BOY-GODS AND GIRL-GODS MIXED UP THERE, DOC.

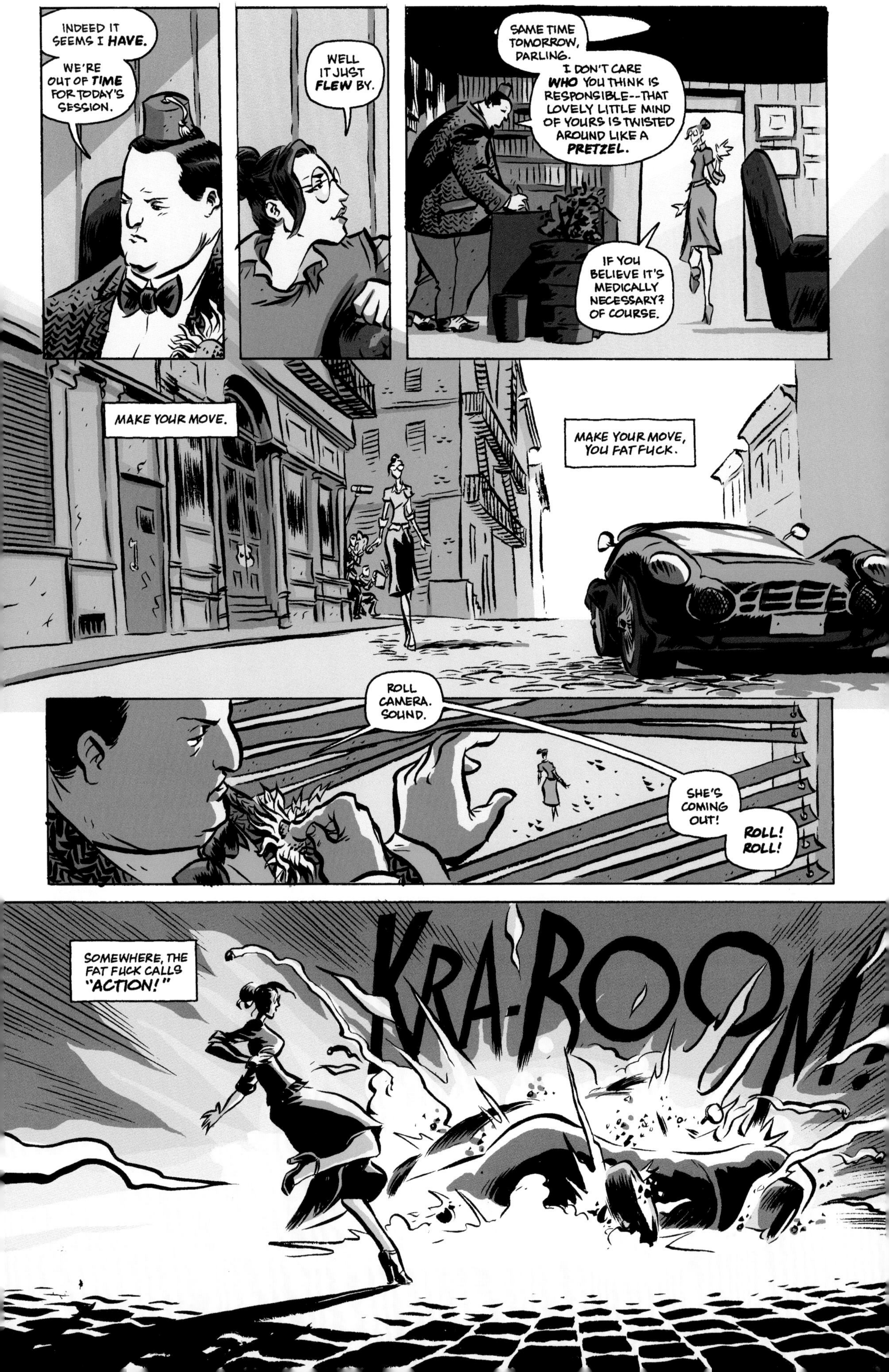
INDEED IT SEEMS I HAVE.
WE'RE OUT OF TIME FOR TODAY'S SESSION.
WELL IT JUST FLEW BY.
SAME TIME TOMORROW, DARLING.
I DON'T CARE WHO YOU THINK IS RESPONSIBLE--THAT LOVELY LITTLE MIND OF YOURS IS TWISTED AROUND LIKE A PRETZEL.
IF YOU BELIEVE IT'S MEDICALLY NECESSARY? OF COURSE.
MAKE YOUR MOVE.
MAKE YOUR MOVE, YOU FAT FUCK.
ROLL CAMERA. SOUND.
SHE'S COMING OUT!
ROLL! ROLL!
SOMEWHERE, THE FAT FUCK CALLS "ACTION!"
KRA-ROOM!

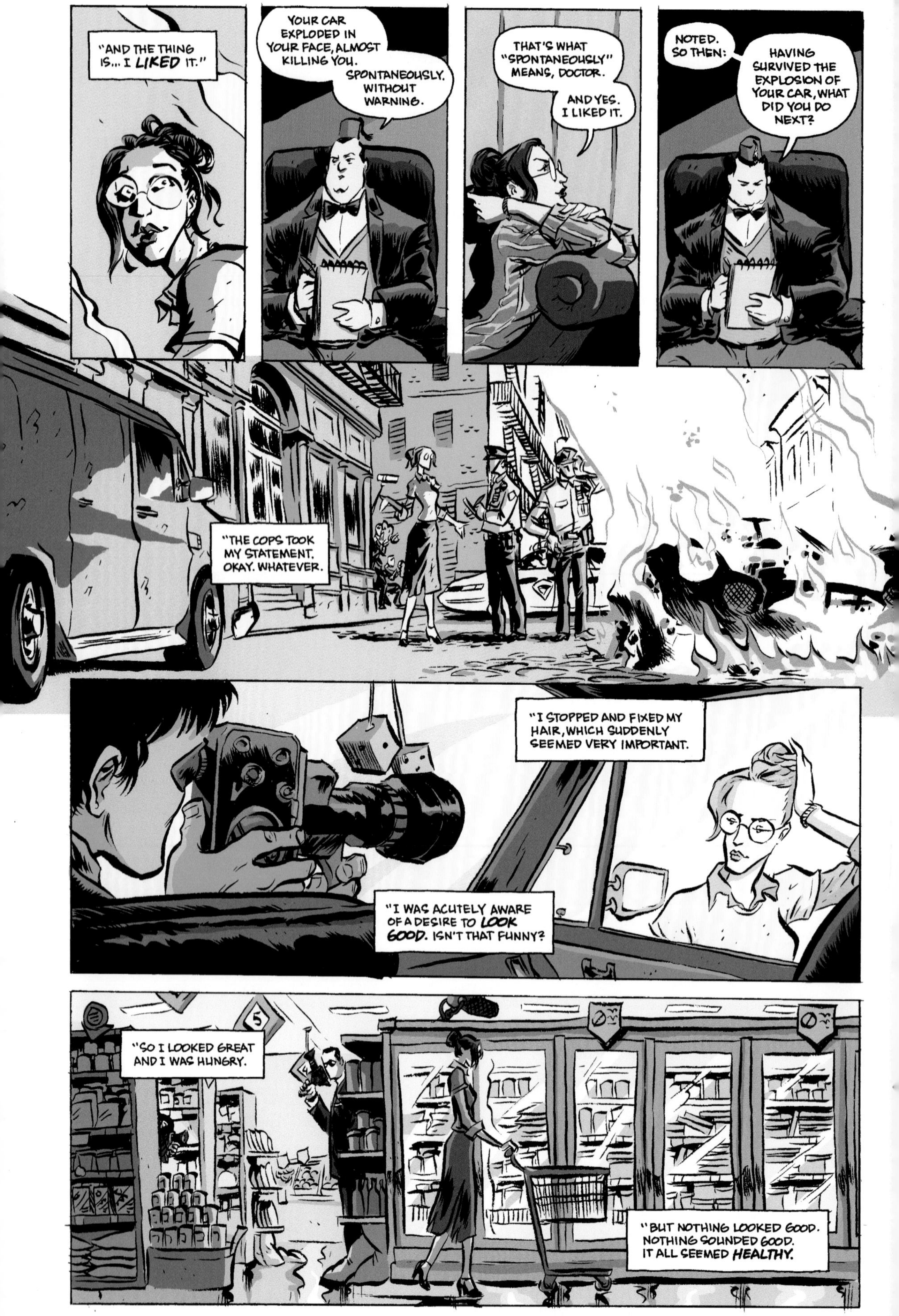
"AND THE THING IS... I LIKED IT."
YOUR CAR EXPLODED IN YOUR FACE, ALMOST KILLING YOU.
SPONTANEOUSLY. WITHOUT WARNING.
THAT'S WHAT "SPONTANEOUSLY" MEANS, DOCTOR.
AND YES. I LIKED IT.
NOTED. SO THEN:
HAVING SURVIVED THE EXPLOSION OF YOUR CAR, WHAT DID YOU DO NEXT?
"THE COPS TOOK MY STATEMENT. OKAY. WHATEVER.
"I STOPPED AND FIXED MY HAIR, WHICH SUDDENLY SEEMED VERY IMPORTANT.
"I WAS ACUTELY AWARE OF A DESIRE TO LOOK GOOD. ISN'T THAT FUNNY?
"SO I LOOKED GREAT AND I WAS HUNGRY.
"BUT NOTHING LOOKED GOOD. NOTHING SOUNDED GOOD. IT ALL SEEMED HEALTHY.

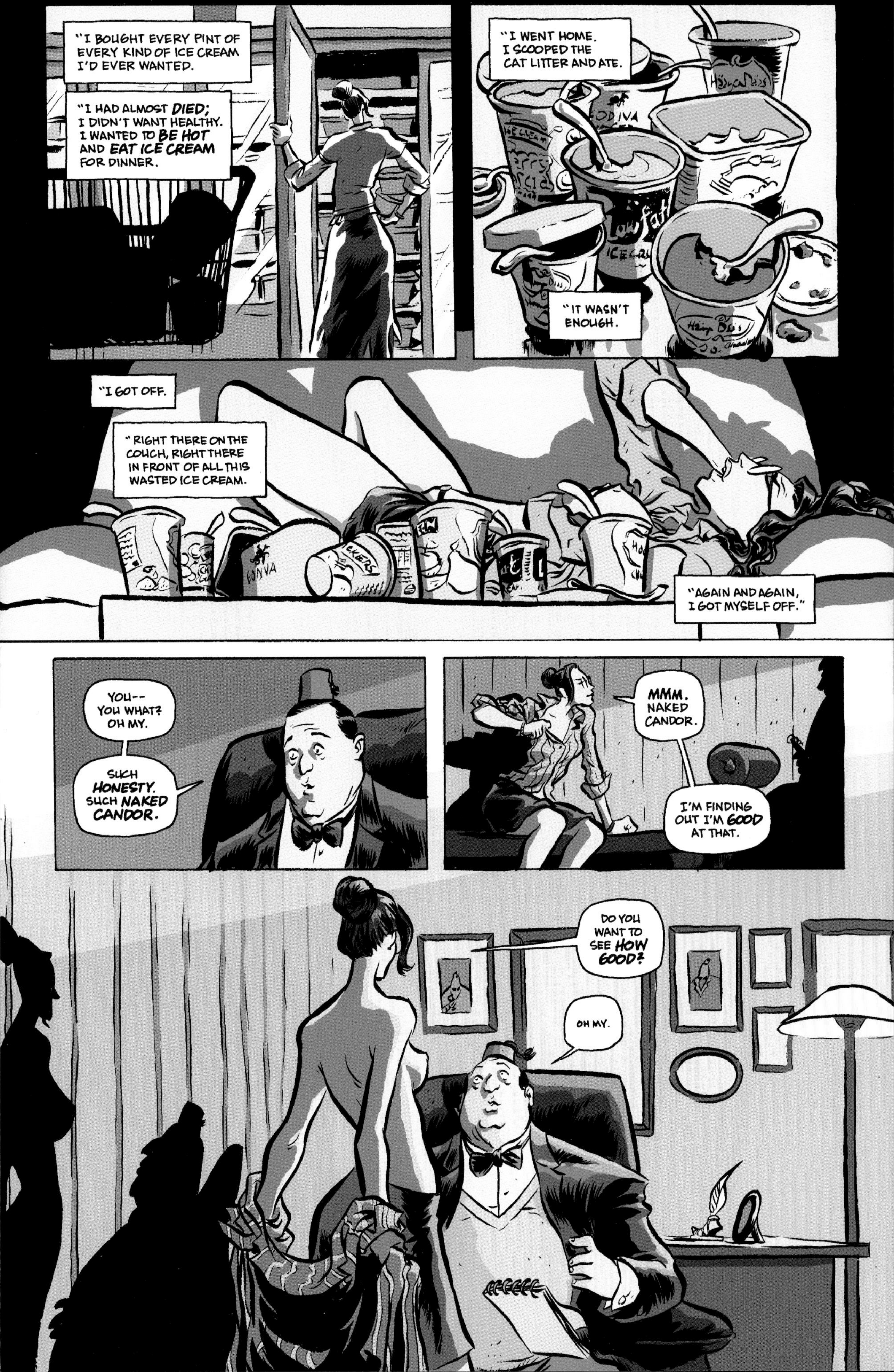
"I BOUGHT EVERY PINT OF EVERY KIND OF ICE CREAM I'D EVER WANTED.
"I HAD ALMOST DIED; I DIDN'T WANT HEALTHY. I WANTED TO BE HOT AND EAT ICE CREAM FOR DINNER.
"I WENT HOME. I SCOOPED THE CAT LITTER AND ATE.
GODIVA
"IT WASN'T ENOUGH.
"I GOT OFF.
"RIGHT THERE ON THE COUCH, RIGHT THERE IN FRONT OF ALL THIS WASTED ICE CREAM.
GODIVA
"AGAIN AND AGAIN, I GOT MYSELF OFF."
YOU-- YOU WHAT? OH MY.
SUCH HONESTY. SUCH NAKED CANDOR.
MMM. NAKED CANDOR.
I'M FINDING OUT I'M GOOD AT THAT.
DO YOU WANT TO SEE HOW GOOD?
OH MY.

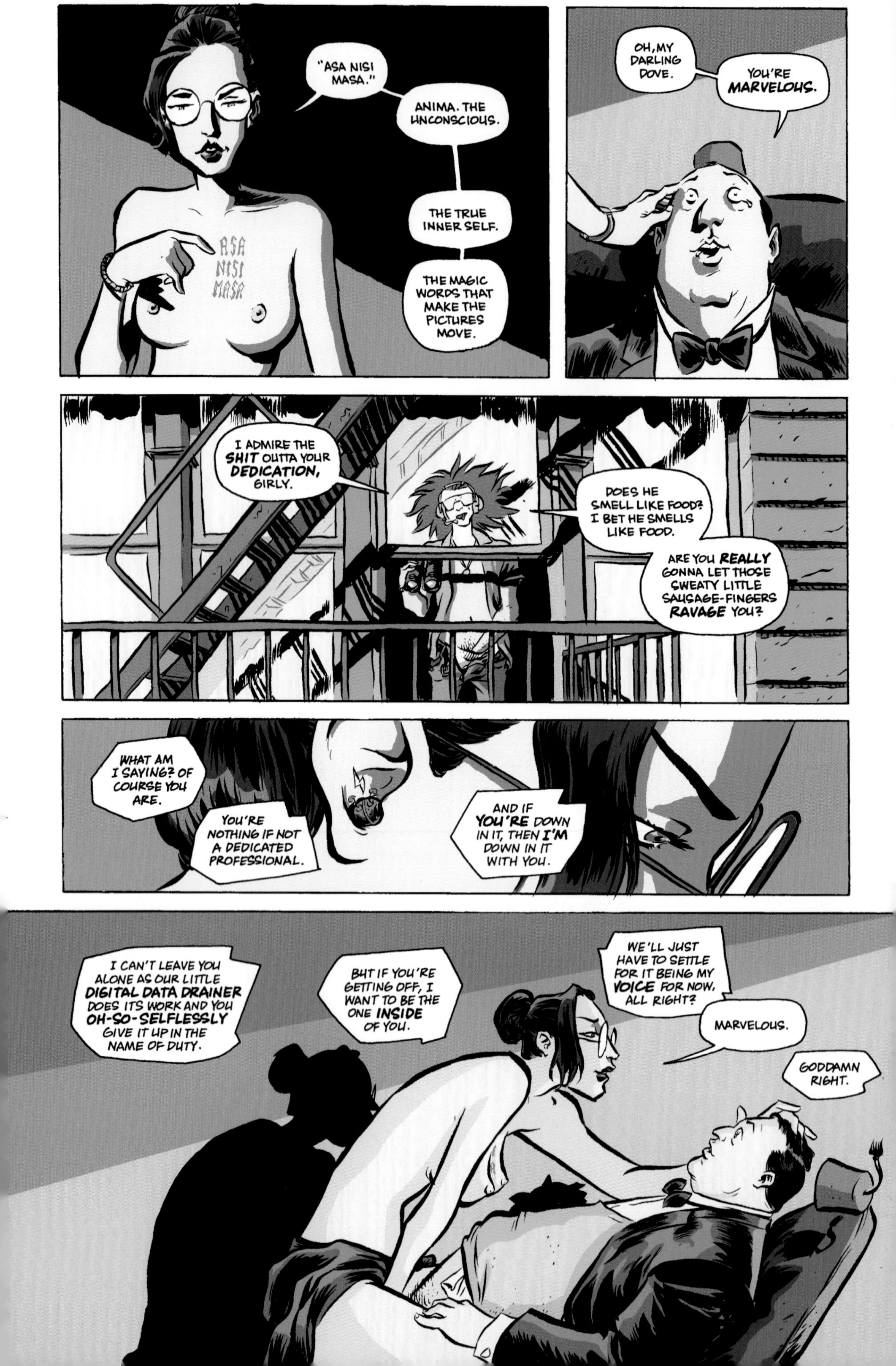
"ASA NISI MASA."
ANIMA. THE UNCONSCIOUS.
THE TRUE INNER SELF.
THE MAGIC WORDS THAT MAKE THE PICTURES MOVE.
ASA NISI MASA
OH, MY DARLING DOVE.
YOU'RE **MARVELOUS.**
I ADMIRE THE **SHIT** OUTTA YOUR **DEDICATION,** GIRLY.
DOES HE SMELL LIKE FOOD? I BET HE SMELLS LIKE FOOD.
ARE YOU **REALLY** GONNA LET THOSE SWEATY LITTLE SAUSAGE-FINGERS **RAVAGE** YOU?
WHAT AM I SAYING? OF COURSE YOU ARE.
YOU'RE NOTHING IF NOT A DEDICATED PROFESSIONAL.
AND IF **YOU'RE** DOWN IN IT, THEN **I'M** DOWN IN IT WITH YOU.
I CAN'T LEAVE YOU ALONE AS OUR LITTLE **DIGITAL DATA DRAINER** DOES ITS WORK AND YOU **OH-SO-SELFLESSLY** GIVE IT UP IN THE NAME OF DUTY.
BUT IF YOU'RE GETTING OFF, I WANT TO BE THE ONE **INSIDE** OF YOU.
WE'LL JUST HAVE TO SETTLE FOR IT BEING MY **VOICE** FOR NOW, ALL RIGHT?
MARVELOUS.
GODDAMN RIGHT.

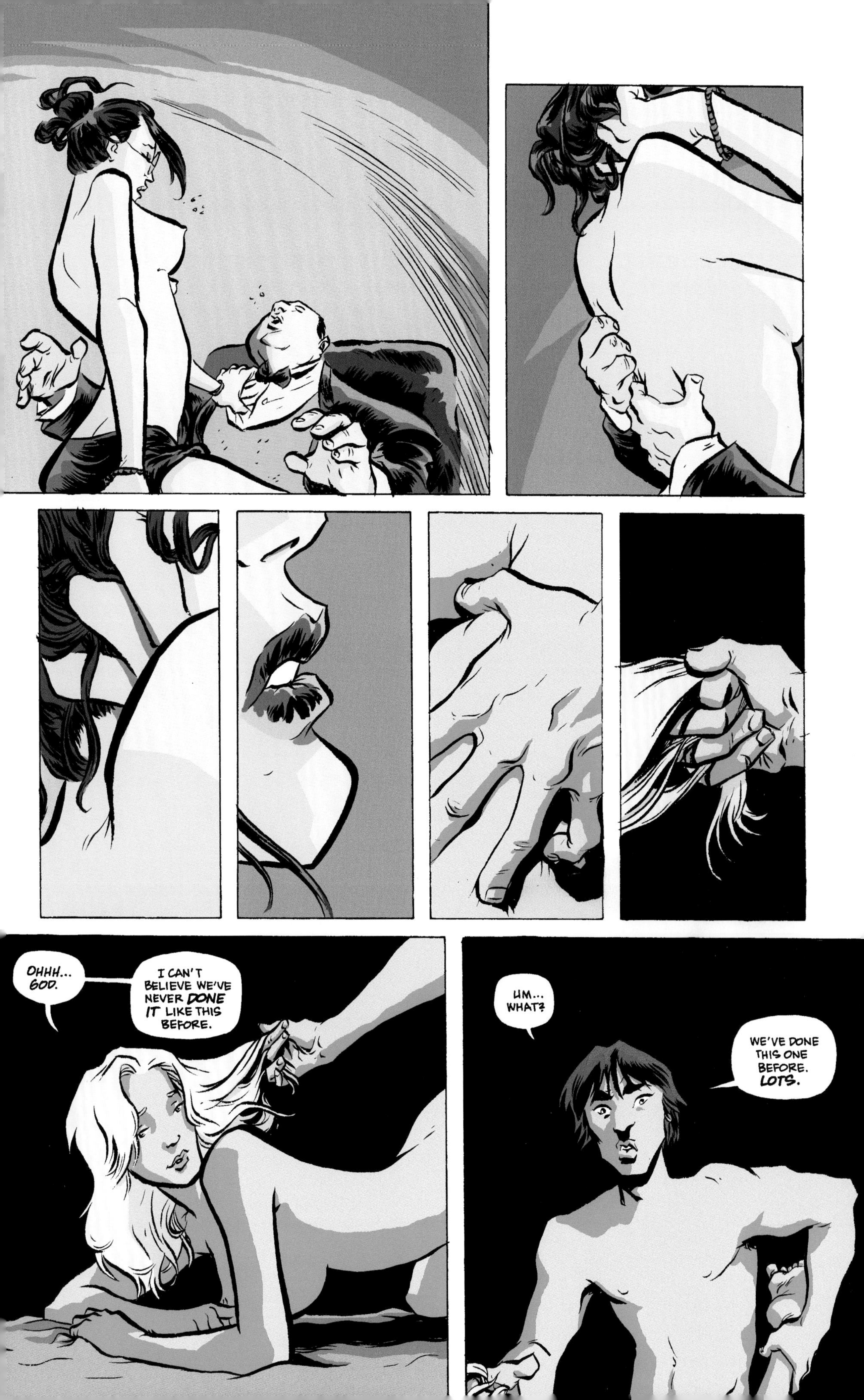
OHHH... GOD.
I CAN'T BELIEVE WE'VE NEVER DONE IT LIKE THIS BEFORE.
UM... WHAT?
WE'VE DONE THIS ONE BEFORE. LOTS.

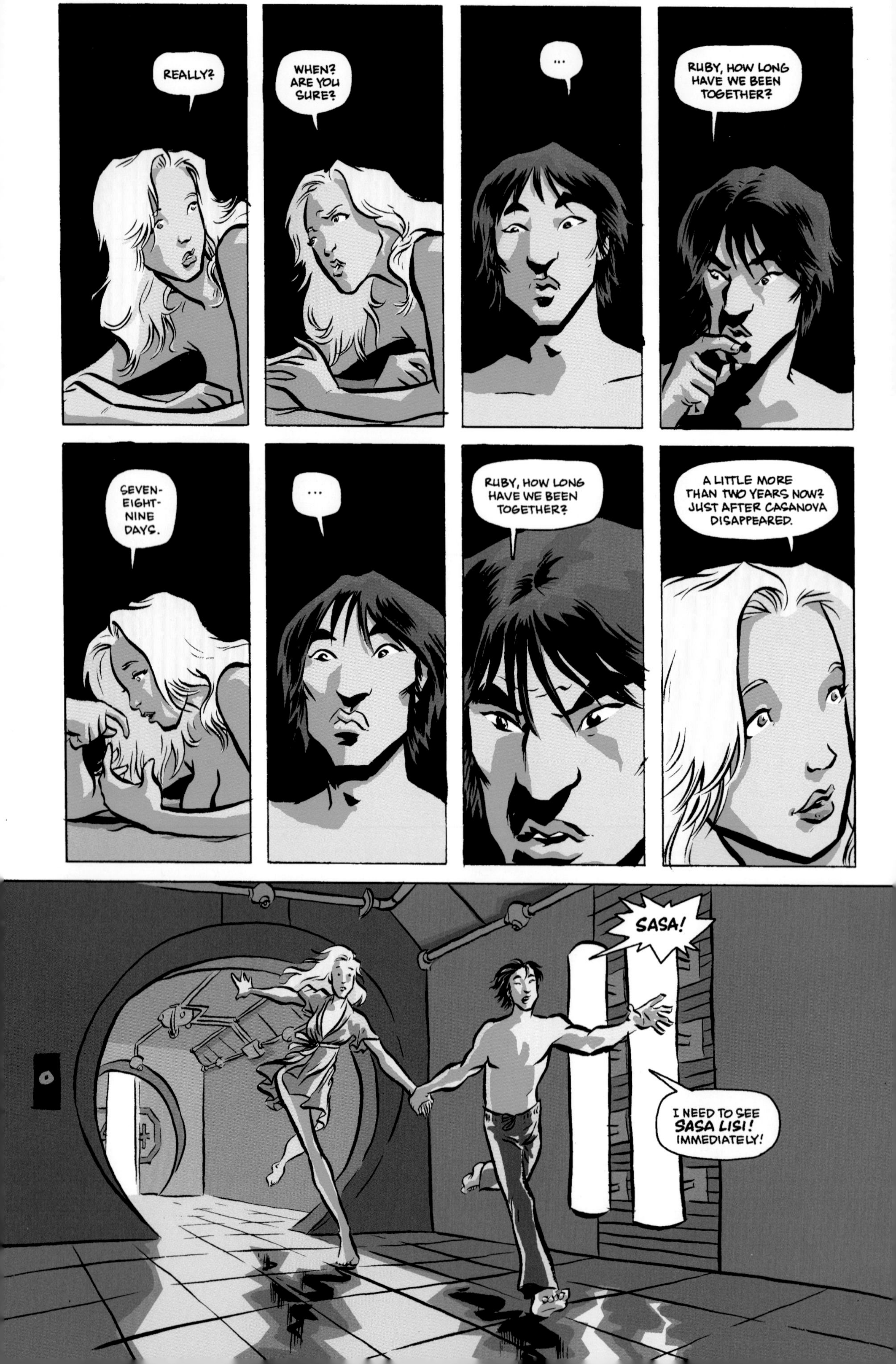
REALLY?
WHEN? ARE YOU SURE?
...
RUBY, HOW LONG HAVE WE BEEN TOGETHER?
SEVEN- EIGHT- NINE DAYS.
...
RUBY, HOW LONG HAVE WE BEEN TOGETHER?
A LITTLE MORE THAN TWO YEARS NOW? JUST AFTER CASANOVA DISAPPEARED.
SASA!
I NEED TO SEE SASA LISI! IMMEDIATELY!

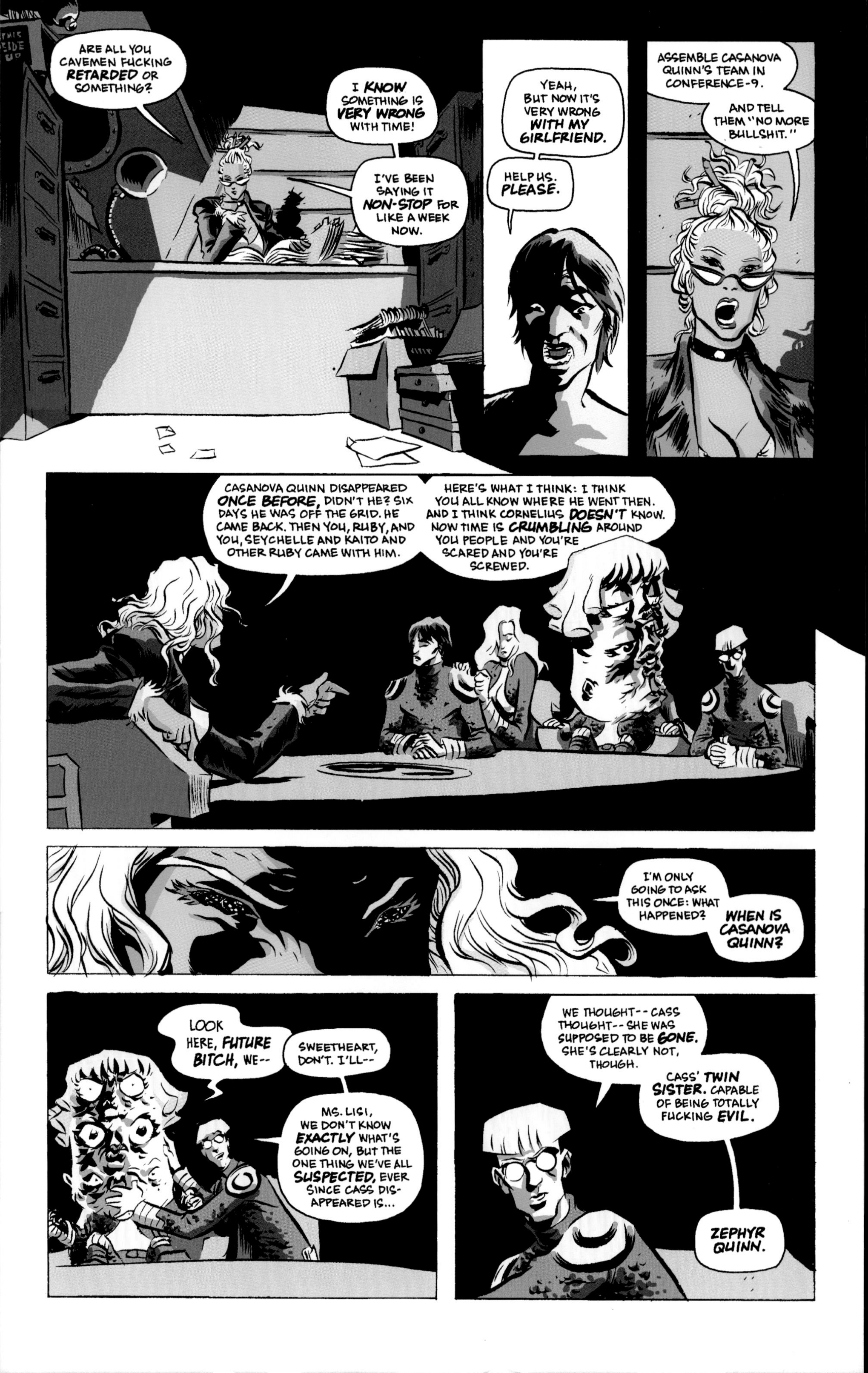
ARE ALL YOU CAVEMEN FUCKING RETARDED OR SOMETHING?
I KNOW SOMETHING IS VERY WRONG WITH TIME!
I'VE BEEN SAYING IT NON-STOP FOR LIKE A WEEK NOW.
YEAH, BUT NOW IT'S VERY WRONG WITH MY GIRLFRIEND.
HELP US. PLEASE.
ASSEMBLE CASANOVA QUINN'S TEAM IN CONFERENCE-9.
AND TELL THEM "NO MORE BULLSHIT."
CASANOVA QUINN DISAPPEARED ONCE BEFORE, DIDN'T HE? SIX DAYS HE WAS OFF THE GRID. HE CAME BACK. THEN YOU, RUBY, AND YOU, SEYCHELLE AND KAITO AND OTHER RUBY CAME WITH HIM.
HERE'S WHAT I THINK: I THINK YOU ALL KNOW WHERE HE WENT THEN. AND I THINK CORNELIUS DOESN'T KNOW. NOW TIME IS CRUMBLING AROUND YOU PEOPLE AND YOU'RE SCARED AND YOU'RE SCREWED.
I'M ONLY GOING TO ASK THIS ONCE: WHAT HAPPENED?
WHEN IS CASANOVA QUINN?
LOOK HERE, FUTURE BITCH, WE--
SWEETHEART, DON'T. I'LL--
MS. LISI, WE DON'T KNOW EXACTLY WHAT'S GOING ON, BUT THE ONE THING WE'VE ALL SUSPECTED, EVER SINCE CASS DIS-APPEARED IS...
WE THOUGHT-- CASS THOUGHT-- SHE WAS SUPPOSED TO BE GONE. SHE'S CLEARLY NOT, THOUGH.
CASS' TWIN SISTER. CAPABLE OF BEING TOTALLY FUCKING EVIL.
ZEPHYR QUINN.

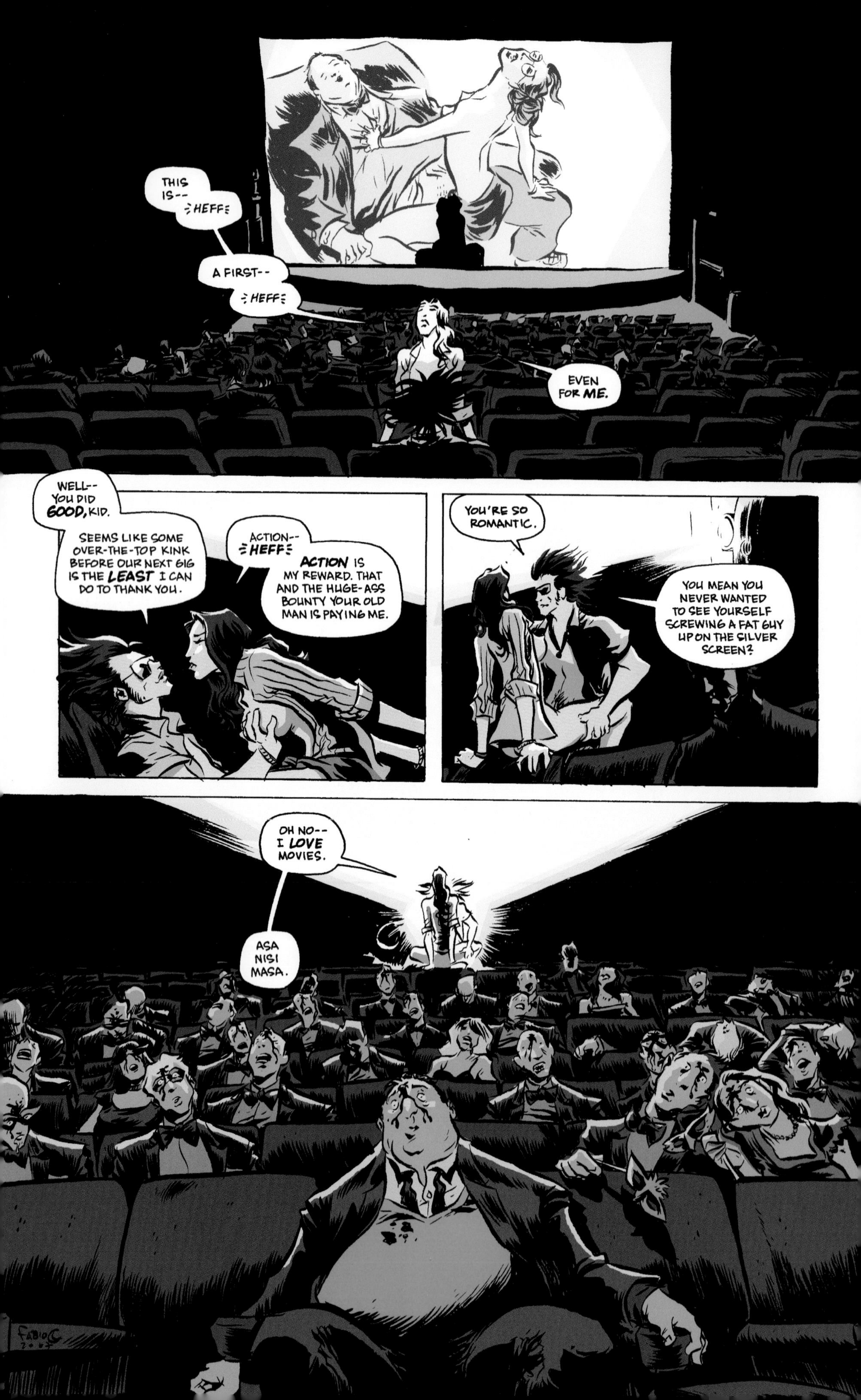
THIS IS-- HEFF
A FIRST-- HEFF
EVEN FOR ME.
WELL-- YOU DID GOOD, KID.
SEEMS LIKE SOME OVER-THE-TOP KINK BEFORE OUR NEXT GIG IS THE LEAST I CAN DO TO THANK YOU.
ACTION-- HEFF
ACTION IS MY REWARD. THAT AND THE HUGE-ASS BOUNTY YOUR OLD MAN IS PAYING ME.
YOU'RE SO ROMANTIC.
YOU MEAN YOU NEVER WANTED TO SEE YOURSELF SCREWING A FAT GUY UP ON THE SILVER SCREEN?
OH NO-- I LOVE MOVIES.
ASA NISI MASA.

IN MEDIAS RES

WHEN THE WOLF COMES HOME

SEVENTEEN

NAOMI I MOAN

FUCK SHIT UP

SOME OF THE THINGS THAT
HAPPENED TO THE MURDERERS
AND MURDERED AMONG US

HALLO SPACEBOY

DIT DIT DIT
DAH DAH DAH
DIT DIT

BACKMATTER

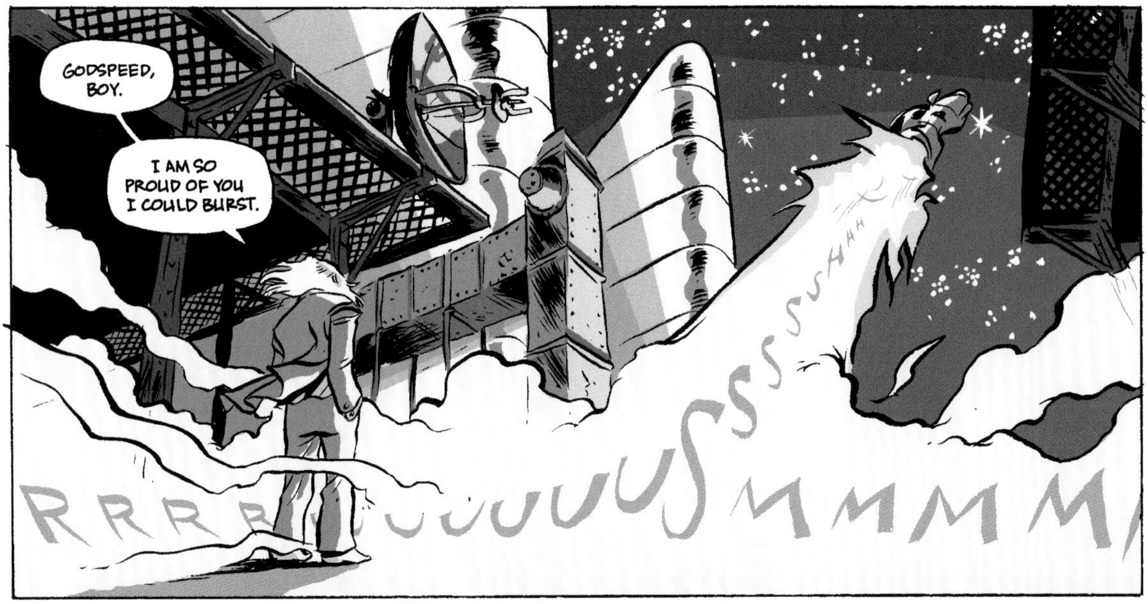
GODSPEED, BOY.
I AM SO PROUD OF YOU I COULD BURST.

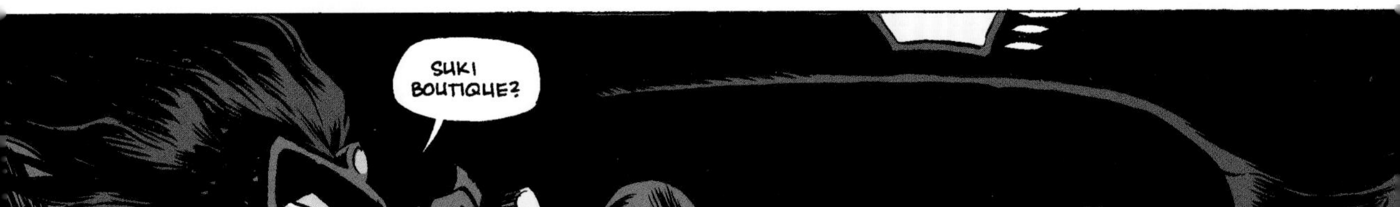
SUKI BOUTIQUE?
SUKI BOUTIQUE.

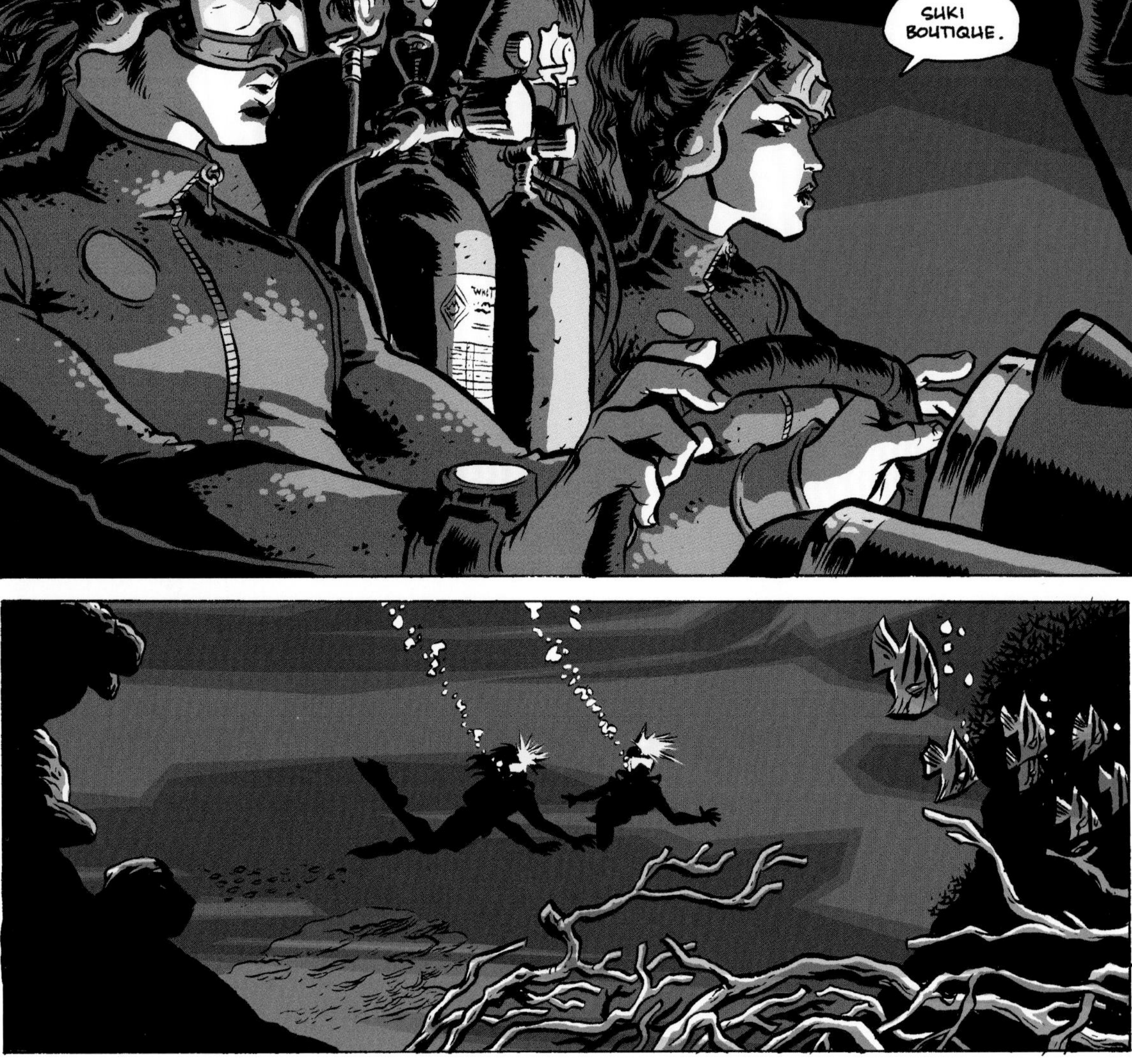

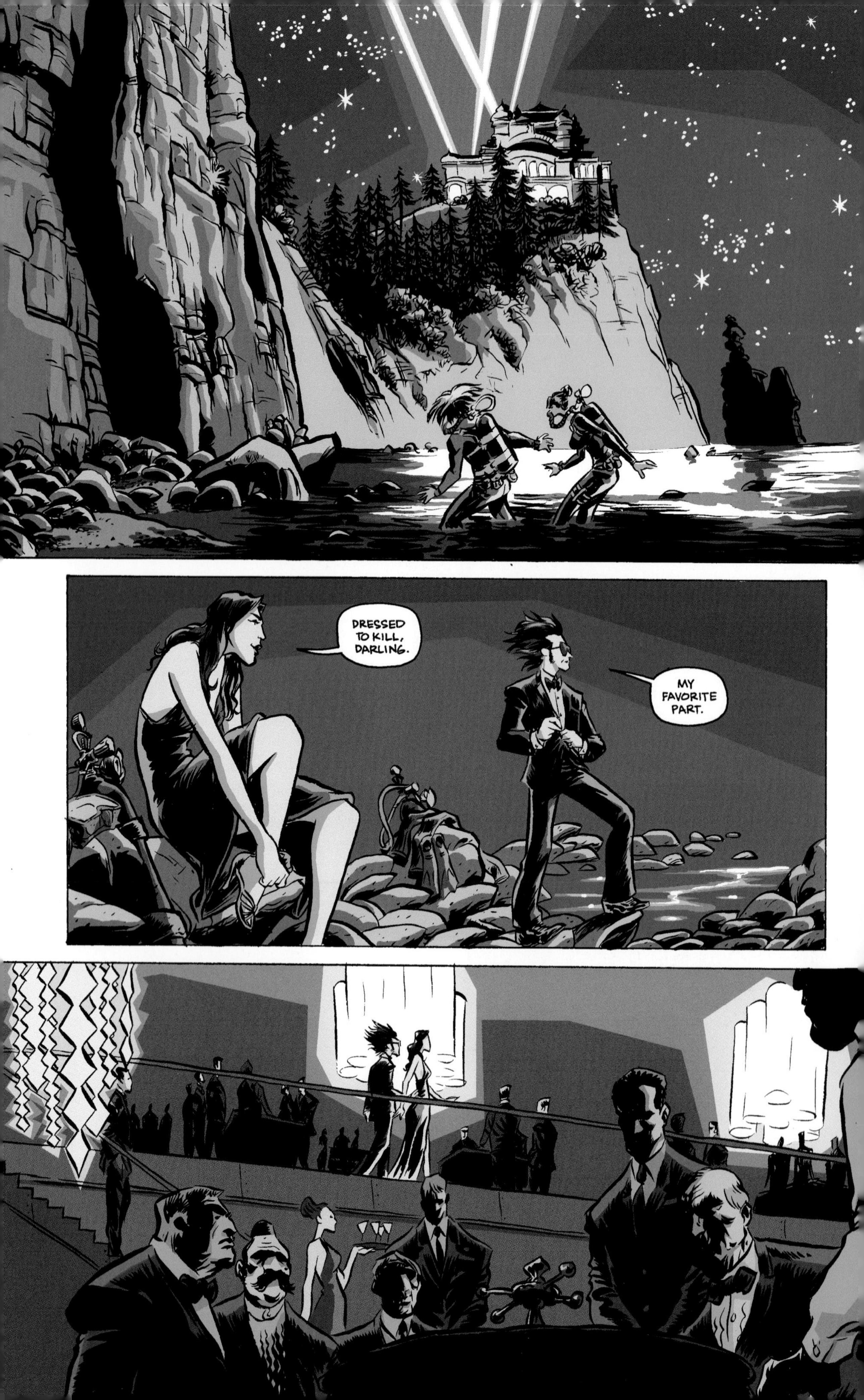
DRESSED TO KILL, DARLING.
MY FAVORITE PART.

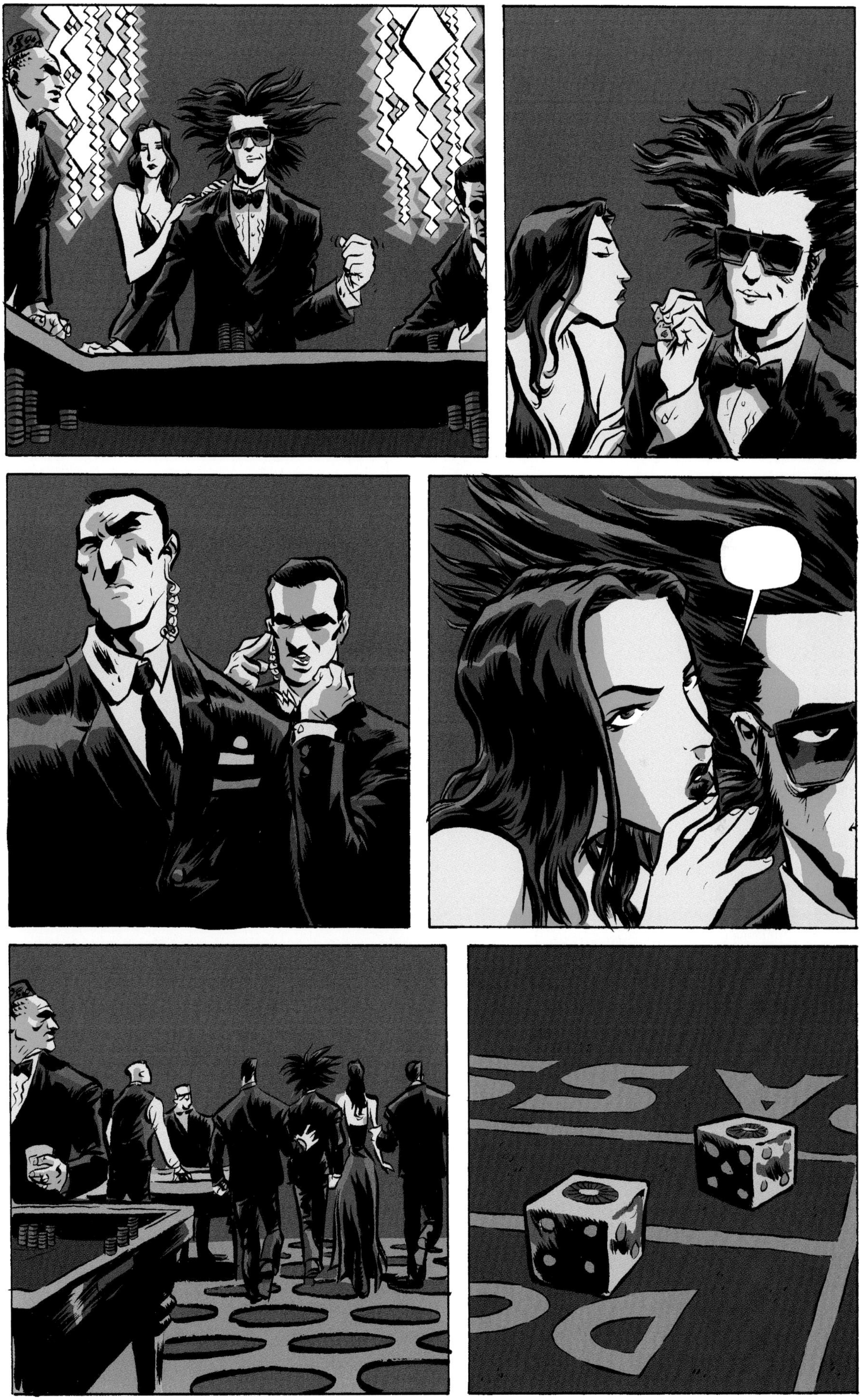

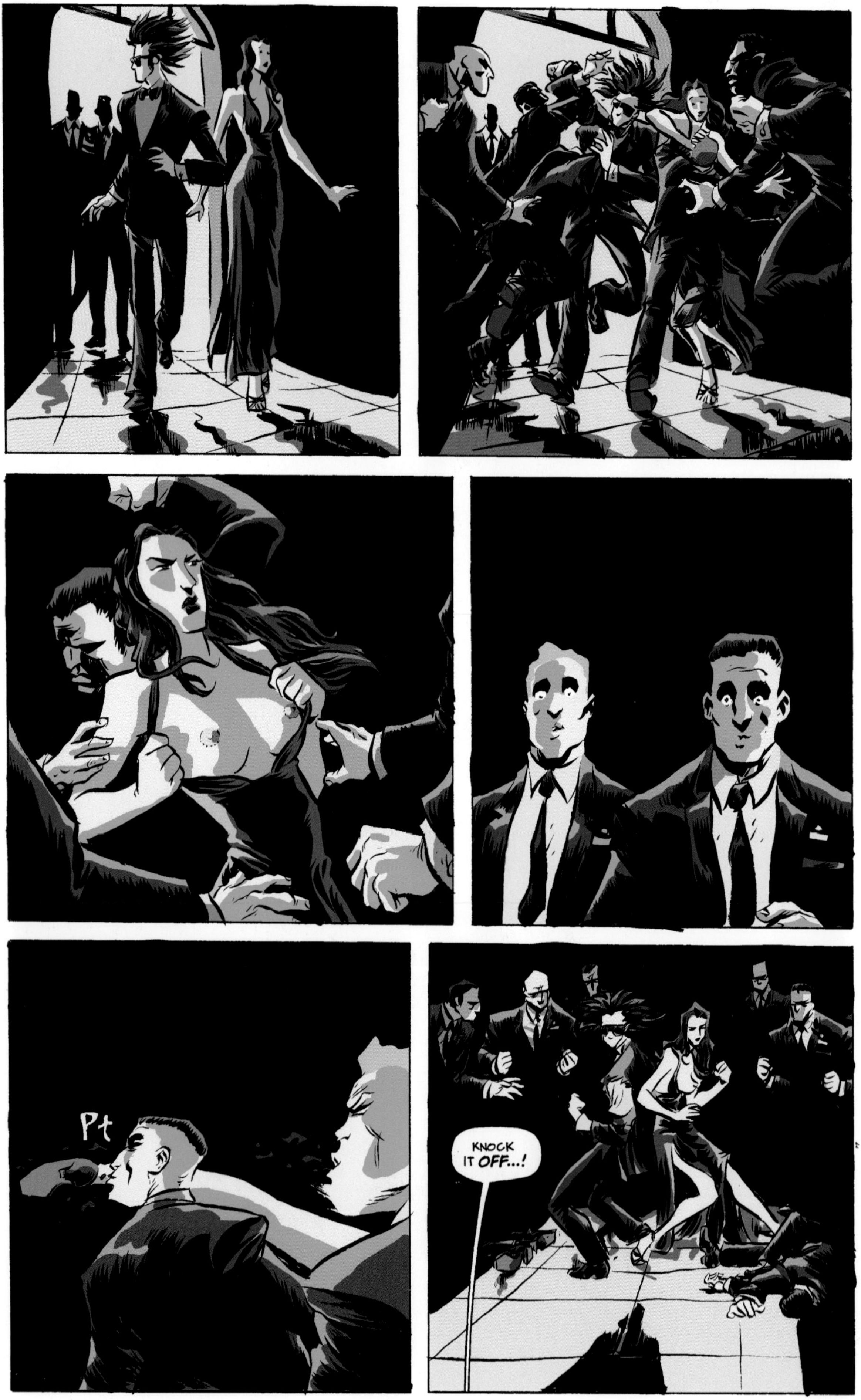
Pt
KNOCK IT OFF...!

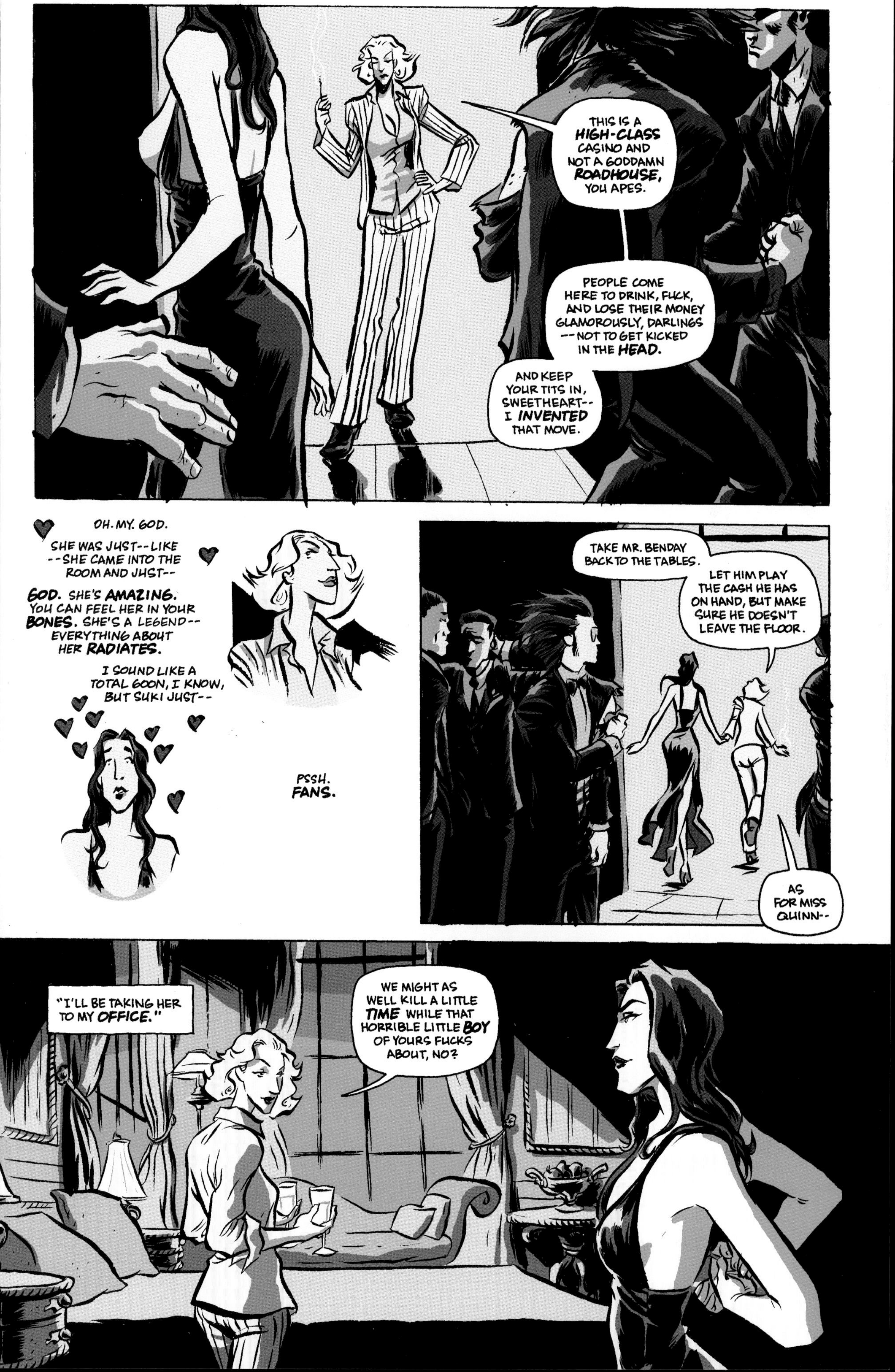
THIS IS A HIGH-CLASS CASINO AND NOT A GODDAMN ROADHOUSE, YOU APES.
PEOPLE COME HERE TO DRINK, FUCK, AND LOSE THEIR MONEY GLAMOROUSLY, DARLINGS --NOT TO GET KICKED IN THE HEAD.
AND KEEP YOUR TITS IN, SWEETHEART-- I INVENTED THAT MOVE.
OH. MY. GOD.
SHE WAS JUST--LIKE --SHE CAME INTO THE ROOM AND JUST--
GOD. SHE'S AMAZING. YOU CAN FEEL HER IN YOUR BONES. SHE'S A LEGEND-- EVERYTHING ABOUT HER RADIATES.
I SOUND LIKE A TOTAL GOON, I KNOW, BUT SUKI JUST--
PSSH. FANS.
TAKE MR. BENDAY BACK TO THE TABLES.
LET HIM PLAY THE CASH HE HAS ON HAND, BUT MAKE SURE HE DOESN'T LEAVE THE FLOOR.
AS FOR MISS QUINN--
"I'LL BE TAKING HER TO MY OFFICE."
WE MIGHT AS WELL KILL A LITTLE TIME WHILE THAT HORRIBLE LITTLE BOY OF YOURS FUCKS ABOUT, NO?

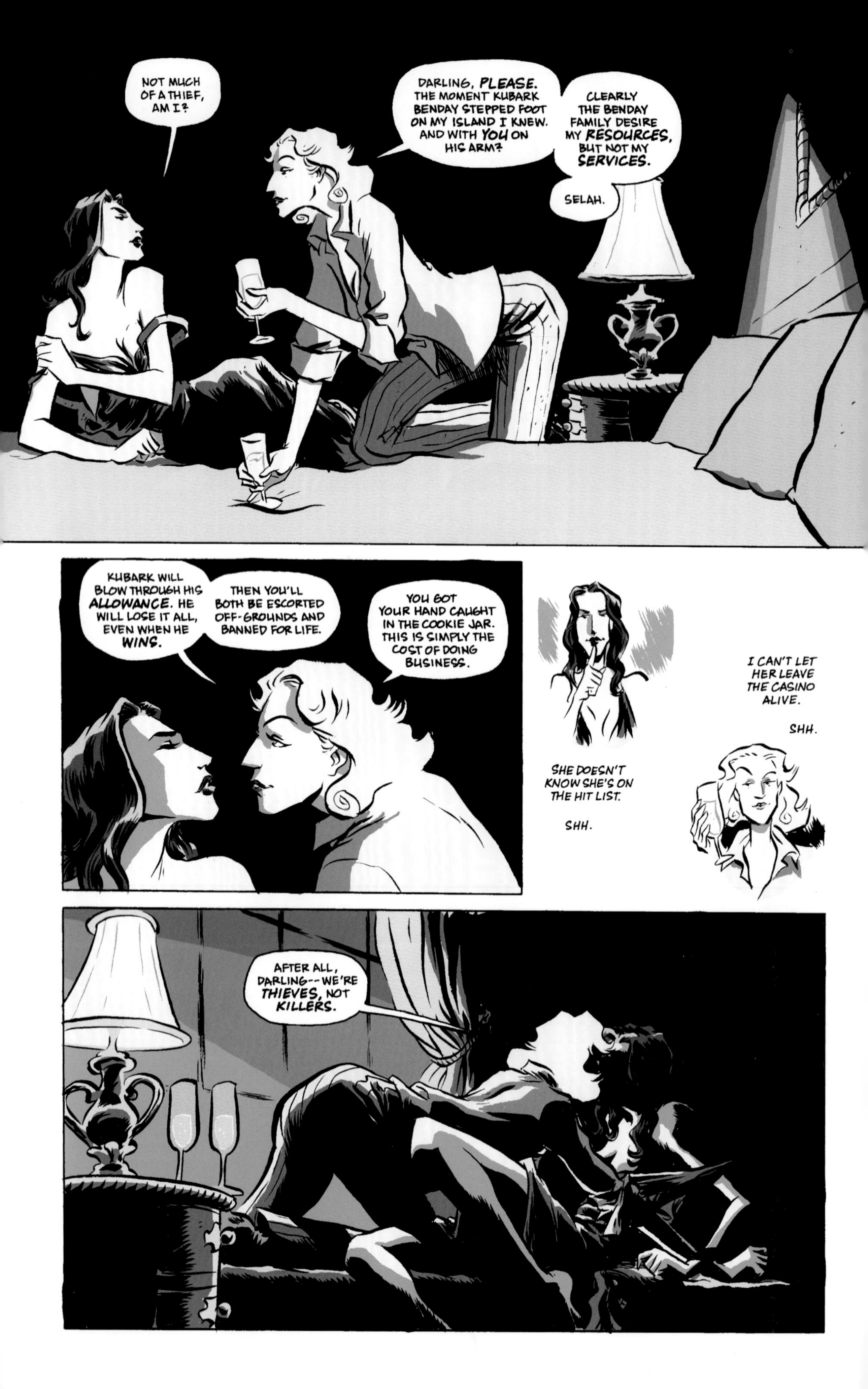
NOT MUCH OF A THIEF, AM I?
DARLING, PLEASE. THE MOMENT KUBARK BENDAY STEPPED FOOT ON MY ISLAND I KNEW. AND WITH YOU ON HIS ARM?
CLEARLY THE BENDAY FAMILY DESIRE MY RESOURCES, BUT NOT MY SERVICES.
SELAH.
KUBARK WILL BLOW THROUGH HIS ALLOWANCE. HE WILL LOSE IT ALL, EVEN WHEN HE WINS.
THEN YOU'LL BOTH BE ESCORTED OFF-GROUNDS AND BANNED FOR LIFE.
YOU GOT YOUR HAND CAUGHT IN THE COOKIE JAR. THIS IS SIMPLY THE COST OF DOING BUSINESS.
I CAN'T LET HER LEAVE THE CASINO ALIVE.
SHH.
SHE DOESN'T KNOW SHE'S ON THE HIT LIST.
SHH.
AFTER ALL, DARLING--WE'RE THIEVES, NOT KILLERS.

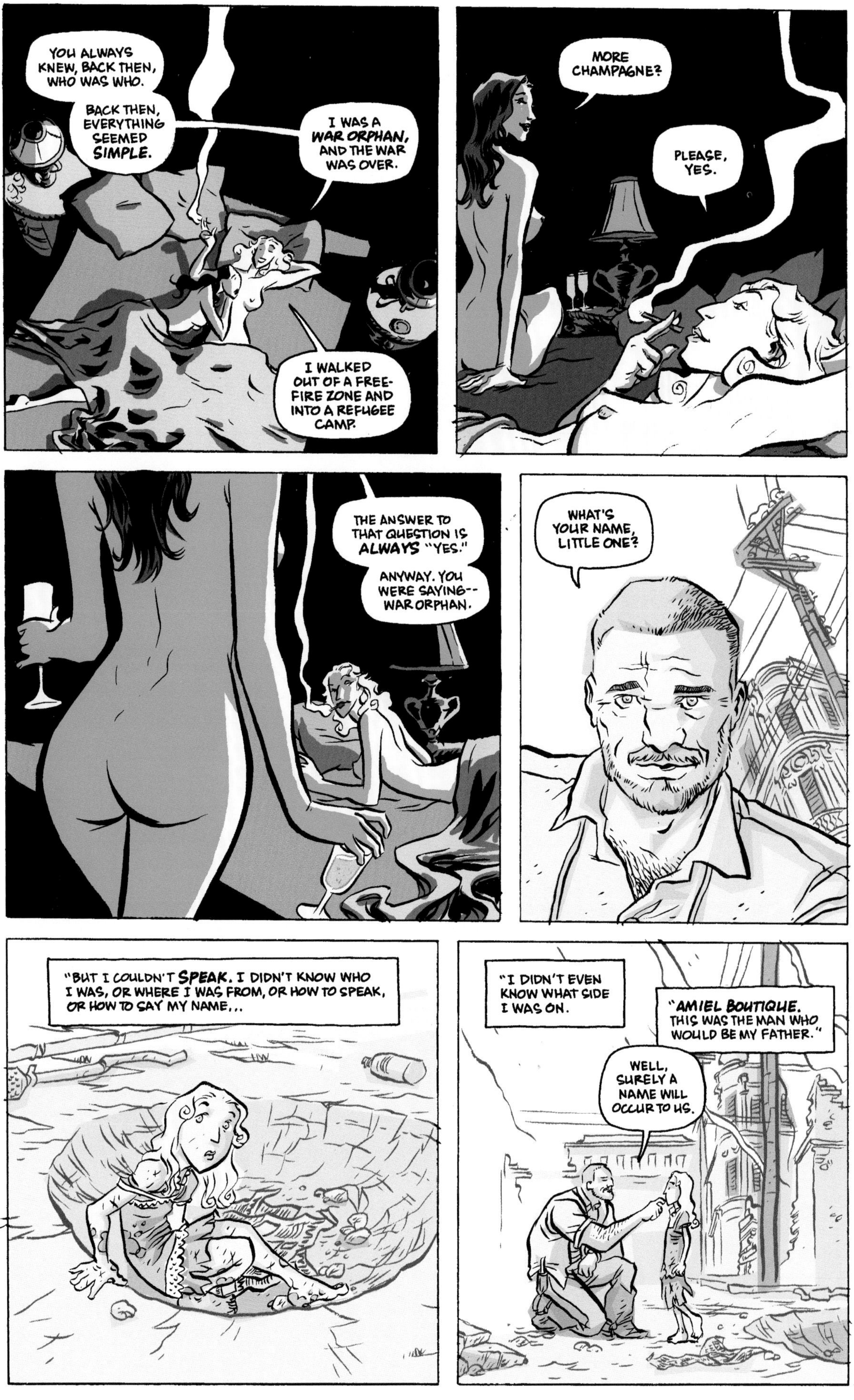
YOU ALWAYS KNEW, BACK THEN, WHO WAS WHO.
BACK THEN, EVERYTHING SEEMED SIMPLE.
I WAS A WAR ORPHAN, AND THE WAR WAS OVER.
I WALKED OUT OF A FREE-FIRE ZONE AND INTO A REFUGEE CAMP.
MORE CHAMPAGNE?
PLEASE, YES.
THE ANSWER TO THAT QUESTION IS ALWAYS "YES."
ANYWAY. YOU WERE SAYING-- WAR ORPHAN.
WHAT'S YOUR NAME, LITTLE ONE?
"BUT I COULDN'T SPEAK. I DIDN'T KNOW WHO I WAS, OR WHERE I WAS FROM, OR HOW TO SPEAK, OR HOW TO SAY MY NAME...
"I DIDN'T EVEN KNOW WHAT SIDE I WAS ON.
"AMIEL BOUTIQUE. THIS WAS THE MAN WHO WOULD BE MY FATHER."
WELL, SURELY A NAME WILL OCCUR TO US.

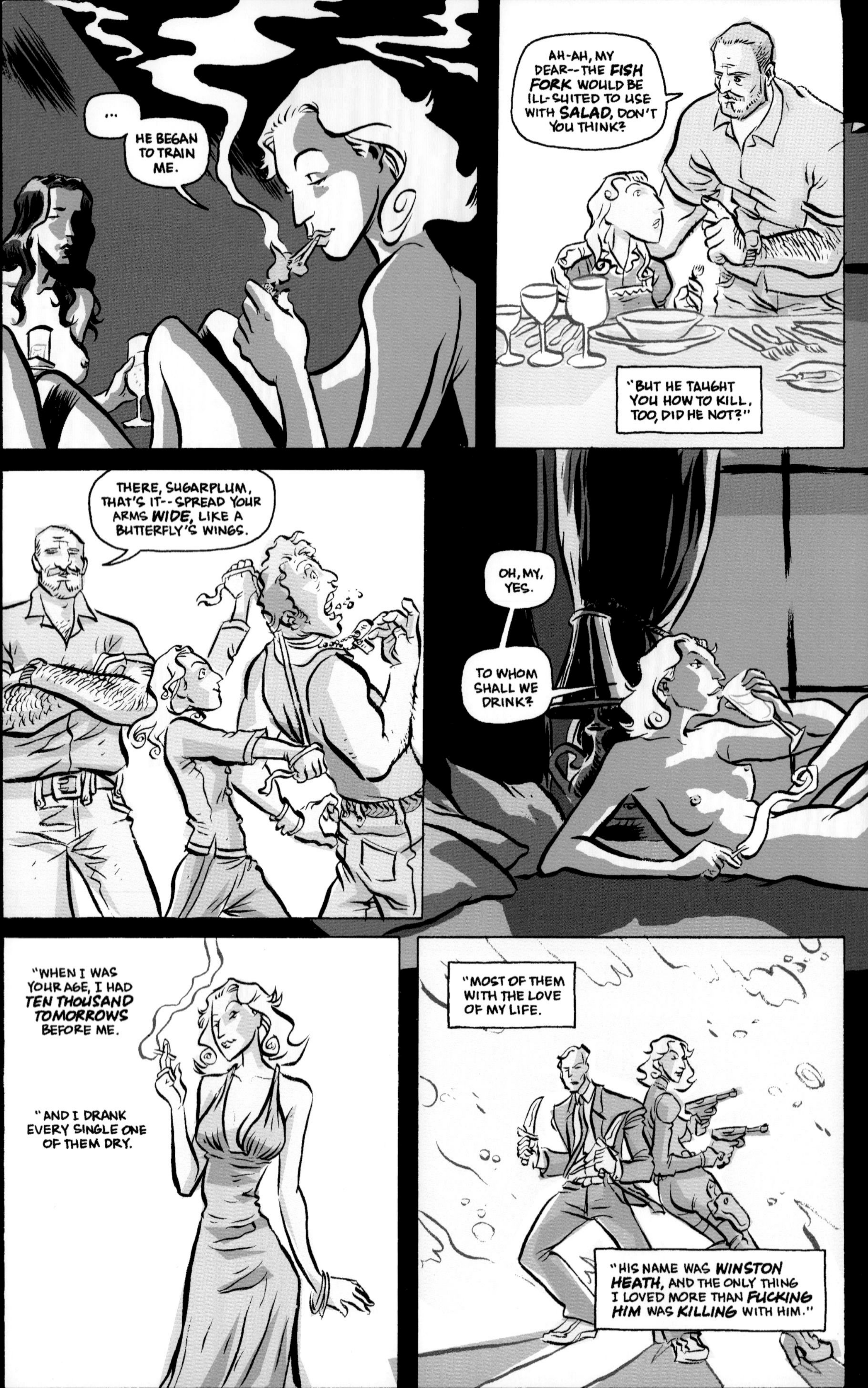
...
HE BEGAN TO TRAIN ME.
AH-AH, MY DEAR--THE FISH FORK WOULD BE ILL-SUITED TO USE WITH SALAD, DON'T YOU THINK?
"BUT HE TAUGHT YOU HOW TO KILL, TOO, DID HE NOT?"
THERE, SUGARPLUM, THAT'S IT--SPREAD YOUR ARMS WIDE, LIKE A BUTTERFLY'S WINGS.
OH, MY, YES.
TO WHOM SHALL WE DRINK?
"WHEN I WAS YOUR AGE, I HAD TEN THOUSAND TOMORROWS BEFORE ME.
"AND I DRANK EVERY SINGLE ONE OF THEM DRY.
"MOST OF THEM WITH THE LOVE OF MY LIFE.
"HIS NAME WAS WINSTON HEATH, AND THE ONLY THING I LOVED MORE THAN FUCKING HIM WAS KILLING WITH HIM."

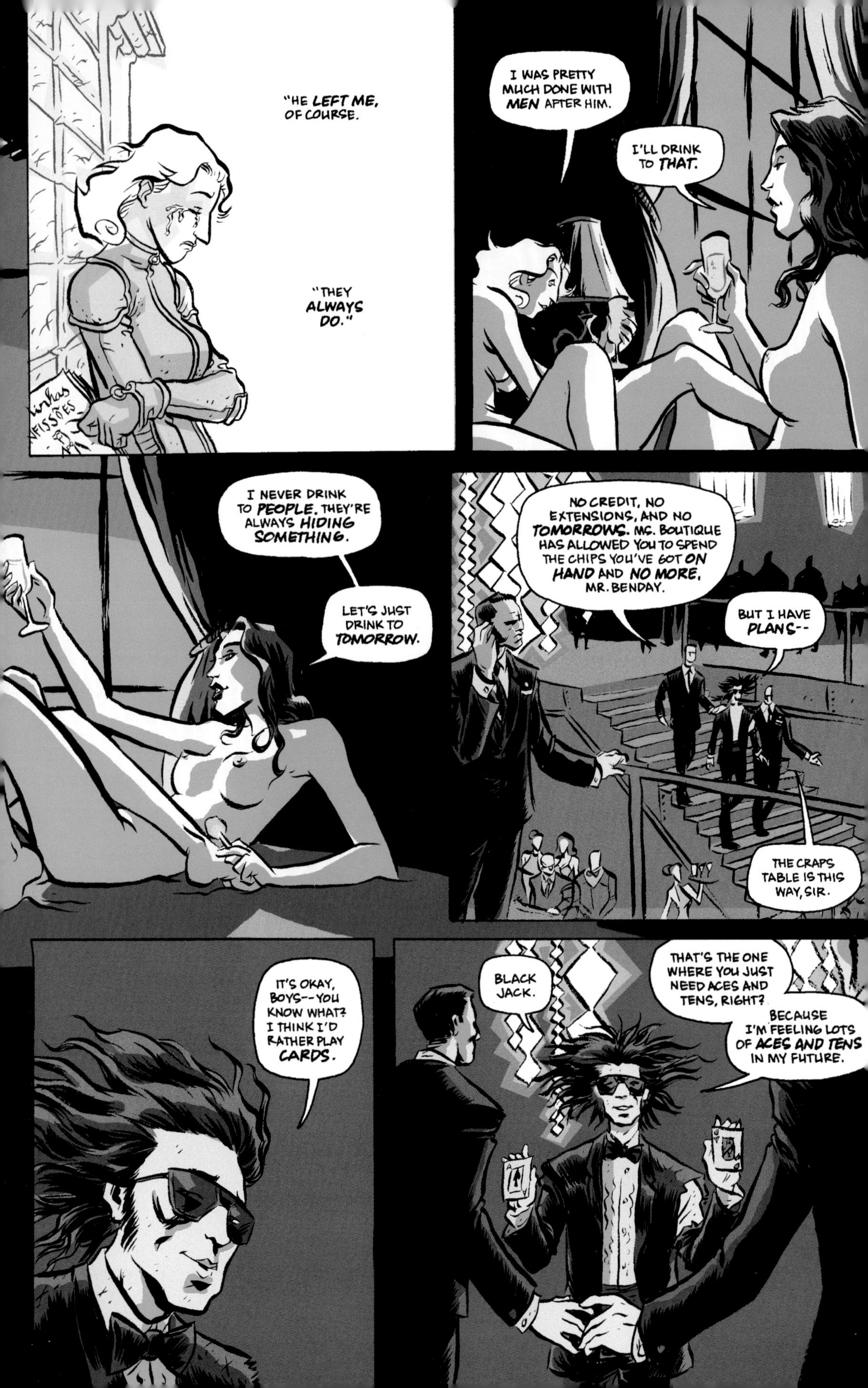
"HE LEFT ME, OF COURSE.
"THEY ALWAYS DO."
I WAS PRETTY MUCH DONE WITH MEN AFTER HIM.
I'LL DRINK TO THAT.
I NEVER DRINK TO PEOPLE. THEY'RE ALWAYS HIDING SOMETHING.
LET'S JUST DRINK TO TOMORROW.
NO CREDIT, NO EXTENSIONS, AND NO TOMORROWS. MS. BOUTIQUE HAS ALLOWED YOU TO SPEND THE CHIPS YOU'VE GOT ON HAND AND NO MORE, MR. BENDAY.
BUT I HAVE PLANS--
THE CRAPS TABLE IS THIS WAY, SIR.
IT'S OKAY, BOYS--YOU KNOW WHAT? I THINK I'D RATHER PLAY CARDS.
BLACK JACK.
THAT'S THE ONE WHERE YOU JUST NEED ACES AND TENS, RIGHT?
BECAUSE I'M FEELING LOTS OF ACES AND TENS IN MY FUTURE.

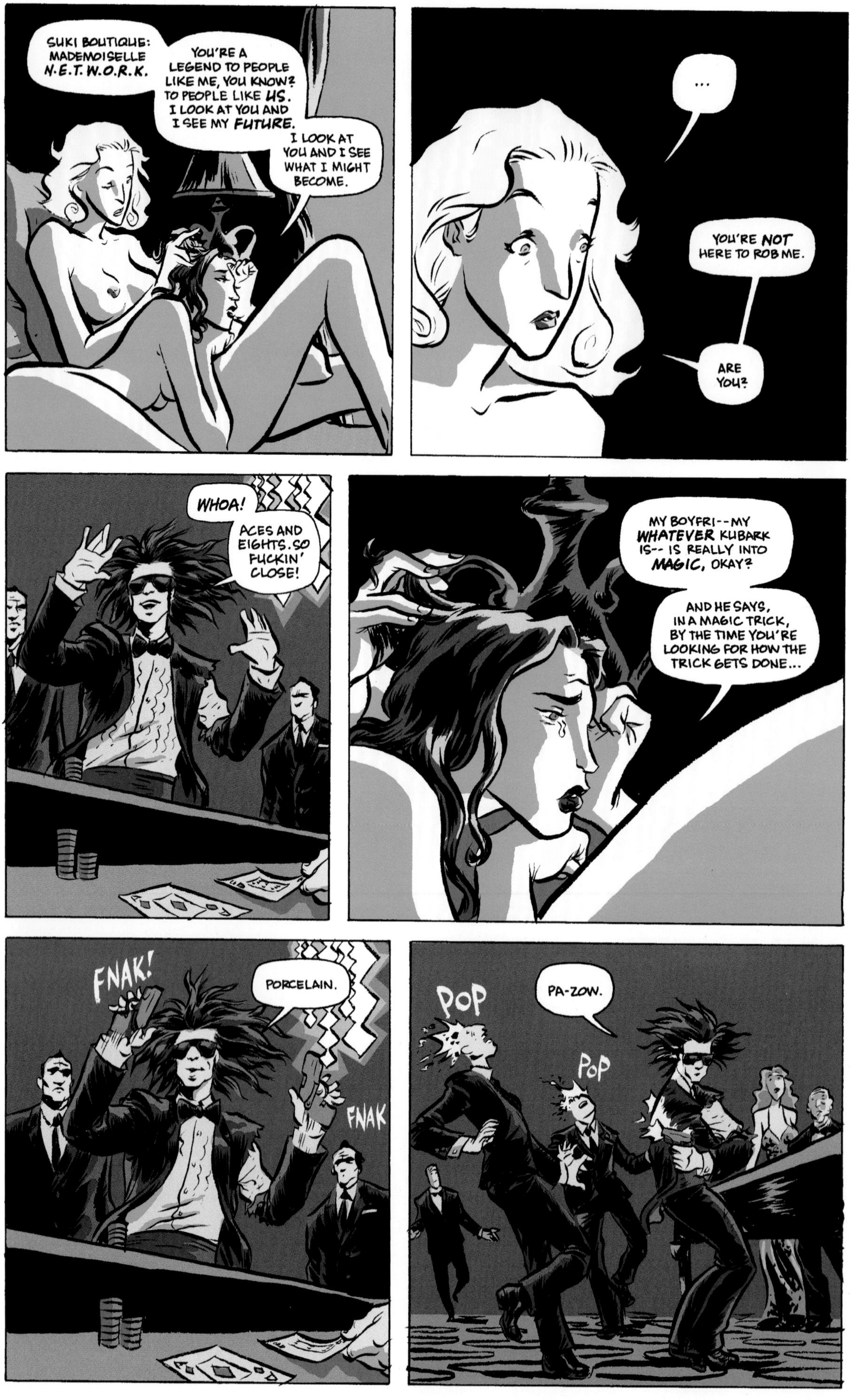
SUKI BOUTIQUE: MADEMOISELLE N.E.T.W.O.R.K.
YOU'RE A LEGEND TO PEOPLE LIKE ME, YOU KNOW? TO PEOPLE LIKE US. I LOOK AT YOU AND I SEE MY FUTURE.
I LOOK AT YOU AND I SEE WHAT I MIGHT BECOME.
...
YOU'RE NOT HERE TO ROB ME.
ARE YOU?
WHOA!
ACES AND EIGHTS. SO FUCKIN' CLOSE!
MY BOYFRI--MY WHATEVER KUBARK IS-- IS REALLY INTO MAGIC, OKAY?
AND HE SAYS, IN A MAGIC TRICK, BY THE TIME YOU'RE LOOKING FOR HOW THE TRICK GETS DONE...
FNAK!
PORCELAIN.
FNAK
POP
PA-ZOW.
POP

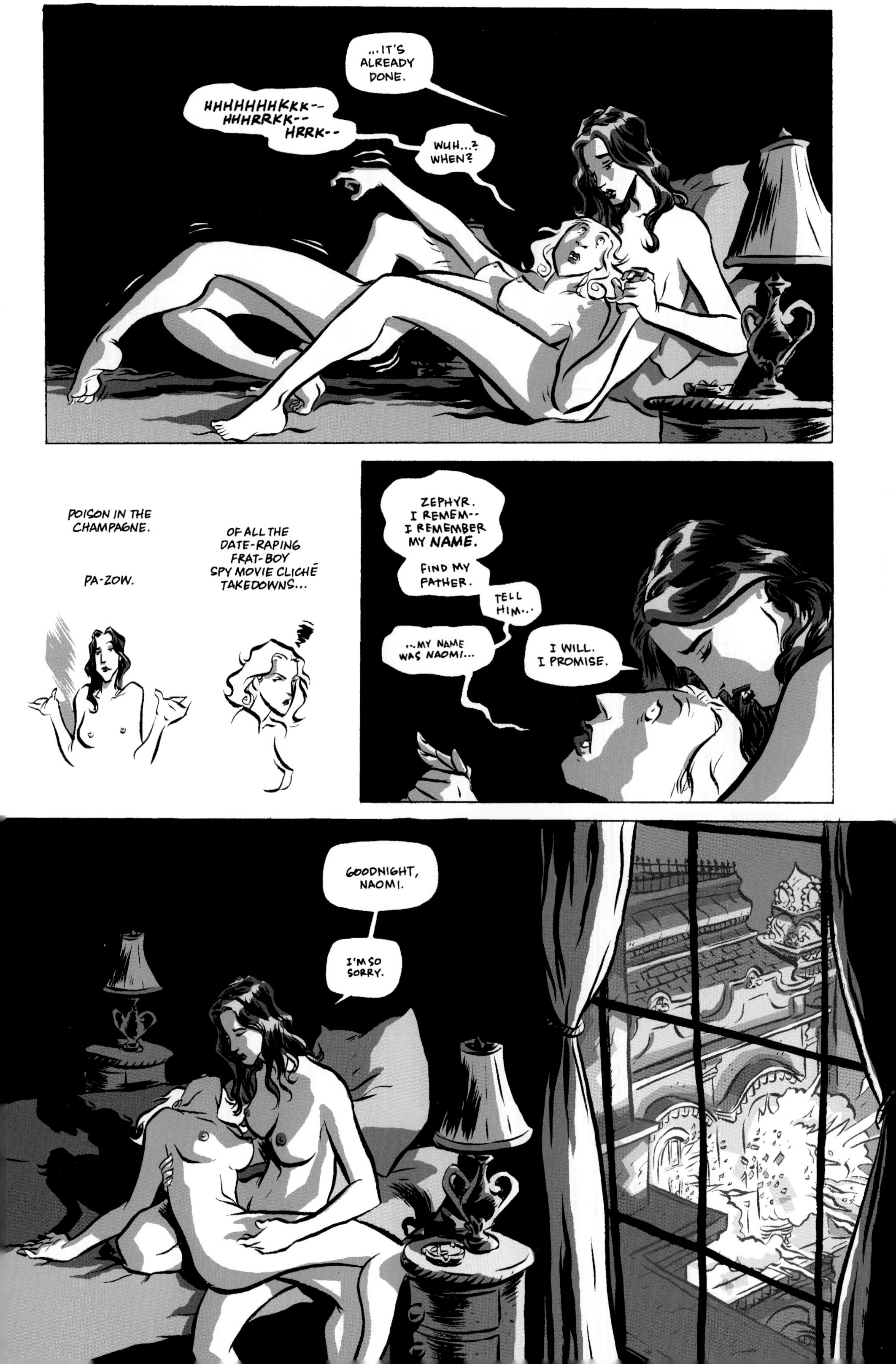
...IT'S ALREADY DONE.
HHHHHHHKKK-- HHHRRKK-- HRRK--
WUH...? WHEN?
POISON IN THE CHAMPAGNE.
PA-ZOW.
OF ALL THE DATE-RAPING FRAT-BOY SPY MOVIE CLICHÉ TAKEDOWNS...
ZEPHYR. I REMEM-- I REMEMBER MY NAME.
FIND MY FATHER.
TELL HIM...
...MY NAME WAS NAOMI...
I WILL. I PROMISE.
GOODNIGHT, NAOMI.
I'M SO SORRY.

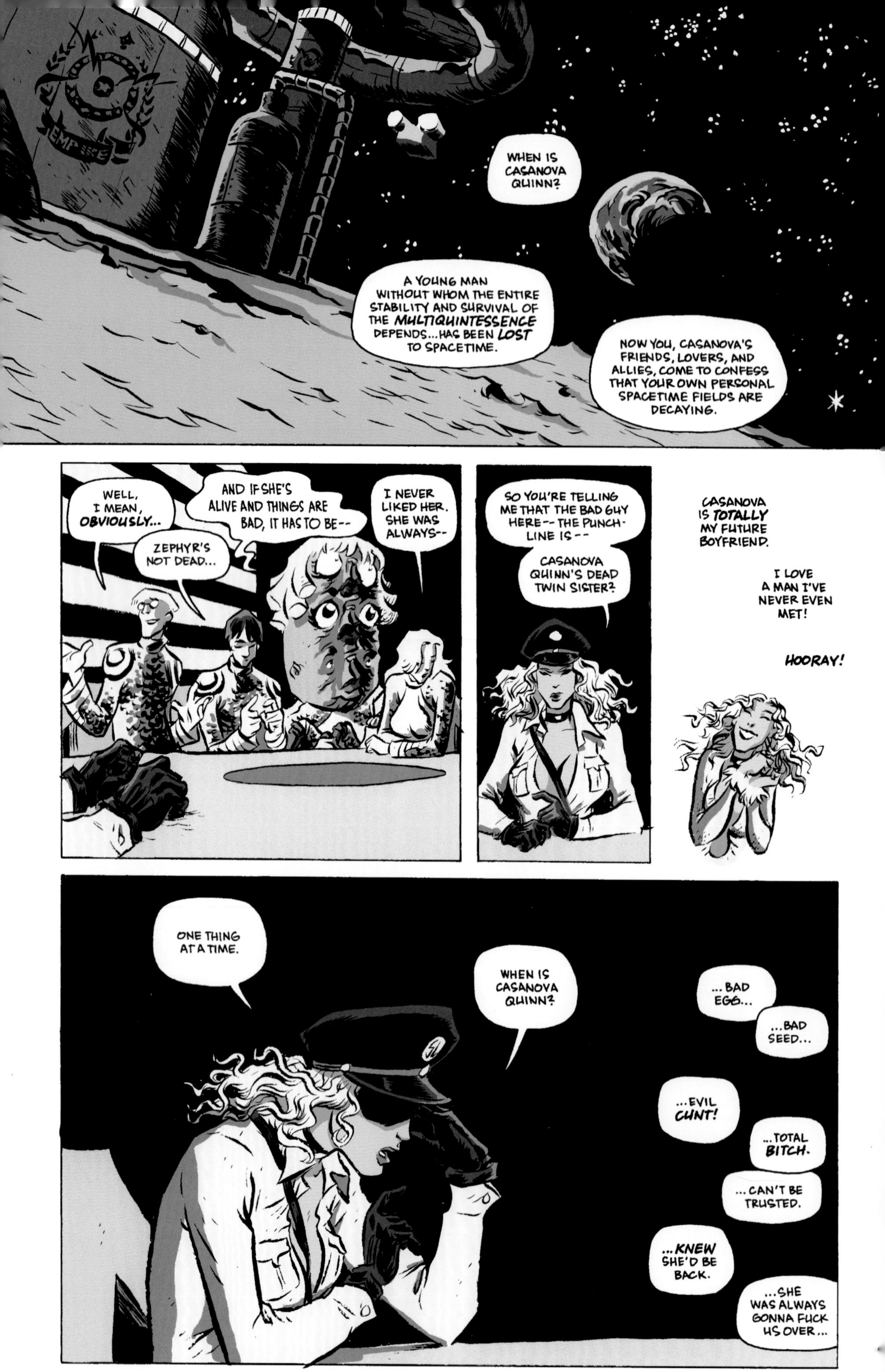
WHEN IS CASANOVA QUINN?
A YOUNG MAN WITHOUT WHOM THE ENTIRE STABILITY AND SURVIVAL OF THE MULTIQUINTESSENCE DEPENDS...HAS BEEN LOST TO SPACETIME.
NOW YOU, CASANOVA'S FRIENDS, LOVERS, AND ALLIES, COME TO CONFESS THAT YOUR OWN PERSONAL SPACETIME FIELDS ARE DECAYING.
WELL, I MEAN, OBVIOUSLY...
ZEPHYR'S NOT DEAD...
AND IF SHE'S ALIVE AND THINGS ARE BAD, IT HAS TO BE--
I NEVER LIKED HER. SHE WAS ALWAYS--
SO YOU'RE TELLING ME THAT THE BAD GUY HERE--THE PUNCH-LINE IS--
CASANOVA QUINN'S DEAD TWIN SISTER?
CASANOVA IS TOTALLY MY FUTURE BOYFRIEND.
I LOVE A MAN I'VE NEVER EVEN MET!
HOORAY!
ONE THING AT A TIME.
WHEN IS CASANOVA QUINN?
...BAD EGG...
...BAD SEED...
...EVIL CUNT!
...TOTAL BITCH.
...CAN'T BE TRUSTED.
...KNEW SHE'D BE BACK.
...SHE WAS ALWAYS GONNA FUCK US OVER...

THE GANG EXPLAINS CASANOVA'S "DISAPPEARANCE".

> THAT MAKES SENSE. I GUESS. THE CASANOVA QUINN I SOUGHT IS *DEAD*, REPLACED BY THE CASANOVA QUINN OF ANOTHER DIMENSION.

> I LOOKED FOR A GOLDEN DELICIOUS IN A PILE OF GRANNY SMITHS.

NEWMAN XENO. W.A.S.T.E. THE FAKEBOOK OF THE COSMOS. BLAH BLAH BLAH.

> YOU DON'T KNOW WHAT THAT MEANS, DO YOU? YOU MIGHT KNOW WHAT IT *IS* BUT YOU DON'T KNOW WHAT IT MEANS...

> IT'S OKAY. I'M HERE TO HELP.

WHAT IS "THE FAKEBOOK OF THE COSMOS"? WHAT DOES THAT MEAN W/R/T WHAT HAPPENED TO CASS?

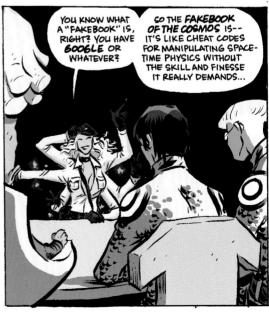

> YOU KNOW WHAT A "FAKEBOOK" IS, RIGHT? YOU HAVE *GOOGLE* OR WHATEVER?

> SO THE *FAKEBOOK OF THE COSMOS* IS-- IT'S LIKE CHEAT CODES FOR MANIPULATING SPACE-TIME PHYSICS WITHOUT THE SKILL AND FINESSE IT REALLY DEMANDS...

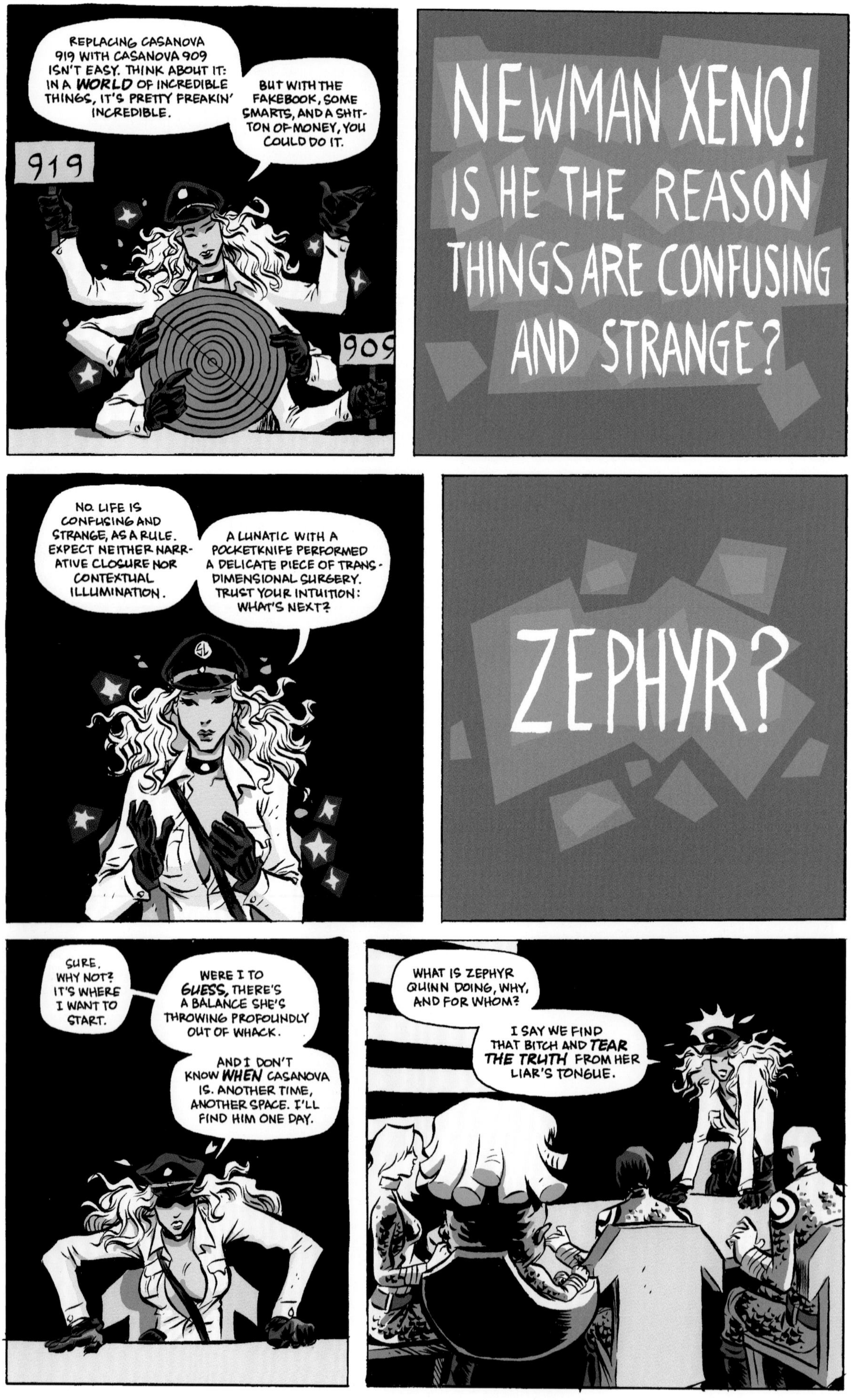
REPLACING CASANOVA 919 WITH CASANOVA 909 ISN'T EASY. THINK ABOUT IT: IN A WORLD OF INCREDIBLE THINGS, IT'S PRETTY FREAKIN' INCREDIBLE.
BUT WITH THE FAKEBOOK, SOME SMARTS, AND A SHIT-TON OF MONEY, YOU COULD DO IT.
919
909
NEWMAN XENO! IS HE THE REASON THINGS ARE CONFUSING AND STRANGE?
NO. LIFE IS CONFUSING AND STRANGE, AS A RULE. EXPECT NEITHER NARRATIVE CLOSURE NOR CONTEXTUAL ILLUMINATION.
A LUNATIC WITH A POCKETKNIFE PERFORMED A DELICATE PIECE OF TRANS-DIMENSIONAL SURGERY. TRUST YOUR INTUITION: WHAT'S NEXT?
ZEPHYR?
SURE. WHY NOT? IT'S WHERE I WANT TO START.
WERE I TO GUESS, THERE'S A BALANCE SHE'S THROWING PROFOUNDLY OUT OF WHACK.
AND I DON'T KNOW WHEN CASANOVA IS. ANOTHER TIME, ANOTHER SPACE. I'LL FIND HIM ONE DAY.
WHAT IS ZEPHYR QUINN DOING, WHY, AND FOR WHOM?
I SAY WE FIND THAT BITCH AND TEAR THE TRUTH FROM HER LIAR'S TONGUE.

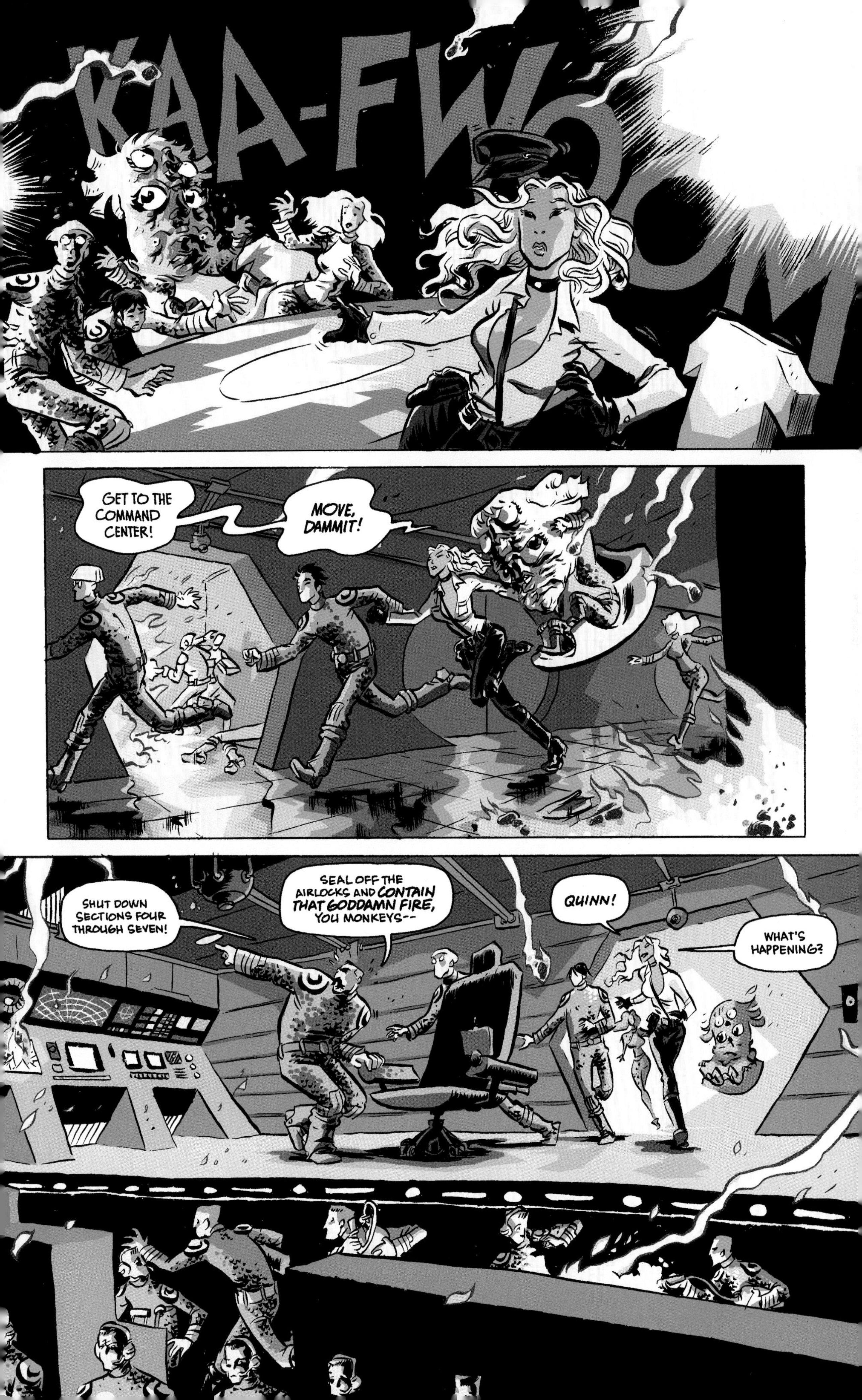
KAA-FWOOM
GET TO THE COMMAND CENTER!
MOVE, DAMMIT!
SHUT DOWN SECTIONS FOUR THROUGH SEVEN!
SEAL OFF THE AIRLOCKS AND CONTAIN THAT GODDAMN FIRE, YOU MONKEYS--
QUINN!
WHAT'S HAPPENING?

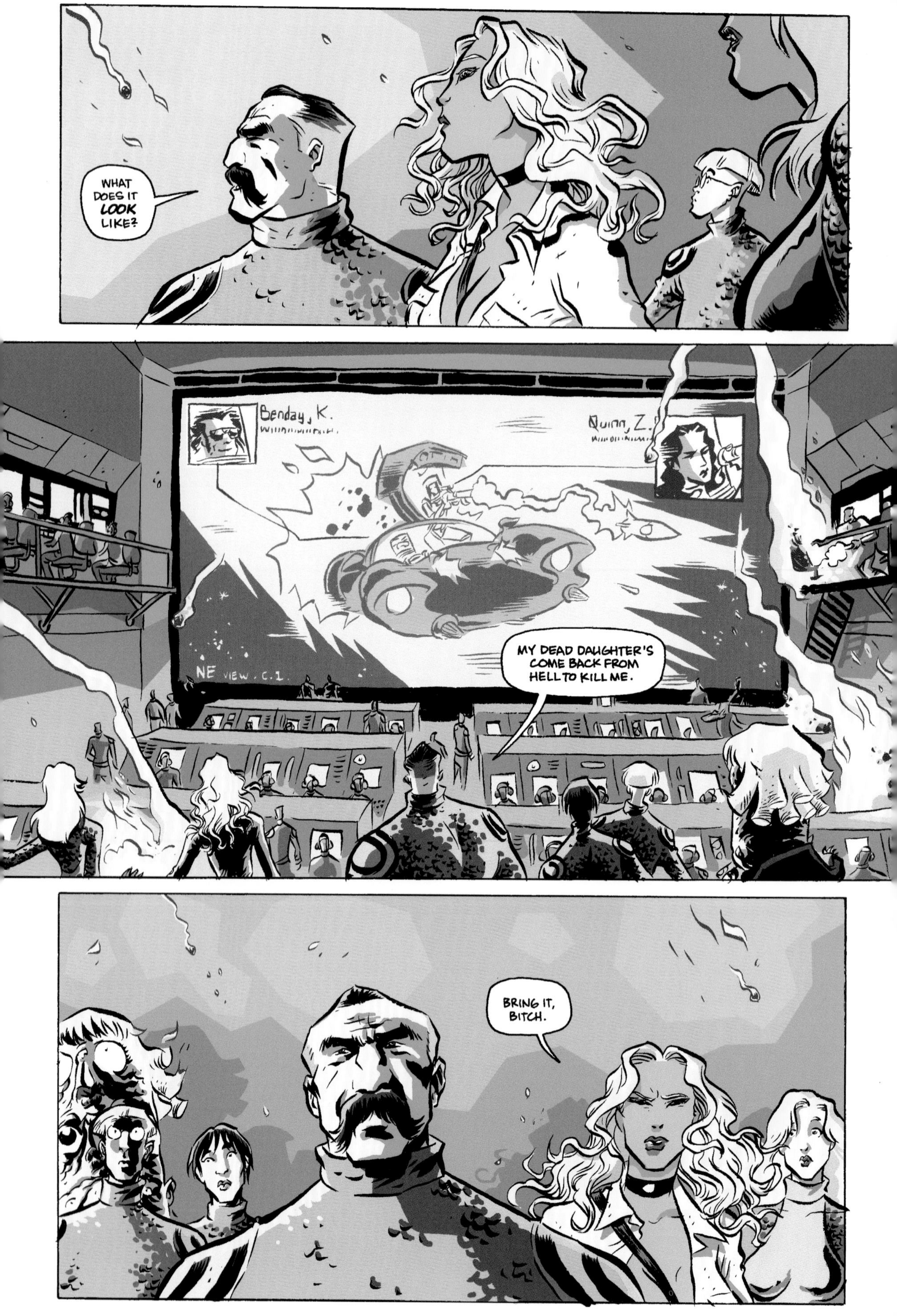
WHAT DOES IT **LOOK** LIKE?
Benday, K.
Quinn, Z.
NE view. C.1
MY DEAD DAUGHTER'S COME BACK FROM HELL TO KILL ME.
BRING IT, BITCH.

IN MEDIAS RES

WHEN THE WOLF COMES HOME

SEVENTEEN

NAOMI I MOAN

FUCK SHIT UP

SOME OF THE THINGS THAT
HAPPENED TO THE MURDERERS
AND MURDERED AMONG US

HALLO SPACEBOY

DIT DIT DIT
DAH DAH DAH
DIT DIT

BACKMATTER

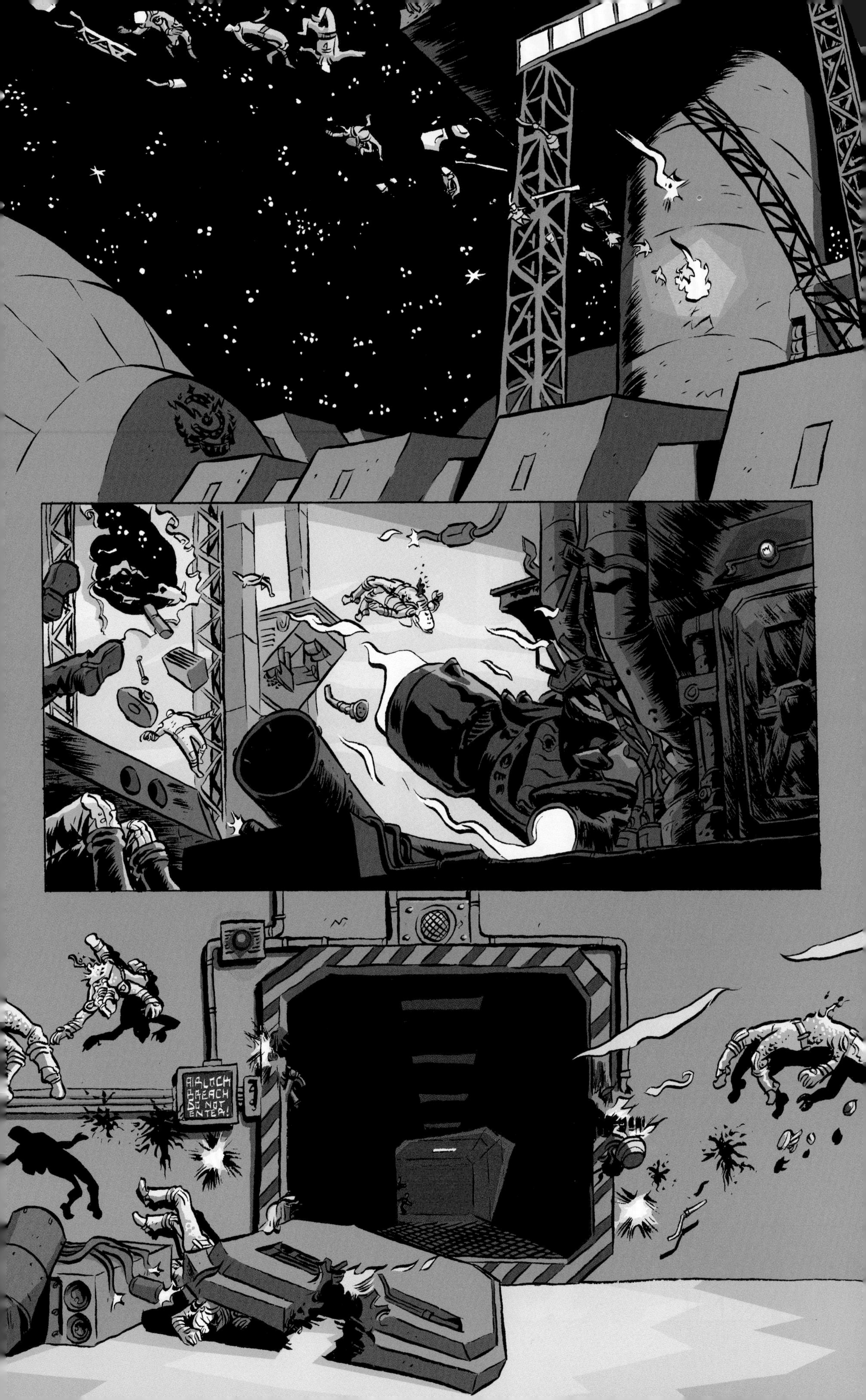
AIRLOCK BREACH DO NOT ENTER!

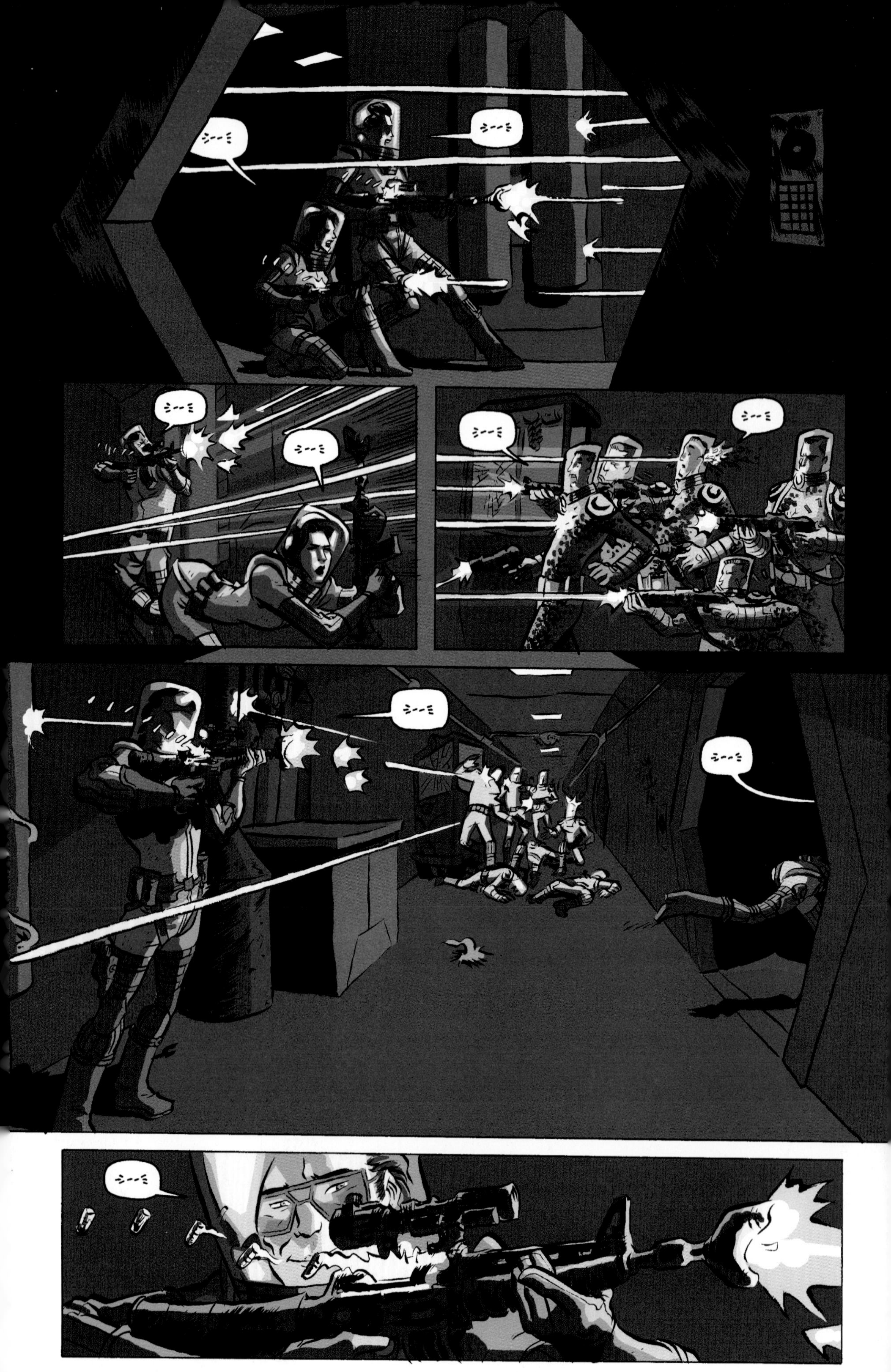

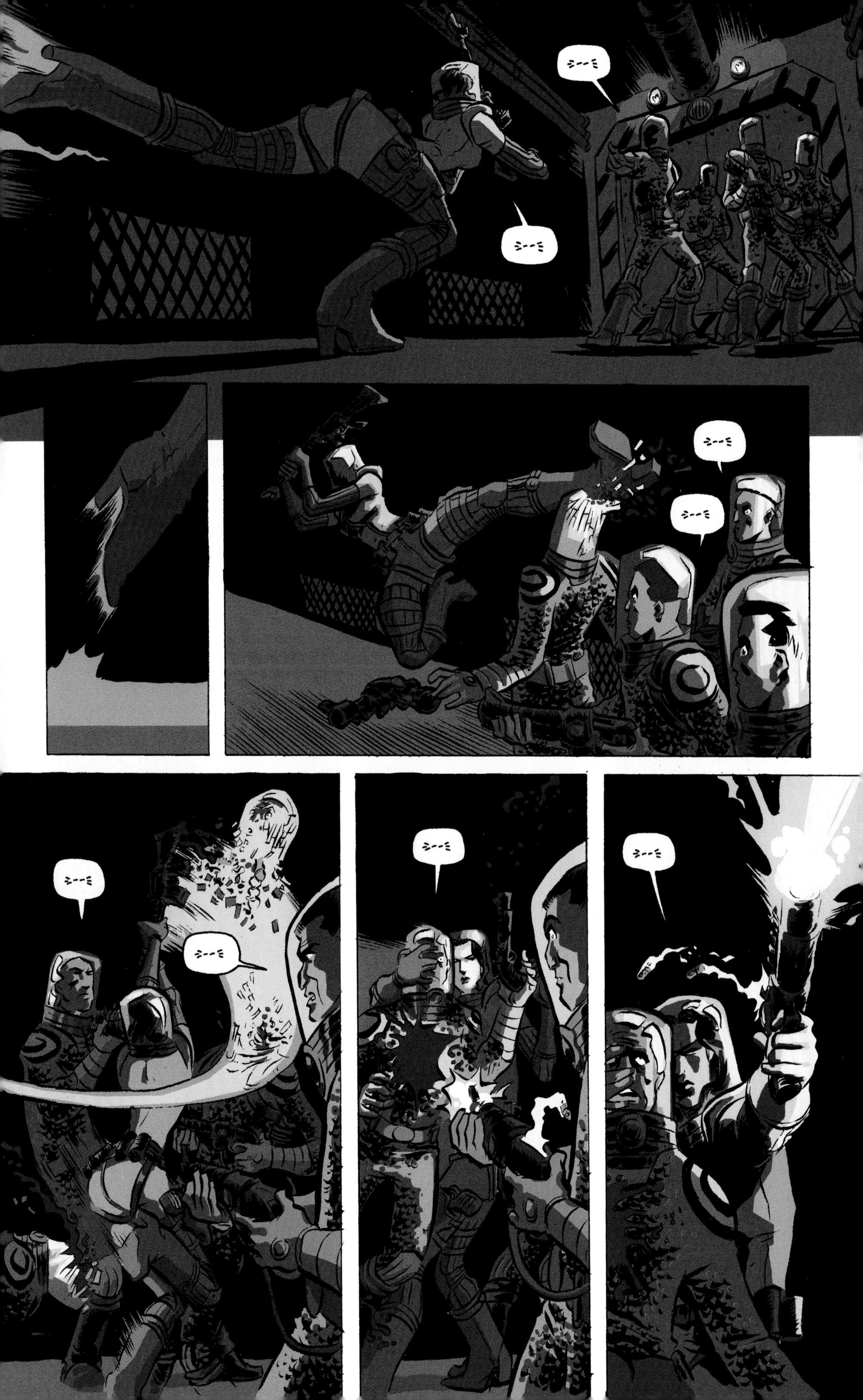

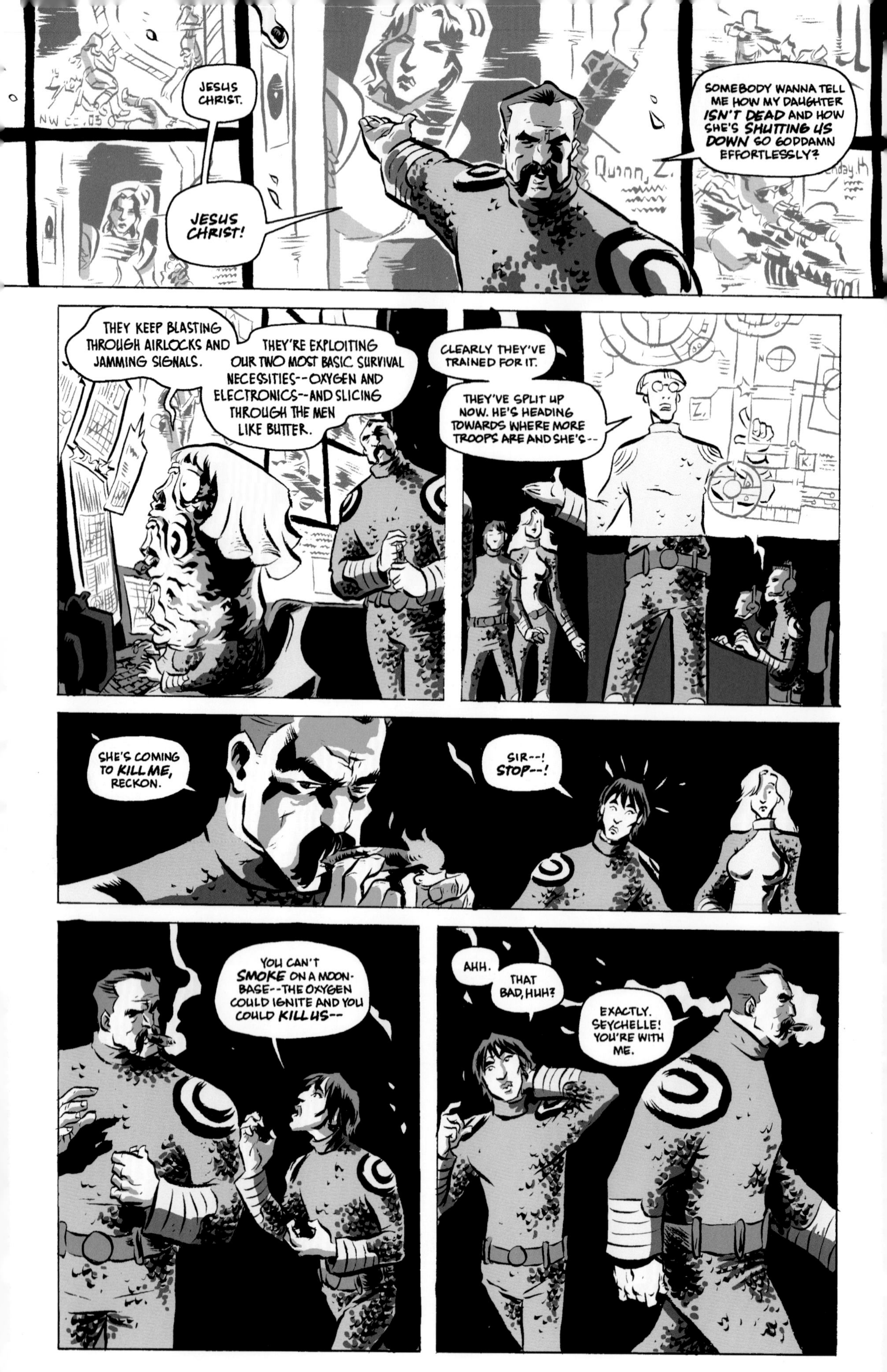

JESUS CHRIST.
JESUS CHRIST!
SOMEBODY WANNA TELL ME HOW MY DAUGHTER ISN'T DEAD AND HOW SHE'S SHUTTING US DOWN SO GODDAMN EFFORTLESSLY?
THEY KEEP BLASTING THROUGH AIRLOCKS AND JAMMING SIGNALS.
THEY'RE EXPLOITING OUR TWO MOST BASIC SURVIVAL NECESSITIES--OXYGEN AND ELECTRONICS--AND SLICING THROUGH THE MEN LIKE BUTTER.
CLEARLY THEY'VE TRAINED FOR IT.
THEY'VE SPLIT UP NOW. HE'S HEADING TOWARDS WHERE MORE TROOPS ARE AND SHE'S--
SHE'S COMING TO KILL ME, RECKON.
SIR--! STOP--!
YOU CAN'T SMOKE ON A MOON-BASE--THE OXYGEN COULD IGNITE AND YOU COULD KILL US--
AHH.
THAT BAD, HUH?
EXACTLY. SEYCHELLE! YOU'RE WITH ME.

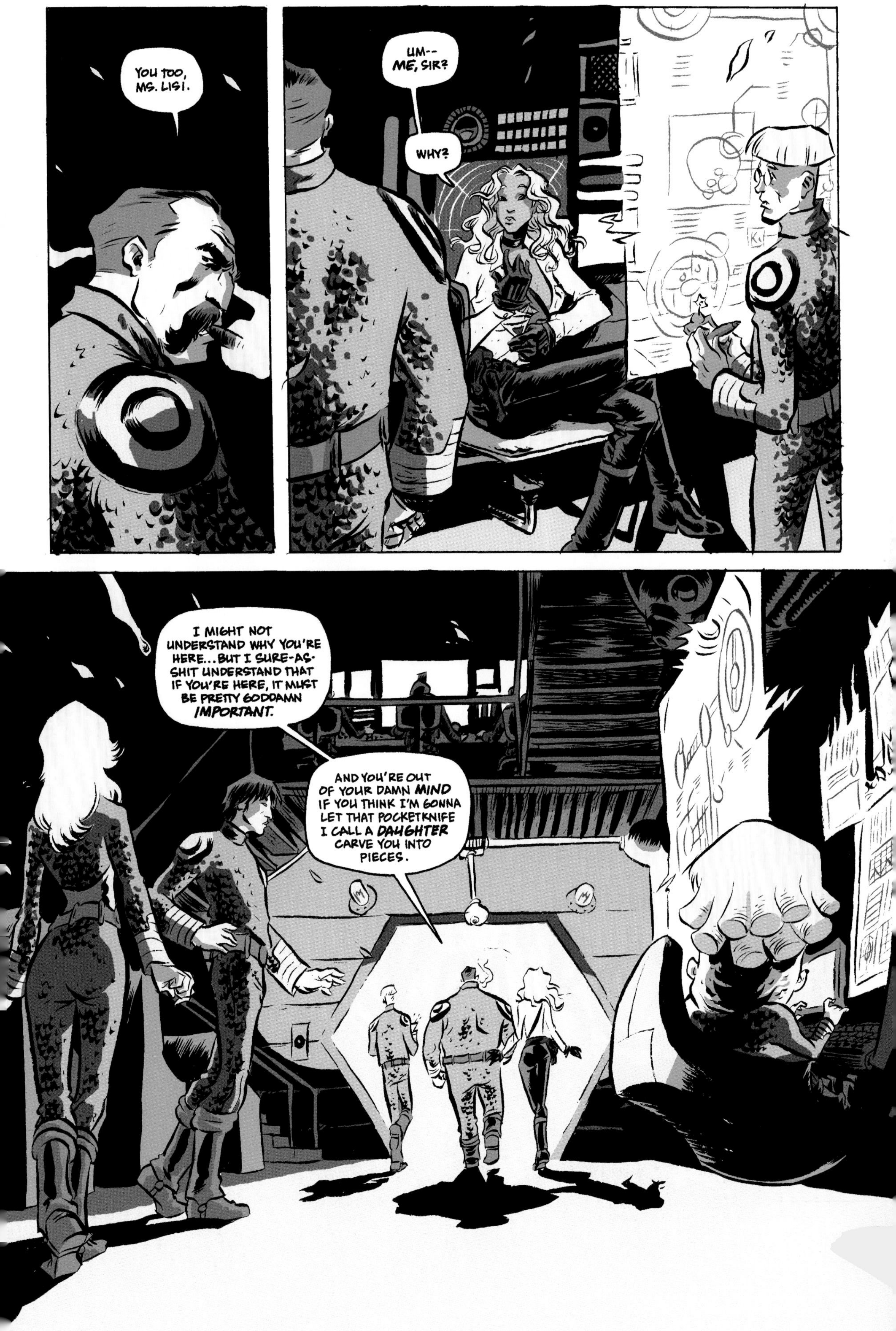
YOU TOO, MS. LISI.
UM-- ME, SIR?
WHY?
I MIGHT NOT UNDERSTAND WHY YOU'RE HERE... BUT I SURE-AS-SHIT UNDERSTAND THAT IF YOU'RE HERE, IT MUST BE PRETTY GODDAMN IMPORTANT.
AND YOU'RE OUT OF YOUR DAMN MIND IF YOU THINK I'M GONNA LET THAT POCKETKNIFE I CALL A DAUGHTER CARVE YOU INTO PIECES.

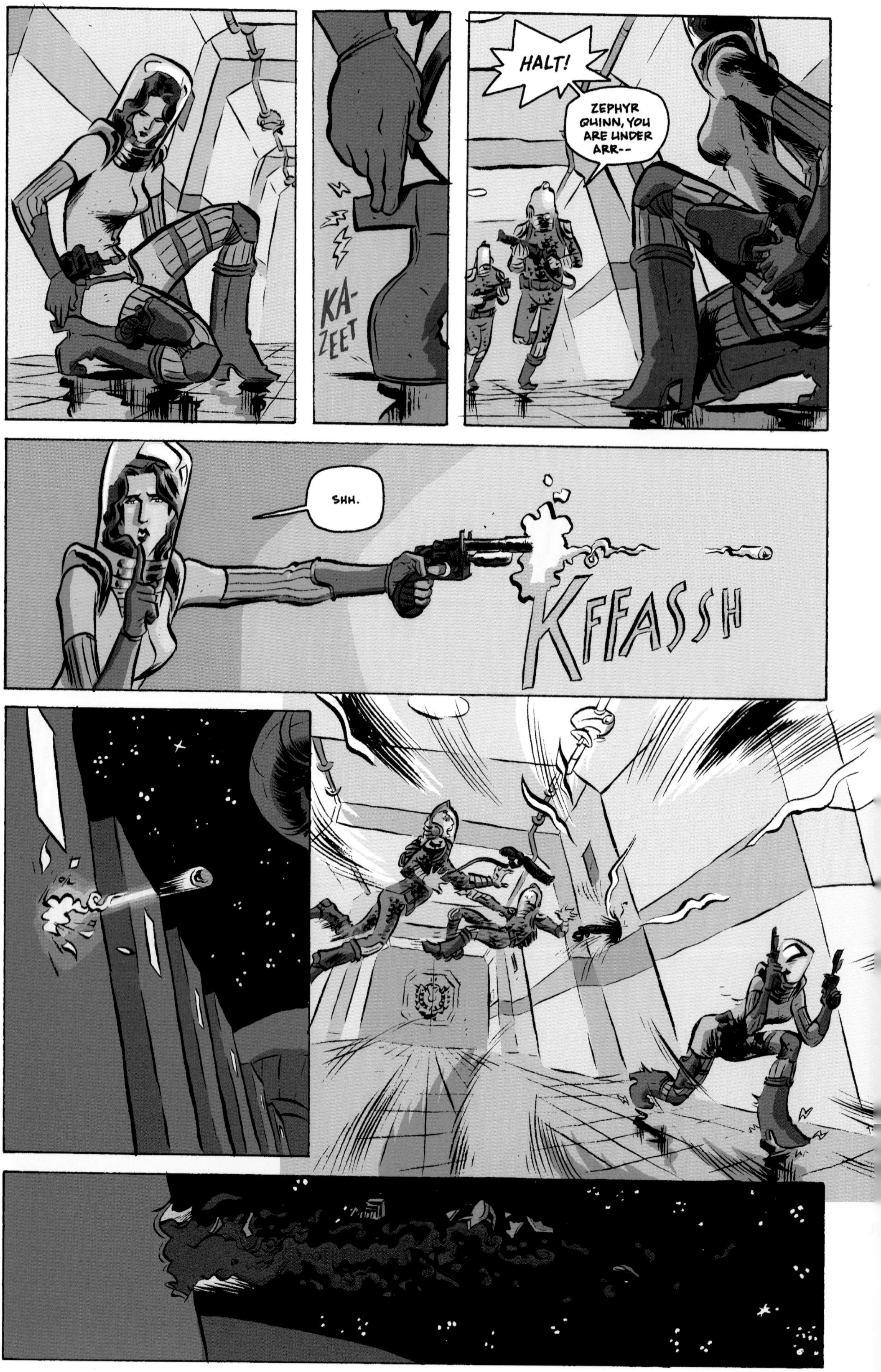
KA-
ZEET
HALT!
ZEPHYR QUINN, YOU ARE UNDER ARR--
SHH.
KFFASSH

MY WORD.

SOMEBODY HAS TO *STOP* HER.

I'M JUST GOING OUTSIDE.

I MAY BE SOME TIME.

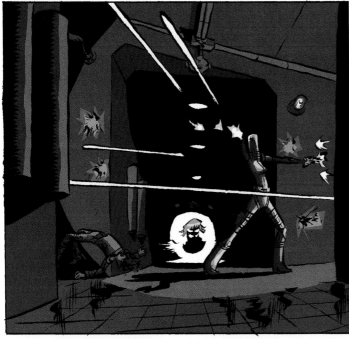

≋WE HAD A DEAL.≋

≋NOTHING GOLD CAN STAY, PONY.≋

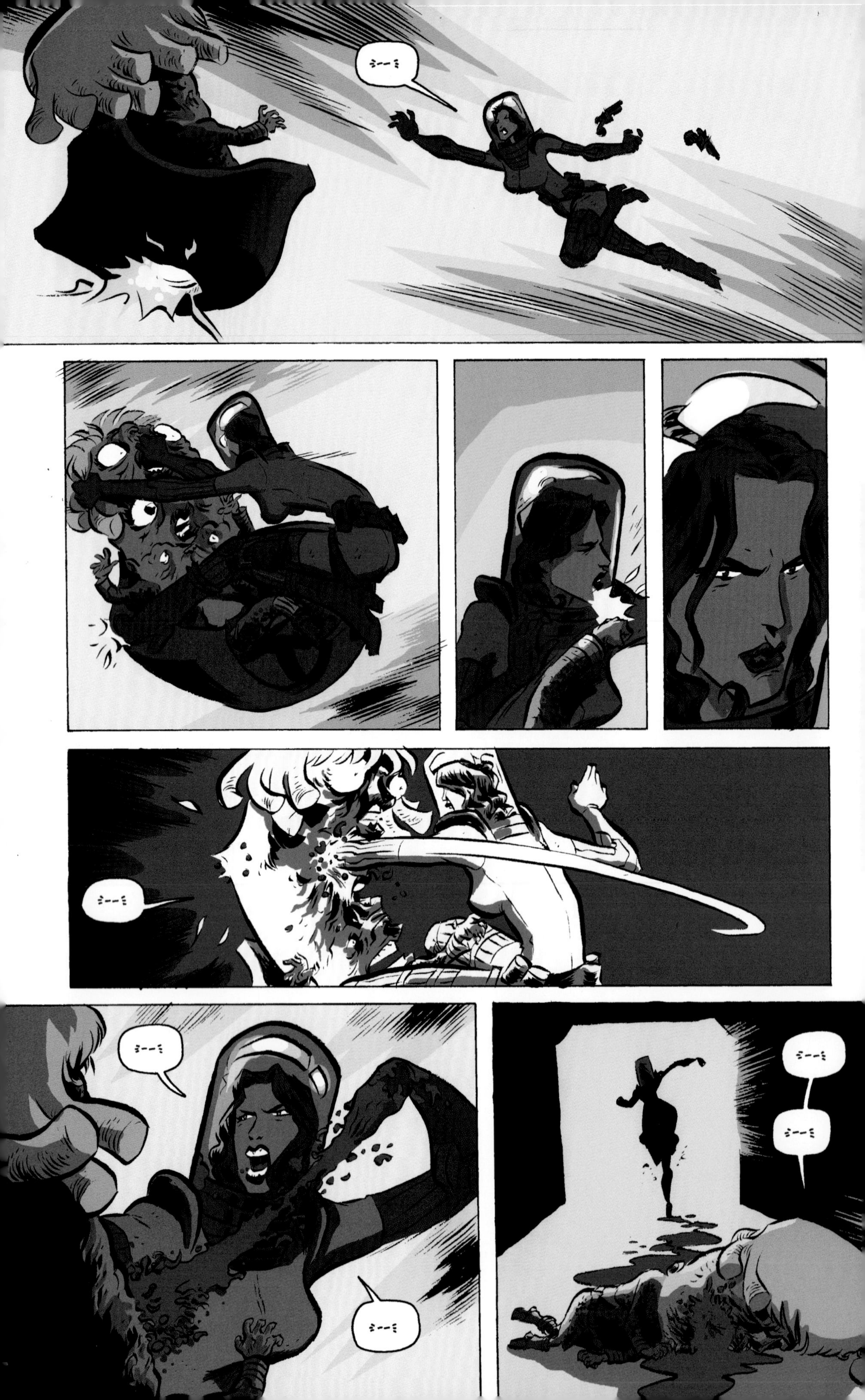

SHE JUST--

SHE JUST--

I KNOW. WE CAN'T--

BABY, WE GOTTA GO STOP ZEPH.

⌇I KNOW.⌇

⌇AND, I KNOW.⌇

⌇WE MIGHT DIE.⌇

⌇I LOVE YOU.⌇

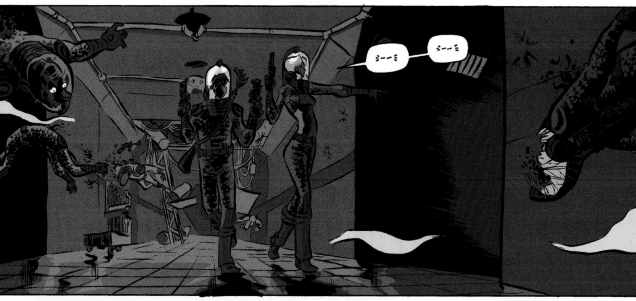
⌇--⌇

⌇--⌇

⌇--⌇

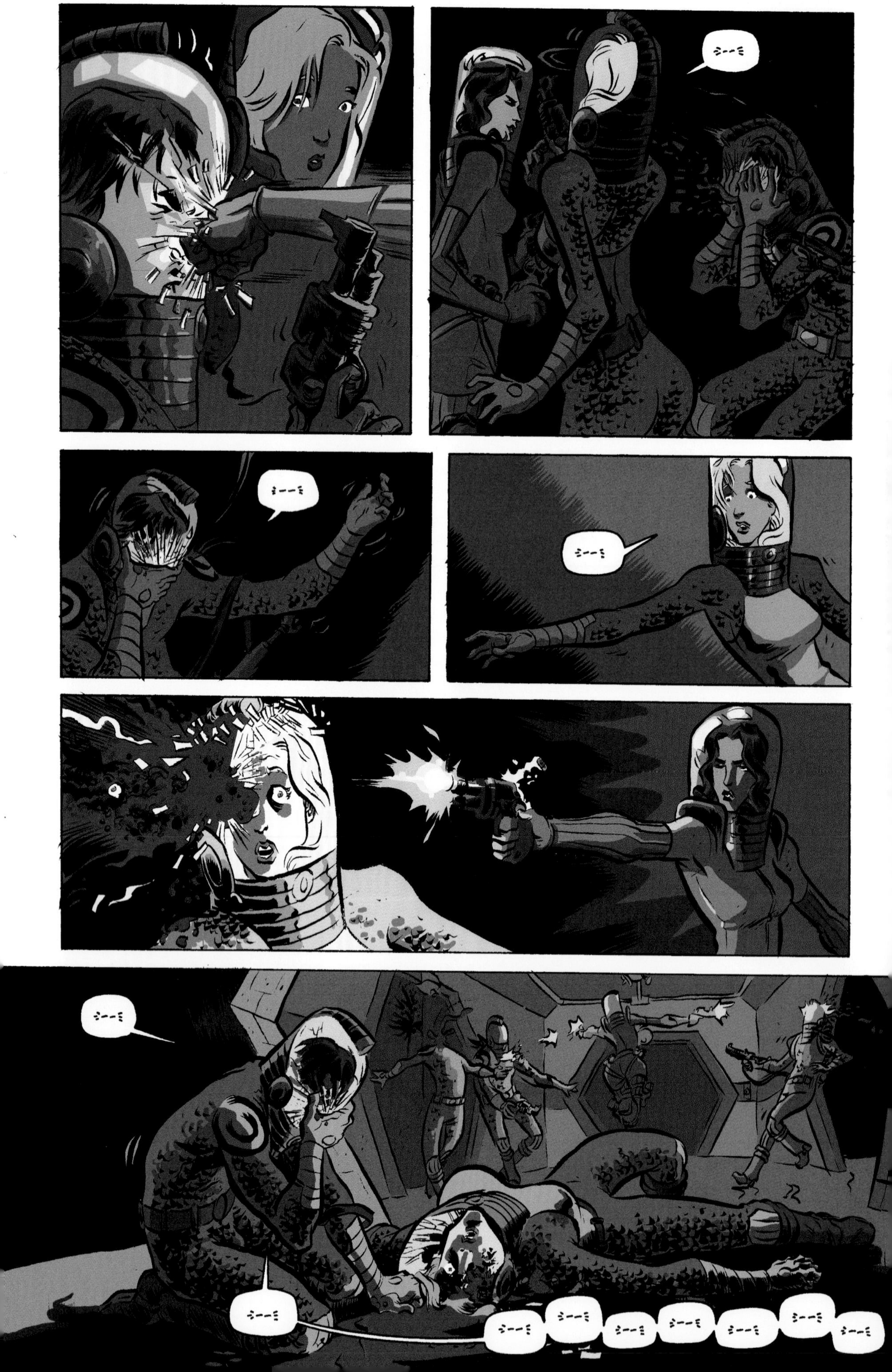

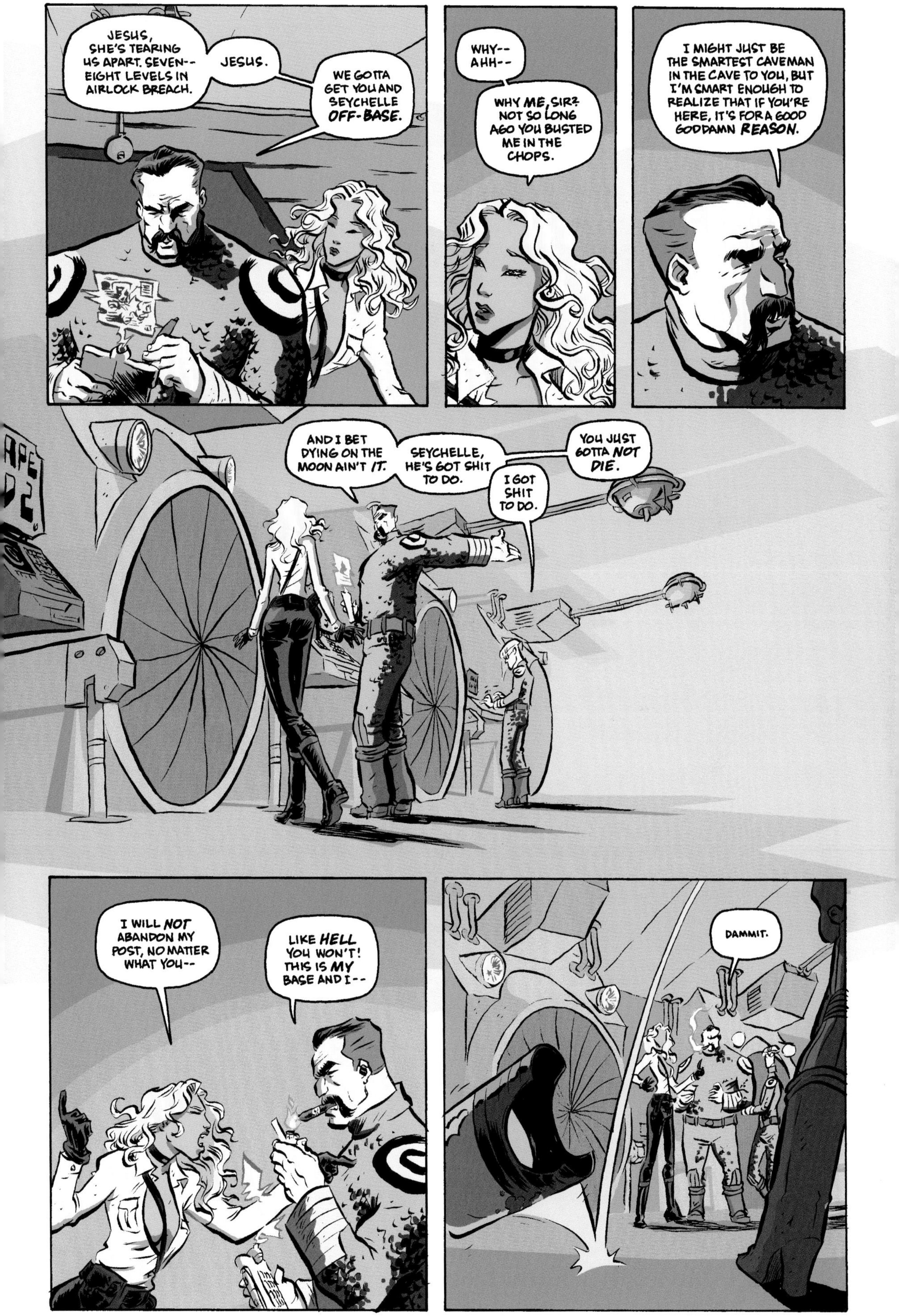

JESUS, SHE'S TEARING US APART. SEVEN-- EIGHT LEVELS IN AIRLOCK BREACH.
JESUS.
WE GOTTA GET YOU AND SEYCHELLE OFF-BASE.
WHY-- AHH--
WHY ME, SIR? NOT SO LONG AGO YOU BUSTED ME IN THE CHOPS.
I MIGHT JUST BE THE SMARTEST CAVEMAN IN THE CAVE TO YOU, BUT I'M SMART ENOUGH TO REALIZE THAT IF YOU'RE HERE, IT'S FOR A GOOD GODDAMN REASON.
AND I BET DYING ON THE MOON AIN'T IT.
SEYCHELLE, HE'S GOT SHIT TO DO.
I GOT SHIT TO DO.
YOU JUST GOTTA NOT DIE.
I WILL NOT ABANDON MY POST, NO MATTER WHAT YOU--
LIKE HELL YOU WON'T! THIS IS MY BASE AND I--
DAMMIT.

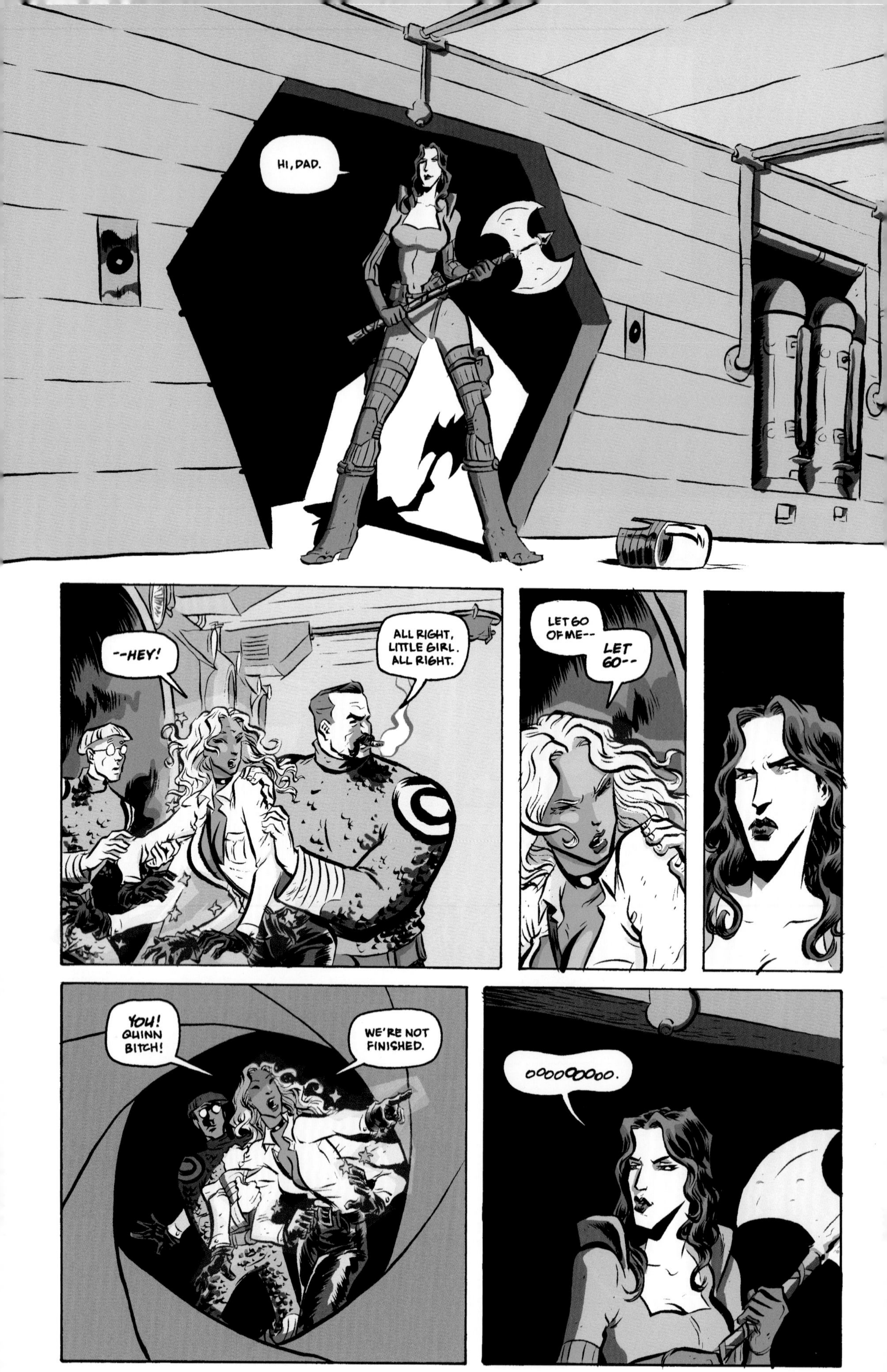
HI, DAD.
--HEY!
ALL RIGHT, LITTLE GIRL. ALL RIGHT.
LET GO OF ME--
LET GO--
YOU! QUINN BITCH!
WE'RE NOT FINISHED.
OOOOOOOOO.

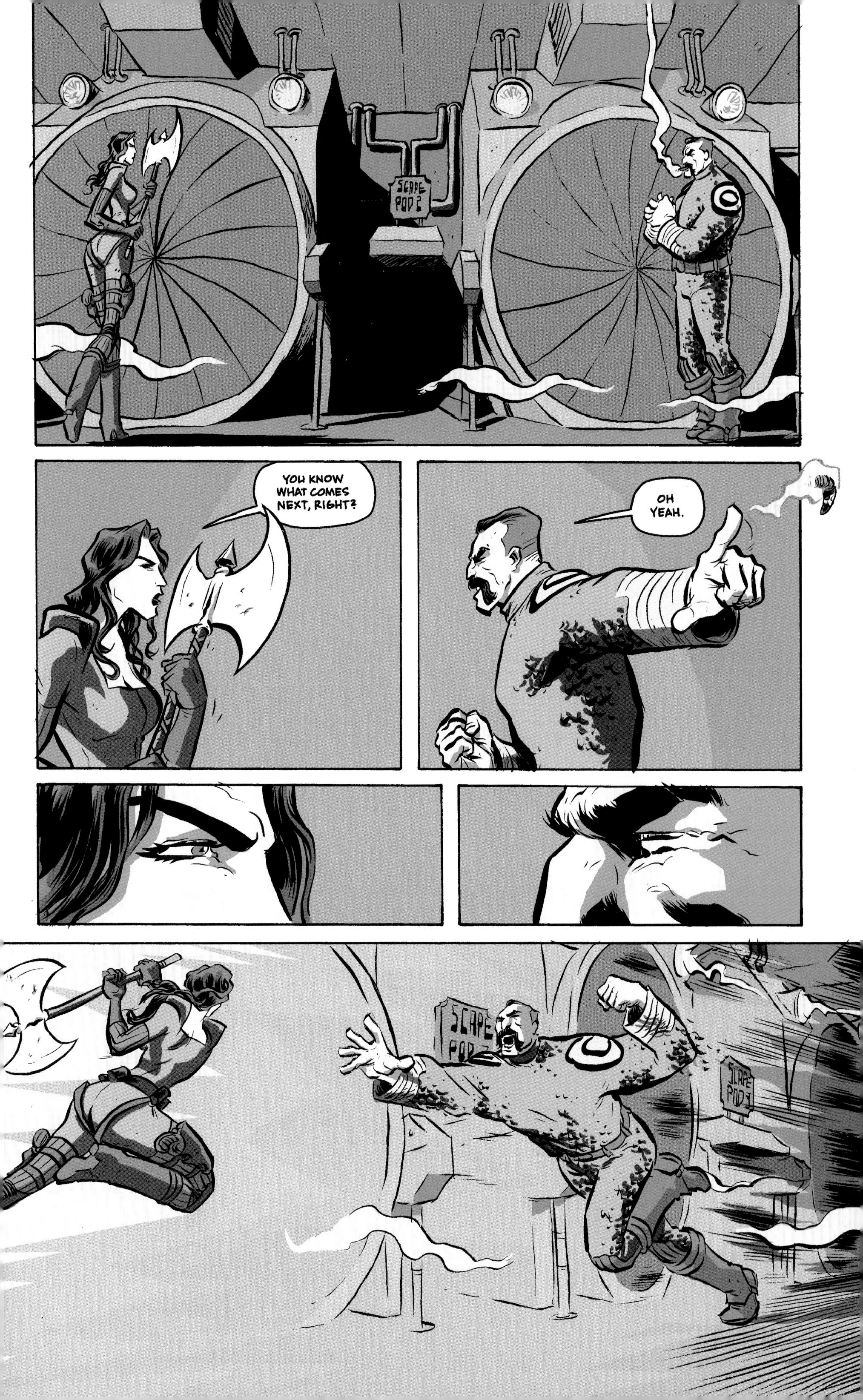
SCAPE POD 2
YOU KNOW WHAT COMES NEXT, RIGHT?
OH YEAH.
SCAPE POD
SCAPE POD 3

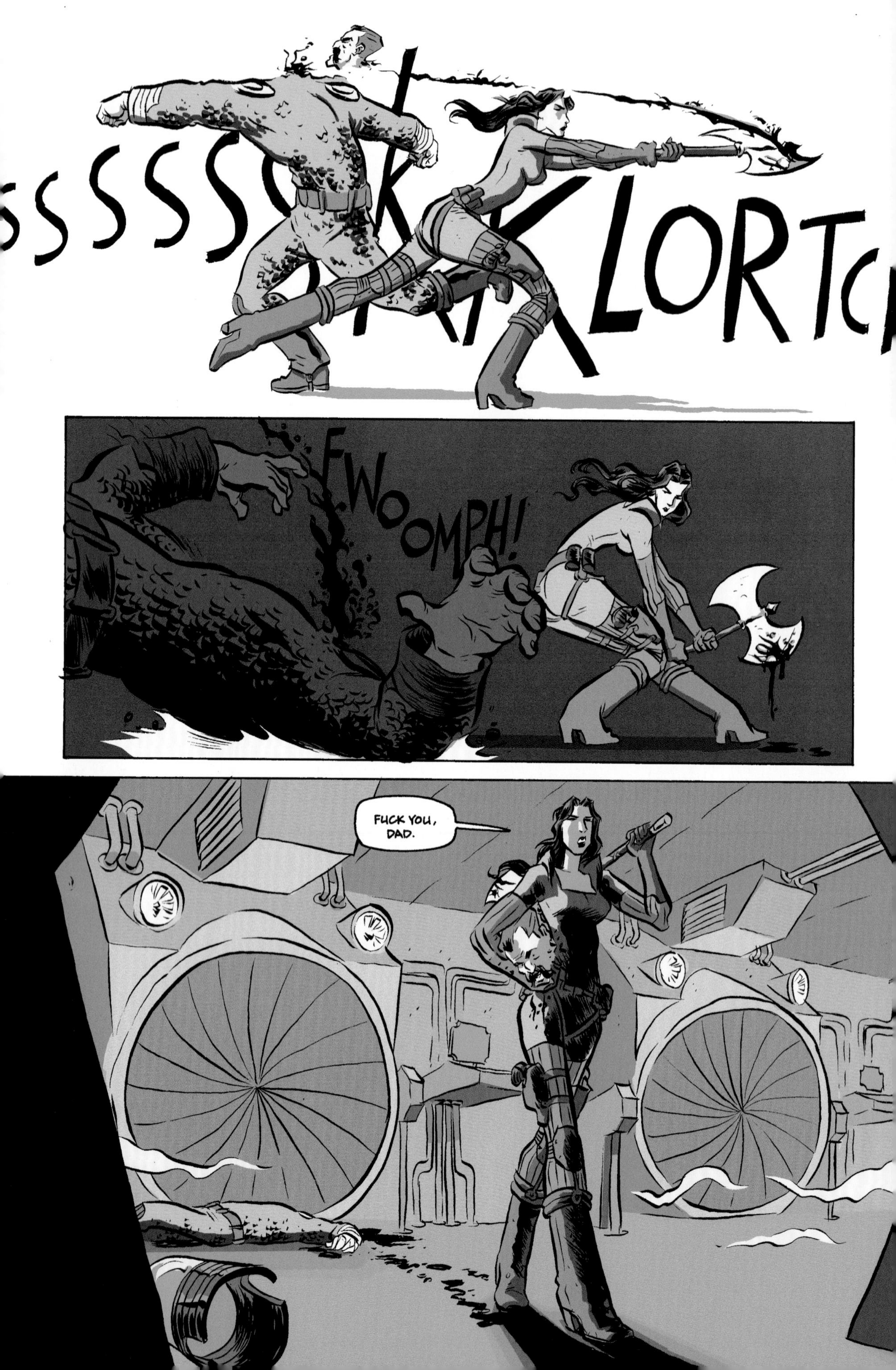
SSSSSSCK
KLORTCH
FWOOMPH!
FUCK YOU, DAD.

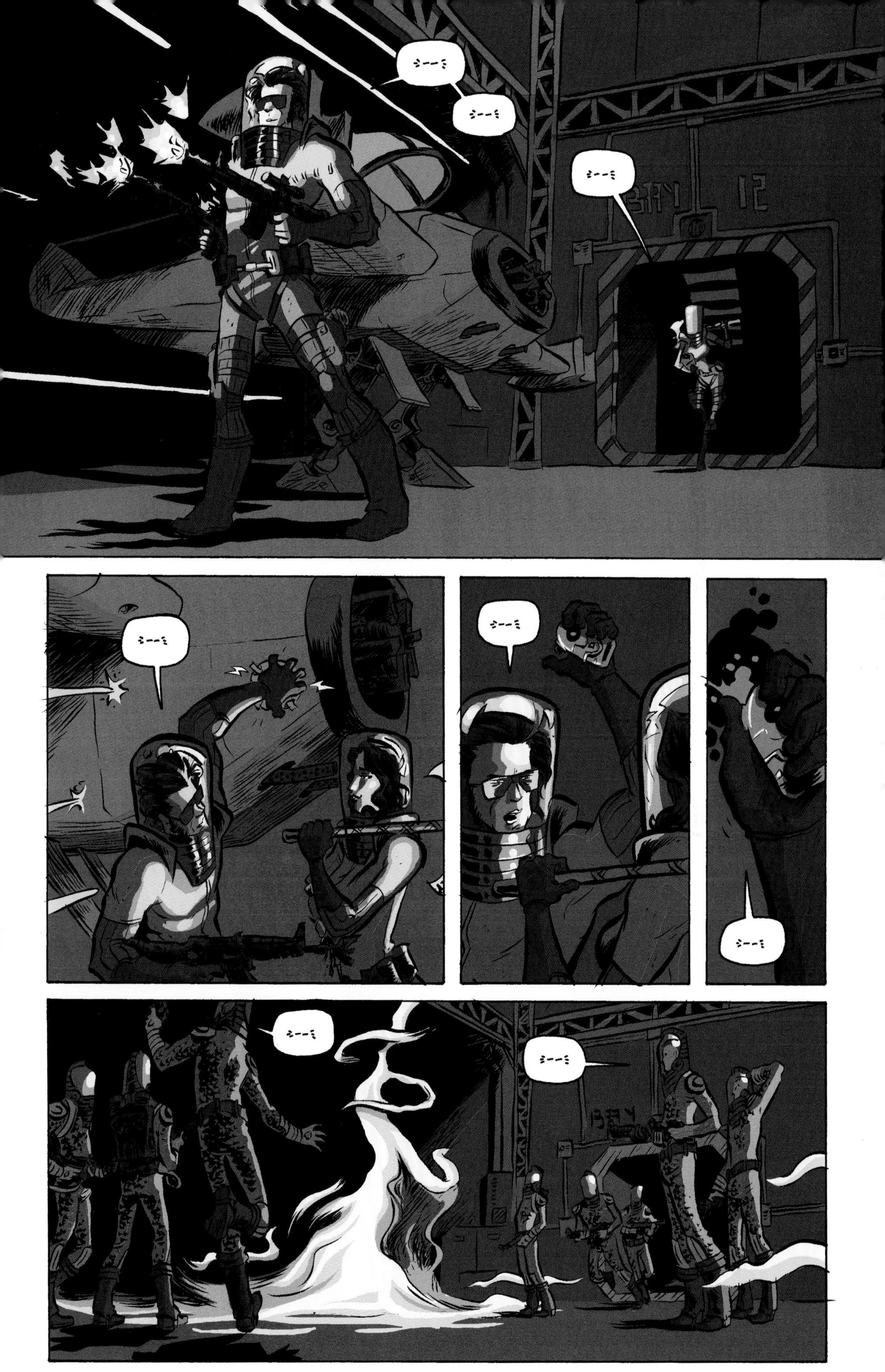

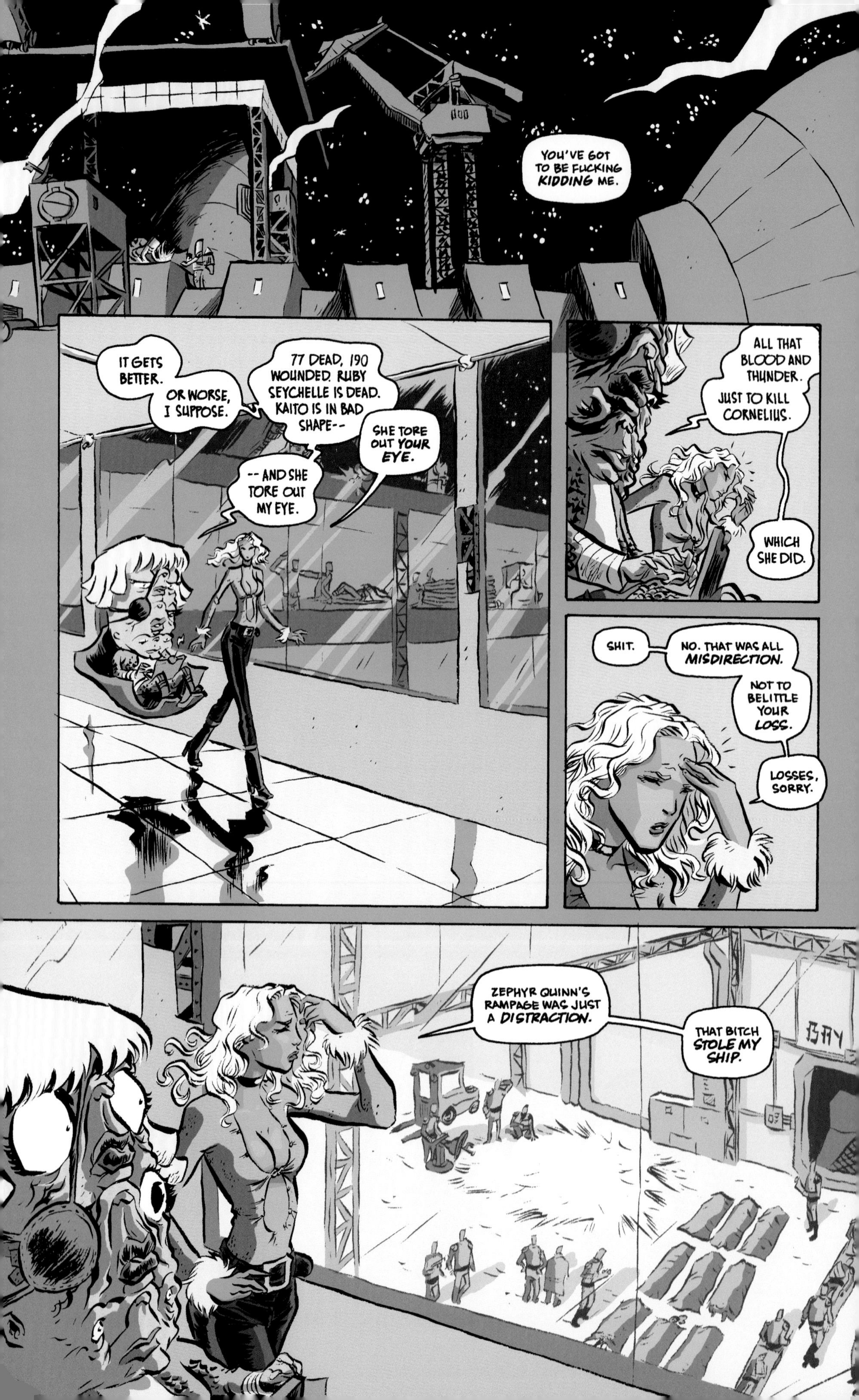
YOU'VE GOT TO BE FUCKING KIDDING ME.
IT GETS BETTER.
OR WORSE, I SUPPOSE.
77 DEAD, 190 WOUNDED. RUBY SEYCHELLE IS DEAD. KAITO IS IN BAD SHAPE--
SHE TORE OUT YOUR EYE.
--AND SHE TORE OUT MY EYE.
ALL THAT BLOOD AND THUNDER.
JUST TO KILL CORNELIUS.
WHICH SHE DID.
SHIT.
NO. THAT WAS ALL MISDIRECTION.
NOT TO BELITTLE YOUR LOSS.
LOSSES, SORRY.
ZEPHYR QUINN'S RAMPAGE WAS JUST A DISTRACTION.
THAT BITCH STOLE MY SHIP.

IN MEDIAS RES

WHEN THE WOLF COMES HOME

SEVENTEEN

NAOMI I MOAN

FUCK SHIT UP

SOME OF THE THINGS THAT
HAPPENED TO THE MURDERERS
AND MURDERED AMONG US

HALLO SPACEBOY

DIT DIT DIT
DAH DAH DAH
DIT DIT

BACKMATTER

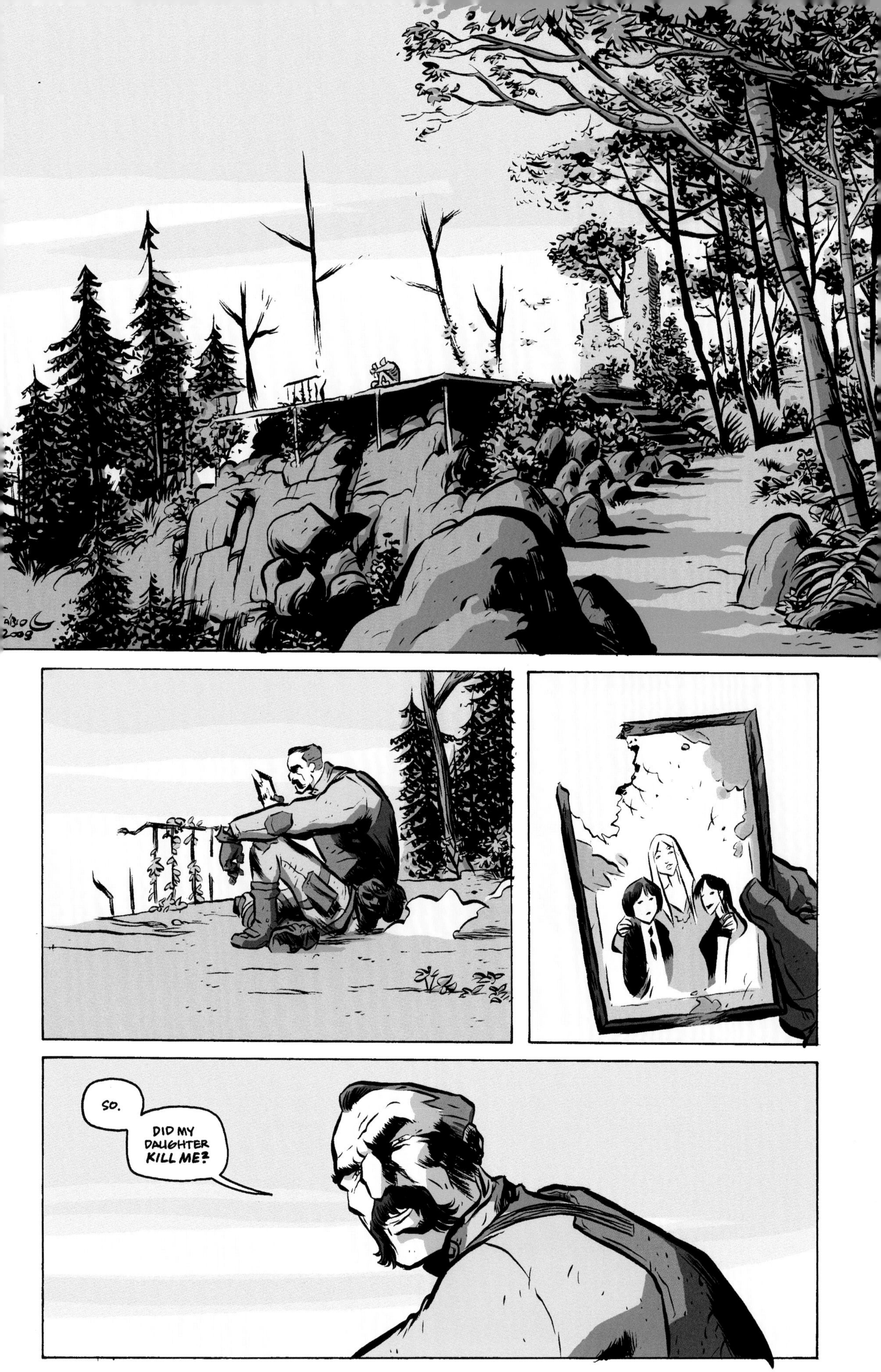
WSO 2008
SO.
DID MY DAUGHTER KILL ME?

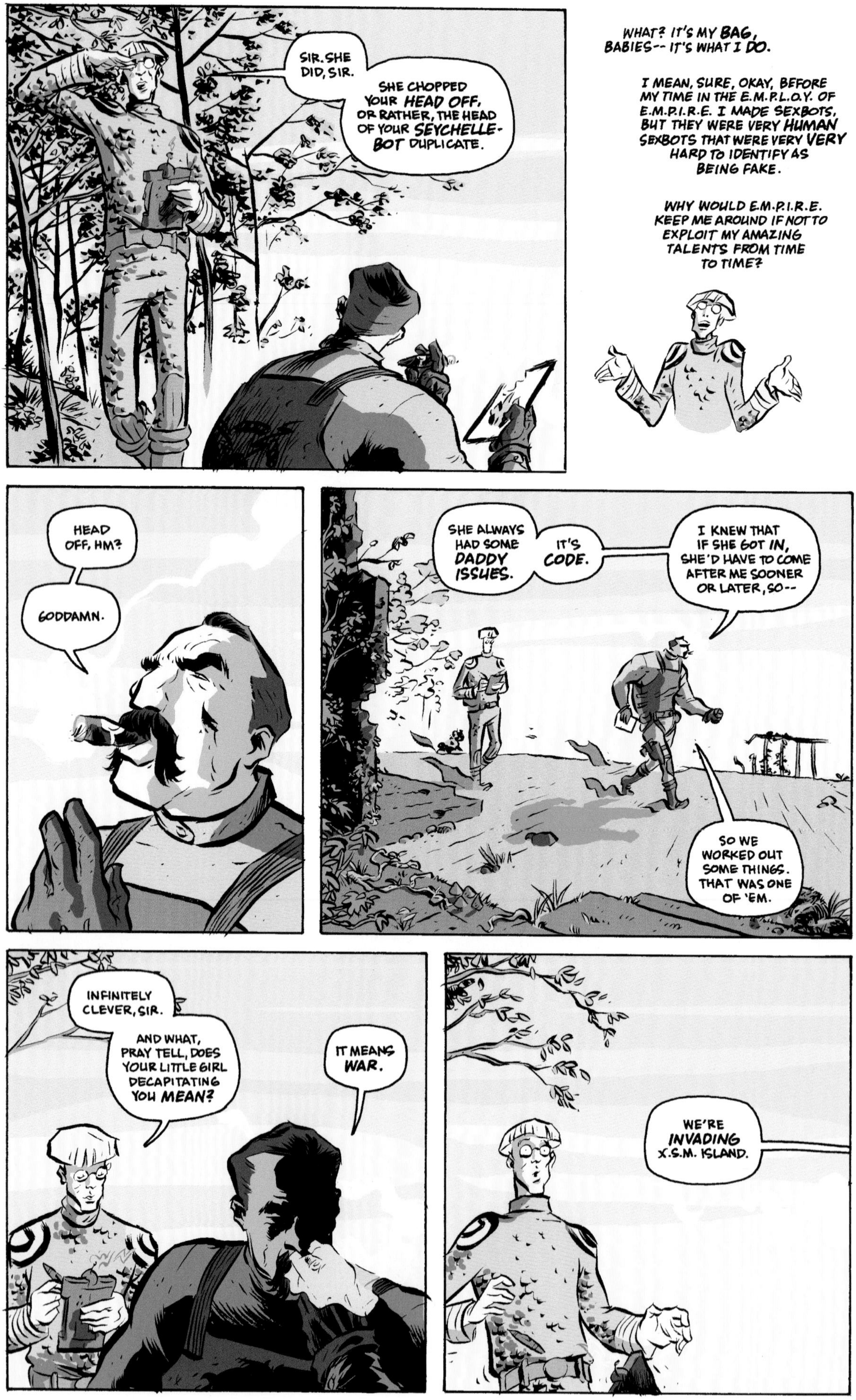

SIR. SHE DID, SIR.
SHE CHOPPED YOUR HEAD OFF, OR RATHER, THE HEAD OF YOUR SEYCHELLE-BOT DUPLICATE.
WHAT? IT'S MY BAG, BABIES-- IT'S WHAT I DO.
I MEAN, SURE, OKAY, BEFORE MY TIME IN THE E.M.P.L.O.Y. OF E.M.P.I.R.E. I MADE SEXBOTS, BUT THEY WERE VERY HUMAN SEXBOTS THAT WERE VERY VERY HARD TO IDENTIFY AS BEING FAKE.
WHY WOULD E.M.P.I.R.E. KEEP ME AROUND IF NOT TO EXPLOIT MY AMAZING TALENTS FROM TIME TO TIME?
HEAD OFF, HM?
GODDAMN.
SHE ALWAYS HAD SOME DADDY ISSUES.
IT'S CODE.
I KNEW THAT IF SHE GOT IN, SHE'D HAVE TO COME AFTER ME SOONER OR LATER, SO--
SO WE WORKED OUT SOME THINGS. THAT WAS ONE OF 'EM.
INFINITELY CLEVER, SIR.
AND WHAT, PRAY TELL, DOES YOUR LITTLE GIRL DECAPITATING YOU MEAN?
IT MEANS WAR.
WE'RE INVADING X.S.M. ISLAND.

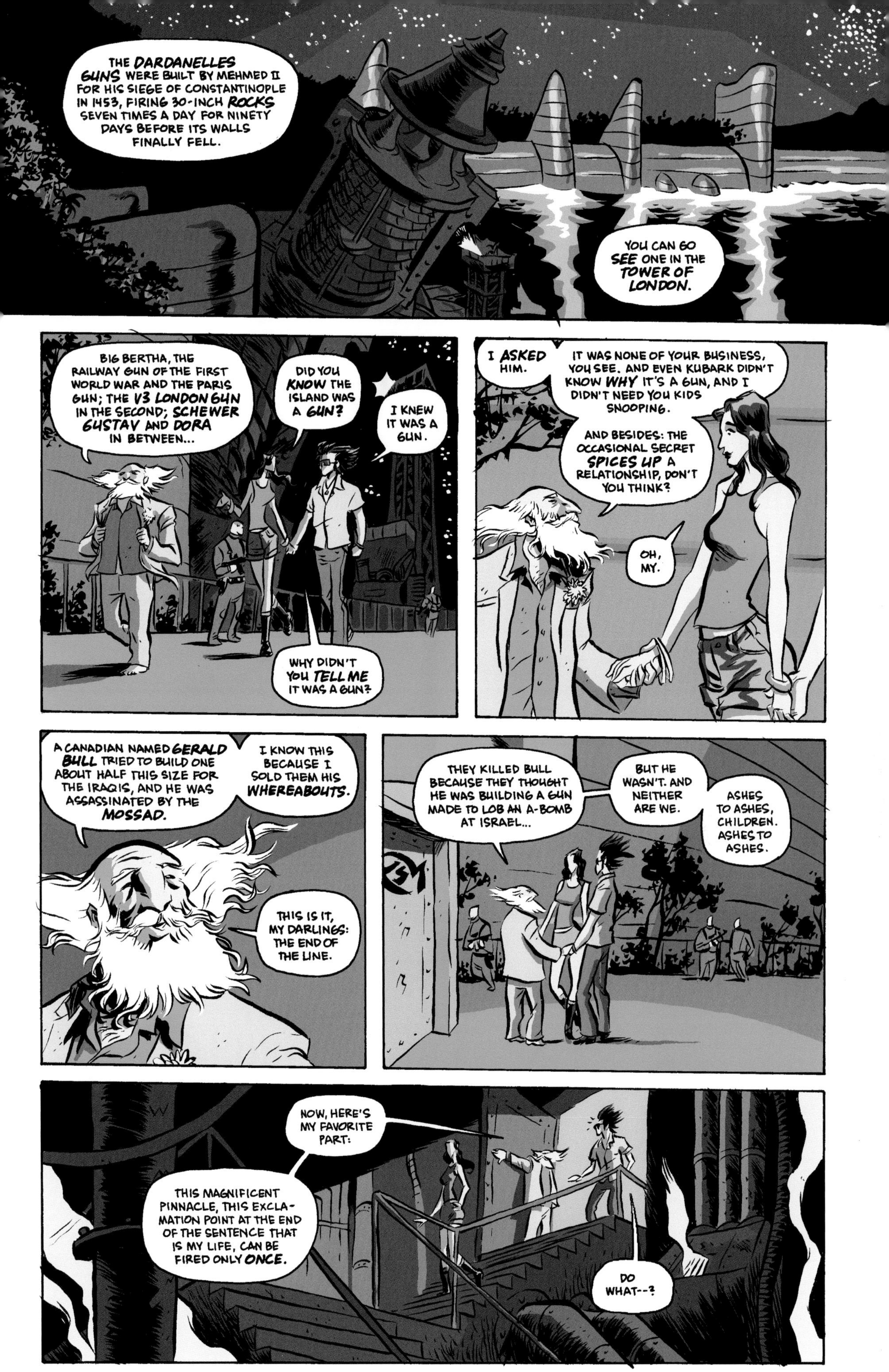
THE DARDANELLES GUNS WERE BUILT BY MEHMED II FOR HIS SIEGE OF CONSTANTINOPLE IN 1453, FIRING 30-INCH ROCKS SEVEN TIMES A DAY FOR NINETY DAYS BEFORE ITS WALLS FINALLY FELL.
YOU CAN GO SEE ONE IN THE TOWER OF LONDON.
BIG BERTHA, THE RAILWAY GUN OF THE FIRST WORLD WAR AND THE PARIS GUN; THE V3 LONDON GUN IN THE SECOND; SCHEWER GUSTAV AND DORA IN BETWEEN...
DID YOU KNOW THE ISLAND WAS A GUN?
I KNEW IT WAS A GUN.
WHY DIDN'T YOU TELL ME IT WAS A GUN?
I ASKED HIM.
IT WAS NONE OF YOUR BUSINESS, YOU SEE. AND EVEN KUBARK DIDN'T KNOW WHY IT'S A GUN, AND I DIDN'T NEED YOU KIDS SNOOPING.
AND BESIDES: THE OCCASIONAL SECRET SPICES UP A RELATIONSHIP, DON'T YOU THINK?
OH, MY.
A CANADIAN NAMED GERALD BULL TRIED TO BUILD ONE ABOUT HALF THIS SIZE FOR THE IRAQIS, AND HE WAS ASSASSINATED BY THE MOSSAD.
I KNOW THIS BECAUSE I SOLD THEM HIS WHEREABOUTS.
THIS IS IT, MY DARLINGS: THE END OF THE LINE.
THEY KILLED BULL BECAUSE THEY THOUGHT HE WAS BUILDING A GUN MADE TO LOB AN A-BOMB AT ISRAEL...
BUT HE WASN'T. AND NEITHER ARE WE.
ASHES TO ASHES, CHILDREN. ASHES TO ASHES.
NOW, HERE'S MY FAVORITE PART:
THIS MAGNIFICENT PINNACLE, THIS EXCLAMATION POINT AT THE END OF THE SENTENCE THAT IS MY LIFE, CAN BE FIRED ONLY ONCE.
DO WHAT--?

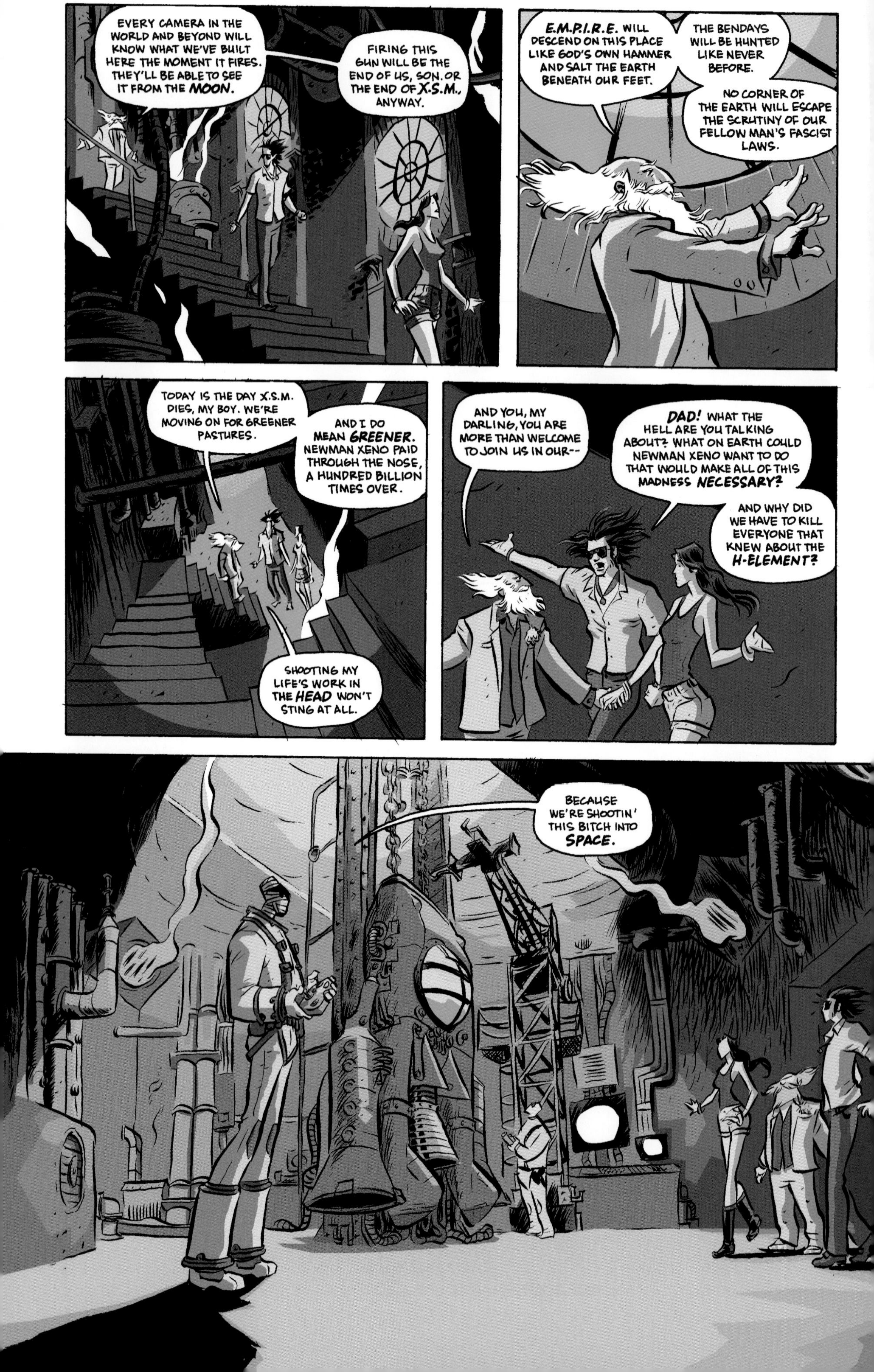
EVERY CAMERA IN THE WORLD AND BEYOND WILL KNOW WHAT WE'VE BUILT HERE THE MOMENT IT FIRES. THEY'LL BE ABLE TO SEE IT FROM THE MOON.
FIRING THIS GUN WILL BE THE END OF US, SON. OR THE END OF X.S.M., ANYWAY.
E.M.P.I.R.E. WILL DESCEND ON THIS PLACE LIKE GOD'S OWN HAMMER AND SALT THE EARTH BENEATH OUR FEET.
THE BENDAYS WILL BE HUNTED LIKE NEVER BEFORE.
NO CORNER OF THE EARTH WILL ESCAPE THE SCRUTINY OF OUR FELLOW MAN'S FASCIST LAWS.
TODAY IS THE DAY X.S.M. DIES, MY BOY. WE'RE MOVING ON FOR GREENER PASTURES.
AND I DO MEAN GREENER. NEWMAN XENO PAID THROUGH THE NOSE, A HUNDRED BILLION TIMES OVER.
SHOOTING MY LIFE'S WORK IN THE HEAD WON'T STING AT ALL.
AND YOU, MY DARLING, YOU ARE MORE THAN WELCOME TO JOIN US IN OUR--
DAD! WHAT THE HELL ARE YOU TALKING ABOUT? WHAT ON EARTH COULD NEWMAN XENO WANT TO DO THAT WOULD MAKE ALL OF THIS MADNESS NECESSARY?
AND WHY DID WE HAVE TO KILL EVERYONE THAT KNEW ABOUT THE H-ELEMENT?
BECAUSE WE'RE SHOOTIN' THIS BITCH INTO SPACE.

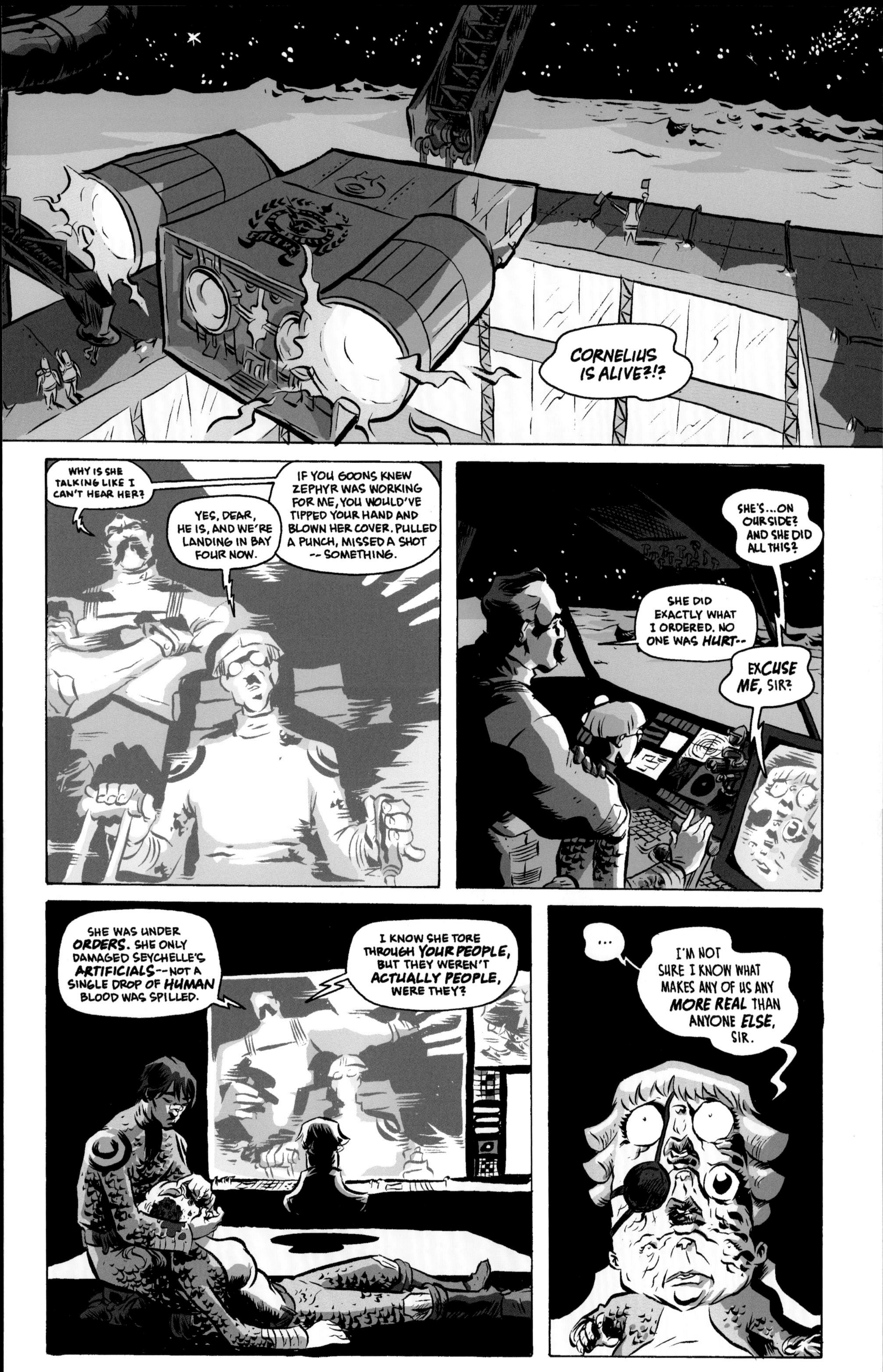
CORNELIUS IS ALIVE?!?
WHY IS SHE TALKING LIKE I CAN'T HEAR HER?
YES, DEAR, HE IS, AND WE'RE LANDING IN BAY FOUR NOW.
IF YOU GOONS KNEW ZEPHYR WAS WORKING FOR ME, YOU WOULD'VE TIPPED YOUR HAND AND BLOWN HER COVER. PULLED A PUNCH, MISSED A SHOT -- SOMETHING.
SHE'S...ON OUR SIDE? AND SHE DID ALL THIS?
SHE DID EXACTLY WHAT I ORDERED. NO ONE WAS HURT--
EXCUSE ME, SIR?
SHE WAS UNDER ORDERS. SHE ONLY DAMAGED SEYCHELLE'S ARTIFICIALS--NOT A SINGLE DROP OF HUMAN BLOOD WAS SPILLED.
I KNOW SHE TORE THROUGH YOUR PEOPLE, BUT THEY WEREN'T ACTUALLY PEOPLE, WERE THEY?
...
I'M NOT SURE I KNOW WHAT MAKES ANY OF US ANY MORE REAL THAN ANYONE ELSE, SIR.

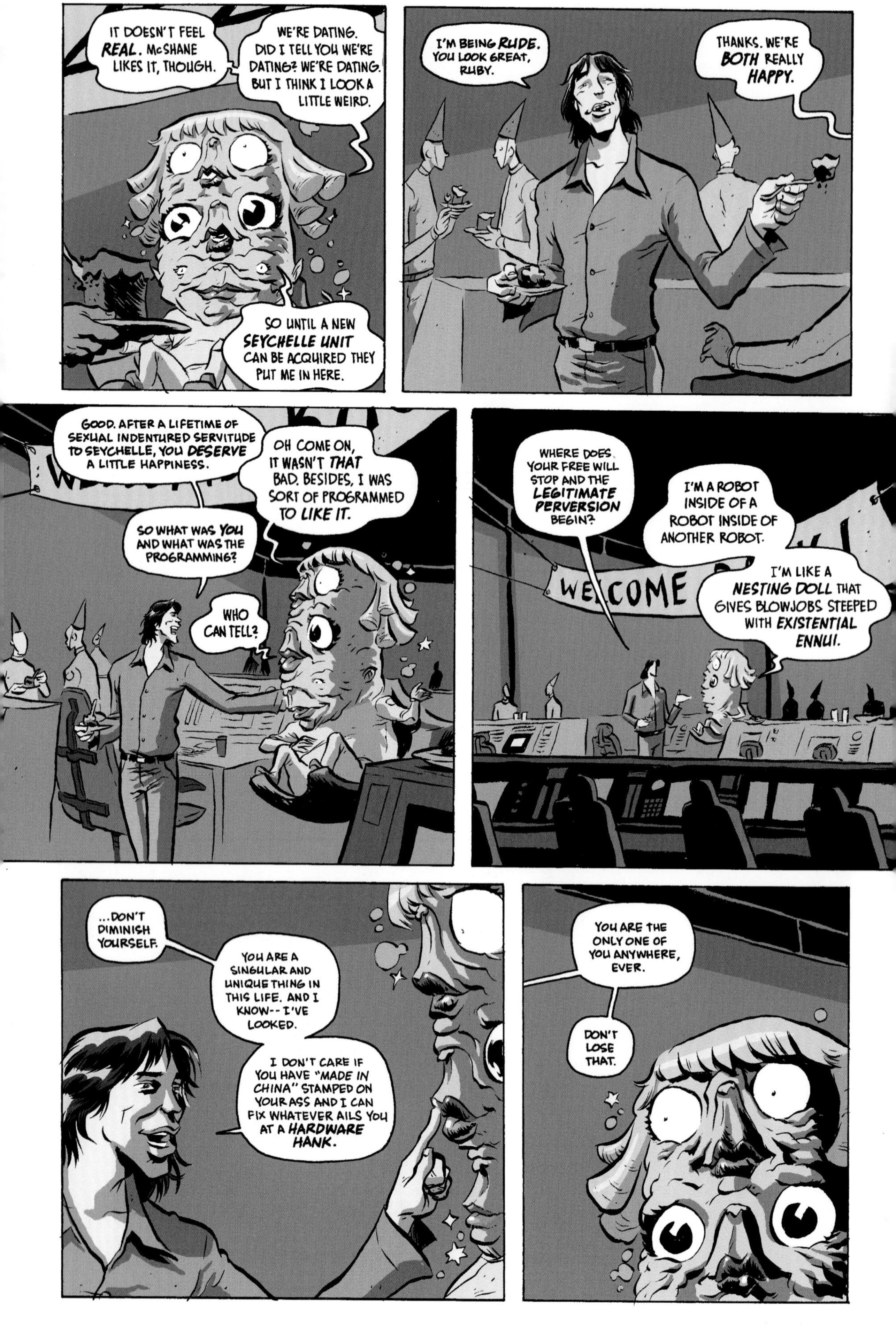
IT DOESN'T FEEL REAL. McSHANE LIKES IT, THOUGH.
WE'RE DATING. DID I TELL YOU WE'RE DATING? WE'RE DATING. BUT I THINK I LOOK A LITTLE WEIRD.
SO UNTIL A NEW SEYCHELLE UNIT CAN BE ACQUIRED THEY PUT ME IN HERE.
I'M BEING RUDE. YOU LOOK GREAT, RUBY.
THANKS. WE'RE BOTH REALLY HAPPY.
GOOD. AFTER A LIFETIME OF SEXUAL INDENTURED SERVITUDE TO SEYCHELLE, YOU DESERVE A LITTLE HAPPINESS.
OH COME ON, IT WASN'T THAT BAD. BESIDES, I WAS SORT OF PROGRAMMED TO LIKE IT.
SO WHAT WAS YOU AND WHAT WAS THE PROGRAMMING?
WHO CAN TELL?
WHERE DOES YOUR FREE WILL STOP AND THE LEGITIMATE PERVERSION BEGIN?
I'M A ROBOT INSIDE OF A ROBOT INSIDE OF ANOTHER ROBOT.
I'M LIKE A NESTING DOLL THAT GIVES BLOWJOBS STEEPED WITH EXISTENTIAL ENNUI.
WELCOME
...DON'T DIMINISH YOURSELF.
YOU ARE A SINGULAR AND UNIQUE THING IN THIS LIFE. AND I KNOW-- I'VE LOOKED.
I DON'T CARE IF YOU HAVE "MADE IN CHINA" STAMPED ON YOUR ASS AND I CAN FIX WHATEVER AILS YOU AT A HARDWARE HANK.
YOU ARE THE ONLY ONE OF YOU ANYWHERE, EVER.
DON'T LOSE THAT.

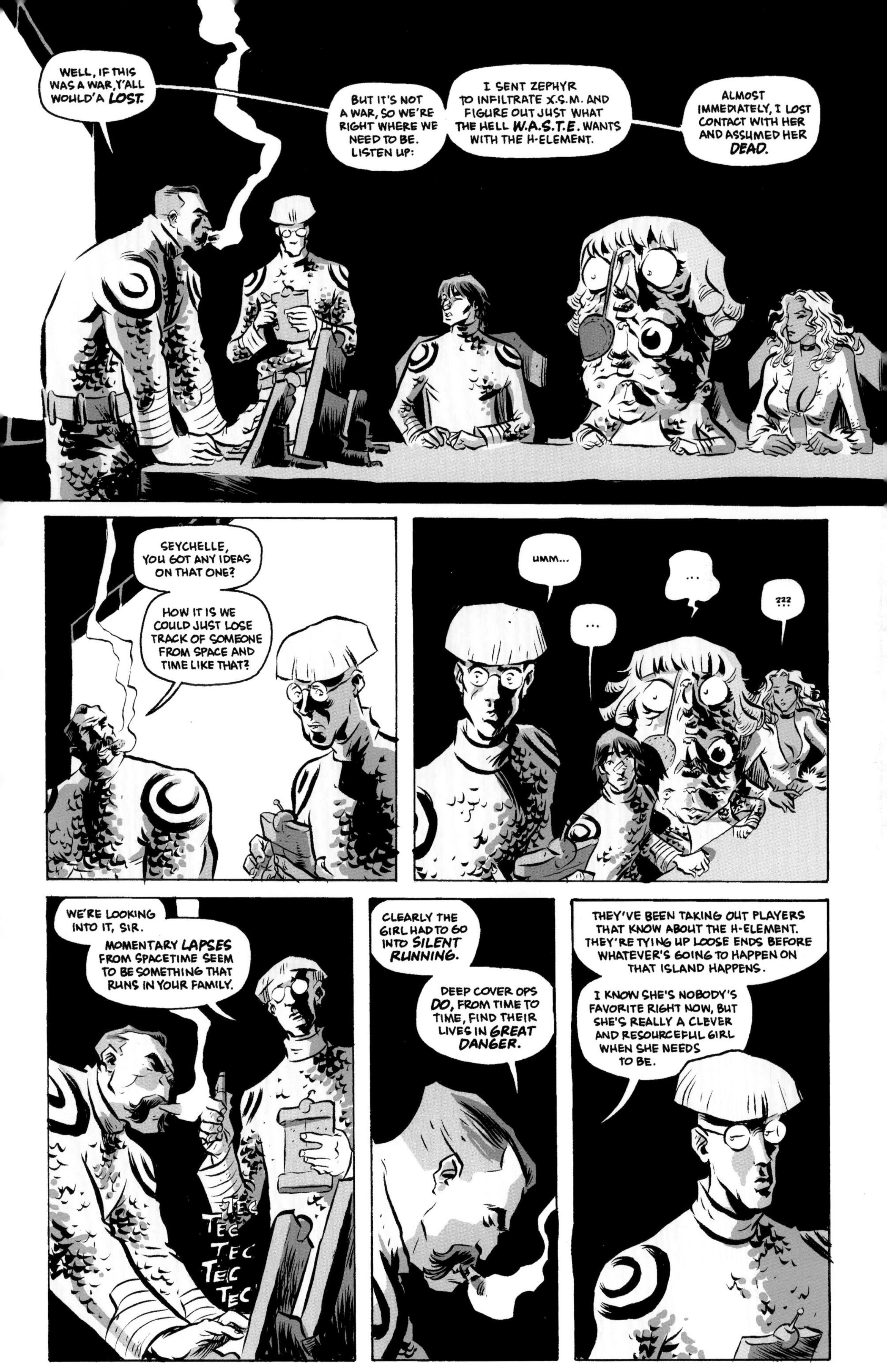
WELL, IF THIS WAS A WAR, Y'ALL WOULD'A LOST.
BUT IT'S NOT A WAR, SO WE'RE RIGHT WHERE WE NEED TO BE. LISTEN UP:
I SENT ZEPHYR TO INFILTRATE X.S.M. AND FIGURE OUT JUST WHAT THE HELL W.A.S.T.E. WANTS WITH THE H-ELEMENT.
ALMOST IMMEDIATELY, I LOST CONTACT WITH HER AND ASSUMED HER DEAD.
SEYCHELLE, YOU GOT ANY IDEAS ON THAT ONE?
HOW IT IS WE COULD JUST LOSE TRACK OF SOMEONE FROM SPACE AND TIME LIKE THAT?
UMM...
...
...
???
WE'RE LOOKING INTO IT, SIR.
MOMENTARY LAPSES FROM SPACETIME SEEM TO BE SOMETHING THAT RUNS IN YOUR FAMILY.
TEC TEC TEC TEC TEC
CLEARLY THE GIRL HAD TO GO INTO SILENT RUNNING.
DEEP COVER OPS DO, FROM TIME TO TIME, FIND THEIR LIVES IN GREAT DANGER.
THEY'VE BEEN TAKING OUT PLAYERS THAT KNOW ABOUT THE H-ELEMENT. THEY'RE TYING UP LOOSE ENDS BEFORE WHATEVER'S GOING TO HAPPEN ON THAT ISLAND HAPPENS.
I KNOW SHE'S NOBODY'S FAVORITE RIGHT NOW, BUT SHE'S REALLY A CLEVER AND RESOURCEFUL GIRL WHEN SHE NEEDS TO BE.

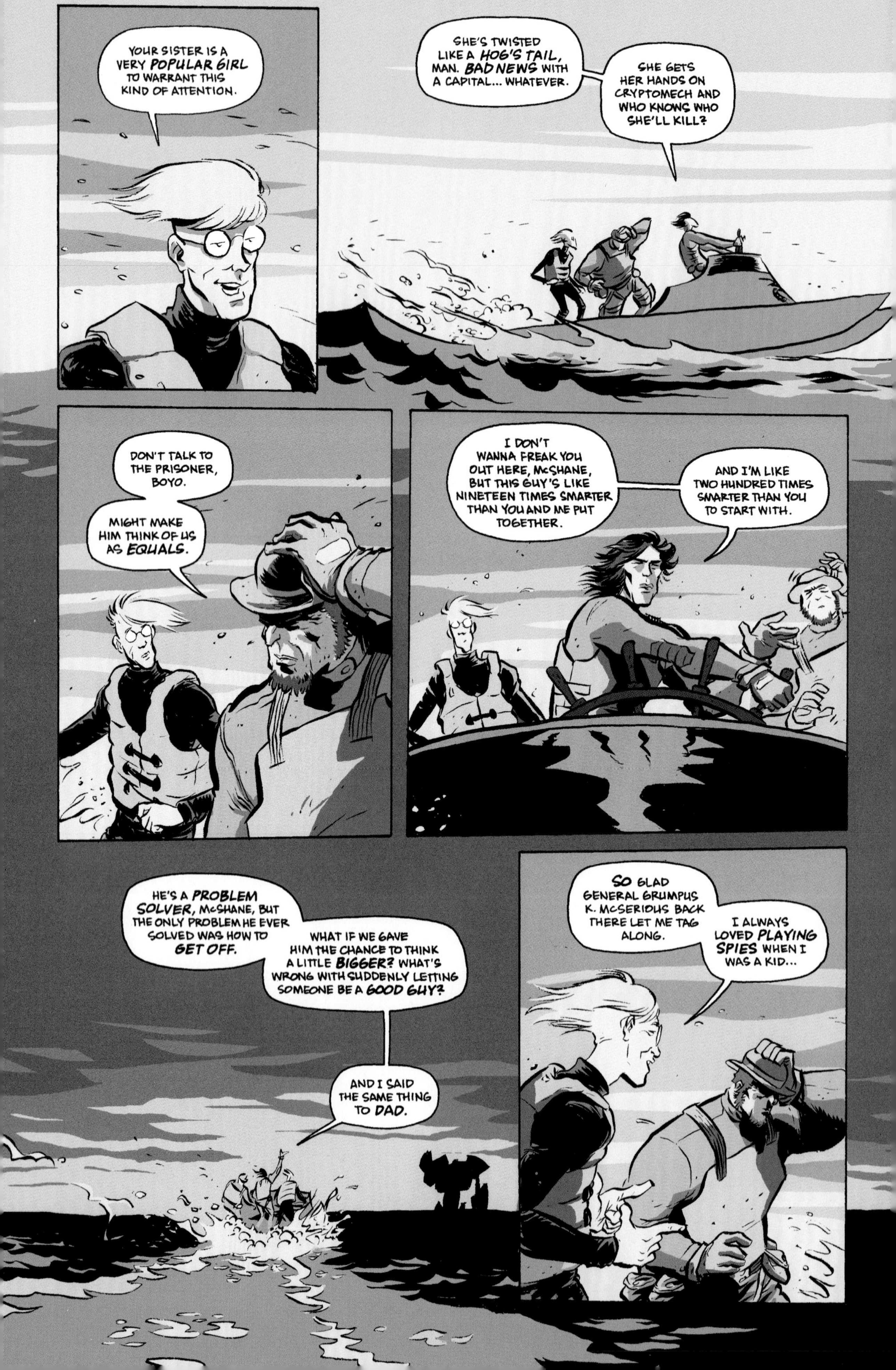
YOUR SISTER IS A VERY POPULAR GIRL TO WARRANT THIS KIND OF ATTENTION.
SHE'S TWISTED LIKE A HOG'S TAIL, MAN. BAD NEWS WITH A CAPITAL... WHATEVER.
SHE GETS HER HANDS ON CRYPTOMECH AND WHO KNOWS WHO SHE'LL KILL?
DON'T TALK TO THE PRISONER, BOYO.
MIGHT MAKE HIM THINK OF US AS EQUALS.
I DON'T WANNA FREAK YOU OUT HERE, McSHANE, BUT THIS GUY'S LIKE NINETEEN TIMES SMARTER THAN YOU AND ME PUT TOGETHER.
AND I'M LIKE TWO HUNDRED TIMES SMARTER THAN YOU TO START WITH.
HE'S A PROBLEM SOLVER, McSHANE, BUT THE ONLY PROBLEM HE EVER SOLVED WAS HOW TO GET OFF.
WHAT IF WE GAVE HIM THE CHANCE TO THINK A LITTLE BIGGER? WHAT'S WRONG WITH SUDDENLY LETTING SOMEONE BE A GOOD GUY?
AND I SAID THE SAME THING TO DAD.
SO GLAD GENERAL GRUMPUS K. McSERIOUS BACK THERE LET ME TAG ALONG.
I ALWAYS LOVED PLAYING SPIES WHEN I WAS A KID...

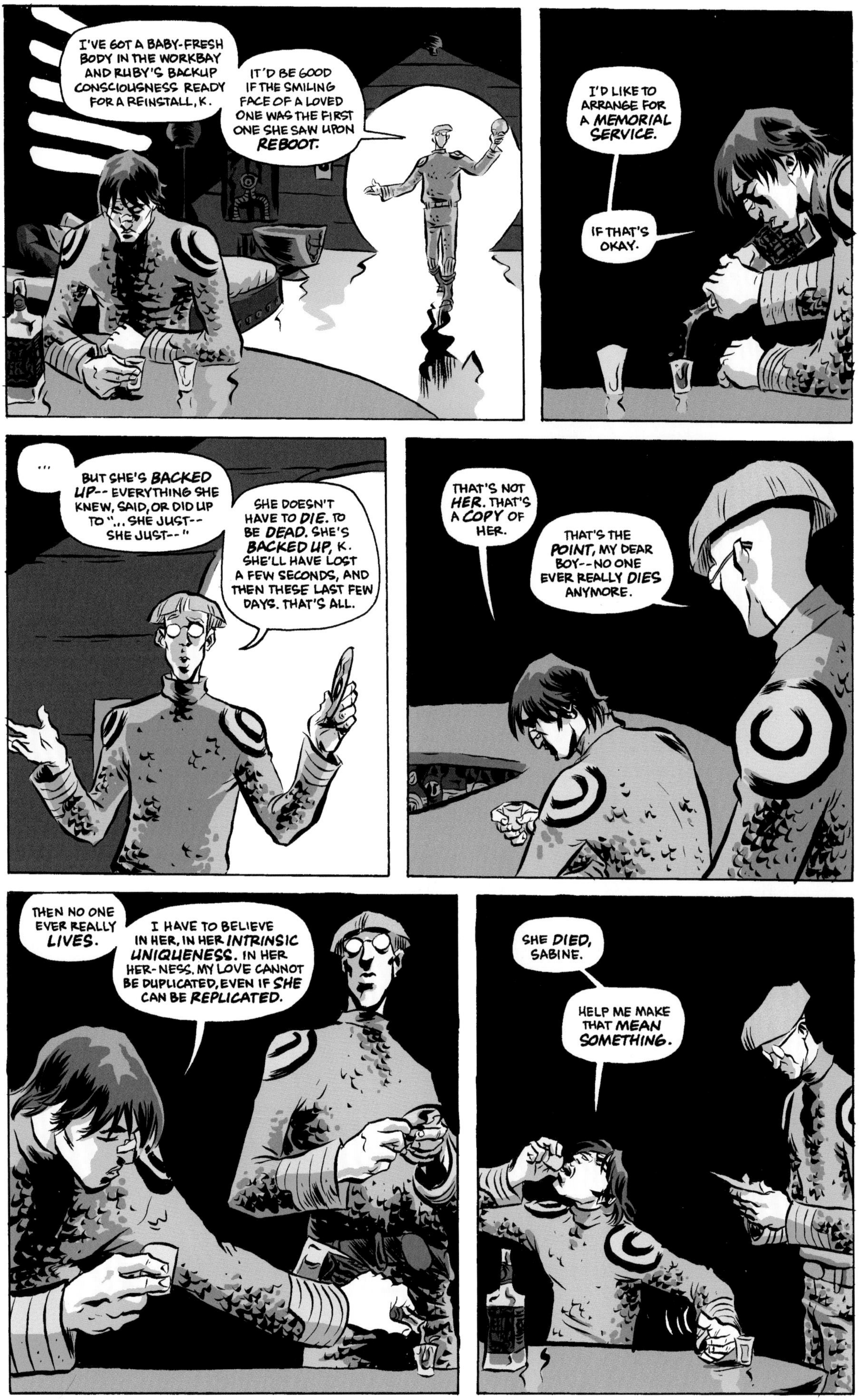
I'VE GOT A BABY-FRESH BODY IN THE WORKBAY AND RUBY'S BACKUP CONSCIOUSNESS READY FOR A REINSTALL, K.
IT'D BE GOOD IF THE SMILING FACE OF A LOVED ONE WAS THE FIRST ONE SHE SAW UPON REBOOT.
I'D LIKE TO ARRANGE FOR A MEMORIAL SERVICE.
IF THAT'S OKAY.
...
BUT SHE'S BACKED UP-- EVERYTHING SHE KNEW, SAID, OR DID UP TO "... SHE JUST-- SHE JUST--"
SHE DOESN'T HAVE TO DIE. TO BE DEAD. SHE'S BACKED UP, K. SHE'LL HAVE LOST A FEW SECONDS, AND THEN THESE LAST FEW DAYS. THAT'S ALL.
THAT'S NOT HER. THAT'S A COPY OF HER.
THAT'S THE POINT, MY DEAR BOY--NO ONE EVER REALLY DIES ANYMORE.
THEN NO ONE EVER REALLY LIVES.
I HAVE TO BELIEVE IN HER, IN HER INTRINSIC UNIQUENESS. IN HER HER-NESS. MY LOVE CANNOT BE DUPLICATED, EVEN IF SHE CAN BE REPLICATED.
SHE DIED, SABINE.
HELP ME MAKE THAT MEAN SOMETHING.

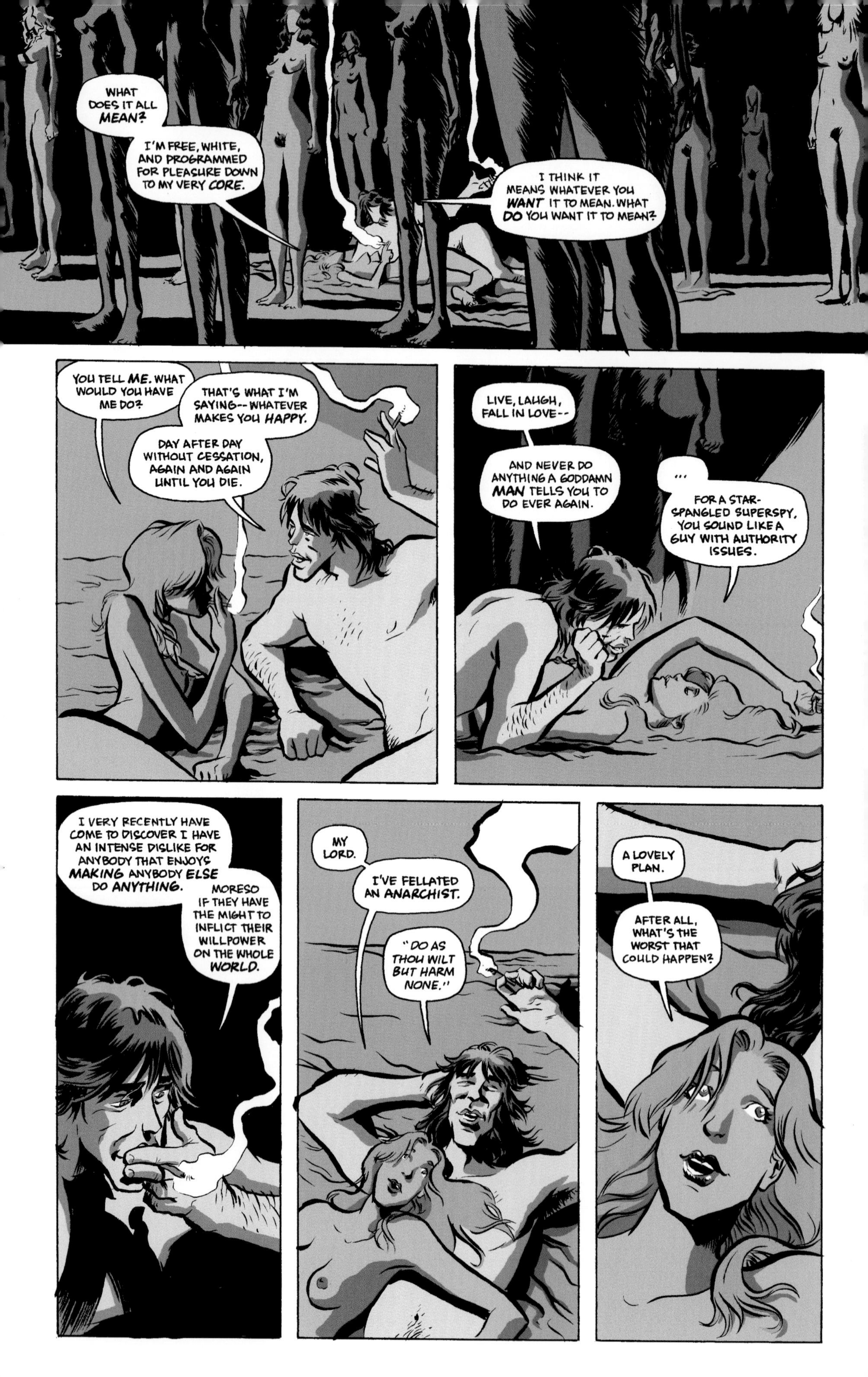
WHAT DOES IT ALL MEAN?
I'M FREE, WHITE, AND PROGRAMMED FOR PLEASURE DOWN TO MY VERY CORE.
I THINK IT MEANS WHATEVER YOU WANT IT TO MEAN. WHAT DO YOU WANT IT TO MEAN?
YOU TELL ME. WHAT WOULD YOU HAVE ME DO?
THAT'S WHAT I'M SAYING--WHATEVER MAKES YOU HAPPY.
DAY AFTER DAY WITHOUT CESSATION, AGAIN AND AGAIN UNTIL YOU DIE.
LIVE, LAUGH, FALL IN LOVE--
AND NEVER DO ANYTHING A GODDAMN MAN TELLS YOU TO DO EVER AGAIN.
...
FOR A STAR-SPANGLED SUPERSPY, YOU SOUND LIKE A GUY WITH AUTHORITY ISSUES.
I VERY RECENTLY HAVE COME TO DISCOVER I HAVE AN INTENSE DISLIKE FOR ANYBODY THAT ENJOYS MAKING ANYBODY ELSE DO ANYTHING.
MORESO IF THEY HAVE THE MIGHT TO INFLICT THEIR WILLPOWER ON THE WHOLE WORLD.
MY LORD.
I'VE FELLATED AN ANARCHIST.
"DO AS THOU WILT BUT HARM NONE."
A LOVELY PLAN.
AFTER ALL, WHAT'S THE WORST THAT COULD HAPPEN?

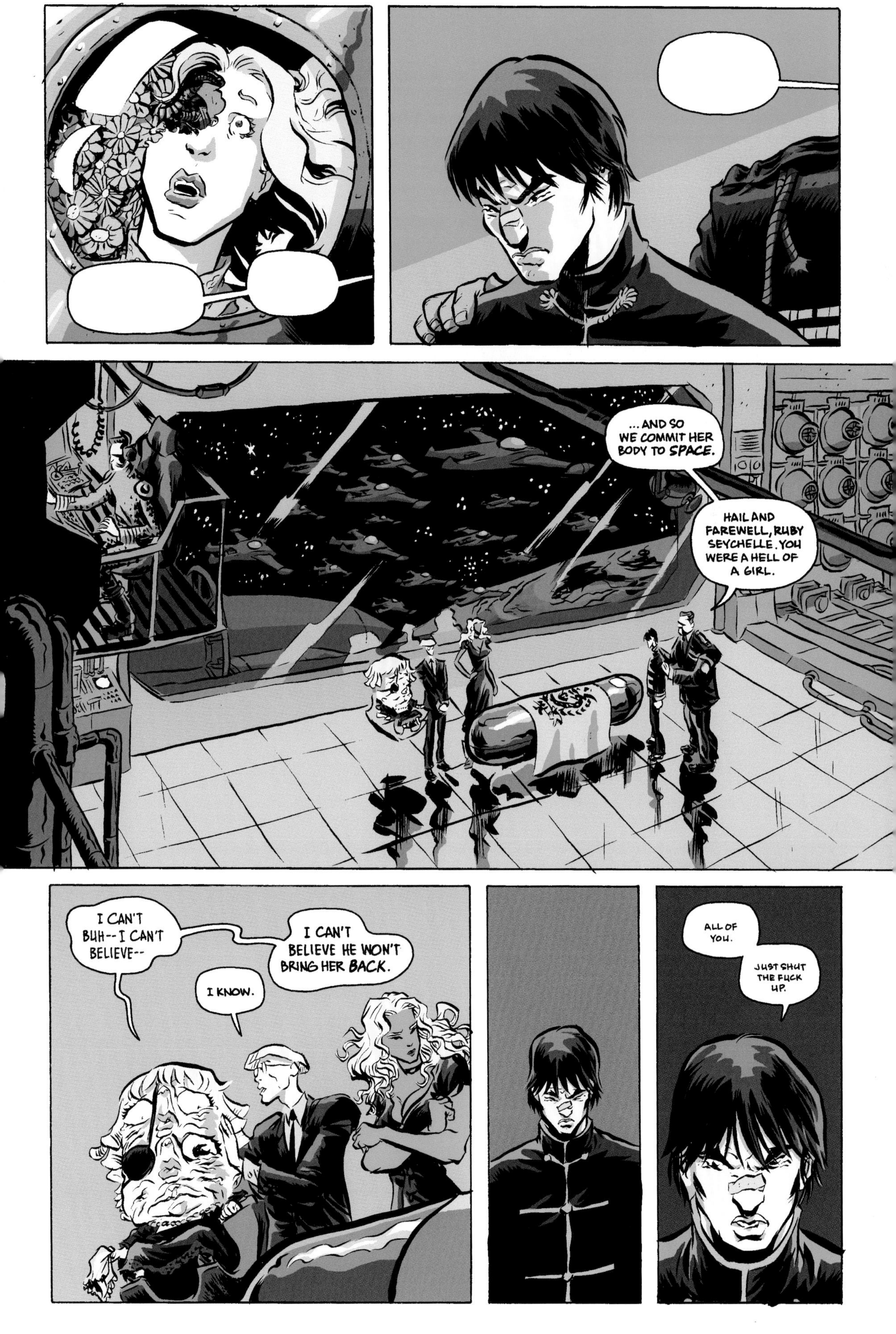
...AND SO WE COMMIT HER BODY TO SPACE.
HAIL AND FAREWELL, RUBY SEYCHELLE. YOU WERE A HELL OF A GIRL.
I CAN'T BUH--I CAN'T BELIEVE--
I CAN'T BELIEVE HE WON'T BRING HER BACK.
I KNOW.
ALL OF YOU.
JUST SHUT THE FUCK UP.

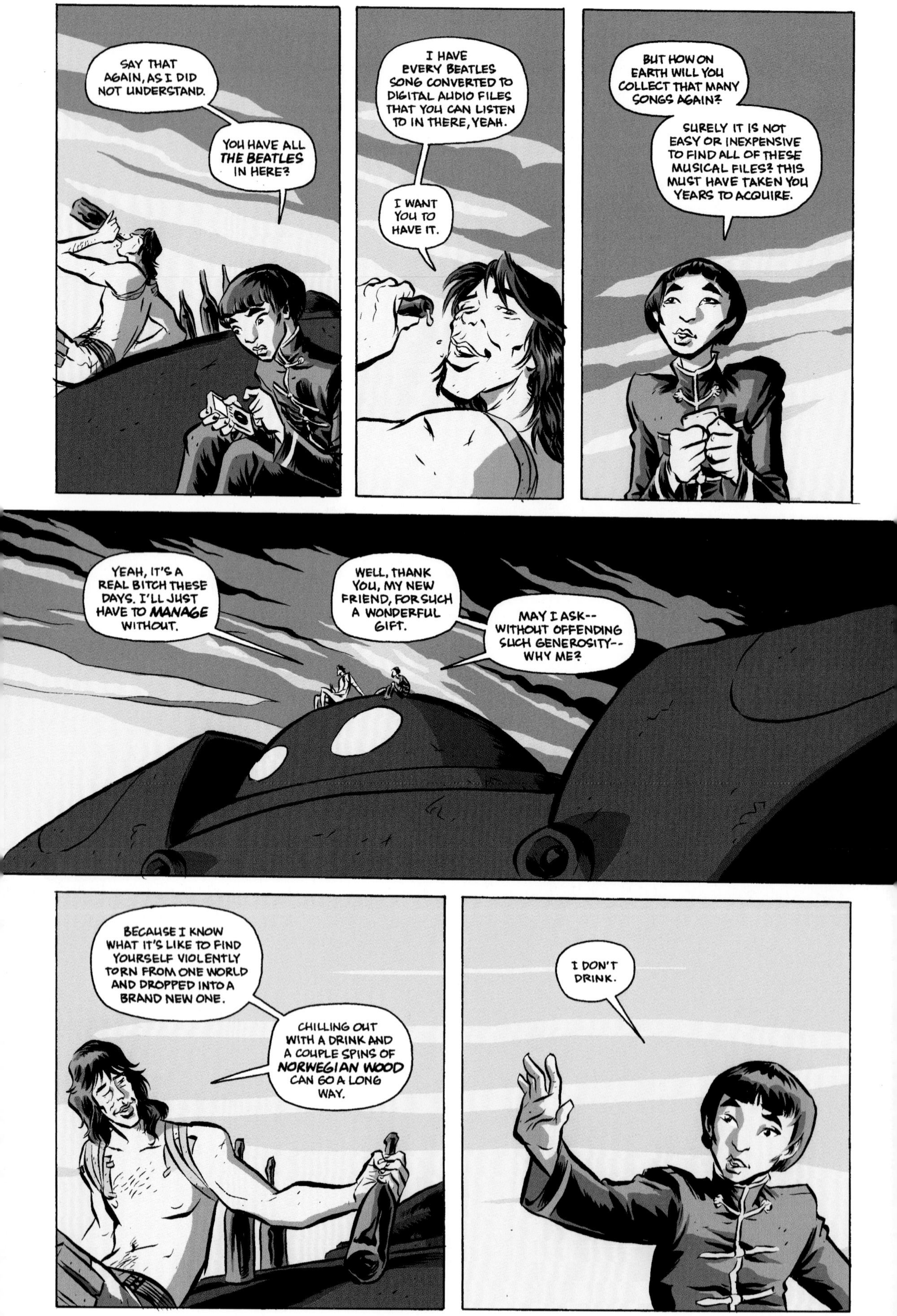
SAY THAT AGAIN, AS I DID NOT UNDERSTAND.
YOU HAVE ALL THE BEATLES IN HERE?
I HAVE EVERY BEATLES SONG CONVERTED TO DIGITAL AUDIO FILES THAT YOU CAN LISTEN TO IN THERE, YEAH.
I WANT YOU TO HAVE IT.
BUT HOW ON EARTH WILL YOU COLLECT THAT MANY SONGS AGAIN?
SURELY IT IS NOT EASY OR INEXPENSIVE TO FIND ALL OF THESE MUSICAL FILES? THIS MUST HAVE TAKEN YOU YEARS TO ACQUIRE.
YEAH, IT'S A REAL BITCH THESE DAYS. I'LL JUST HAVE TO MANAGE WITHOUT.
WELL, THANK YOU, MY NEW FRIEND, FOR SUCH A WONDERFUL GIFT.
MAY I ASK-- WITHOUT OFFENDING SUCH GENEROSITY-- WHY ME?
BECAUSE I KNOW WHAT IT'S LIKE TO FIND YOURSELF VIOLENTLY TORN FROM ONE WORLD AND DROPPED INTO A BRAND NEW ONE.
CHILLING OUT WITH A DRINK AND A COUPLE SPINS OF NORWEGIAN WOOD CAN GO A LONG WAY.
I DON'T DRINK.

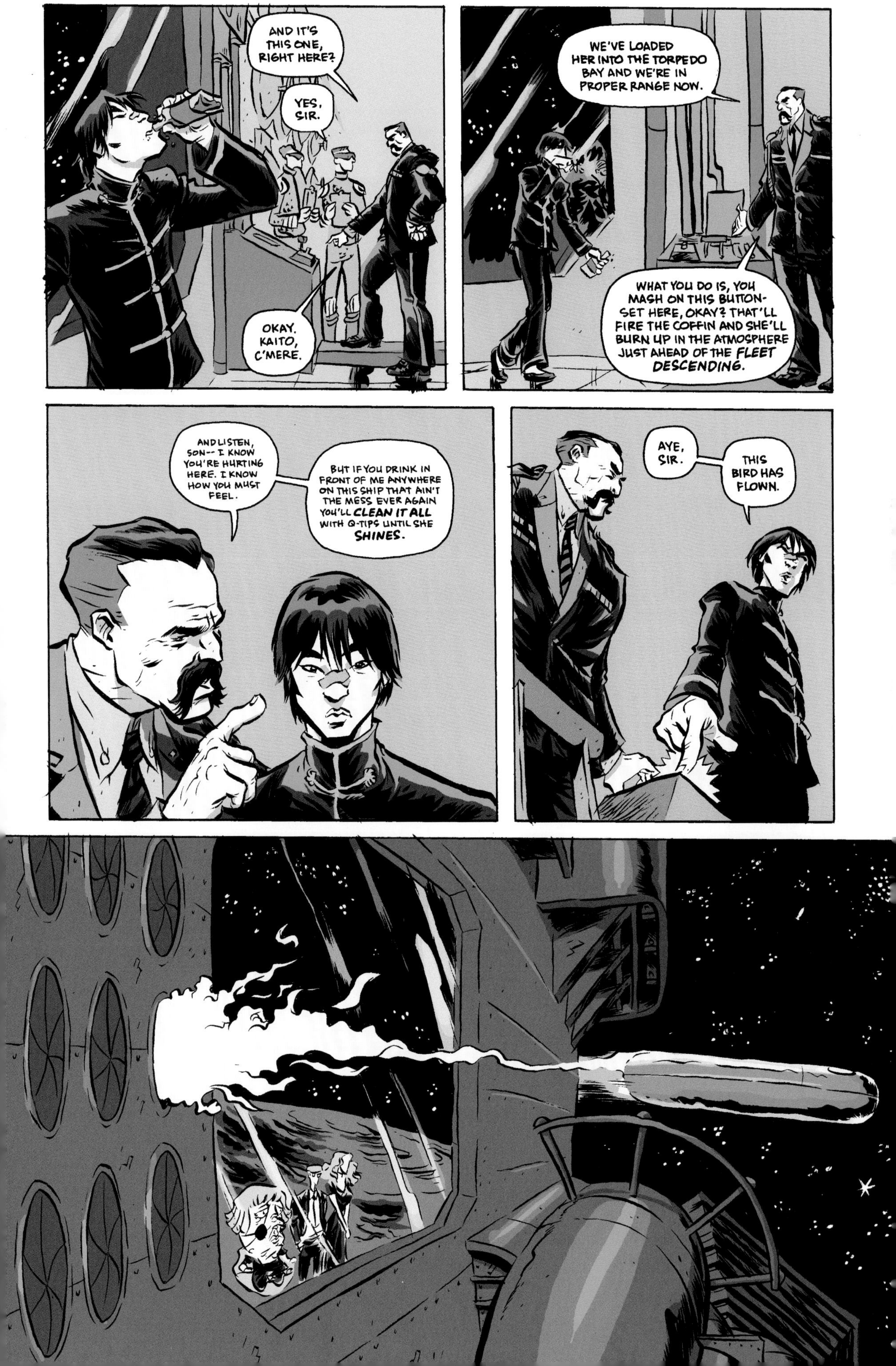
AND IT'S THIS ONE, RIGHT HERE?
YES, SIR.
OKAY. KAITO, C'MERE.
WE'VE LOADED HER INTO THE TORPEDO BAY AND WE'RE IN PROPER RANGE NOW.
WHAT YOU DO IS, YOU MASH ON THIS BUTTON-SET HERE, OKAY? THAT'LL FIRE THE COFFIN AND SHE'LL BURN UP IN THE ATMOSPHERE JUST AHEAD OF THE FLEET DESCENDING.
AND LISTEN, SON-- I KNOW YOU'RE HURTING HERE. I KNOW HOW YOU MUST FEEL.
BUT IF YOU DRINK IN FRONT OF ME ANYWHERE ON THIS SHIP THAT AIN'T THE MESS EVER AGAIN YOU'LL CLEAN IT ALL WITH Q-TIPS UNTIL SHE SHINES.
AYE, SIR.
THIS BIRD HAS FLOWN.

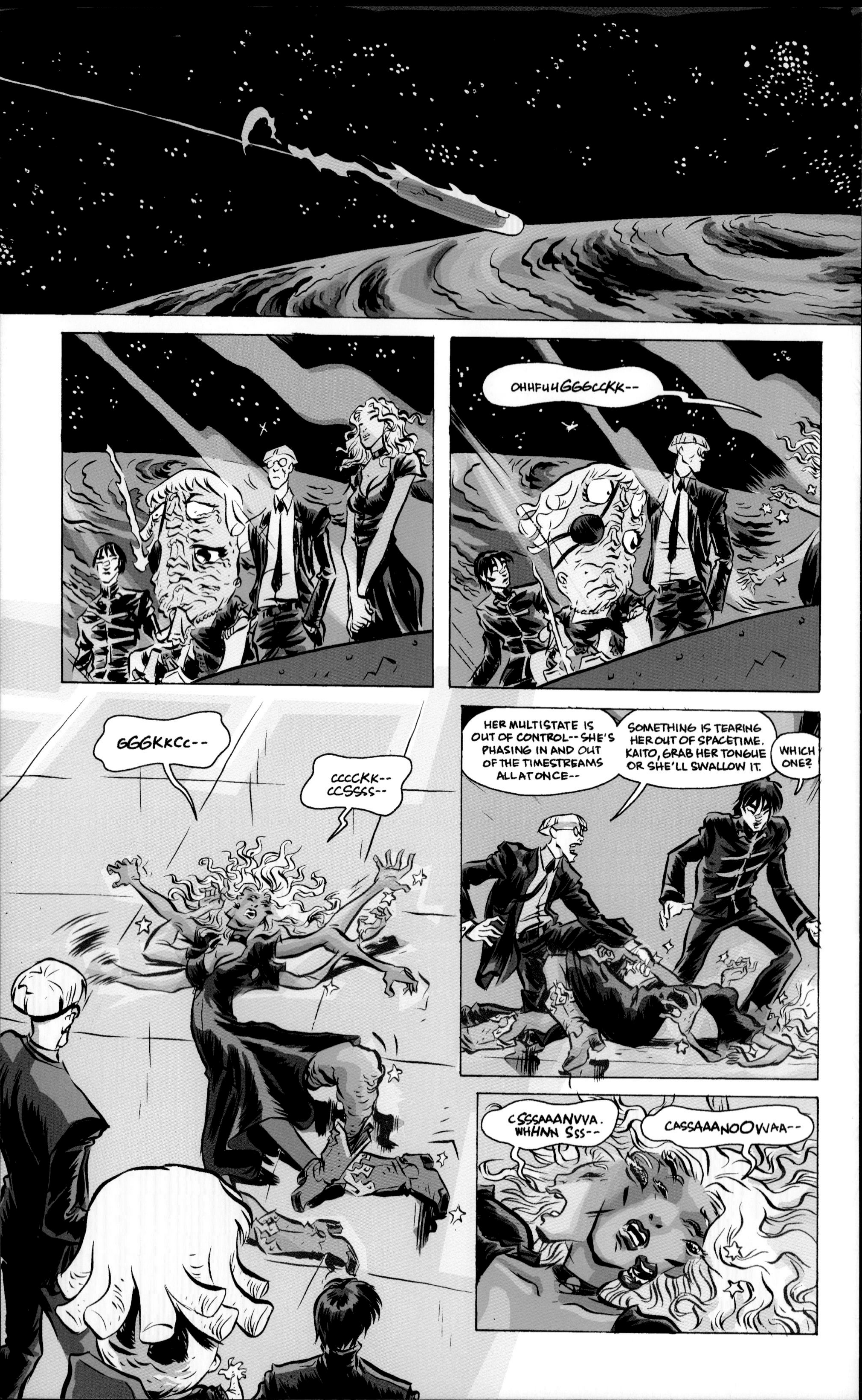
OHHFUUGGGCCKK--
GGGKKCc--
CCCCKK-- CCSSSS--
HER MULTISTATE IS OUT OF CONTROL--SHE'S PHASING IN AND OUT OF THE TIMESTREAMS ALL AT ONCE--
SOMETHING IS TEARING HER OUT OF SPACETIME. KAITO, GRAB HER TONGUE OR SHE'LL SWALLOW IT.
WHICH ONE?
CSSSAAANVVA. WHHNN SSS--
CASSAAANOOWAA--

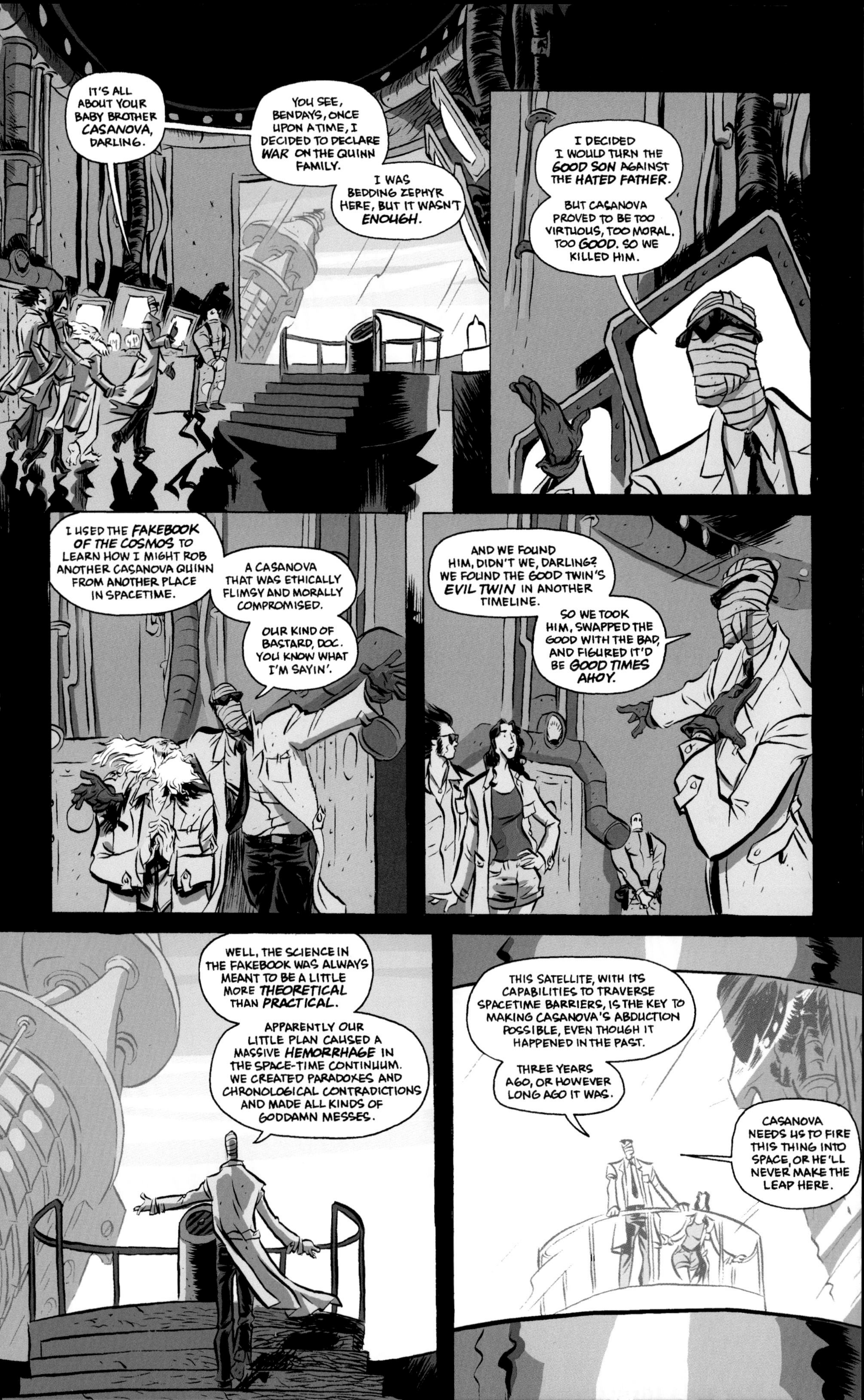
IT'S ALL ABOUT YOUR BABY BROTHER CASANOVA, DARLING.
YOU SEE, BENDAYS, ONCE UPON A TIME, I DECIDED TO DECLARE WAR ON THE QUINN FAMILY.
I WAS BEDDING ZEPHYR HERE, BUT IT WASN'T ENOUGH.
I DECIDED I WOULD TURN THE GOOD SON AGAINST THE HATED FATHER.
BUT CASANOVA PROVED TO BE TOO VIRTUOUS, TOO MORAL. TOO GOOD. SO WE KILLED HIM.
I USED THE FAKEBOOK OF THE COSMOS TO LEARN HOW I MIGHT ROB ANOTHER CASANOVA QUINN FROM ANOTHER PLACE IN SPACETIME.
A CASANOVA THAT WAS ETHICALLY FLIMSY AND MORALLY COMPROMISED.
OUR KIND OF BASTARD, DOC. YOU KNOW WHAT I'M SAYIN'.
AND WE FOUND HIM, DIDN'T WE, DARLING? WE FOUND THE GOOD TWIN'S EVIL TWIN IN ANOTHER TIMELINE.
SO WE TOOK HIM, SWAPPED THE GOOD WITH THE BAD, AND FIGURED IT'D BE GOOD TIMES AHOY.
WELL, THE SCIENCE IN THE FAKEBOOK WAS ALWAYS MEANT TO BE A LITTLE MORE THEORETICAL THAN PRACTICAL.
APPARENTLY OUR LITTLE PLAN CAUSED A MASSIVE HEMORRHAGE IN THE SPACE-TIME CONTINUUM. WE CREATED PARADOXES AND CHRONOLOGICAL CONTRADICTIONS AND MADE ALL KINDS OF GODDAMN MESSES.
THIS SATELLITE, WITH ITS CAPABILITIES TO TRAVERSE SPACETIME BARRIERS, IS THE KEY TO MAKING CASANOVA'S ABDUCTION POSSIBLE, EVEN THOUGH IT HAPPENED IN THE PAST.
THREE YEARS AGO, OR HOWEVER LONG AGO IT WAS.
CASANOVA NEEDS US TO FIRE THIS THING INTO SPACE, OR HE'LL NEVER MAKE THE LEAP HERE.

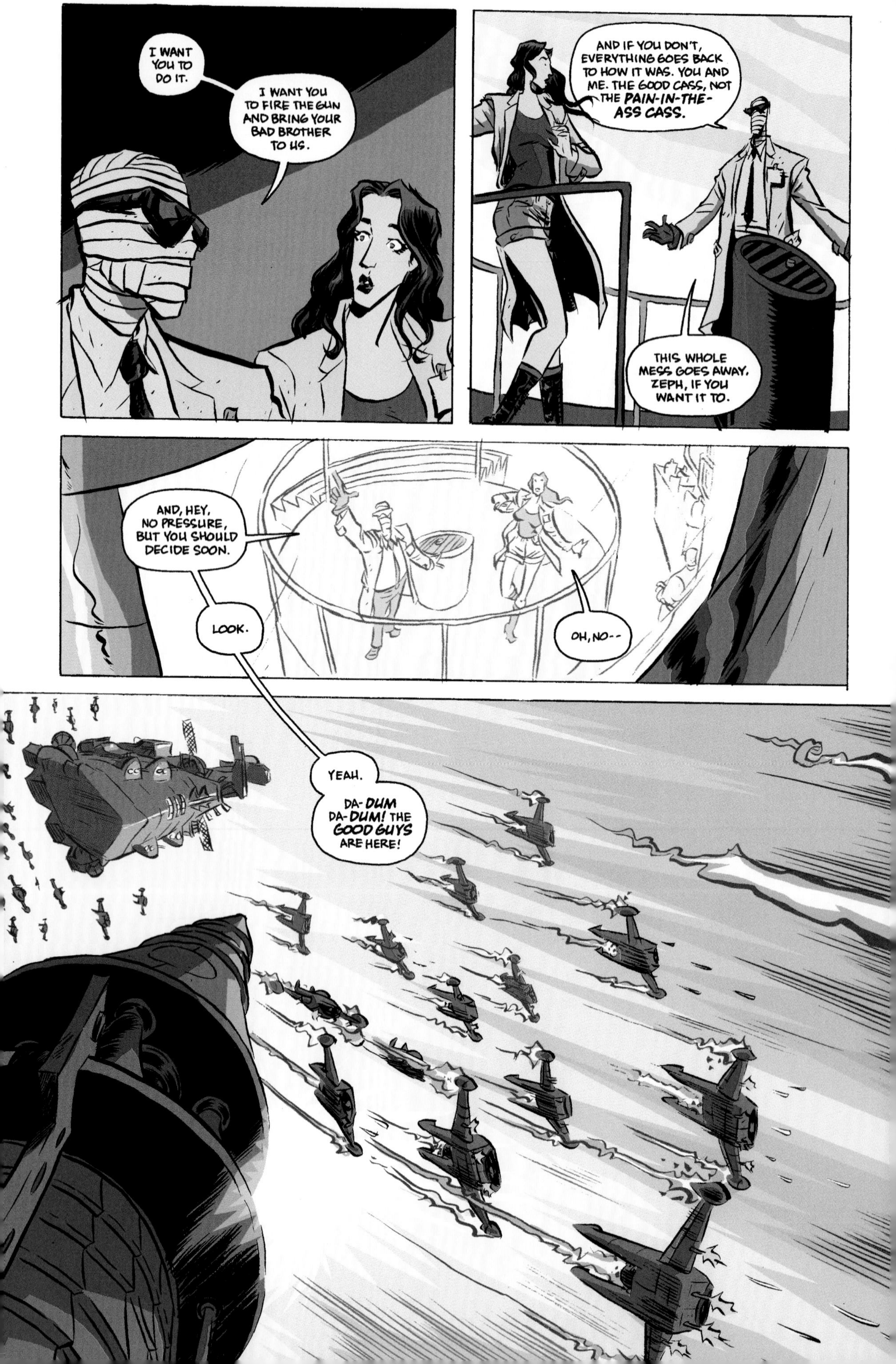
I WANT YOU TO DO IT.
I WANT YOU TO FIRE THE GUN AND BRING YOUR BAD BROTHER TO US.
AND IF YOU DON'T, EVERYTHING GOES BACK TO HOW IT WAS. YOU AND ME. THE GOOD CASS, NOT THE PAIN-IN-THE-ASS CASS.
THIS WHOLE MESS GOES AWAY, ZEPH, IF YOU WANT IT TO.
AND, HEY, NO PRESSURE, BUT YOU SHOULD DECIDE SOON.
LOOK.
OH, NO--
YEAH.
DA-DUM DA-DUM! THE GOOD GUYS ARE HERE!

IN MEDIAS RES

WHEN THE WOLF COMES HOME

SEVENTEEN

NAOMI I MOAN

FUCK SHIT UP

SOME OF THE THINGS THAT
HAPPENED TO THE MURDERERS
AND MURDERED AMONG US

HALLO SPACEBOY

DIT DIT DIT
DAH DAH DAH
DIT DIT

BACKMATTER

1: Paper Planes (3:24)

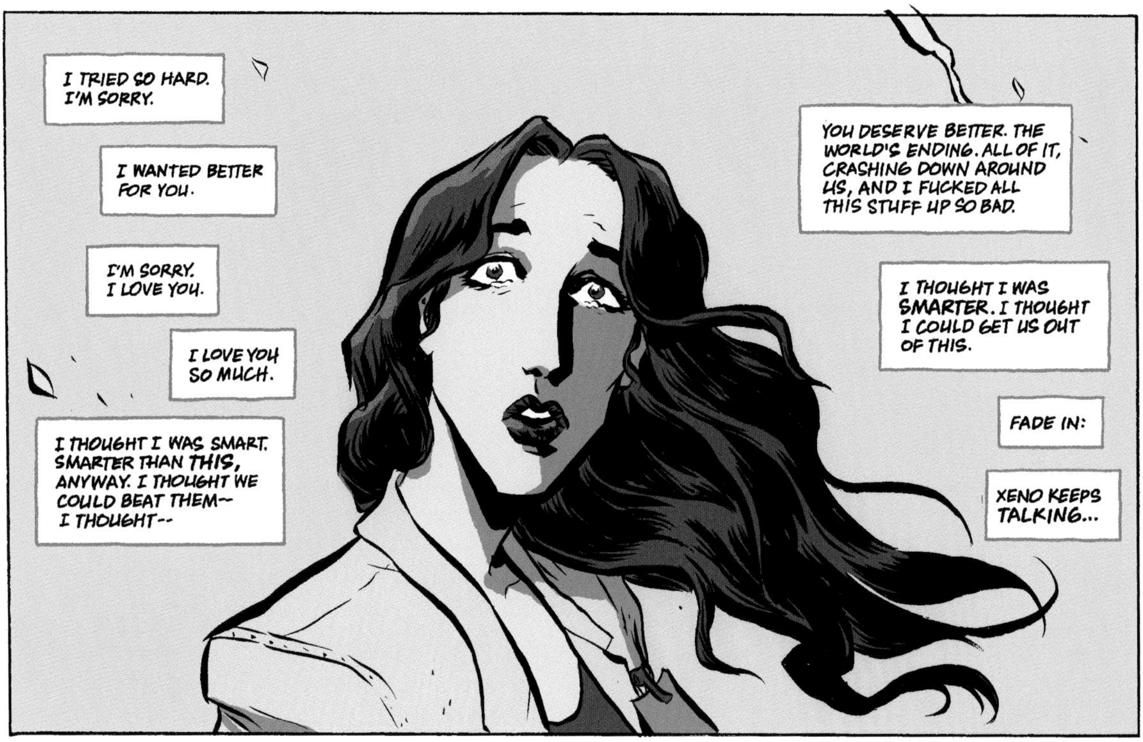
I TRIED SO HARD. I'M SORRY.
I WANTED BETTER FOR YOU.
I'M SORRY. I LOVE YOU.
I LOVE YOU SO MUCH.
I THOUGHT I WAS SMART. SMARTER THAN THIS, ANYWAY. I THOUGHT WE COULD BEAT THEM-- I THOUGHT--
YOU DESERVE BETTER. THE WORLD'S ENDING. ALL OF IT, CRASHING DOWN AROUND US, AND I FUCKED ALL THIS STUFF UP SO BAD.
I THOUGHT I WAS SMARTER. I THOUGHT I COULD GET US OUT OF THIS.
FADE IN:
XENO KEEPS TALKING...

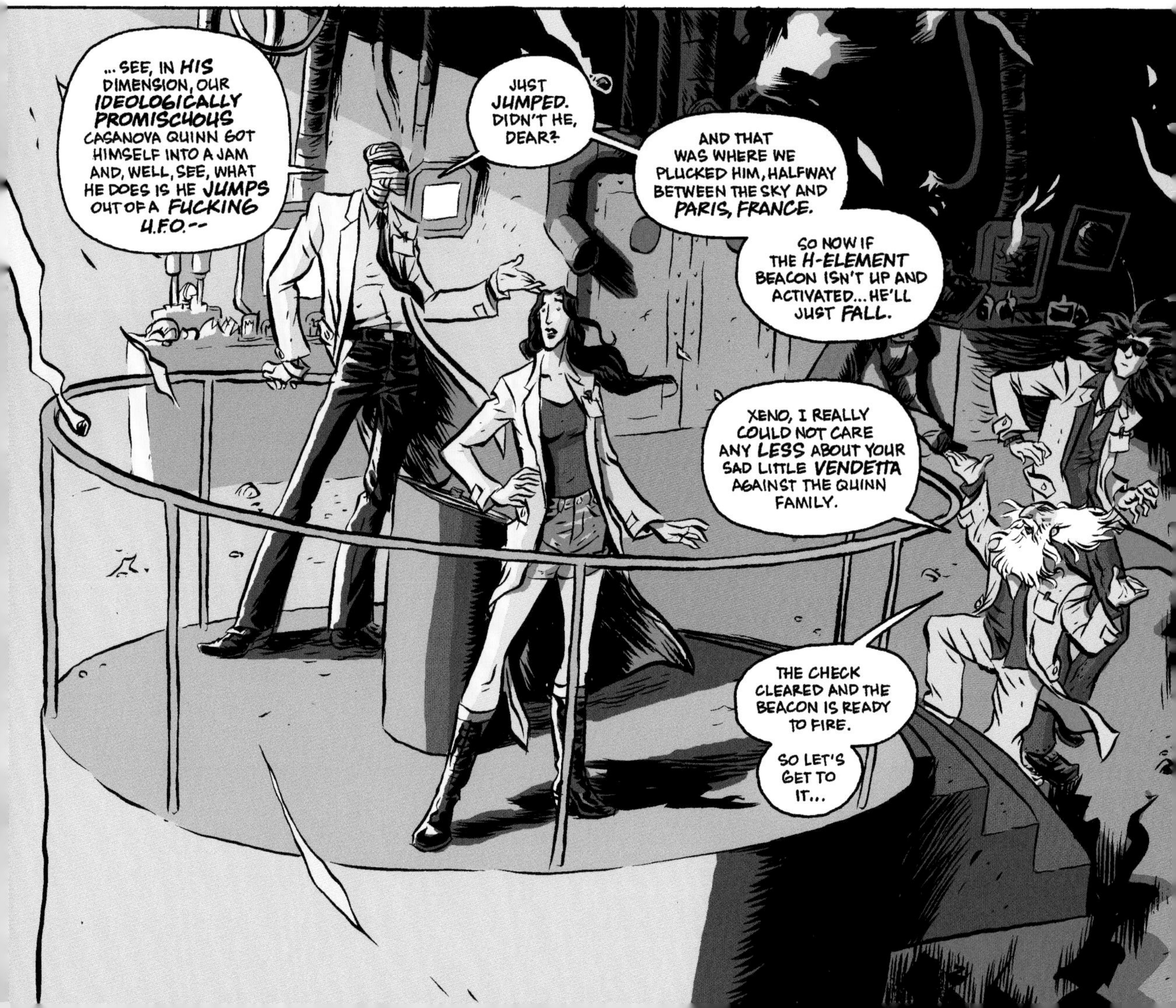
...SEE, IN HIS DIMENSION, OUR IDEOLOGICALLY PROMISCUOUS CASANOVA QUINN GOT HIMSELF INTO A JAM AND, WELL, SEE, WHAT HE DOES IS HE JUMPS OUT OF A FUCKING U.F.O.--
JUST JUMPED. DIDN'T HE, DEAR?
AND THAT WAS WHERE WE PLUCKED HIM, HALFWAY BETWEEN THE SKY AND PARIS, FRANCE.
SO NOW IF THE H-ELEMENT BEACON ISN'T UP AND ACTIVATED... HE'LL JUST FALL.
XENO, I REALLY COULD NOT CARE ANY LESS ABOUT YOUR SAD LITTLE VENDETTA AGAINST THE QUINN FAMILY.
THE CHECK CLEARED AND THE BEACON IS READY TO FIRE.
SO LET'S GET TO IT...

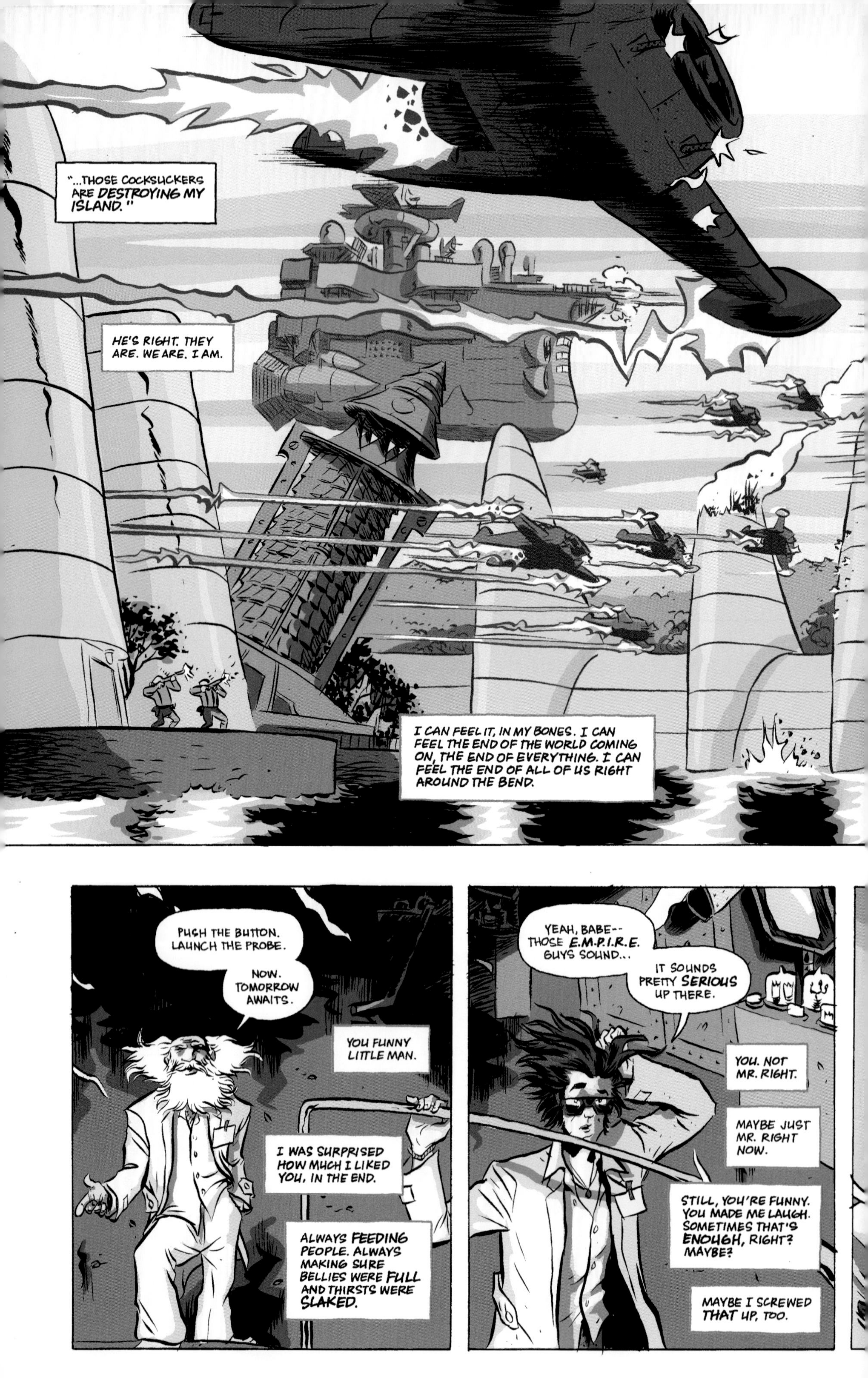
"...THOSE COCKSUCKERS ARE DESTROYING MY ISLAND."
HE'S RIGHT. THEY ARE. WE ARE. I AM.
I CAN FEEL IT, IN MY BONES. I CAN FEEL THE END OF THE WORLD COMING ON, THE END OF EVERYTHING. I CAN FEEL THE END OF ALL OF US RIGHT AROUND THE BEND.
PUSH THE BUTTON. LAUNCH THE PROBE.
NOW. TOMORROW AWAITS.
YOU FUNNY LITTLE MAN.
I WAS SURPRISED HOW MUCH I LIKED YOU, IN THE END.
ALWAYS FEEDING PEOPLE. ALWAYS MAKING SURE BELLIES WERE FULL AND THIRSTS WERE SLAKED.
YEAH, BABE-- THOSE E.M.P.I.R.E. GUYS SOUND...
IT SOUNDS PRETTY SERIOUS UP THERE.
YOU. NOT MR. RIGHT.
MAYBE JUST MR. RIGHT NOW.
STILL, YOU'RE FUNNY. YOU MADE ME LAUGH. SOMETIMES THAT'S ENOUGH, RIGHT? MAYBE?
MAYBE I SCREWED THAT UP, TOO.

GOD. ALL THIS WORK. THIS WHOLE LIFETIME, REAL OR IMAGINED...

ALL OF IT GONE.

CHRIST. WAS IT WORTH IT?

WHAT COULD POSSIBLY BE WORTH ALL THIS?

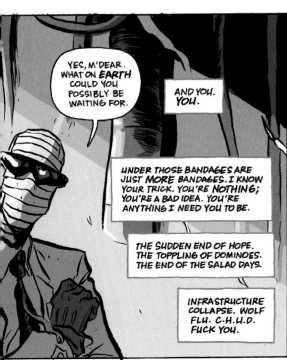

YES, M'DEAR. WHAT ON EARTH COULD YOU POSSIBLY BE WAITING FOR.

AND YOU. YOU.

UNDER THOSE BANDAGES ARE JUST MORE BANDAGES. I KNOW YOUR TRICK. YOU'RE NOTHING; YOU'RE A BAD IDEA. YOU'RE ANYTHING I NEED YOU TO BE.

THE SUDDEN END OF HOPE. THE TOPPLING OF DOMINOES. THE END OF THE SALAD DAYS.

INFRASTRUCTURE COLLAPSE. WOLF FLU. C.H.U.D. FUCK YOU.

I LOVE YOU. I LOVE YOU ALL. YOU DESERVED SO MUCH BETTER. BETTER THAN ME, ANYWAY.

WELL? WHAT ARE WE WAITING FOR? DOLLY BACK, GIRL. FADE TO BLACK...

YEAH.

YEAH, YOU GUYS ARE ALL UNDER ARREST.

PA-ZOW.

2: Young Folks (4:39)

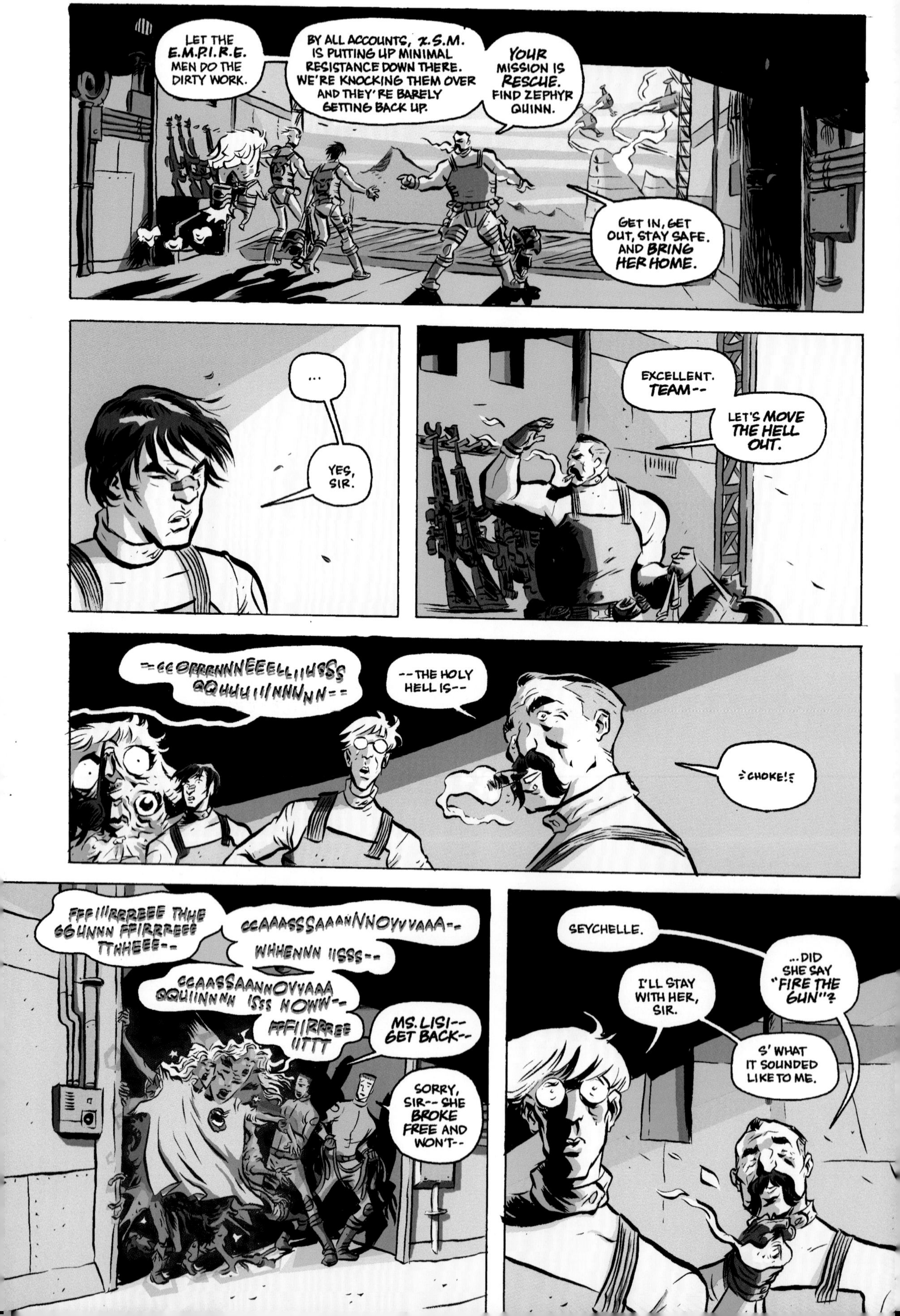

LET THE E.M.P.I.R.E. MEN DO THE DIRTY WORK.
BY ALL ACCOUNTS, X.S.M. IS PUTTING UP MINIMAL RESISTANCE DOWN THERE. WE'RE KNOCKING THEM OVER AND THEY'RE BARELY GETTING BACK UP.
YOUR MISSION IS RESCUE. FIND ZEPHYR QUINN.
GET IN, GET OUT, STAY SAFE. AND BRING HER HOME.
...
YES, SIR.
EXCELLENT. TEAM--
LET'S MOVE THE HELL OUT.
==CCORRRNNNEEELLIIUSSS QQUUUIIINNNNN==
--THE HOLY HELL IS--
=CHOKE!=
FFFIIIRRREEE THHE GGUNNN FFIRRREEE TTHHEEE--
CCAAAASSSAAANNNOVVVAAA--
WHHENNN IISSS--
CCAASSAANNOVVAAA QQUIINNNNN ISSS NOWW--
FFFIIRRREEE IITTT
MS. LISI-- GET BACK--
SORRY, SIR-- SHE BROKE FREE AND WON'T--
SEYCHELLE.
I'LL STAY WITH HER, SIR.
...DID SHE SAY "FIRE THE GUN"?
S' WHAT IT SOUNDED LIKE TO ME.

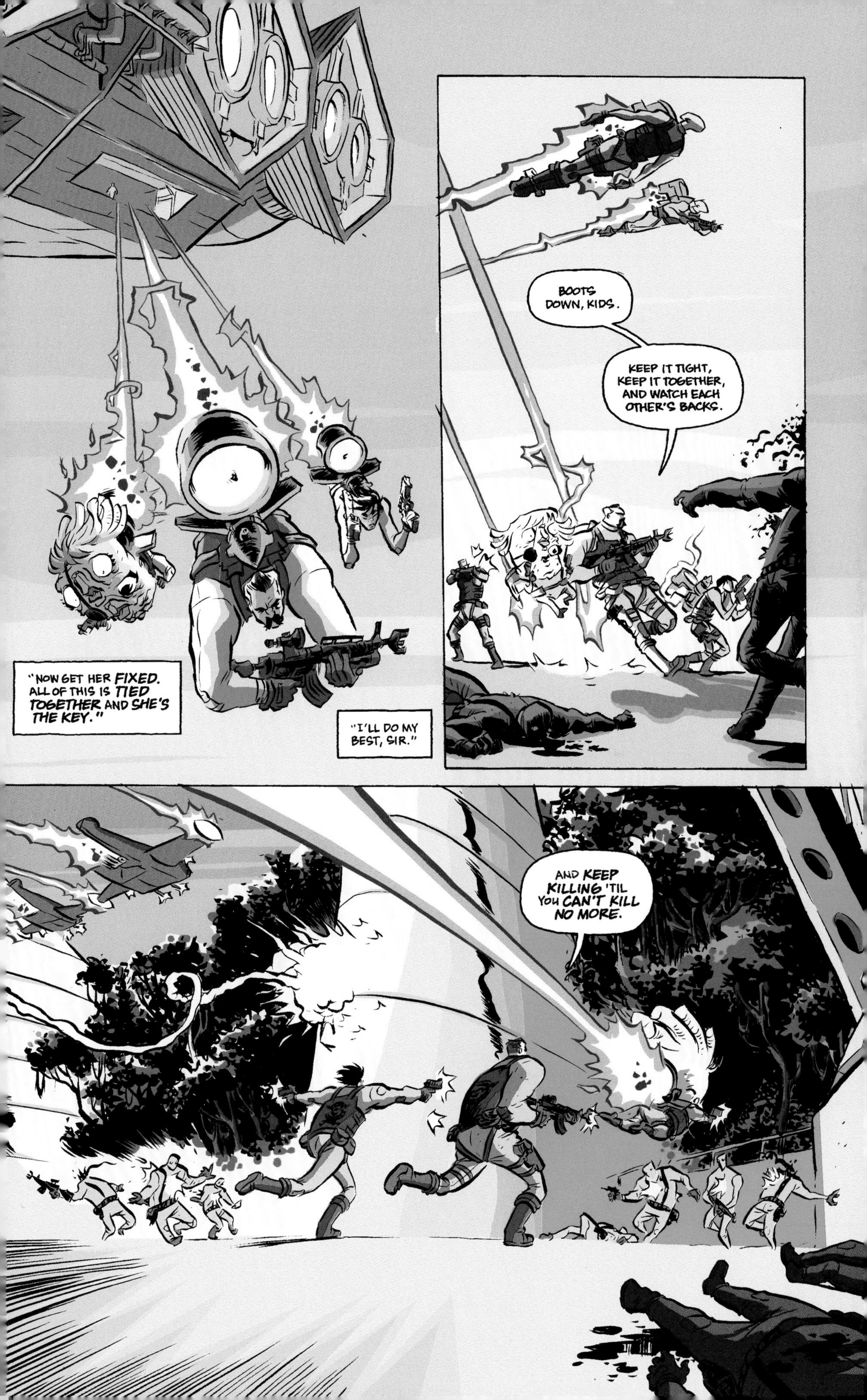
"NOW GET HER FIXED. ALL OF THIS IS TIED TOGETHER AND SHE'S THE KEY."
"I'LL DO MY BEST, SIR."
BOOTS DOWN, KIDS.
KEEP IT TIGHT, KEEP IT TOGETHER, AND WATCH EACH OTHER'S BACKS.
AND KEEP KILLING 'TIL YOU CAN'T KILL NO MORE.

3: You Only Live Once (3:05)

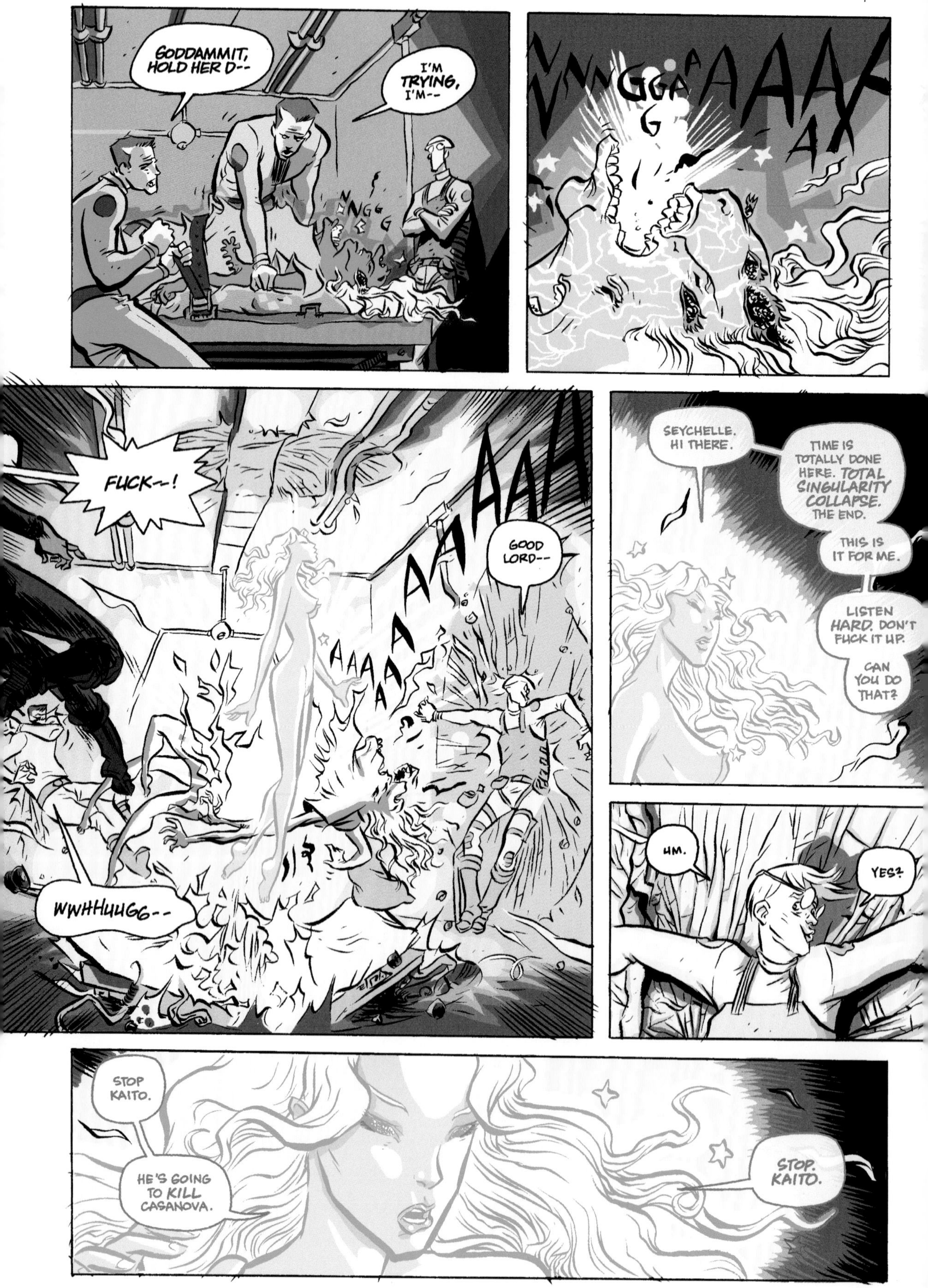
GODDAMMIT, HOLD HER D--
I'M TRYING, I'M--
NNGGG
NNNGGAAAAAAAAAAAAX
FUCK--!
GOOD LORD--
AAAAAAAAAAAAA
WWHHUUGG--
SEYCHELLE. HI THERE.
TIME IS TOTALLY DONE HERE. TOTAL SINGULARITY COLLAPSE. THE END.
THIS IS IT FOR ME.
LISTEN HARD. DON'T FUCK IT UP.
CAN YOU DO THAT?
UM.
YES?
STOP KAITO.
HE'S GOING TO KILL CASANOVA.
STOP. KAITO.

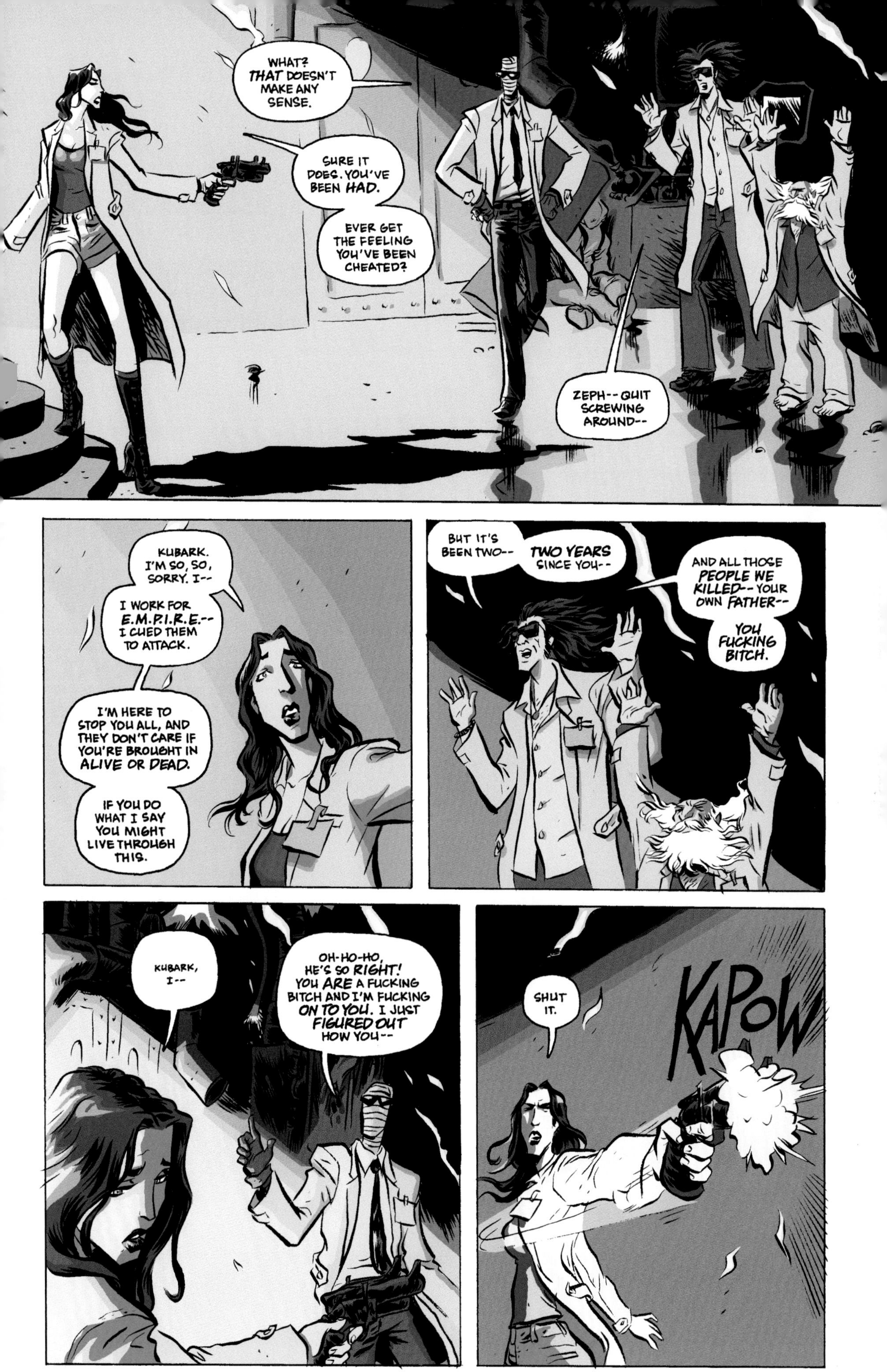
WHAT? THAT DOESN'T MAKE ANY SENSE.
SURE IT DOES. YOU'VE BEEN HAD.
EVER GET THE FEELING YOU'VE BEEN CHEATED?
ZEPH-- QUIT SCREWING AROUND--
KUBARK. I'M SO, SO, SORRY. I--
I WORK FOR E.M.P.I.R.E.-- I CUED THEM TO ATTACK.
I'M HERE TO STOP YOU ALL, AND THEY DON'T CARE IF YOU'RE BROUGHT IN ALIVE OR DEAD.
IF YOU DO WHAT I SAY YOU MIGHT LIVE THROUGH THIS.
BUT IT'S BEEN TWO--
TWO YEARS SINCE YOU--
AND ALL THOSE PEOPLE WE KILLED-- YOUR OWN FATHER--
YOU FUCKING BITCH.
KUBARK, I--
OH-HO-HO, HE'S SO RIGHT! YOU ARE A FUCKING BITCH AND I'M FUCKING ON TO YOU. I JUST FIGURED OUT HOW YOU--
SHUT IT.
KAPOW

4: The Beat That My Heart Skipped (3:48)

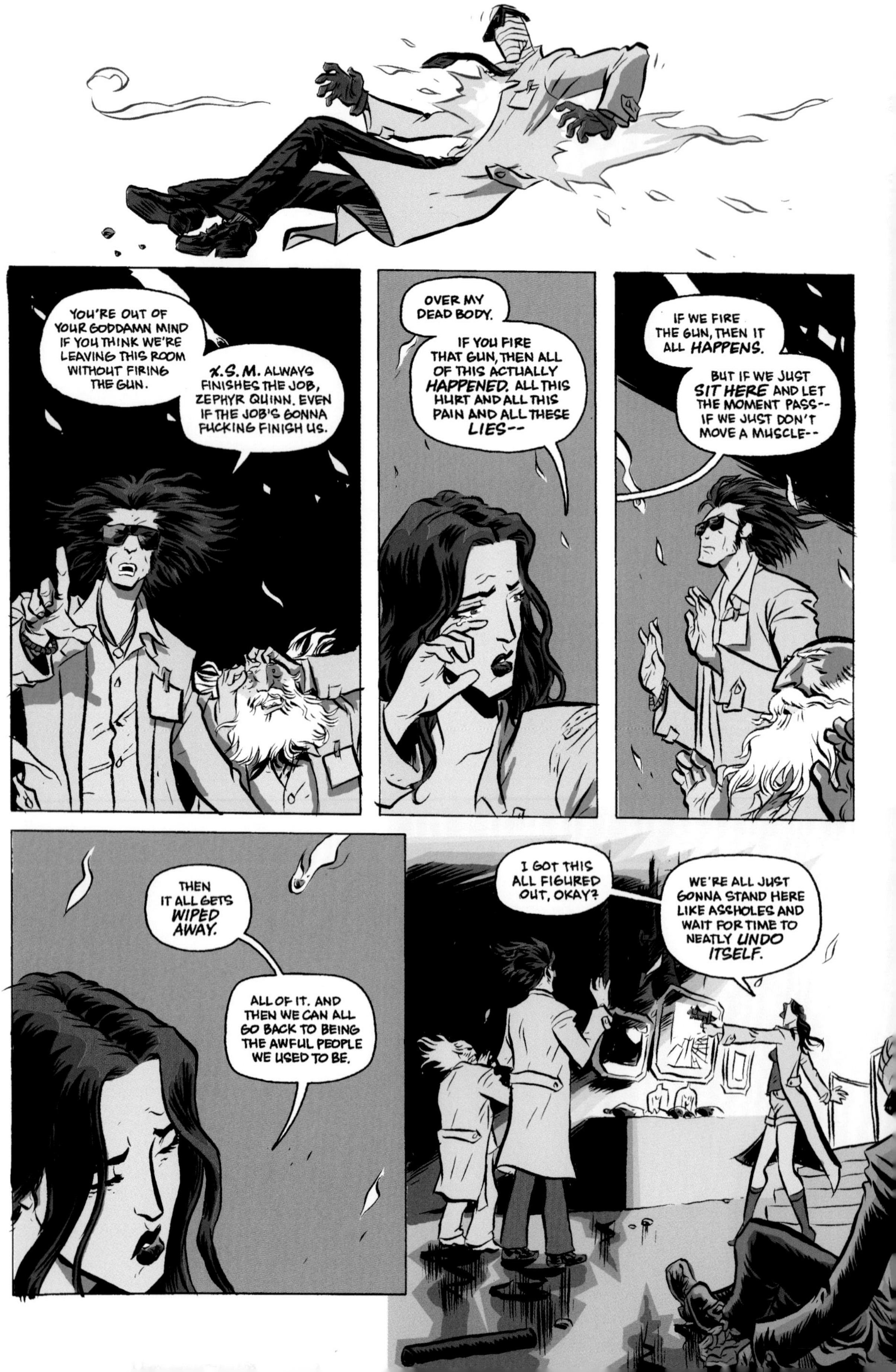
YOU'RE OUT OF YOUR GODDAMN MIND IF YOU THINK WE'RE LEAVING THIS ROOM WITHOUT FIRING THE GUN.
X.S.M. ALWAYS FINISHES THE JOB, ZEPHYR QUINN. EVEN IF THE JOB'S GONNA FUCKING FINISH US.
OVER MY DEAD BODY.
IF YOU FIRE THAT GUN, THEN ALL OF THIS ACTUALLY HAPPENED. ALL THIS HURT AND ALL THIS PAIN AND ALL THESE LIES--
IF WE FIRE THE GUN, THEN IT ALL HAPPENS.
BUT IF WE JUST SIT HERE AND LET THE MOMENT PASS-- IF WE JUST DON'T MOVE A MUSCLE--
THEN IT ALL GETS WIPED AWAY.
ALL OF IT. AND THEN WE CAN ALL GO BACK TO BEING THE AWFUL PEOPLE WE USED TO BE.
I GOT THIS ALL FIGURED OUT, OKAY?
WE'RE ALL JUST GONNA STAND HERE LIKE ASSHOLES AND WAIT FOR TIME TO NEATLY UNDO ITSELF.

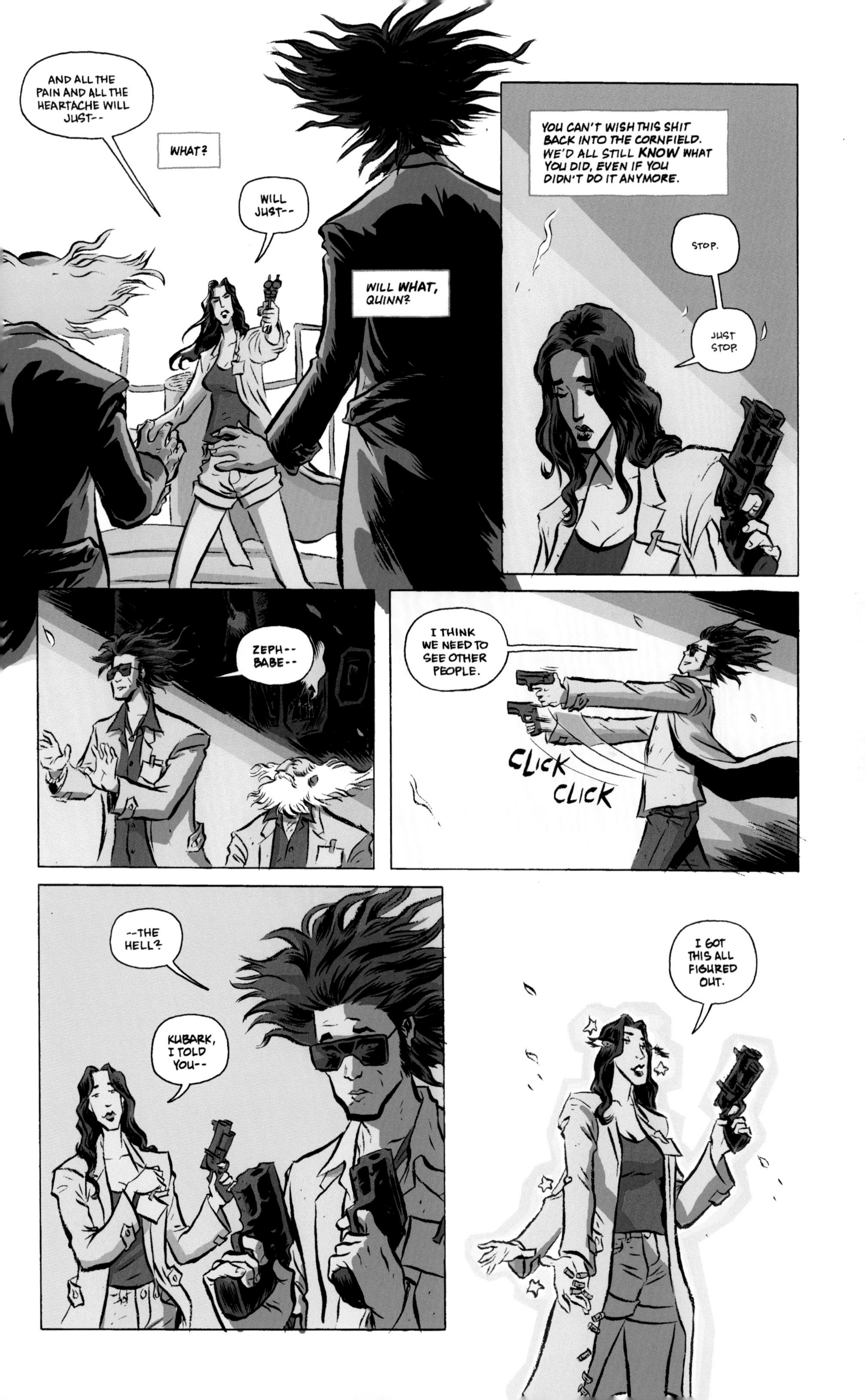
AND ALL THE PAIN AND ALL THE HEARTACHE WILL JUST--
WHAT?
WILL JUST--
WILL WHAT, QUINN?
YOU CAN'T WISH THIS SHIT BACK INTO THE CORNFIELD. WE'D ALL STILL KNOW WHAT YOU DID, EVEN IF YOU DIDN'T DO IT ANYMORE.
STOP.
JUST STOP.
ZEPH-- BABE--
I THINK WE NEED TO SEE OTHER PEOPLE.
CLICK
CLICK
--THE HELL?
KUBARK, I TOLD YOU--
I GOT THIS ALL FIGURED OUT.

5: Ashes To Ashes (4:28)

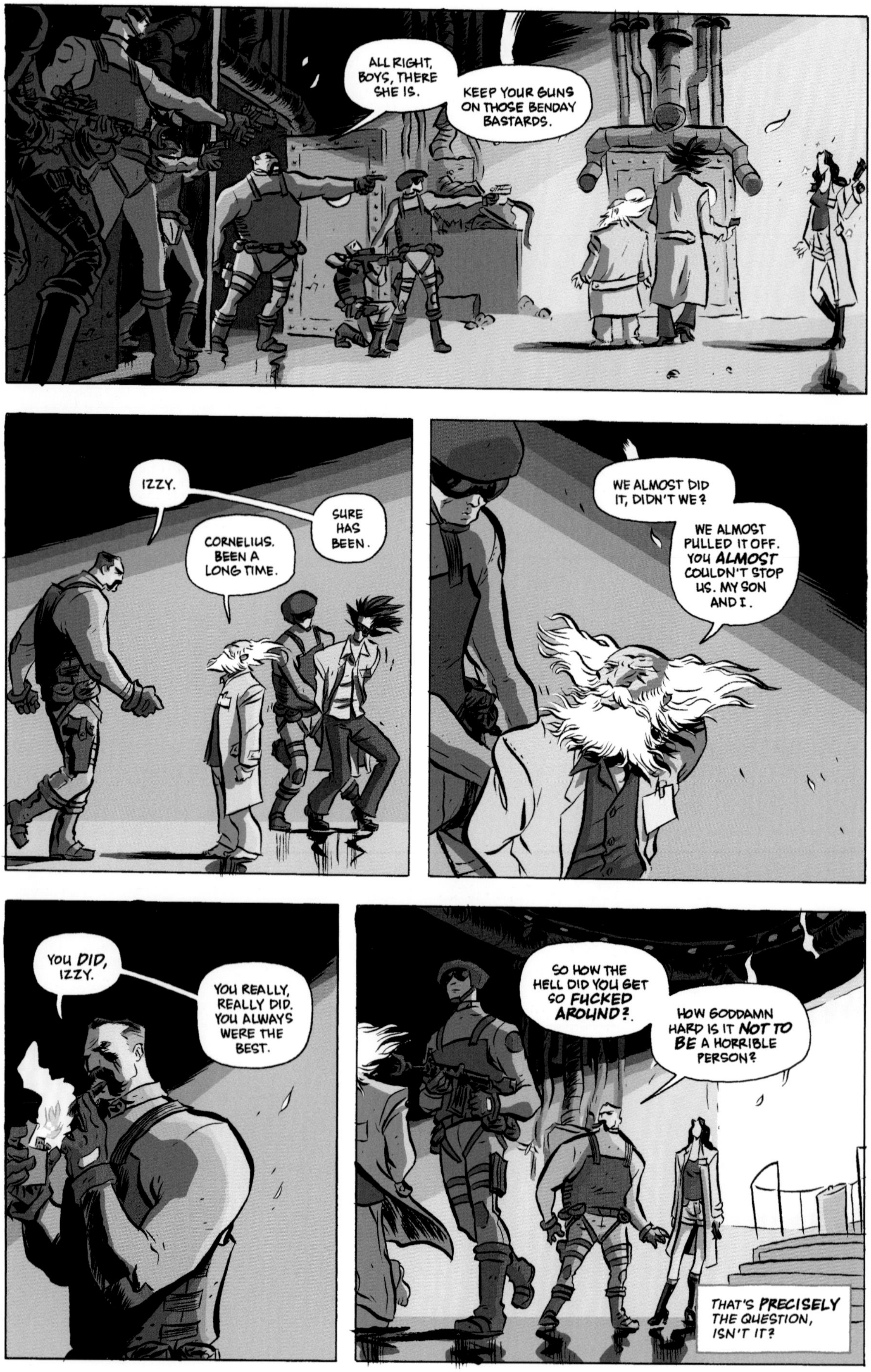
ALL RIGHT, BOYS, THERE SHE IS.
KEEP YOUR GUNS ON THOSE BENDAY BASTARDS.
IZZY.
CORNELIUS. BEEN A LONG TIME.
SURE HAS BEEN.
WE ALMOST DID IT, DIDN'T WE?
WE ALMOST PULLED IT OFF. YOU ALMOST COULDN'T STOP US. MY SON AND I.
YOU DID, IZZY.
YOU REALLY, REALLY DID. YOU ALWAYS WERE THE BEST.
SO HOW THE HELL DID YOU GET SO FUCKED AROUND?
HOW GODDAMN HARD IS IT NOT TO BE A HORRIBLE PERSON?
THAT'S PRECISELY THE QUESTION, ISN'T IT?

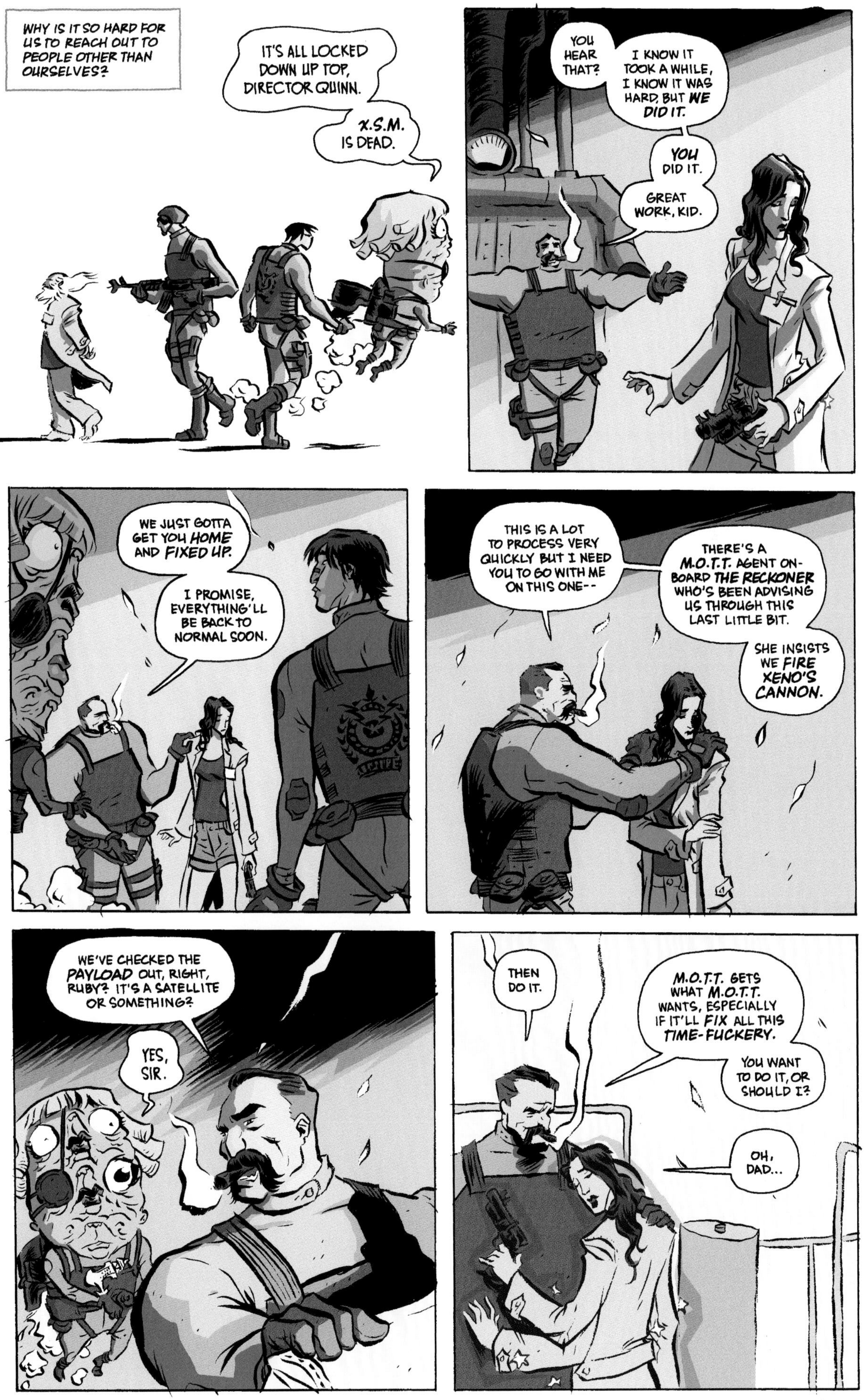
WHY IS IT SO HARD FOR US TO REACH OUT TO PEOPLE OTHER THAN OURSELVES?
IT'S ALL LOCKED DOWN UP TOP, DIRECTOR QUINN.
X.S.M. IS DEAD.
YOU HEAR THAT?
I KNOW IT TOOK A WHILE, I KNOW IT WAS HARD, BUT WE DID IT.
YOU DID IT.
GREAT WORK, KID.
WE JUST GOTTA GET YOU HOME AND FIXED UP.
I PROMISE, EVERYTHING'LL BE BACK TO NORMAL SOON.
THIS IS A LOT TO PROCESS VERY QUICKLY BUT I NEED YOU TO GO WITH ME ON THIS ONE--
THERE'S A M.O.T.T. AGENT ON-BOARD THE RECKONER WHO'S BEEN ADVISING US THROUGH THIS LAST LITTLE BIT.
SHE INSISTS WE FIRE XENO'S CANNON.
WE'VE CHECKED THE PAYLOAD OUT, RIGHT, RUBY? IT'S A SATELLITE OR SOMETHING?
YES, SIR.
THEN DO IT.
M.O.T.T. GETS WHAT M.O.T.T. WANTS, ESPECIALLY IF IT'LL FIX ALL THIS TIME-FUCKERY.
YOU WANT TO DO IT, OR SHOULD I?
OH, DAD...

6: 7 Stars (3:47)

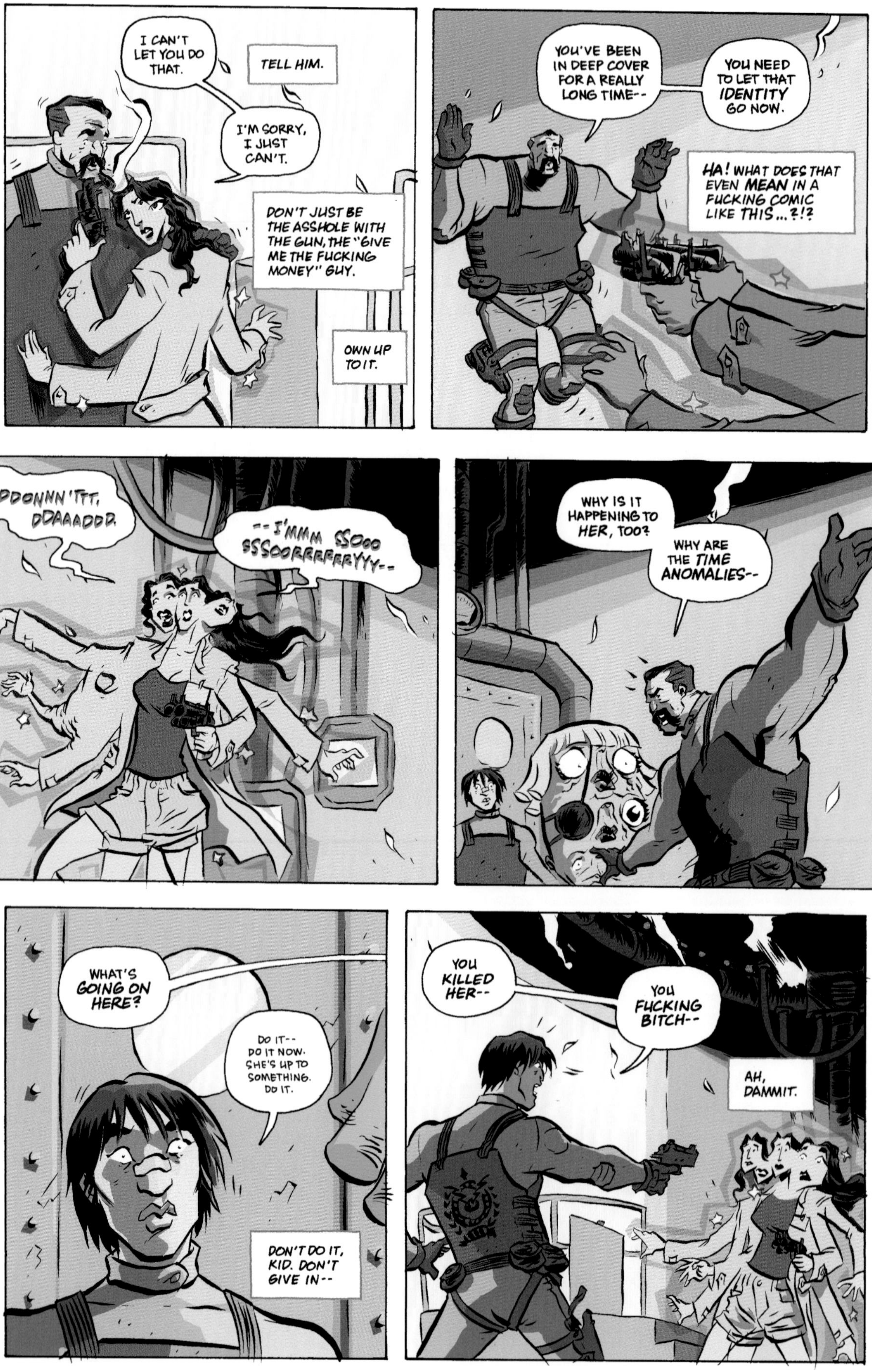

I CAN'T LET YOU DO THAT.
TELL HIM.
I'M SORRY, I JUST CAN'T.
DON'T JUST BE THE ASSHOLE WITH THE GUN, THE "GIVE ME THE FUCKING MONEY" GUY.
OWN UP TO IT.
YOU'VE BEEN IN DEEP COVER FOR A REALLY LONG TIME--
YOU NEED TO LET THAT IDENTITY GO NOW.
HA! WHAT DOES THAT EVEN MEAN IN A FUCKING COMIC LIKE THIS...?!?
DDONNN'TTT, DDAAAADDD.
--I'MMM SSOoo SSSOORRRRRRRYYY--
WHY IS IT HAPPENING TO HER, TOO?
WHY ARE THE TIME ANOMALIES--
WHAT'S GOING ON HERE?
DO IT-- DO IT NOW. SHE'S UP TO SOMETHING. DO IT.
DON'T DO IT, KID. DON'T GIVE IN--
YOU KILLED HER--
YOU FUCKING BITCH--
AH, DAMMIT.

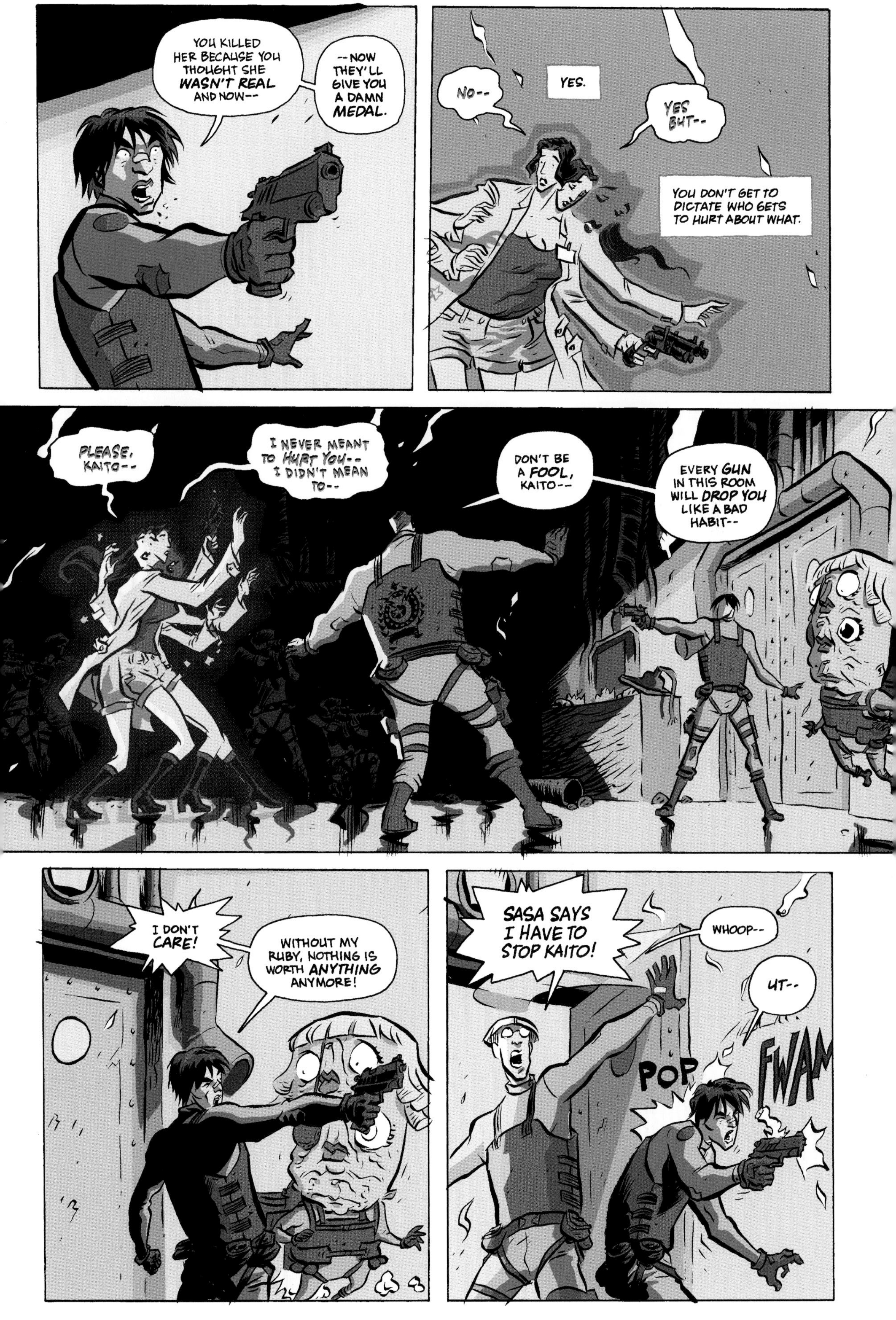
YOU KILLED HER BECAUSE YOU THOUGHT SHE WASN'T REAL AND NOW--
--NOW THEY'LL GIVE YOU A DAMN MEDAL.
NO--
YES.
YES BUT--
YOU DON'T GET TO DICTATE WHO GETS TO HURT ABOUT WHAT.
PLEASE, KAITO--
I NEVER MEANT TO HURT YOU-- I DIDN'T MEAN TO--
DON'T BE A FOOL, KAITO--
EVERY GUN IN THIS ROOM WILL DROP YOU LIKE A BAD HABIT--
I DON'T CARE!
WITHOUT MY RUBY, NOTHING IS WORTH ANYTHING ANYMORE!
SASA SAYS I HAVE TO STOP KAITO!
WHOOP--
UT--
POP
FWAM

7: Woke Up New (2:57)

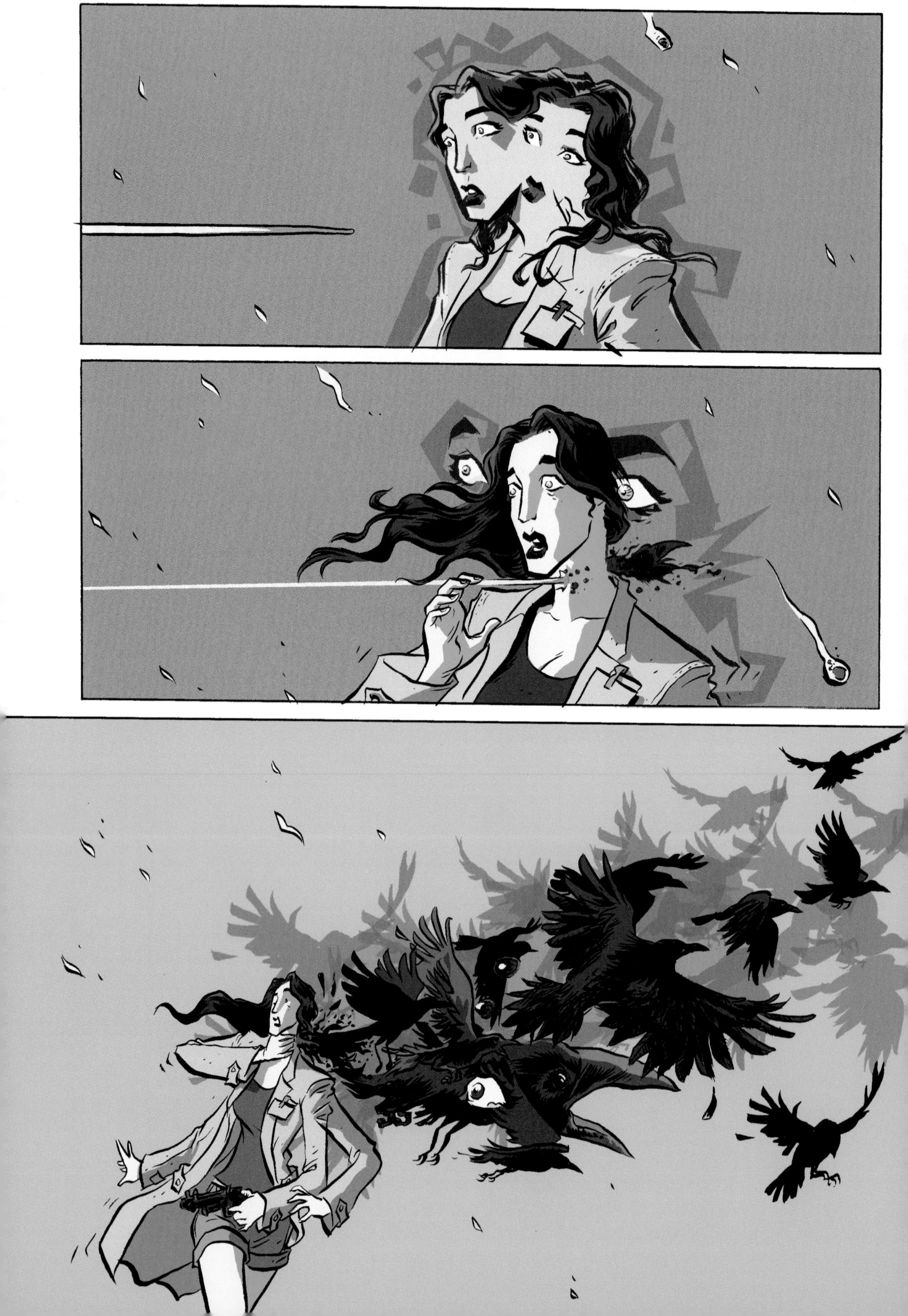

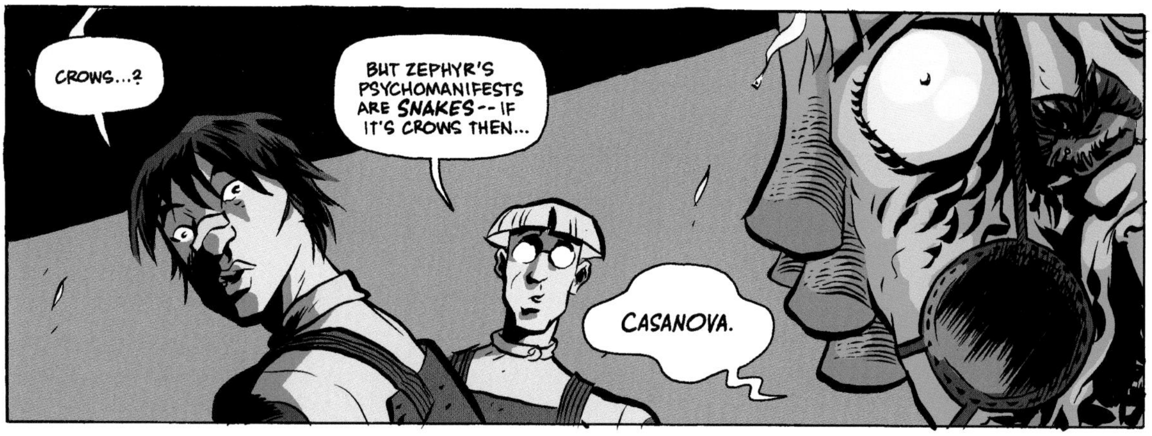
CROWS...?
BUT ZEPHYR'S PSYCHOMANIFESTS ARE SNAKES--IF IT'S CROWS THEN...
CASANOVA.

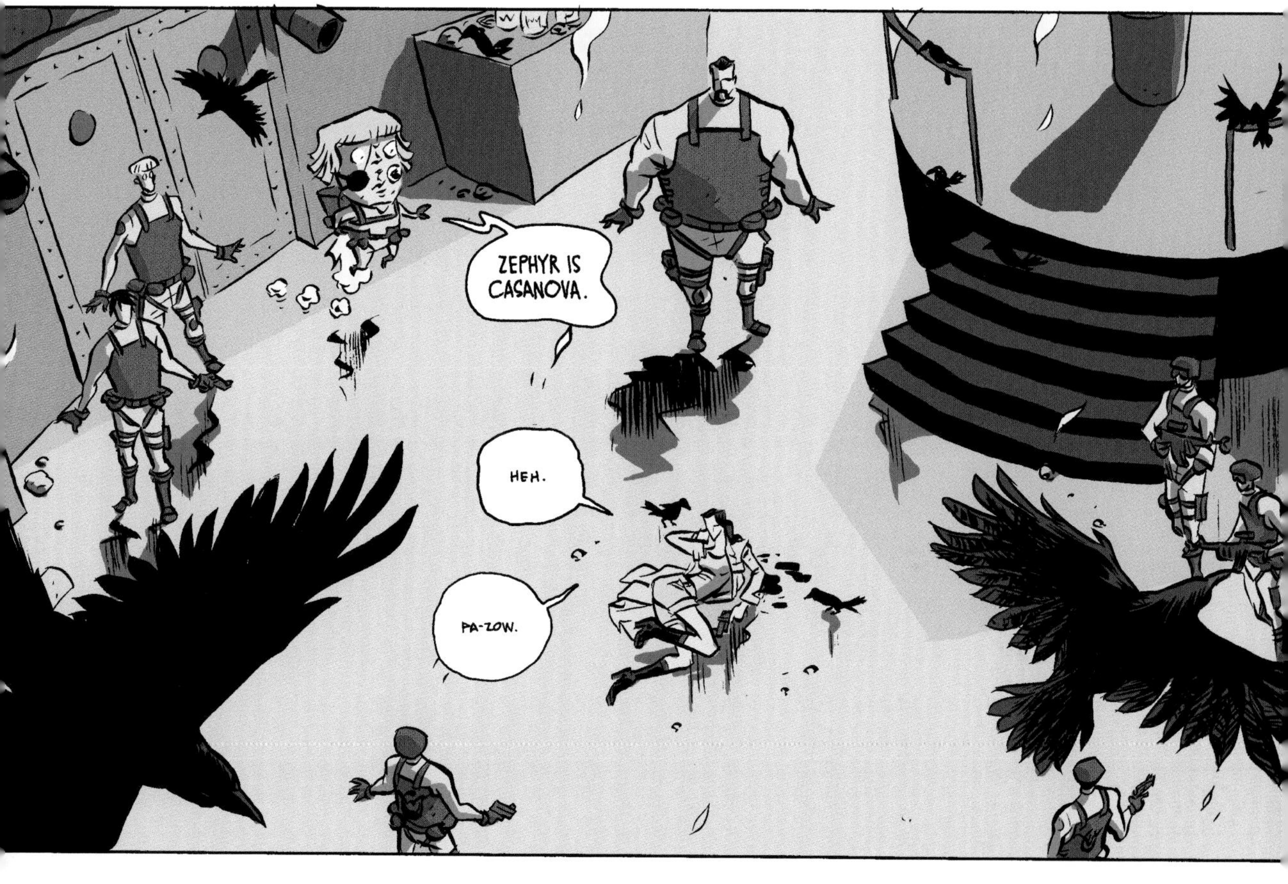
ZEPHYR IS CASANOVA.
HEH.
PA-ZOW.

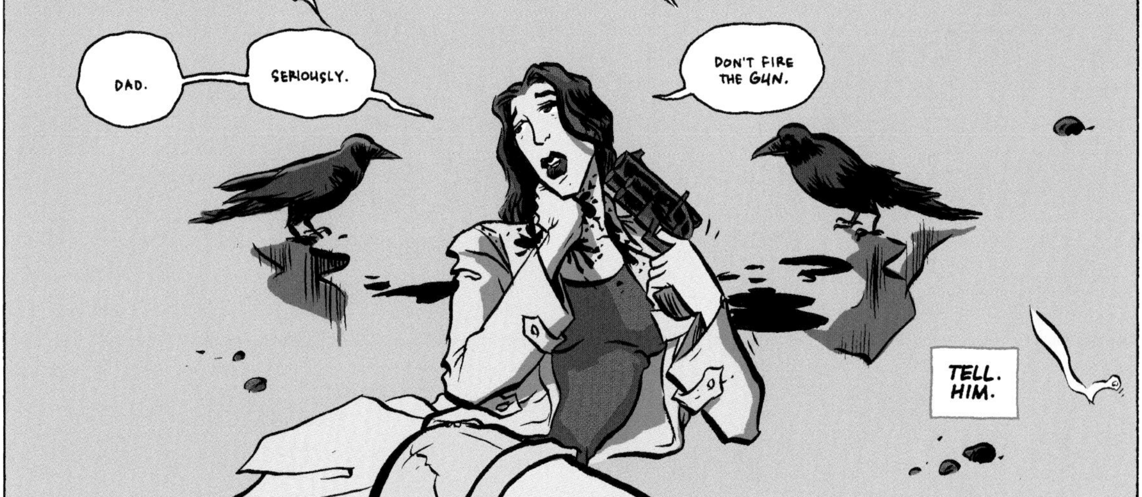
DAD.
SERIOUSLY.
DON'T FIRE THE GUN.
TELL. HIM.

8: Evil Will Prevail (3:46)

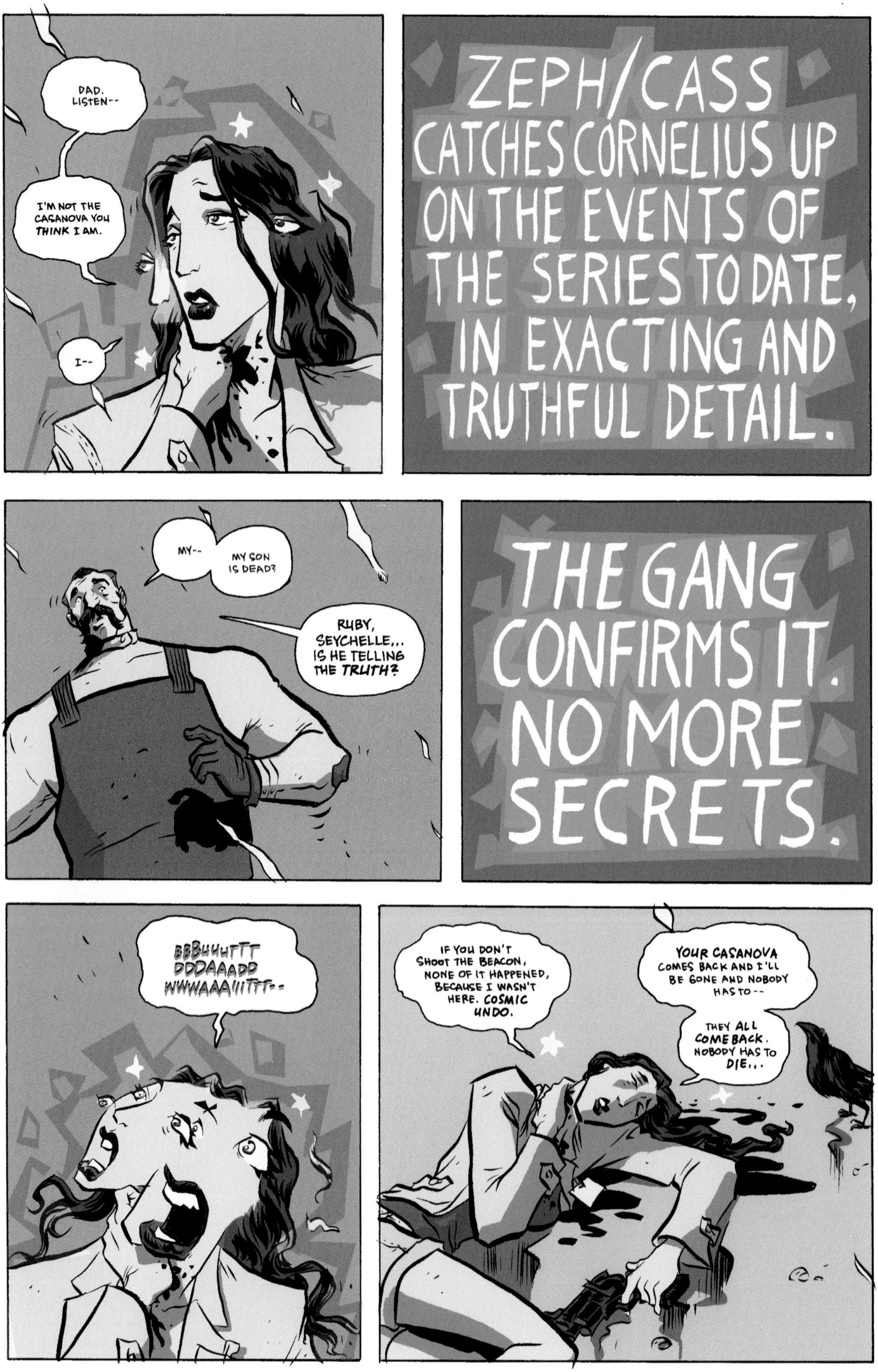
DAD. LISTEN--
I'M NOT THE CASANOVA YOU THINK I AM.
I--
ZEPH/CASS CATCHES CORNELIUS UP ON THE EVENTS OF THE SERIES TO DATE, IN EXACTING AND TRUTHFUL DETAIL.
MY--
MY SON IS DEAD?
RUBY, SEYCHELLE... IS HE TELLING THE TRUTH?
THE GANG CONFIRMS IT. NO MORE SECRETS.
BBBUUUTTT DDDAAADD WWWAAAIIITTT--
IF YOU DON'T SHOOT THE BEACON, NONE OF IT HAPPENED, BECAUSE I WASN'T HERE. COSMIC UNDO.
YOUR CASANOVA COMES BACK AND I'LL BE GONE AND NOBODY HAS TO--
THEY ALL COME BACK. NOBODY HAS TO DIE...

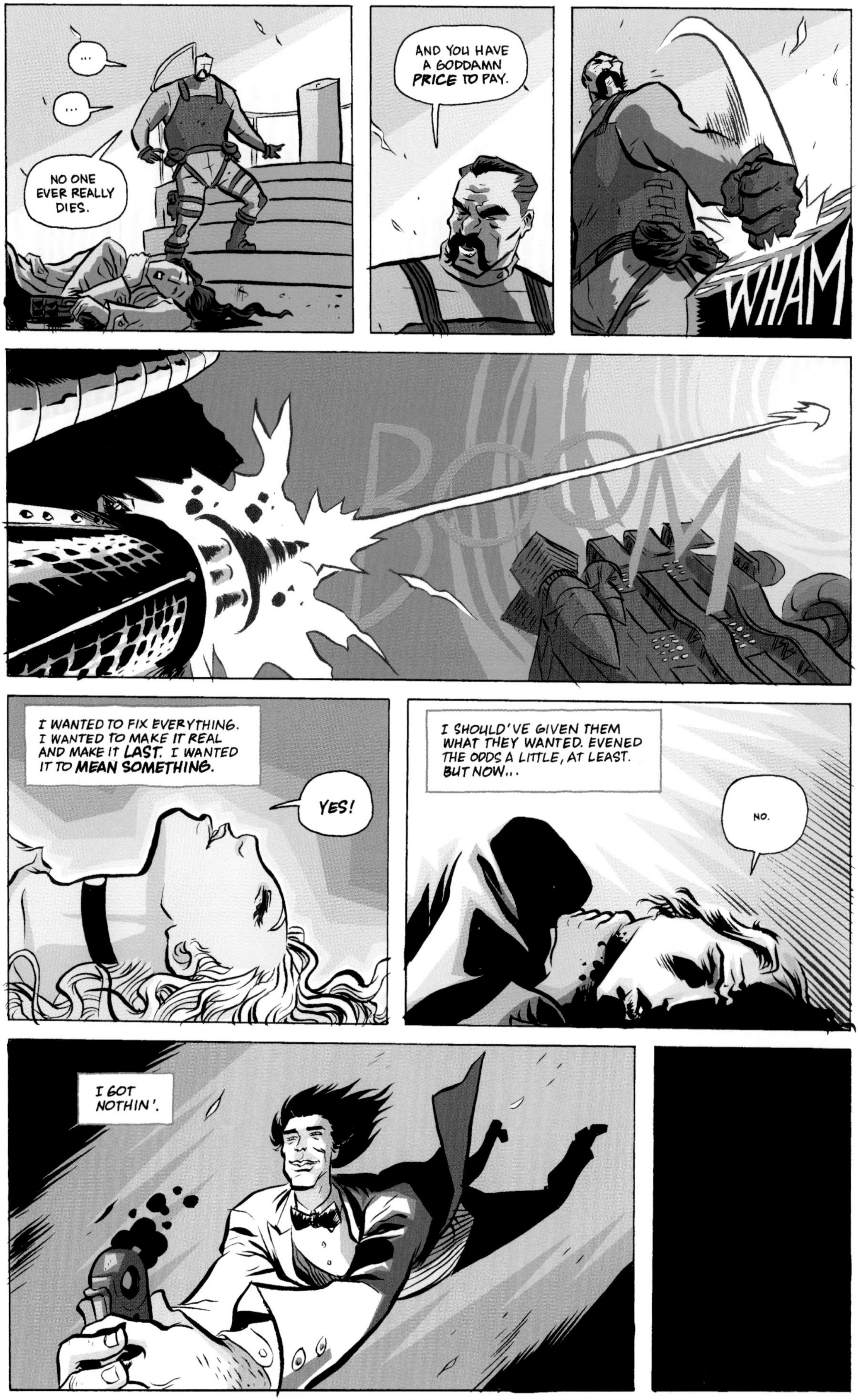
...
...
NO ONE EVER REALLY DIES.
AND YOU HAVE A GODDAMN PRICE TO PAY.
WHAM
BOOM
I WANTED TO FIX EVERYTHING. I WANTED TO MAKE IT REAL AND MAKE IT LAST. I WANTED IT TO MEAN SOMETHING.
YES!
I SHOULD'VE GIVEN THEM WHAT THEY WANTED. EVENED THE ODDS A LITTLE, AT LEAST. BUT NOW...
NO.
I GOT NOTHIN'.

9: Six Days (5:02)

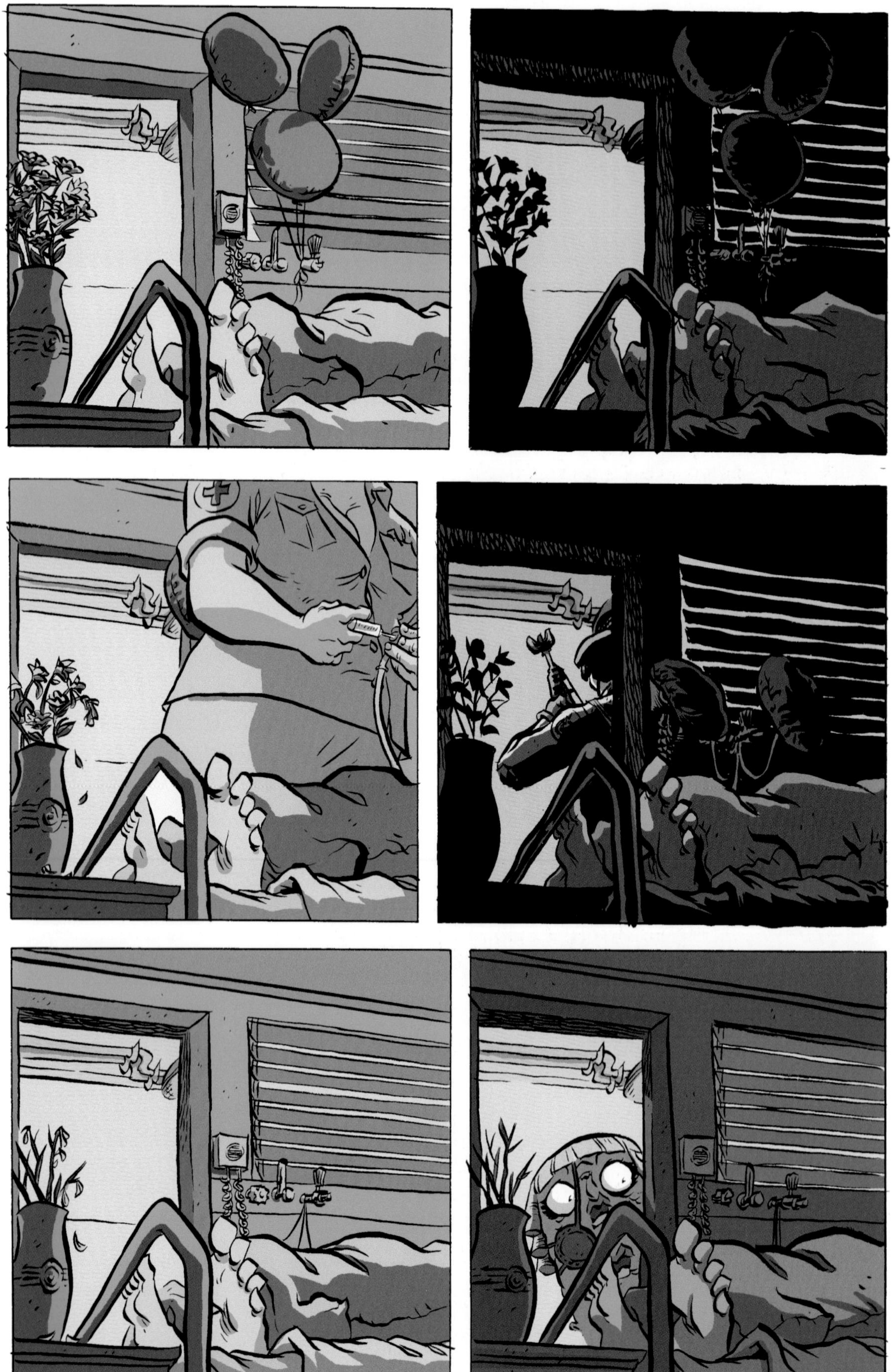

WELL, FOR A GUY THAT WAS A GIRL AND NOW IS A GUY AGAIN, I GOTTA SAY, YOU *ABSOLUTELY* LOOK LIKE A GUY AGAIN.

THEY GET YOUR *JUNK* WORKING, TOO?

I--

I'M *KIDDING*. DON'T TRY AND SPEAK IF YOU DON'T *HAVE TO,* CASS.

KAITO'S SHOT GOT YOUR THROAT PRETTY GOOD, SO YOU SHOULD REST YOUR VOICE AS MUCH AS YOU CAN.

RUBY, I'M SO--

YEAH.

YOU'RE NOT SUCH A BAD SHOT YOURSELF, ARE YOU?

SEYCHELLE OFFERED TO MAKE ME A *REPLACEMENT EYE* BUT I--

BUT I WANT TO REMEMBER.

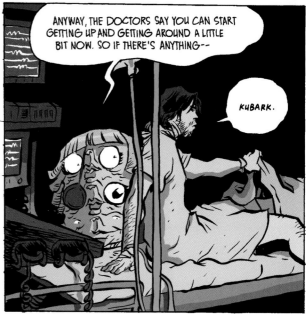

ANYWAY, THE DOCTORS SAY YOU CAN START GETTING UP AND GETTING AROUND A LITTLE BIT NOW. SO IF THERE'S ANYTHING--

KUBARK.

10: River Deep, Mountain High (3:39)

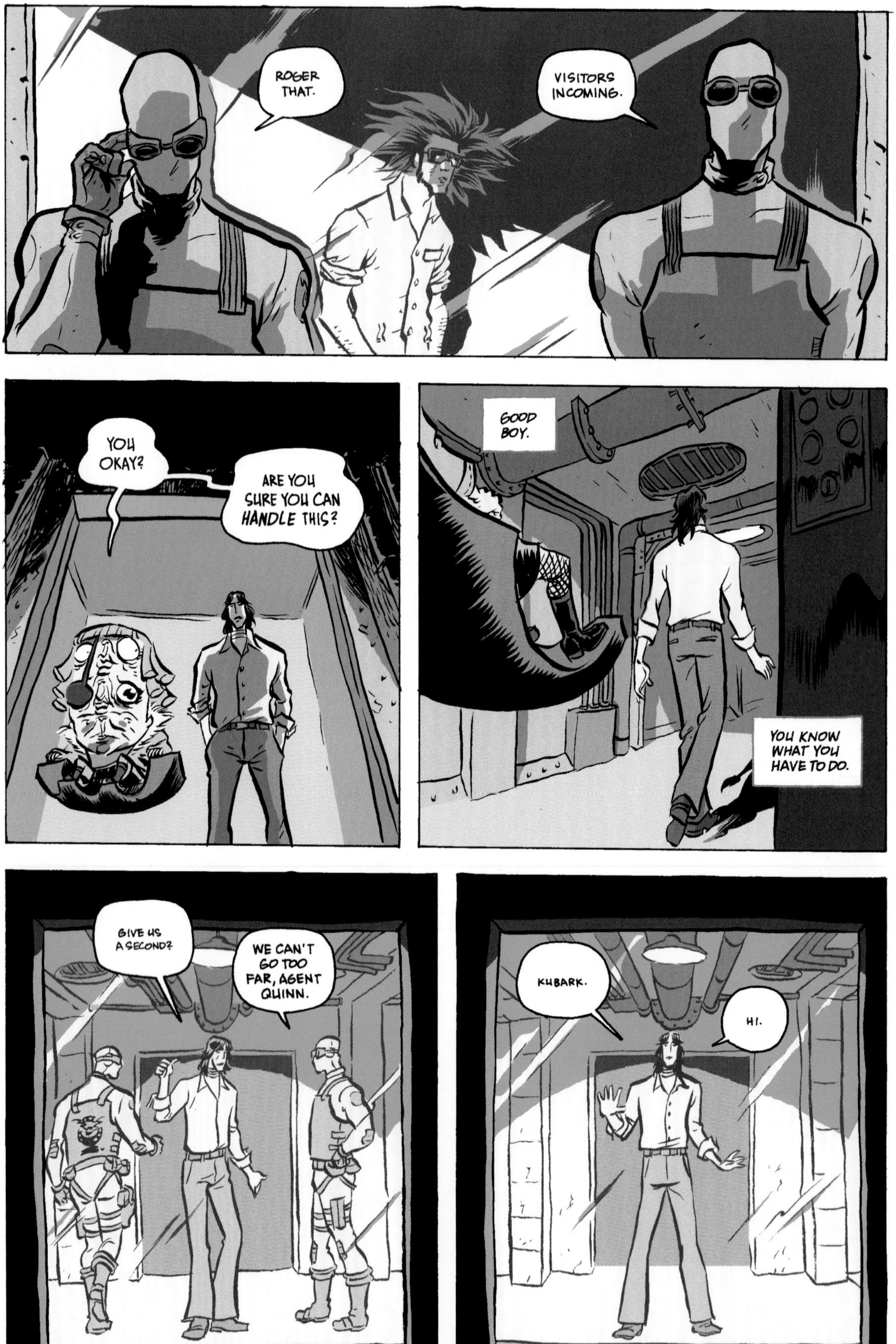
ROGER THAT.
VISITORS INCOMING.
YOU OKAY?
ARE YOU SURE YOU CAN HANDLE THIS?
GOOD BOY.
YOU KNOW WHAT YOU HAVE TO DO.
GIVE US A SECOND?
WE CAN'T GO TOO FAR, AGENT QUINN.
KUBARK.
HI.

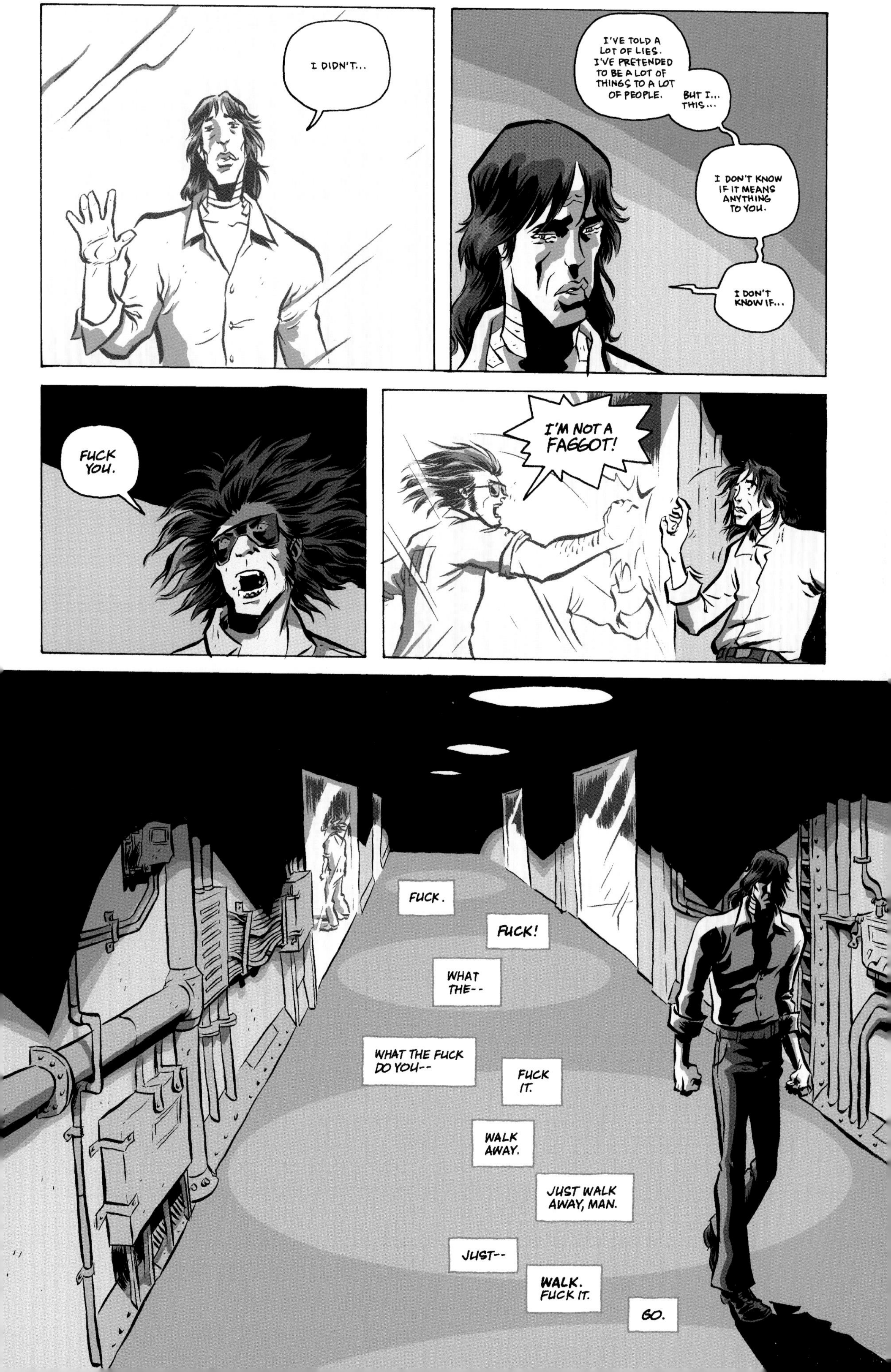

I DIDN'T...
I'VE TOLD A LOT OF LIES. I'VE PRETENDED TO BE A LOT OF THINGS TO A LOT OF PEOPLE.
BUT I... THIS...
I DON'T KNOW IF IT MEANS ANYTHING TO YOU.
I DON'T KNOW IF...
FUCK YOU.
I'M NOT A FAGGOT!
FUCK.
FUCK!
WHAT THE--
WHAT THE FUCK DO YOU--
FUCK IT.
WALK AWAY.
JUST WALK AWAY, MAN.
JUST--
WALK. FUCK IT.
GO.

11: To Catch A Thief (3:17)

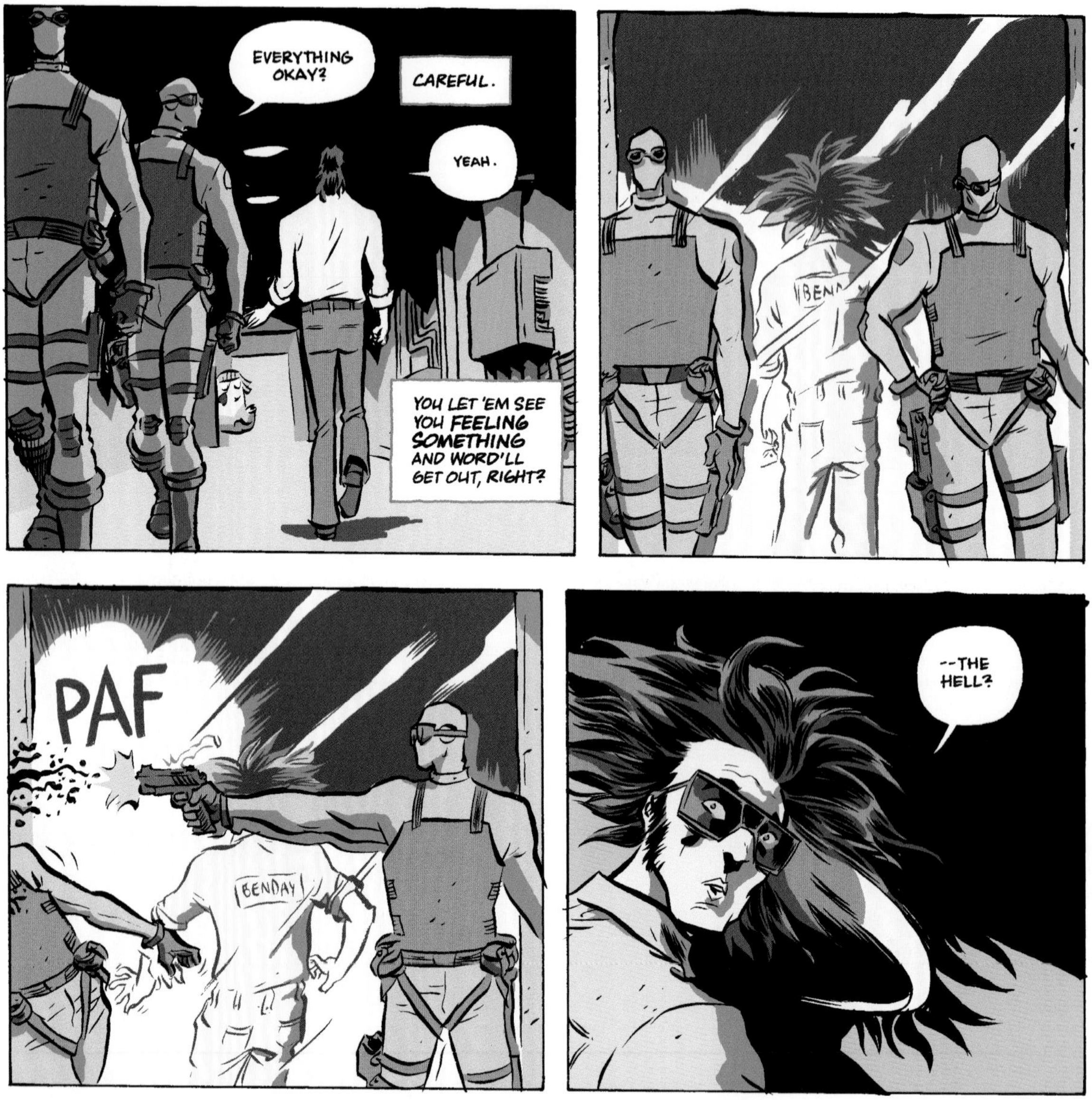
EVERYTHING OKAY?
CAREFUL.
YEAH.
YOU LET 'EM SEE YOU FEELING SOMETHING AND WORD'LL GET OUT, RIGHT?
BENDAY
PAF
--THE HELL?

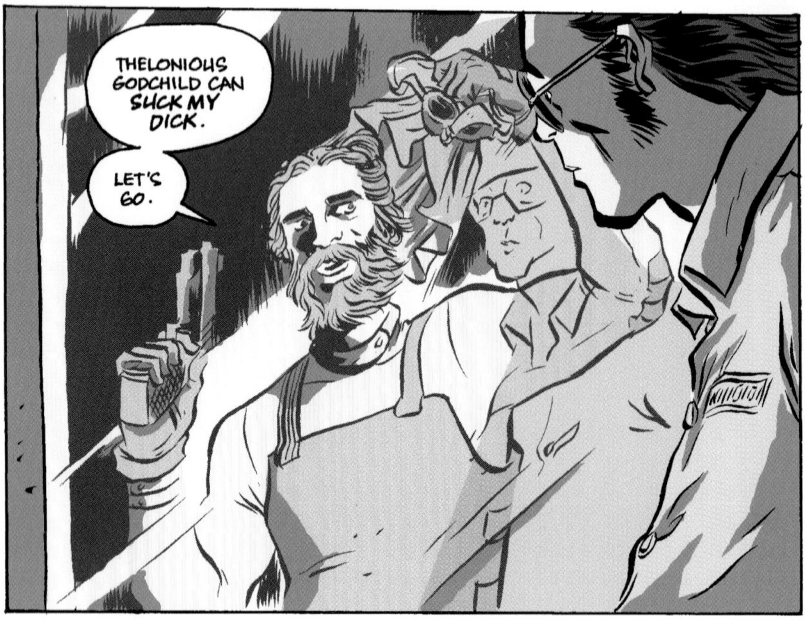
THELONIOUS GODCHILD CAN SUCK MY DICK.
LET'S GO.

HI, EVERYBODY. DAVID X, ESCAPE MESSIAH EXTRAORDINAIRE.

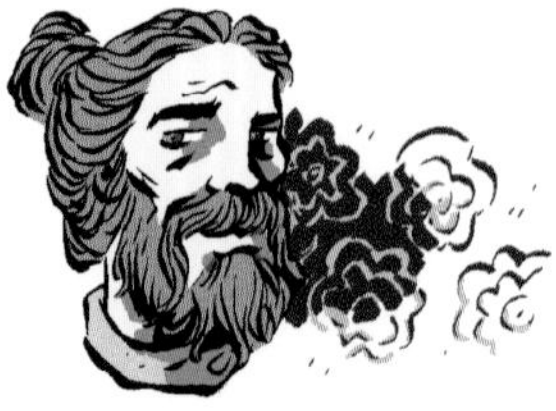

YOU LAST SAW ME GETTING MURDERED IN GULA #1. AND BEFORE THAT, I WAS IN... LUXURIA #3 MAYBE? I THINK IT WAS #3.

ANYWAY. HI.

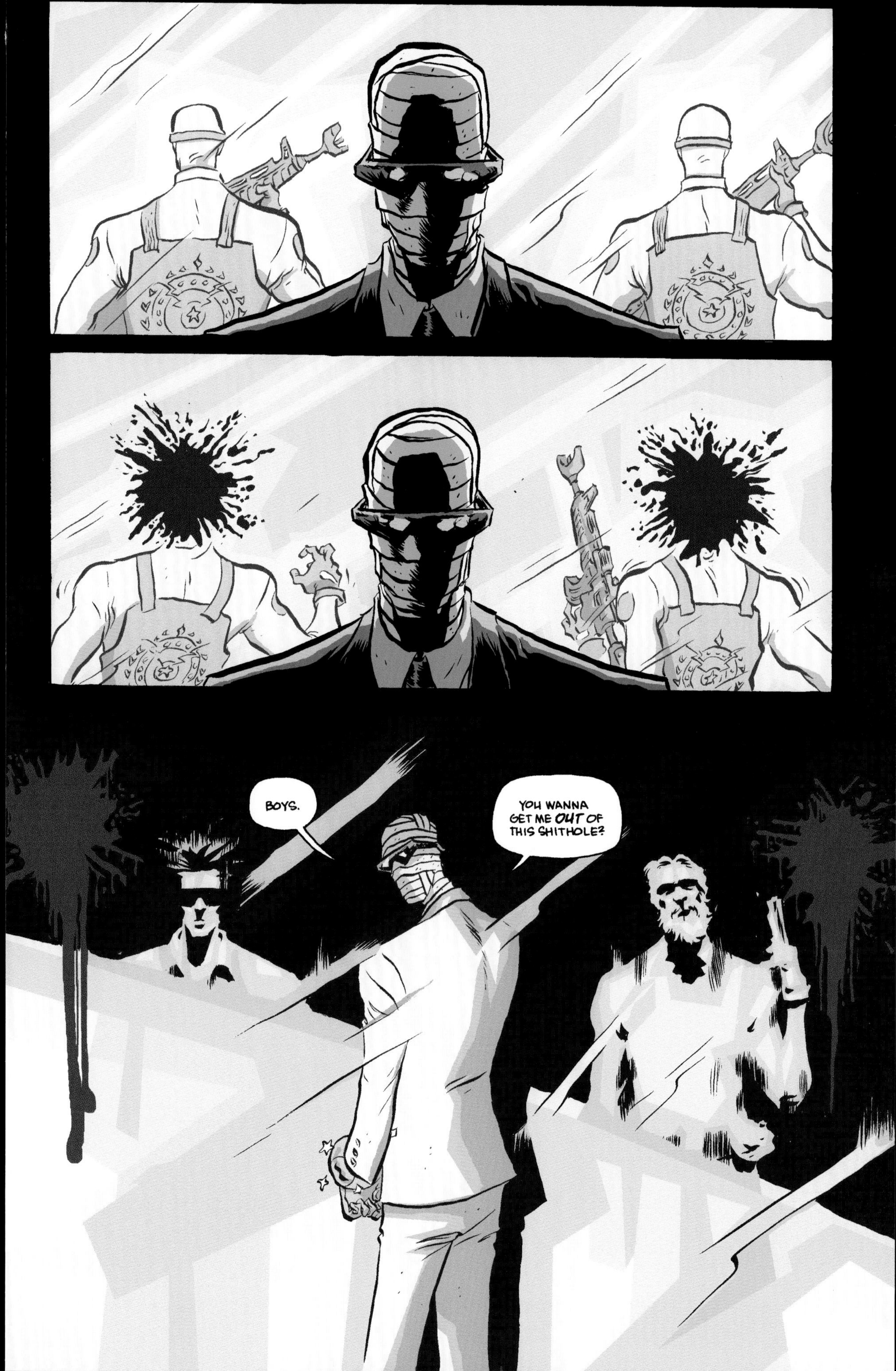
BOYS.
YOU WANNA GET ME OUT OF THIS SHITHOLE?

12: She Will Only Bring You Happiness (3:28)

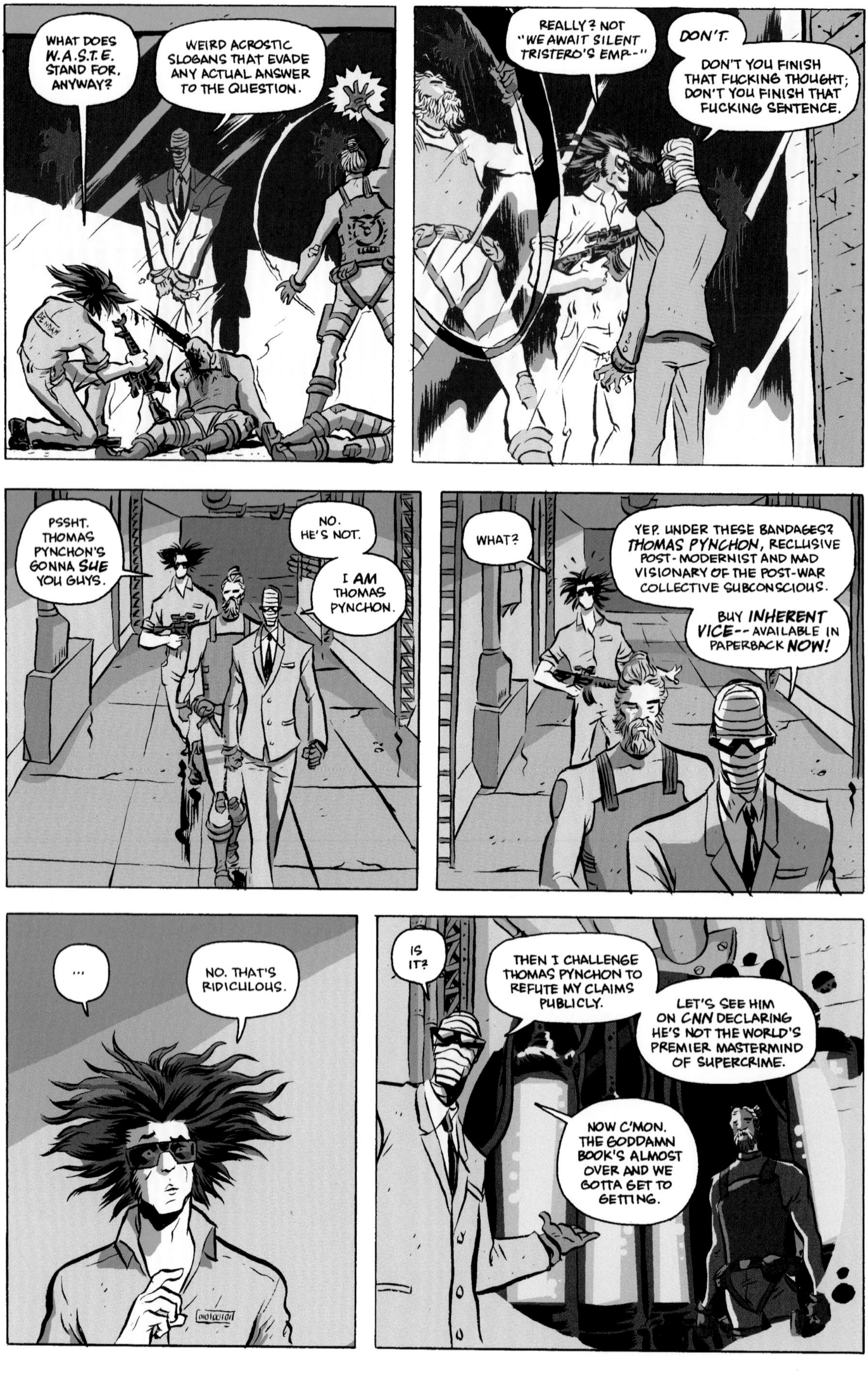
WHAT DOES W.A.S.T.E. STAND FOR, ANYWAY?
WEIRD ACROSTIC SLOGANS THAT EVADE ANY ACTUAL ANSWER TO THE QUESTION.
REALLY? NOT "WE AWAIT SILENT TRISTERO'S EMP--"
DON'T.
DON'T YOU FINISH THAT FUCKING THOUGHT; DON'T YOU FINISH THAT FUCKING SENTENCE.
PSSHT. THOMAS PYNCHON'S GONNA SUE YOU GUYS.
NO. HE'S NOT.
I AM THOMAS PYNCHON.
WHAT?
YEP. UNDER THESE BANDAGES? THOMAS PYNCHON, RECLUSIVE POST-MODERNIST AND MAD VISIONARY OF THE POST-WAR COLLECTIVE SUBCONSCIOUS.
BUY INHERENT VICE-- AVAILABLE IN PAPERBACK NOW!
...
NO. THAT'S RIDICULOUS.
IS IT?
THEN I CHALLENGE THOMAS PYNCHON TO REFUTE MY CLAIMS PUBLICLY.
LET'S SEE HIM ON CNN DECLARING HE'S NOT THE WORLD'S PREMIER MASTERMIND OF SUPERCRIME.
NOW C'MON. THE GODDAMN BOOK'S ALMOST OVER AND WE GOTTA GET TO GETTING.

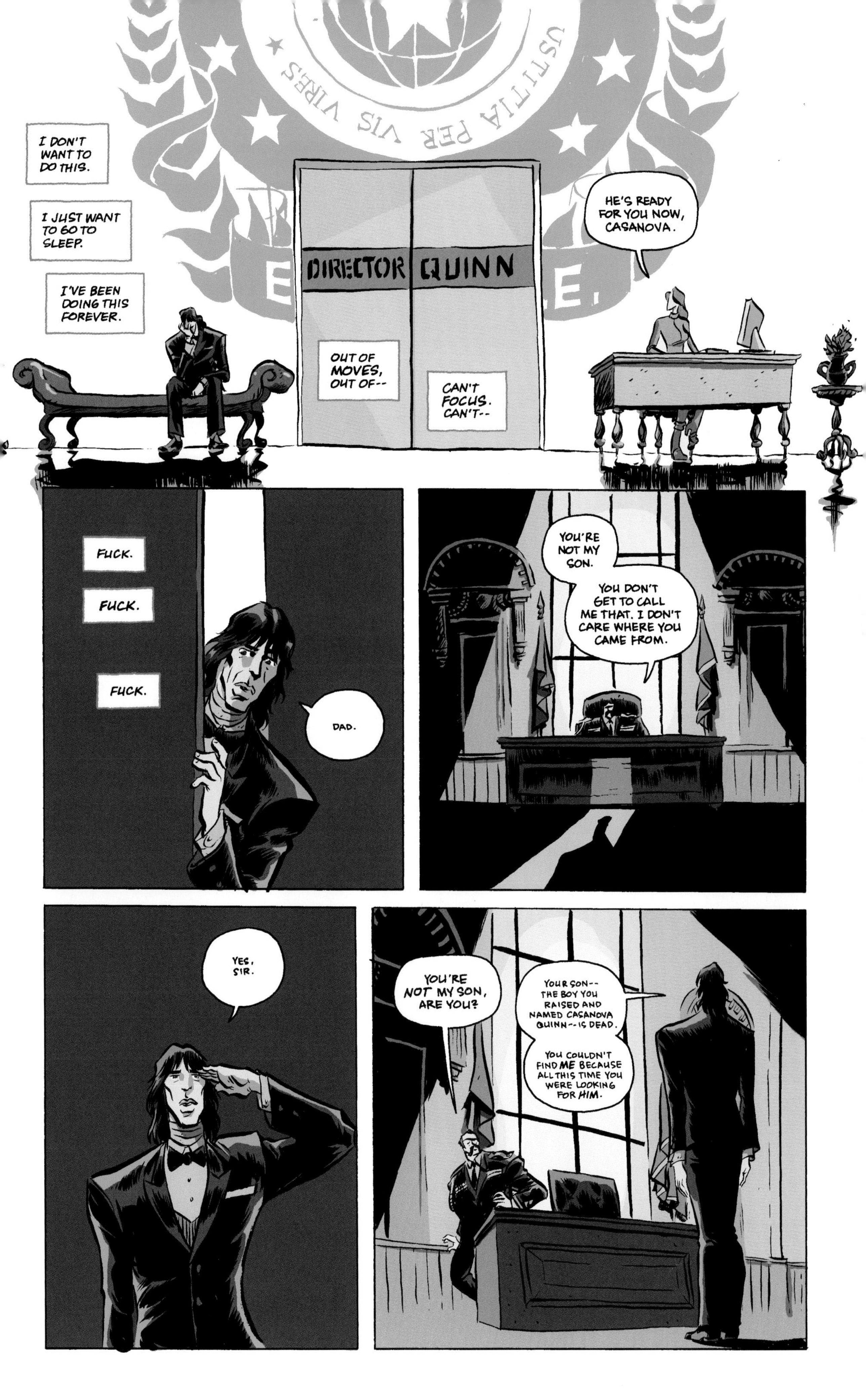

USTITIA PER VIS VIRES
I DON'T WANT TO DO THIS.
I JUST WANT TO GO TO SLEEP.
I'VE BEEN DOING THIS FOREVER.
DIRECTOR QUINN
OUT OF MOVES, OUT OF--
CAN'T FOCUS. CAN'T--
HE'S READY FOR YOU NOW, CASANOVA.
FUCK.
FUCK.
FUCK.
DAD.
YOU'RE NOT MY SON.
YOU DON'T GET TO CALL ME THAT. I DON'T CARE WHERE YOU CAME FROM.
YES, SIR.
YOU'RE NOT MY SON, ARE YOU?
YOUR SON-- THE BOY YOU RAISED AND NAMED CASANOVA QUINN--IS DEAD.
YOU COULDN'T FIND ME BECAUSE ALL THIS TIME YOU WERE LOOKING FOR HIM.

13: Taxman (2:39)

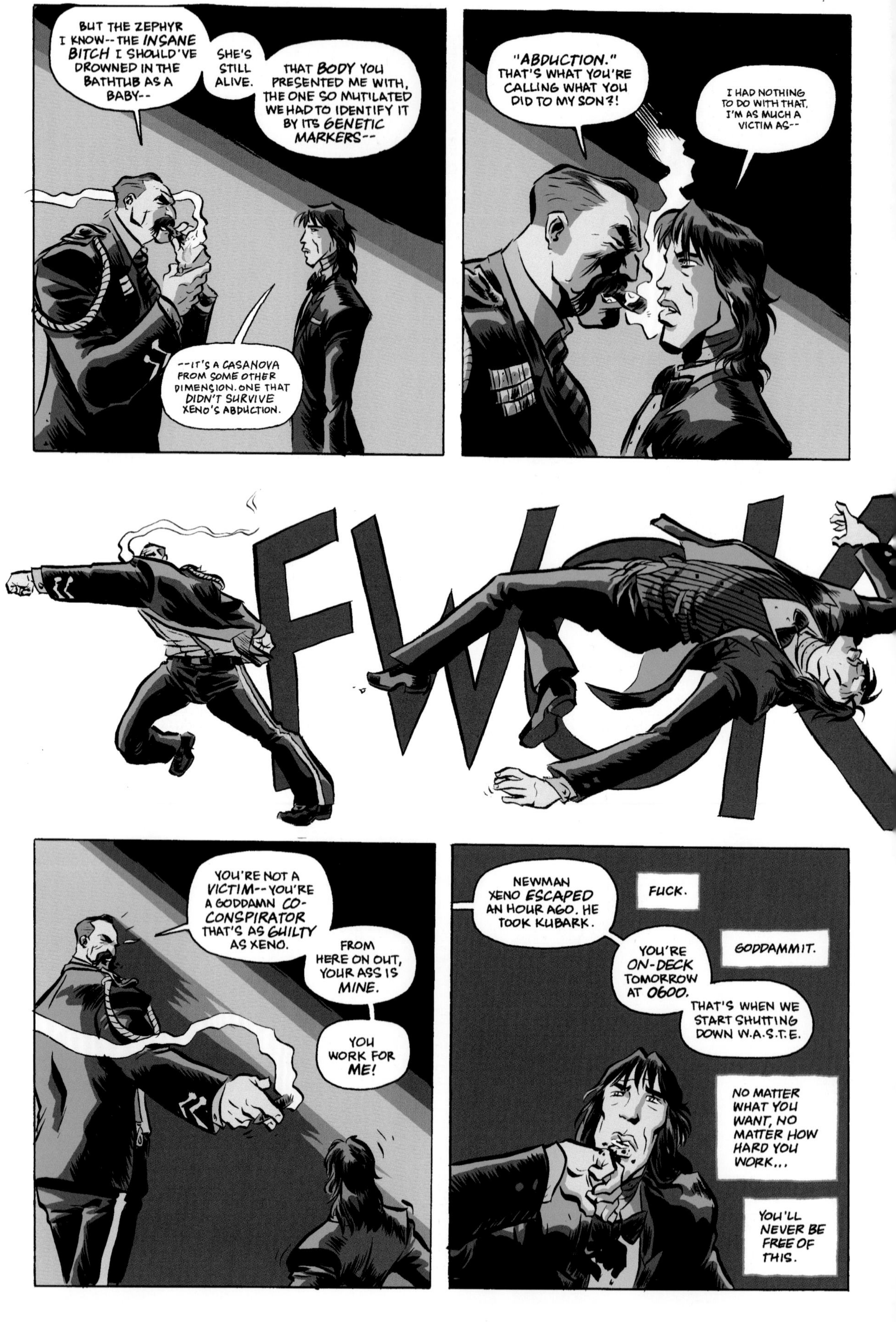

BUT THE ZEPHYR I KNOW--THE INSANE BITCH I SHOULD'VE DROWNED IN THE BATHTUB AS A BABY--
SHE'S STILL ALIVE.
THAT BODY YOU PRESENTED ME WITH, THE ONE SO MUTILATED WE HAD TO IDENTIFY IT BY ITS GENETIC MARKERS--
--IT'S A CASANOVA FROM SOME OTHER DIMENSION. ONE THAT DIDN'T SURVIVE XENO'S ABDUCTION.
"ABDUCTION." THAT'S WHAT YOU'RE CALLING WHAT YOU DID TO MY SON?!
I HAD NOTHING TO DO WITH THAT, I'M AS MUCH A VICTIM AS--
YOU'RE NOT A VICTIM--YOU'RE A GODDAMN CO-CONSPIRATOR THAT'S AS GUILTY AS XENO.
FROM HERE ON OUT, YOUR ASS IS MINE.
YOU WORK FOR ME!
NEWMAN XENO ESCAPED AN HOUR AGO. HE TOOK KUBARK.
FUCK.
YOU'RE ON-DECK TOMORROW AT 0600.
GODDAMMIT.
THAT'S WHEN WE START SHUTTING DOWN W.A.S.T.E.
NO MATTER WHAT YOU WANT, NO MATTER HOW HARD YOU WORK...
YOU'LL NEVER BE FREE OF THIS.

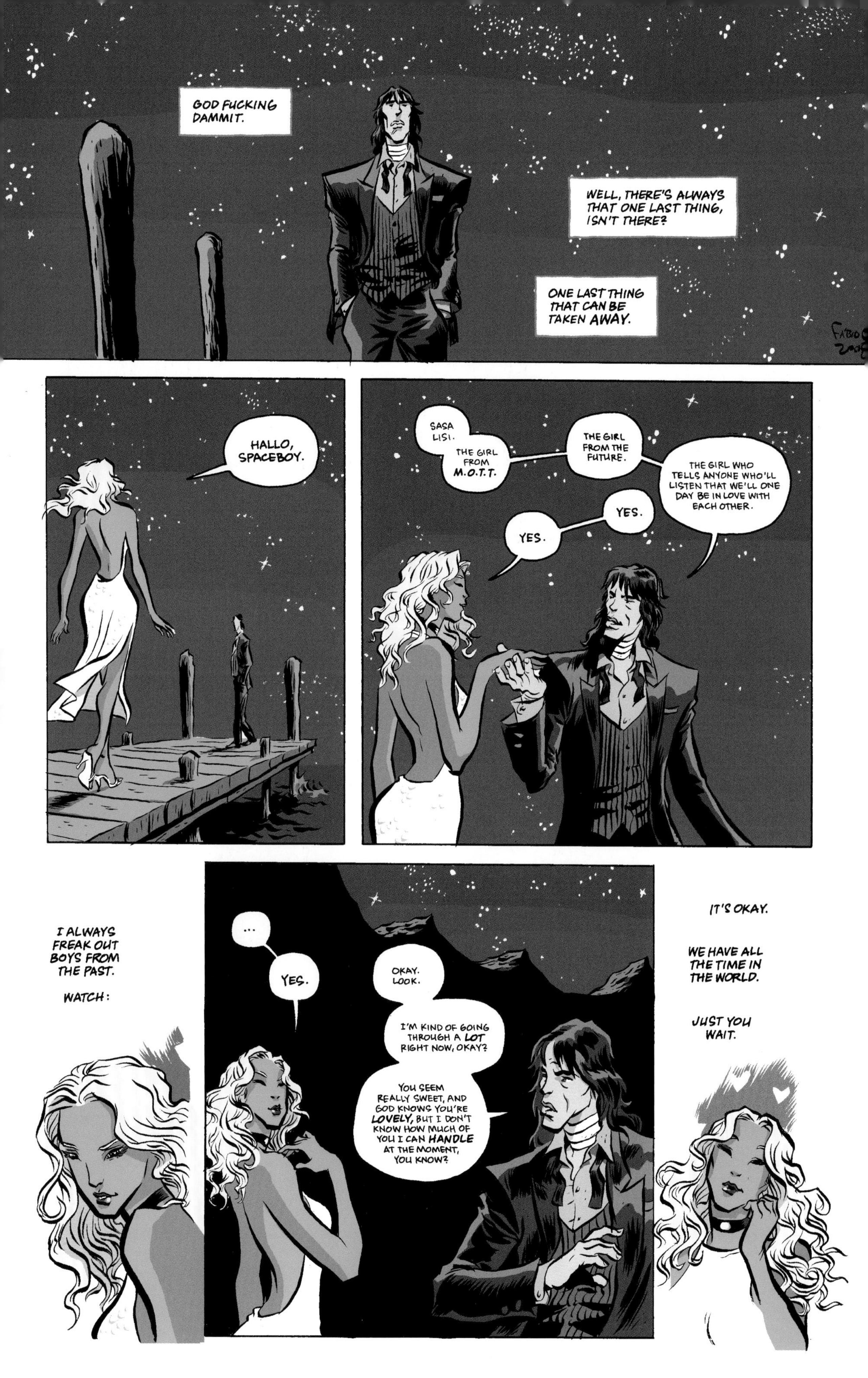
GOD FUCKING DAMMIT.
WELL, THERE'S ALWAYS THAT ONE LAST THING, ISN'T THERE?
ONE LAST THING THAT CAN BE TAKEN AWAY.
FABIO
HALLO, SPACEBOY.
SASA LISI.
THE GIRL FROM M.O.T.T.
THE GIRL FROM THE FUTURE.
THE GIRL WHO TELLS ANYONE WHO'LL LISTEN THAT WE'LL ONE DAY BE IN LOVE WITH EACH OTHER.
YES.
YES.
I ALWAYS FREAK OUT BOYS FROM THE PAST.
WATCH:
...
YES.
OKAY. LOOK.
I'M KIND OF GOING THROUGH A LOT RIGHT NOW, OKAY?
YOU SEEM REALLY SWEET, AND GOD KNOWS YOU'RE LOVELY, BUT I DON'T KNOW HOW MUCH OF YOU I CAN HANDLE AT THE MOMENT, YOU KNOW?
IT'S OKAY.
WE HAVE ALL THE TIME IN THE WORLD.
JUST YOU WAIT.

14: Execution Day (3:00)

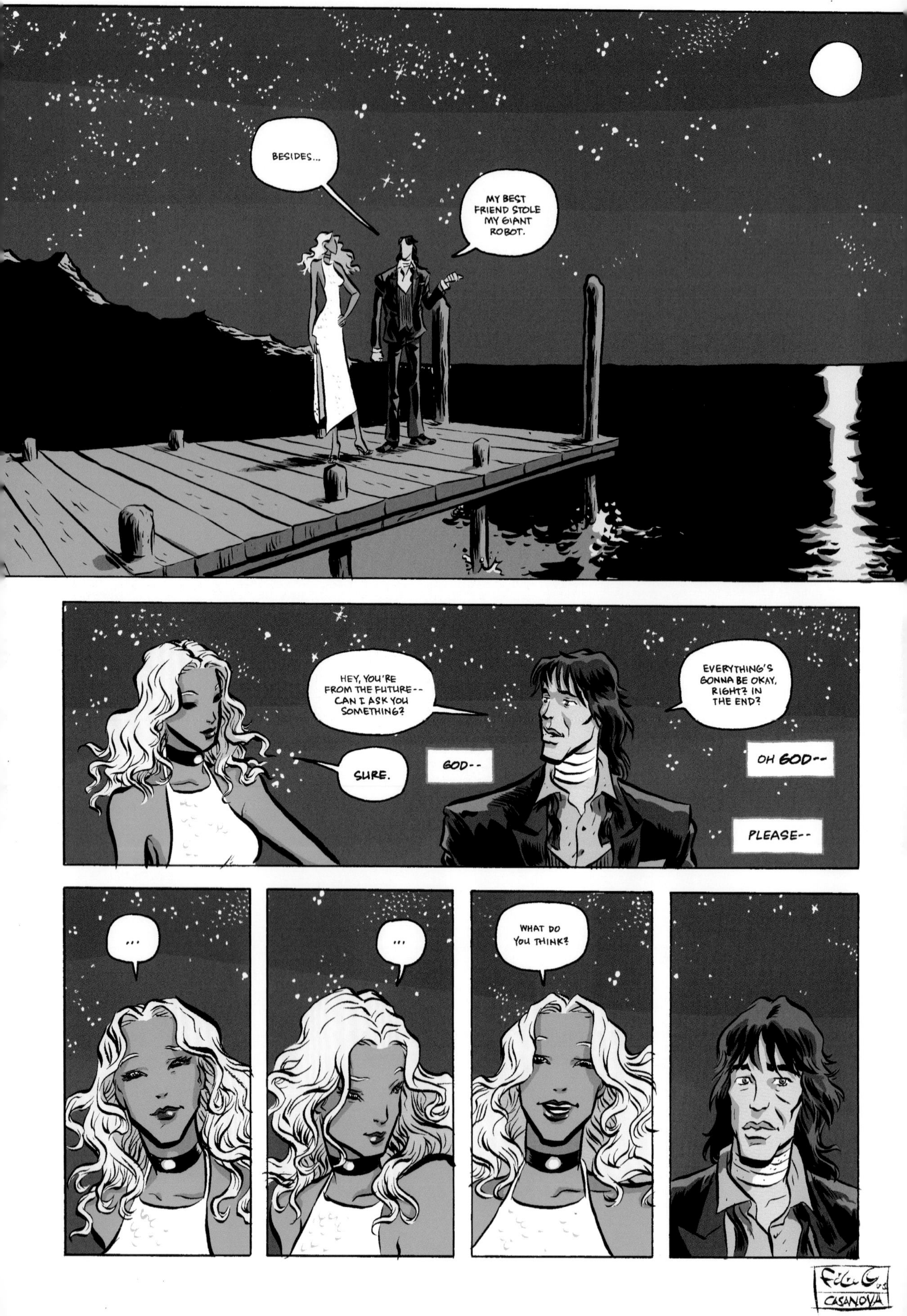

BESIDES...
MY BEST FRIEND STOLE MY GIANT ROBOT.
HEY, YOU'RE FROM THE FUTURE-- CAN I ASK YOU SOMETHING?
SURE.
GOD--
EVERYTHING'S GONNA BE OKAY, RIGHT? IN THE END?
OH GOD--
PLEASE--
...
...
WHAT DO YOU THINK?
CASANOVA

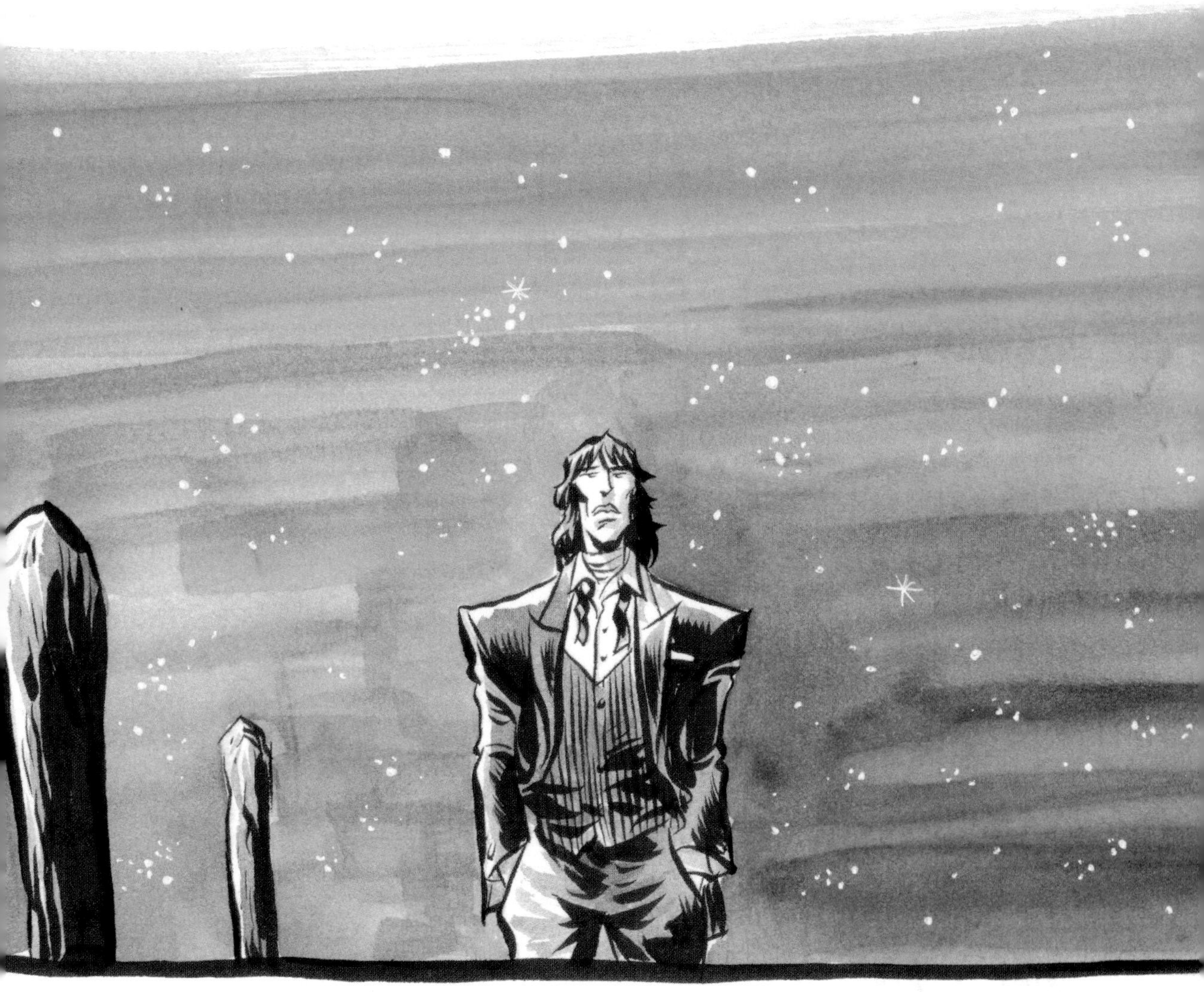

IN MEDIAS RES

WHEN THE WOLF COMES HOME

SEVENTEEN

NAOMI I MOAN

FUCK SHIT UP

SOME OF THE THINGS THAT
HAPPENED TO THE MURDERERS
AND MURDERED AMONG US

HALLO SPACEBOY

**DIT DIT DIT
DAH DAH DAH
DIT DIT**

BACKMATTER

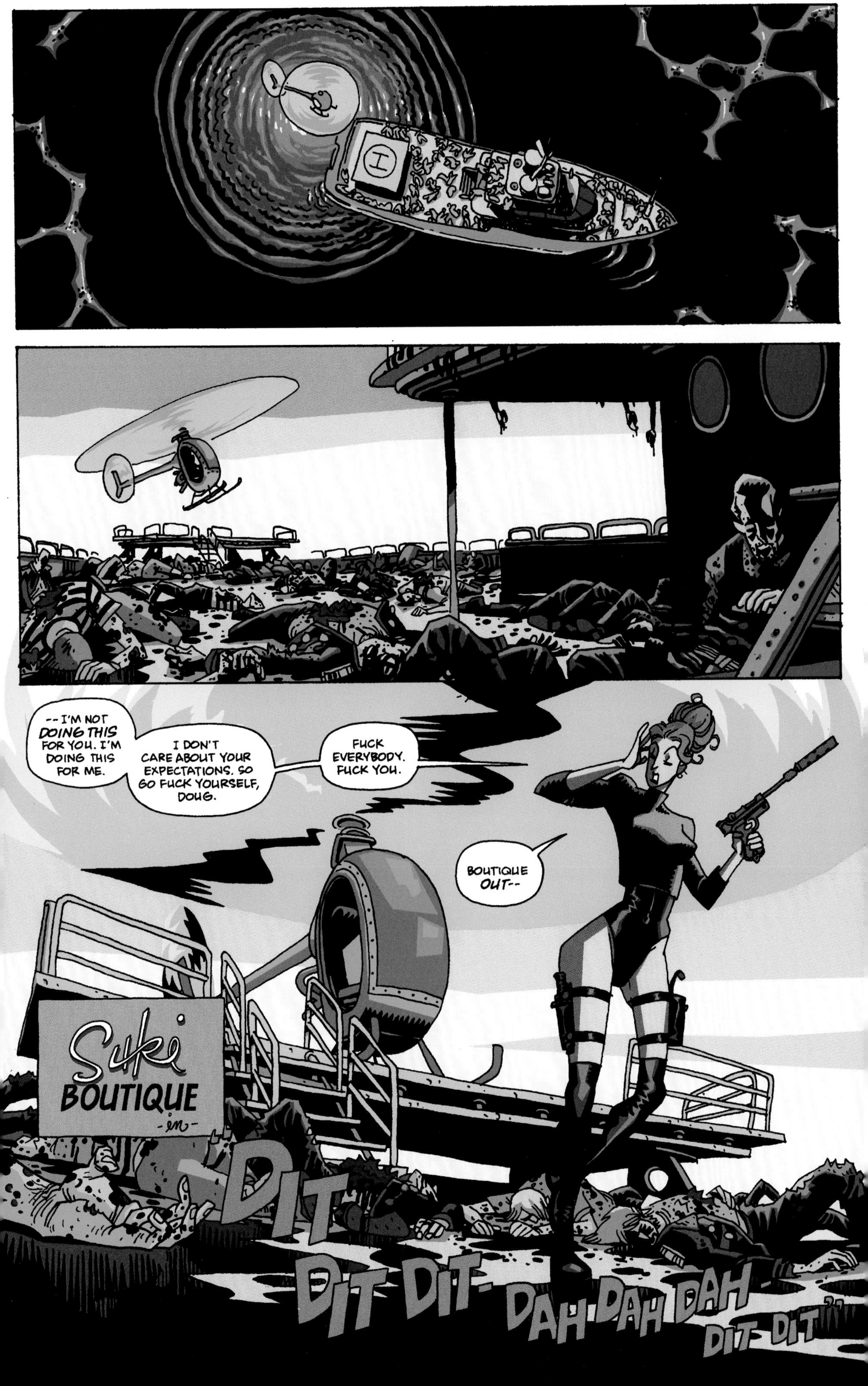

-- I'M NOT DOING THIS FOR YOU. I'M DOING THIS FOR ME.
I DON'T CARE ABOUT YOUR EXPECTATIONS. SO GO FUCK YOURSELF, DOUG.
FUCK EVERYBODY. FUCK YOU.
BOUTIQUE OUT--
Suki BOUTIQUE -in-
DIT
DIT DIT- DAH DAH DAH DIT DIT

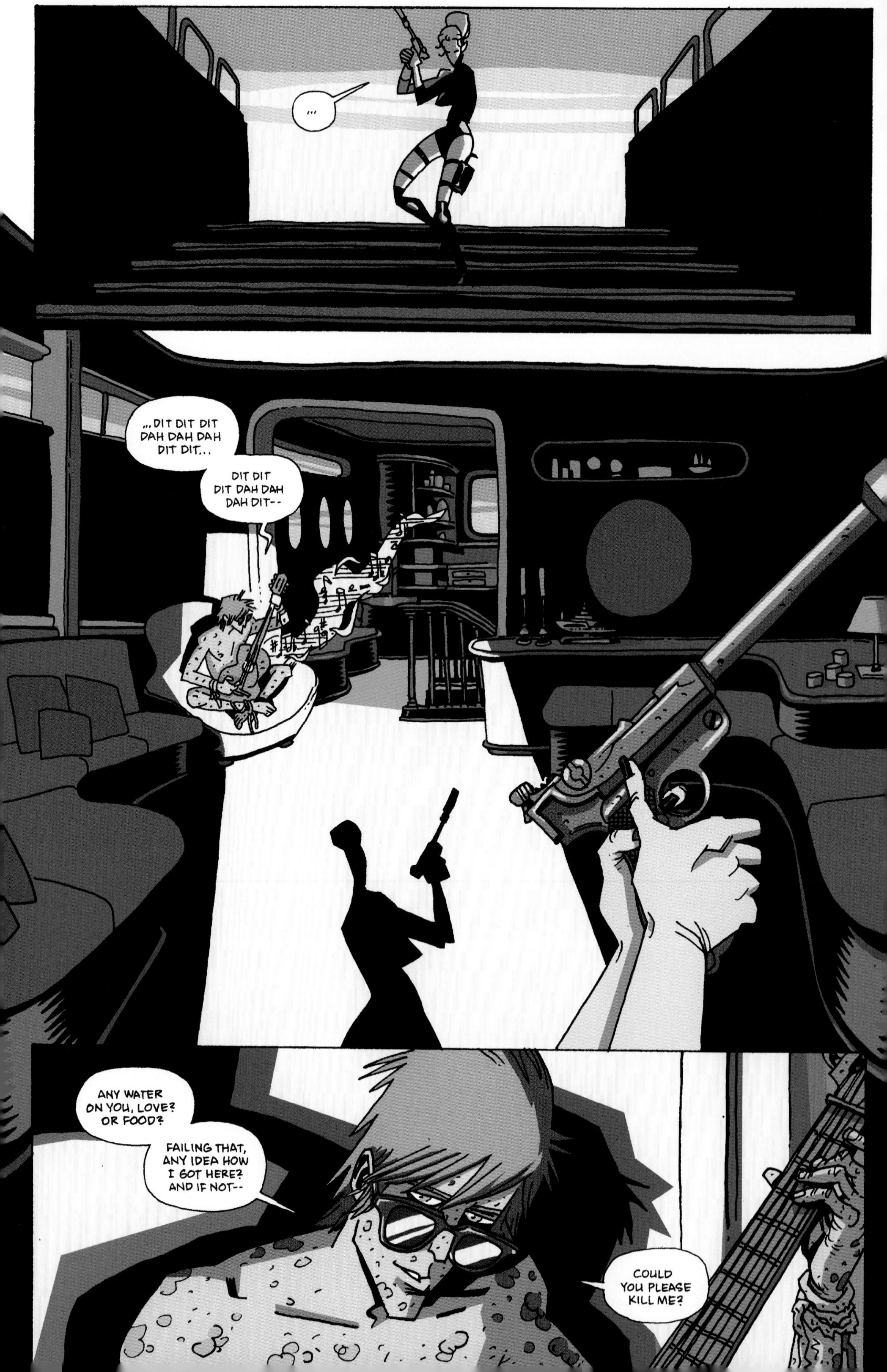
...
...DIT DIT DIT
DAH DAH DAH
DIT DIT...
DIT DIT
DIT DAH DAH
DAH DIT--
ANY WATER
ON YOU, LOVE?
OR FOOD?
FAILING THAT,
ANY IDEA HOW
I GOT HERE?
AND IF NOT--
COULD
YOU PLEASE
KILL ME?

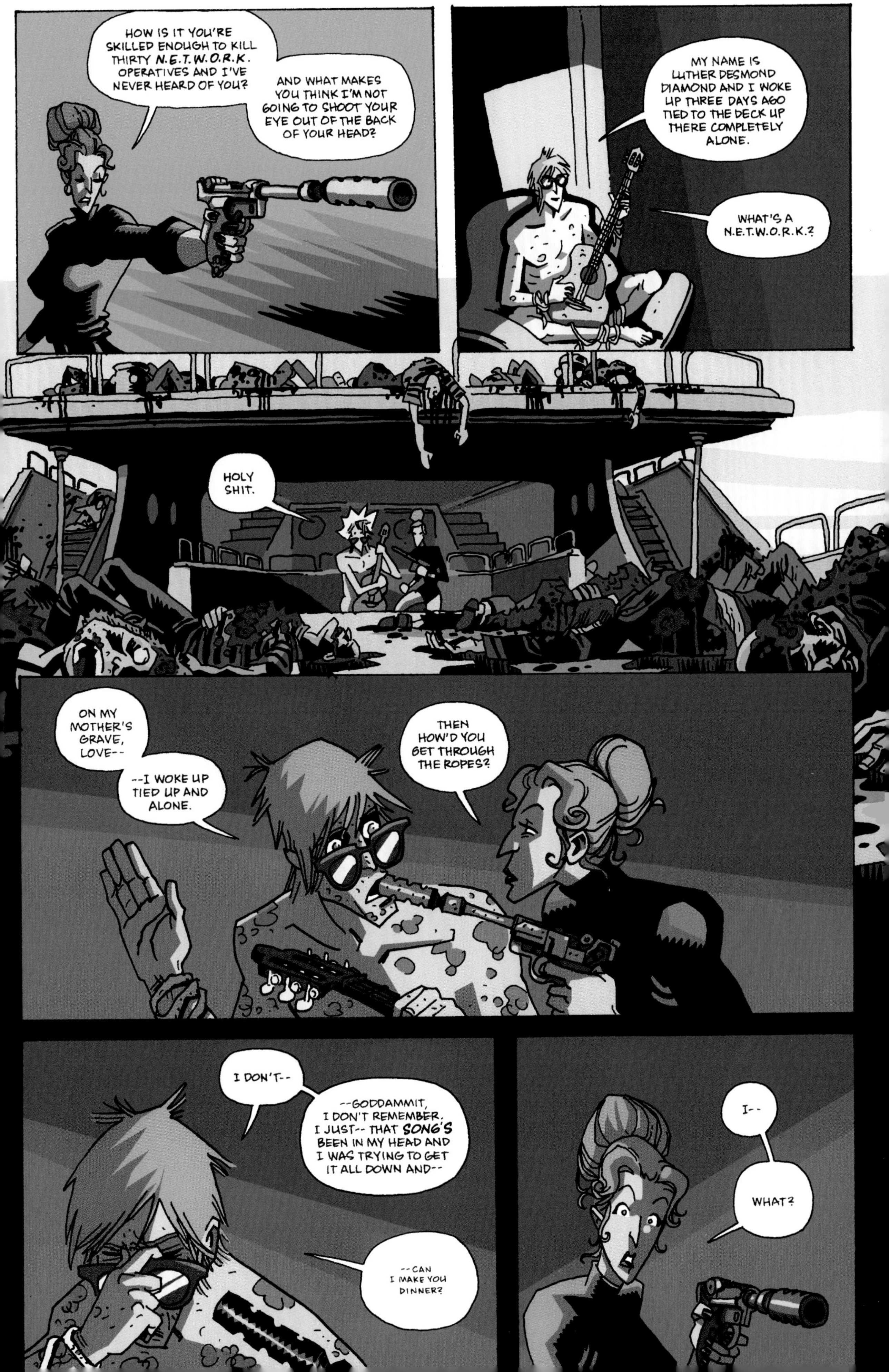

HOW IS IT YOU'RE SKILLED ENOUGH TO KILL THIRTY N.E.T.W.O.R.K. OPERATIVES AND I'VE NEVER HEARD OF YOU?
AND WHAT MAKES YOU THINK I'M NOT GOING TO SHOOT YOUR EYE OUT OF THE BACK OF YOUR HEAD?
MY NAME IS LUTHER DESMOND DIAMOND AND I WOKE UP THREE DAYS AGO TIED TO THE DECK UP THERE COMPLETELY ALONE.
WHAT'S A N.E.T.W.O.R.K.?
HOLY SHIT.
ON MY MOTHER'S GRAVE, LOVE--
--I WOKE UP TIED UP AND ALONE.
THEN HOW'D YOU GET THROUGH THE ROPES?
I DON'T--
--GODDAMMIT, I DON'T REMEMBER. I JUST-- THAT SONG'S BEEN IN MY HEAD AND I WAS TRYING TO GET IT ALL DOWN AND--
--CAN I MAKE YOU DINNER?
I--
WHAT?

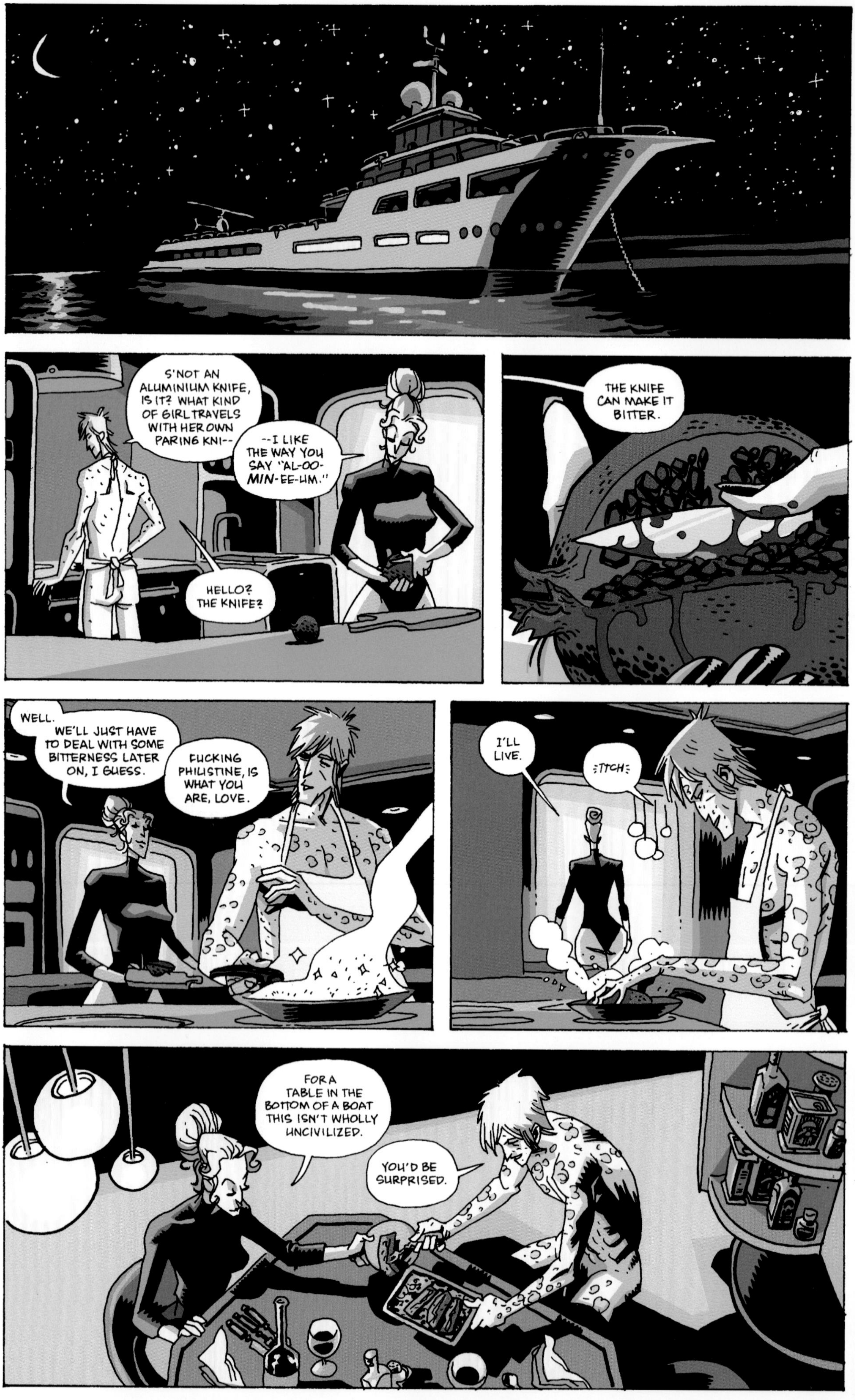
S'NOT AN ALUMINIUM KNIFE, IS IT? WHAT KIND OF GIRL TRAVELS WITH HER OWN PARING KNI--
--I LIKE THE WAY YOU SAY "AL-OO-MIN-EE-UM."
HELLO? THE KNIFE?
THE KNIFE CAN MAKE IT BITTER.
WELL. WE'LL JUST HAVE TO DEAL WITH SOME BITTERNESS LATER ON, I GUESS.
FUCKING PHILISTINE, IS WHAT YOU ARE, LOVE.
I'LL LIVE.
TTCH
FOR A TABLE IN THE BOTTOM OF A BOAT THIS ISN'T WHOLLY UNCIVILIZED.
YOU'D BE SURPRISED.

Y'KNOW, I'M **ENGLISH**--I'VE NEVER REALLY HAD A PROPER TROPICAL SUNBURN BEFORE.

YOU SAY THAT LIKE IT'S AN ACQUISITIVE ACHIEVEMENT.

WELL, AN **EXPERIENTIAL** ACHIEVEMENT, ANYWAY.

S'WHAT IT'S ABOUT, RIGHT?

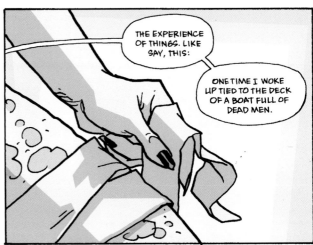

THE EXPERIENCE OF THINGS. LIKE SAY, THIS:

ONE TIME I WOKE UP TIED TO THE DECK OF A BOAT FULL OF DEAD MEN.

NO CLUE HOW I GOT THERE.

I SWEAR. BUT THEN--

THEN THIS CRAZY BIRD LANDS IN A HELICHIPPER AND SAYS I DID IT. AND I'M TELLING YOU, I CAN'T REMEMBER SHIT ABOUT FUCK RIGHT NOW BUT SO--

SO-- SO THEN I--

SO THEN I POISON HER. I SUDDENLY REMEMBER I KNOW HOW TO DO THAT.

I POISON HER AND SHE DOESN'T DIE.

ISN'T THAT THE CRAZIEST THING YOU'VE EVER HEARD?

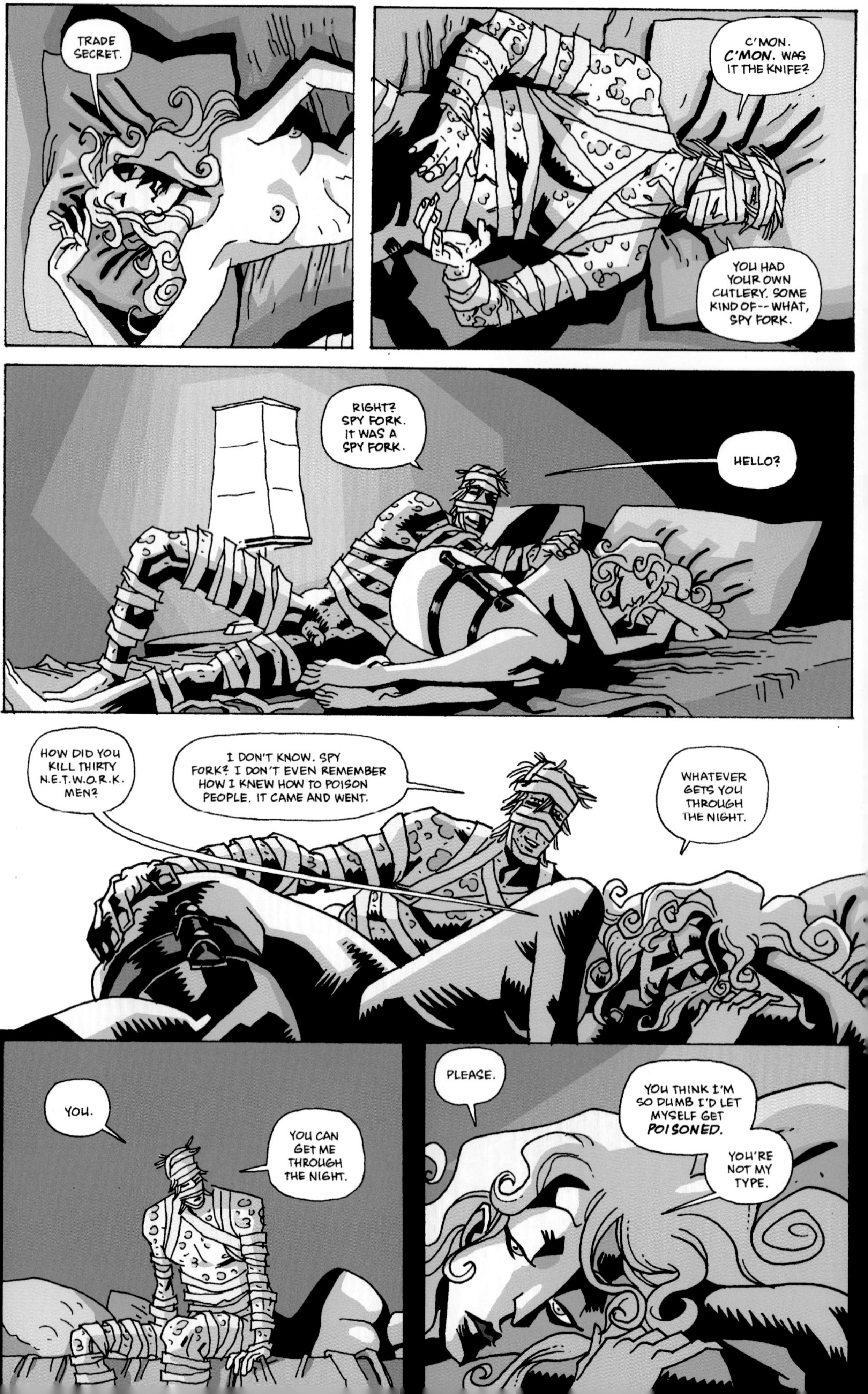
TRADE SECRET.
C'MON. C'MON. WAS IT THE KNIFE?
YOU HAD YOUR OWN CUTLERY. SOME KIND OF-- WHAT, SPY FORK.
RIGHT? SPY FORK. IT WAS A SPY FORK.
HELLO?
HOW DID YOU KILL THIRTY N.E.T.W.O.R.K. MEN?
I DON'T KNOW. SPY FORK? I DON'T EVEN REMEMBER HOW I KNEW HOW TO POISON PEOPLE. IT CAME AND WENT.
WHATEVER GETS YOU THROUGH THE NIGHT.
YOU.
YOU CAN GET ME THROUGH THE NIGHT.
PLEASE.
YOU THINK I'M SO DUMB I'D LET MYSELF GET POISONED.
YOU'RE NOT MY TYPE.

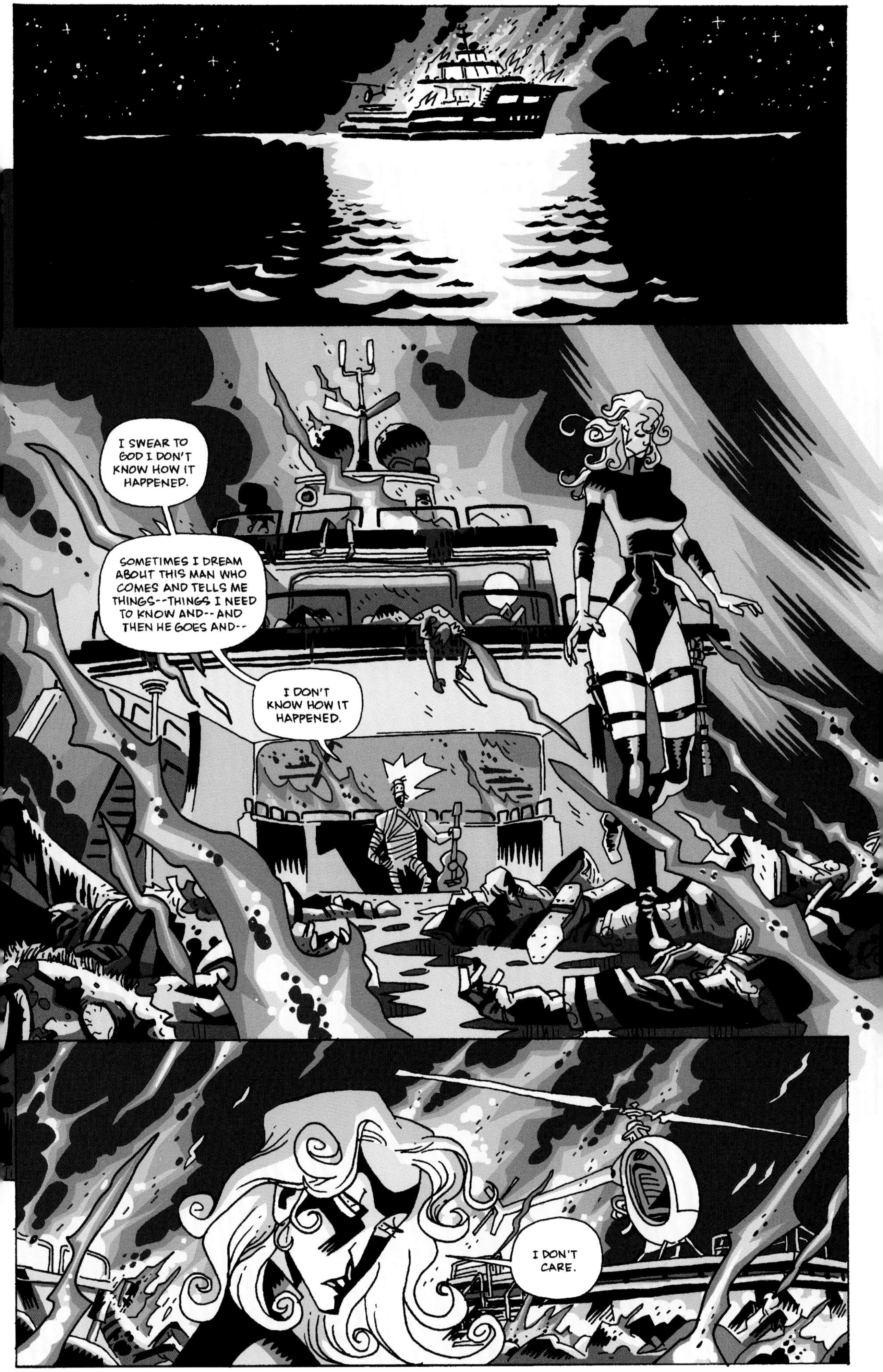
I SWEAR TO GOD I DON'T KNOW HOW IT HAPPENED.
SOMETIMES I DREAM ABOUT THIS MAN WHO COMES AND TELLS ME THINGS--THINGS I NEED TO KNOW AND--AND THEN HE GOES AND--
I DON'T KNOW HOW IT HAPPENED.
I DON'T CARE.

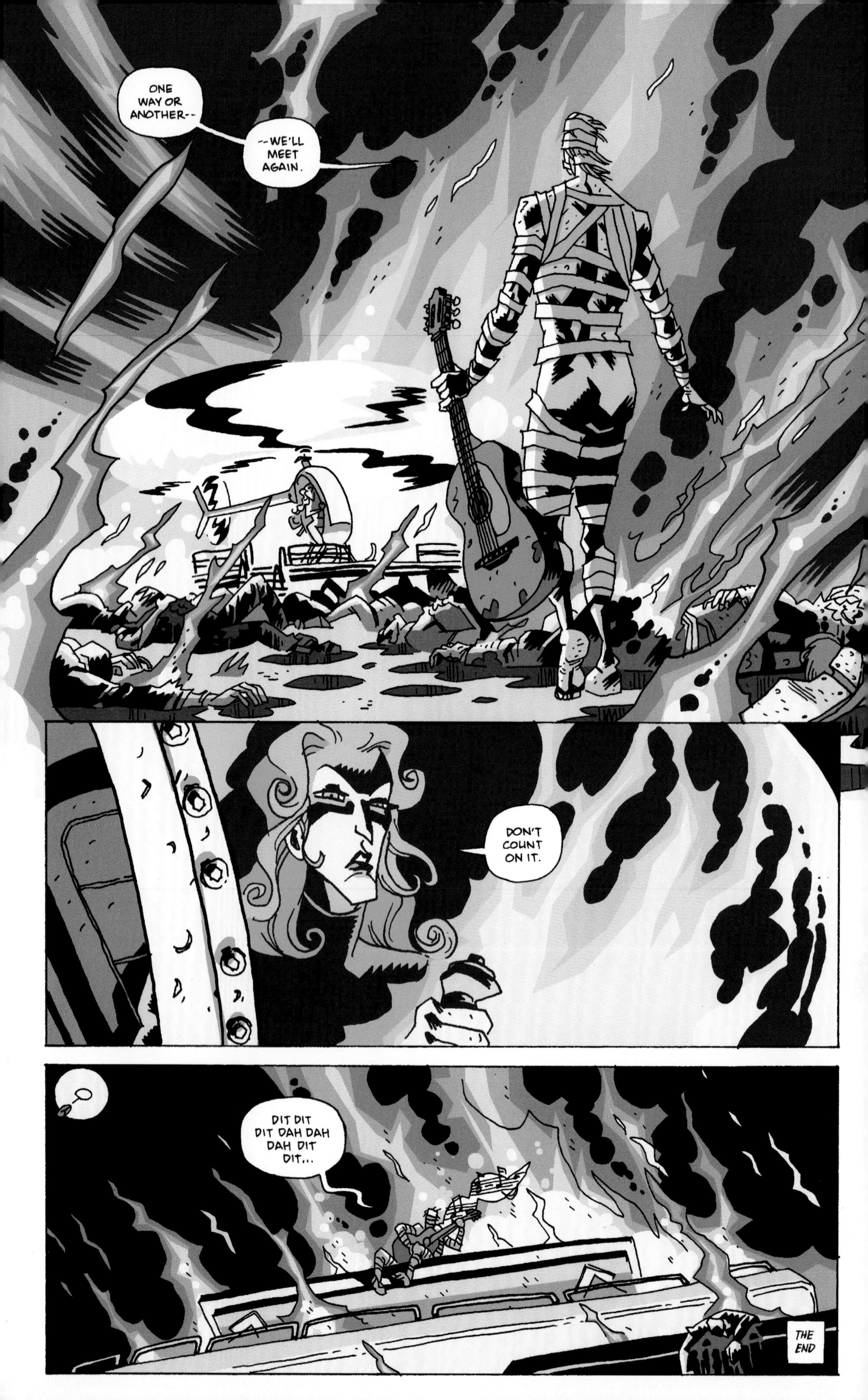
ONE WAY OR ANOTHER--
--WE'LL MEET AGAIN.
DON'T COUNT ON IT.
DIT DIT DIT DAH DAH DAH DIT DIT...
THE END

IN MEDIAS RES

WHEN THE WOLF COMES HOME

SEVENTEEN

NAOMI I MOAN

FUCK SHIT UP

SOME OF THE THINGS THAT
HAPPENED TO THE MURDERERS
AND MURDERED AMONG US

HALLO SPACEBOY

DIT DIT DIT
DAH DAH DAH
DIT DIT

BACKMATTER

GULA 1, Issue 8[1] (Image Comics, 2007)

Hiyah Earthmen Indeed.

Oh, god, how I regretted what I said in there pages when we last spoke.

When we last spoke[2], I was raising my defiant fist to Stupid Heaven and screaming that I, in my Elton John best, was Still Standin', yeah yeah yeah, and that I was at one with my process and CASANOVA's place in it; that I was it and it was me and dammit, if I'd gotten through everything I got through on my way to the finish line then—well, I believe I said something like "bring your weak ass on." To, you know. The infinite.

In these pages, I had declared to the cosmic powers I had become convinced pulsed through the veins of CASANOVA that they were, in fact, total pussies[3] and whatever they could dish out, I could take, so bang on, you total pussy[4], bang on.

Four days later, I was in an Emergency Room in Florida, on Christmas Day, sicker than I've been in I don't know how long, wanting an OK from a doctor to make sure I could fly home the next day.

I couldn't really talk, but I took notes[5].

I watched a woman find out her mother had been killed in a car crash, six feet in front of me. A triage nurse confessed to me how much she hated working Christmas Day, while over her shoulder I watched a man struggle and scream against his restraints. The dead woman, the girl's mother, was his wife. I was told she was gone before he was told he was a widower[6]. That seems extraordinarily wrong[7].

"We are what we pretend to be, so we must be careful what we pretend to be," wrote Kurt Vonnegut Jr., once upon a time. And god bless you, Mr. Vonnegut—the world is more boring for your absence. Merry Christmas—you gave me the opening to my dumb little magic comic book.

Everything medical Cass sees or hears in these pages—except, you know, the comic book stuff—happened to me as shown, with one-to-one parity. And that was just the beginning of my year[8].

I wrote the first scene, or at least sketched it out. I thought—oh! Well, you've decided to make Cass sick, so write the scene where he gets away from the horrible hospital. I sketched it out, roughly, and let it sit.

Things didn't get better.

It got worse and worse, the bad news piling on more and more relentlessly, the work never stopping. I would be in a hospital three times before my health would finally come back, on and off antibiotics, in and out of ill health.

In L.A., sick and on more drugs and without a voice again[9], I wrote what came next—Cass on the "beach" with beautiful Ruby. A subtle shift in my thinking: don't just write him sick. Write him well, dumbass. So I did, and I finally got better[10]. You can titter and call that coincidental all you like; but as a friend or mine like to point out, there's a reason comics writers go crazy.

In all that time I, and my family, dealt with all nature of horrible stuff, culminating with my wife's grandmother dying in hospice care at her home, in Florida, where I had been so sick at the holiday. The whole family, myself included, gathered to be at her side through her transition[11].

I wasn't sure how to deal with that, honestly. I was glad to be there for my wife, and happy to help her family, but that's a wholly alien operating procedure than what I know. It was the end of the first brutal quarter of a new year and I was exhausted by felt useless. Mostly I just tried to open doors for people and stay out of the way.

That's the same reason I regretted what I wrote here in #7—not because I was embarrassed at daring to believe in something considerably more powerful and infinite than myself—but rather, because it wasn't me being Cutsey McGee and trying to avoid talking

---

1   In its original publication scheme, CASANOVA existed as 16 pages of story with one color (a kind of lima bean green for LUXURIA and a radiant, eye-searing cyan for GULA) and this blather at the back in a package for two bucks. Later this story was reprinted two at a time in full color and with new lettering from another publisher. So the contents of this issue, for example, appeared under the appellations CASANOVA #8 and CASANOVA: GULA #1 (which also collected what was once CASANOVA #9). So ICON GULA 1 was IMAGE GULA 8 and 9; ICON GULA 2 was IMAGE GULA 10 and 11; ICON GULA 3 was IMAGE GULA 12 and 13; and ICON GULA 4 was IMAGE GULA 14 and the bonus short DIT DIT DIT DAH DAH DAH DIT DIT.

2   I literally have not read this since I proofread it for its original publication. Oh boy!

3   Jesus, Matt.

4   JESUS, MATT.

5   Somewhere around here, this note is reproduced. I kept it.

6   My immediate thought? "If that was me, I'd go get drunk." It was that thought that finally sent me into a recovery program for addiction to drugs and alcohol four days later. I'd been clean for a few years but, as thinking like that betrays, I was anything but sober.

7   This was also the day that James Brown died. Ho ho ho.

8   This would've been six months or so after I left the safety of my old career behind for the explosive wealth, eternal security, and unimaginable power synonymous with the job of "comic book writer." So a stress-induced catastrophic health collapse was pretty much a gimme.

9   I had a sinus infection that pretty much lasted three years.

10   I wonder if I knew this was bullshit at the time? I wouldn't "get better" until 2010.

11   The other half of that side of the family tree went this year. Jesus, it's been a decade.

about craft by cross-referencing my DVD collection with, I dunno, whatever Brian Wilson had for lunch in 1967. By my nature, I tend to isolate. Being forced out into the open where everybody's looking at you as you feel stuff tends to make me want to tear my face off and run screaming. And even more that how shitty it is to be relentlessly sick, or relentlessly depressed or relentlessly ANYTHING—having to deal with a relentless barrage of feeling stuff is just the worst. I'm not a fully formed enough human being to know how to parse all that out.[12]

And ever since I allowed myself to write what I wrote in CASANOVA #7, it had just been nonstop.

Three months to the day of my ER visit, I sat out of the way on the front porch and finished CASANOVA #8. The sketched out scene became a finished script in one aching and manic burst. I started early; I finished late; my hands throbbed by my book was done.

I wanted to stay out of the way. I wanted to isolate. I wanted not feel stuff for just a few goddamn minutes and, finally, finally, thank Christ finally be finished with it.

Two days later, my wife's grandmother passed away, surrounded by her family.

Two days after that, my wife and I entered the second trimester of our second pregnancy.

So it's not been all bad, this feeling stuff.

Sometimes feeling stuff can feel pretty good, if you just let it.

The baby's due on September 21st[13].

Bang on.

•

So, then. This issue.

We should've called it: FUCK CASANOVA.

By making fun of the whole of the first album[14], I hope you'll join us in marshaling in this new beast in all its glitter and glory. Super-condensing the formula scenes that showed up in the chapters of LUXURIA time and time again (T.A.M.I. Opening! Ridiculous Mission! Turnaround! Elliptical philosophy masquerading as character development! Exploding brainbirds! Touching moment where Cass reveals his humanity, beneath the hedonistic shell! Partying! Throwaway characters! Ruby! Overwhelming fictional technobabble masquerading as plot development! Everybody talking like Cool Prick Catchphrase was their native tongue!) meant crushing all that down into a half-issue mockery[15] of all that came before as our exorcism to out all of LUXURIA'S ghosts and to free us from it. This issue is our needle drag across the record that's played for our last seven issues. CASANOVA is dead. Long live CASANOVA[16]. We have all new formulas to meet, use, and abuse. New story, new timeframe, new characters (that lovely lady on the last page? I've been trying to shoehorn her into CASANOVA since #3 and I just couldn't fit her in…), and best of all, new life.

•

Oh! And new art.

It's funny that the book you're reading, about evil twins and whatnot, was visually hatched by twins.

Fábio Moon has the art on this second album of CASANOVA and I couldn't be more thrilled. He was, in fact, the brother I went after in the first place. He and Bá—currently drawing the excellent THE UMBRELLA ACADEMY, as written by Mr. Gerard Way and published by Mr. Dark Horse this fall—discussed the matter between themselves and informed me that Bá was the one to launch CASANOVA. Okay,

---

12   This is a lie. Well – this is obfuscation. And the truth of it all is shot through the rest of the backmatter stuff in CASANOVA, the truth of it all goes right to the heart of why I wanted to stop writing it all together, and, if I'm being honest, the truth of it affects me still. And I'm trying to figure out how to write about it now, because, fuck it, why not, and I'm not sure how, and I'm not sure I want to, anyway, and besides, who, but me, cares?

What happened was this: my wife was pregnant. And then we lost the baby. It gave me a change of heart – several, really – about a lot of things in my life. What kind of man I was, what kind of husband, what kind of person. How I wrote. What I wrote. And the end of CASANOVA #7, the first thing I had to write in the wake of the miscarriage.

And because the rules of CASANOVA were the rules of CASANOVA, I wrote about it (in what was the backmatter of CASANOVA: LUXURIA #7).

And then someone wrote me about it and said I deserved it. That *we* deserved it.

I suppose my punchline, then, is that *someone was mean to me on the internet* but that's not really the whole of it; *someone was mean to me on the internet and I started to think I deserved it* is maybe more on-point. Because I couldn't protect my wife and children born, unborn, or otherwise from that kind of shit, and even worse I felt like I couldn't punch back. Or rather – I felt punching back would've been a mistake. And I like craft and I like talking about craft and thinking about it and reading about it but that suddenly wasn't about that at all; it was just some anonymous shitbag being mean because they didn't like me and thought our miscarriage was, I dunno, *funny*. Or at least *fair game*.

I felt and feel otherwise and if I'm being honest, here's the point where I start pulling up the drawbridges and arming the ramparts against the outside world, started to self-negate and self-immolate by way of apologizing for *the nerve of me* daring to *talk about my shit*.

Maybe you could've handled it differently. Good for you.

13   He was twelve days early.

14   See?

15   But it wasn't.

16   This part, at least, is accurate. By design I wanted every arc of CASANOVA to be different, to feel different, to read differently than what came before. Every chapter, every act. It means having to reinvent the goddamn thing every time a new story starts but that's the rules of the game. Well of this particular game anyway.

I thought, and never once disagreed. When an un-say-no-able opportunity like THE UMBRELLA ACADEMY[17] comes along, and Bá and I realized he'd not likely be drawing 8-15, I immediately thought back to Fábio. I dunno if Bá did or not, but I remember talking it over with the boys at San Diego, trying to convince them it was the right move. Surely if anyone could follow Bá, it'd be the third man present at the book's birth, and the project's godfather. AND we'd have that whole cutesy-pie twin thing going on behind the scenes that just tickled me to no fucking end.[18]

I don't envy him the job, especially with an issue like this.

But the second I saw Kaito go splashing through the woods, cursing. I new we'd be in great shape.

Casanovanauts! Meet your new art hero, and mine, Mr. Fábio Moon[19]:

"I must be crazy, taking over the art duties on this book" crossed my mind a million times every time Matt and I chatted about me replacing my brother. I followed close the production of every page of Casanova and, besides Bá, I was the only one looking at the complete process, from the early pencils he sent to Matt and the production crew, to more detailed pencils, to final inks. I was there when he chose that weird green. I saw the zillions sketches he made of each character, of each gun, of each weird thing Matt would write on each script[20]. I was the first one to say, "Bá is perfect for this book," and after he did it, I was the first to say, "I can't imagine anyone else drawing it but him."

Now I'm drawing it.

Damn.

I spend seven issues and one year worth of work reading Matt tell in the backmatter how everything in his life could influence what he'd write in the book, and that was certainly true about how Bá approached the art as well, but for me, it's like the opposite. I fell like I'm inside a Casanova episode where I began as a reader of my evil twin's work and now I'm on a different timeline where I'm the twin in charge.

I am my own evil twin!

•

And so that's our song-and-dance this time around, Casanovanauts. If you want in on the e-newsletter supersecret CASANOVA society, drop us a line at casanovaquinn@gmail.com[21]. Put something charming and sexy in the subject line. This gluttonous new era demands nothing less of you.

Welcome back, and thanks.

Fraction
KC MO
05.14.07

GULA 2, Issue 9 (Image Comics, 2007)

Hiyah, earthmen,

"Thelonius Godchild[22]" is another one of those characters I've been trying to shoehorn in since, I dunno, CASANOVA #2, I think. I couldn't find space for him until this mention. I was walking the dogs[23] and listening to The Apples in Stereo; the entirety of Kubark's monologue fell into my head. I didn't even need to write it down: the cadence, the beats, even his kicker—"the old pa-ZOW," which would be pronounced "pa-zeeeaaaaaaooow'—bloop. There is was. Thelonius was so excited to materialize, even in this acorporeal[24] form, that he brought along Kubark's into speech with him.

•

Orson Welles' mentalist was teaching me how to disappear cards. Always a difficult student, instead of asking questions about the gag, I kept focusing on the bigger-picture issues. Audience manipulation, stagecraft, theory—never mind making the fucking card vanish, I wanted to know about tipping points and nonverbal cues and all that noise.

There's a thematic thing going on with magic and performers in this book. It started in our last album with David X, who may or may not

---

17   For a long time only Gerard Way (who wrote UMBRELLA) and I were the only people that knew Bá and Moon didn't really *need* to work with writers, they were just *deigning* to work with writers. And then the boys did DAYTRIPPER and now the whole world knows. Gerard and I still laugh about it.

18   I don't remember it like this at all now. In my mind it was always going to be rotational but... well, shit, who knows.

19   This is legitimately written by Fábio. Me, deflecting. *Let's fill these pages with someone else.*

20   The most trenchant observation anyone's ever made about my writing were the boys, talking about my CASANOVA scripts: "The first line you write (of a panel description) is for us. The rest is just for you."

21   I long since stopped looking at that email address. In fact, I missed Michael Chabon reaching out as a fan to that email address.

22   See CASANOVA: ACEDIA #2, coming in 2015.

23   In fact, the whole twist of GULA came while walking those goddamn dogs. But more on that during the wrap-up.

24   Is that a word.

meet his end here, and continues on. We'll get back to that later in the book—especially in #11—but it's clearly a theme I'm thinking about and I have to confess I'm not sure why[25].

Eventually, I got to the point where the cards would disappear. I'd keep one in my pocket, so I'd have something to do with my hands. Out and about in the world, I'd surreptitiously do it for little kids when nobody else was looking.

•

Kubarn, Ahhh, Kubark. Before I go on, here's a note from Fábio about designing the family Benday:

Kubark was supposed to have afro hair, but I just couldn't do it. I tried (and Matt and Bá will be the only witness to that sketch), but it didn't look right. It didn't look bad-ass, and Kubark is the bad-ass sexy guy. White dude with afro hair? Not sexy. So I started thinking about how to keep the giant crazy hair idea and do something different, and I also tried to think about how I would draw his father, another crazy villan, and how to make them similar. The crazy hair got out of control—literally—I came to the final versions of the family duo.

Kubark went all the way to my teenager years, when I read Akira and thought Tetsuo was a crazy cool bad guy with that punk hair. I then noticed that crazy hair on bad guys of the fashion world, mostly photographers, and then I decided crazy hair was cool. So Kubark, our cool bad guy, needed that crazy hair.

Even if he now looks like Dragonball Wolverine.

Doctor Benday was easier because I had already defined the crazy hair for his son. I just made him bald on the top and gave him a crazy mustache and beard. Oh, and crazy eyebrows (which will get crazier as issues pass), which any decent mastermind must have. I instantly fell in love with his design, and also it instantly reminded me of another Manga reading of mine: Itto Ogami's nemesis, Retsudo Yagiu. Since father and son made me think of probably my only Manga influences, I decided I was on the right track and went crazy with them.

Now, every time I look at Doctor Benday, I think of Warren Ellis. I never met Warren Ellis, but I imagine him looking like this. I know he's very tall, but my little doctor of evil reminds me of him and I blame it all on Matt for knowing Warren and talking about him and stuff.

So there, Retsudo Warren Ellis and Dragonball Wolverine are now ready to take over the world.

•

"White dude with afro hair not sexy," Fábio? Really? Say hello to Sam Fucking Humphries:

This is my pal Sam[26], the visual inspiration in the script for Kubark. I think someone (Fábio) owes someone else (Sam) an apology.

So, "Kubark" as a word is explained next issue, for those of you not into Google, but 'Benday' might need some explanation, too, for those of you not wholly obsessed with the minutiae of comics.

"Benday Dots" were the names of the dots that produced the coloring effects used by 4-color comics in the fifties and sixties. They're the little, overlapping, tightly or loosely spaced colored dots that make everyone—Roy Lichtenstein included—think "comic book!" when they see them. They were named after the illustrator Benjamin Day, and I couldn't imagine a more perfect surname for my comic book character[27].

•

Oh! Yeah, so, Zeph is back.

I remember, maybe a couple weeks into this album, getting up and running, after Fábio had sent me a sketchbook page or two of Casanova, that I needed to break the news to him that Casanova was really off the table for the foreseeable future and what he really needed to get used to drawing was Zeph.

I wrote her wearing some kind of, I don't know, Emma Peel dress in this scene—something about a woman in a long gown and a gun— so I have no idea where Fábio got this heart-covered pajama top look for her. In my head? She totally looked way sluttier[28].

•

High atop ever-churning Turkey Creek is waydowntown Miriam, Kansas, a man named Russell Sifers carries the unholy burden that has

---

25   It's still there. I think I have a story about magicians in me somewhere.

26   That's Sam Humphries, author of, among other things, OUR LOVE IS REAL, SACRIFICE, and, currently, THE LEGENDARY STAR-LORD.

27   In this digital age, in this age of printing presses that are not giant pieces of crap, Benday dots are a relic of the past. And like digital grain added to high-definitions video footage, digital comickers have started to mimic the effect but, like that digital grain, it's too mathematically perfect, too geometric. Benday dots gave comics a kind of tooth, a grit, a texture that we've obliterated in an era of smoother paper and better printers. I think comics these days tend to look like little boys forced into blazers and clip-on ties on Easter Sunday.

28   In case I am unclear: he was right, I was wrong, his way is better. This is the joy of collaboration: your partners make you look better, smarter, more elevated, more mature, than you actually are.

defined his family for six generations now—he makes candies. VALOMILK candies, to be specific[29]. Or chocolates? I'm not sure what the proper nomenclature is, but I know that they are delicious, that I love them, and that you life is a hollowed-out candy-less shell if you, too, have not had to deal with a Valomilk dribble down your goddamn chin.

The thing is, Valomilk's are made by hand, one batch at a time, with fresh ingredients with as much of the original equipment as they can. Add to that the killer design on the wrapper and you might as well be back in 1931.

You know how your grandparents (or parents, or whomever) complain about things not tasting the way they used to? [30]I didn't get that until I tried a Valomilk.

Kansas City, where I live, was a workingman's town, the midway point between Chicago and Texas, and a goddamn lot of livestock—cows and pigs and whatever else—came through here. Pig, as a rule, is cheaper than cow. All that means KC is sorta known for its barbecue, but if I had my druthers it's be the Valomilk town all the way.

Words can't express how much I love Siefer's VAL-O-MILK candies. They are as orgasmically great as Kubark Benday describes.

You can visit the Sifers on the web at

http://www.valomilk.com

And order 'em online here

http://www.oldtimecandy.com/valomilk.htm[31]

•

The setup:

Two bulls, a young one and an old one, are standing on a hill, overlooking all these hot young cows in the pasture below.

"Hey," says the young bull, "I'm gonna run down this hill and fuck one of them cows."

•

Man, if you ever find yourself writing your comic and feeling like, boy, I sure could spruce up the pace a little bit, might I suggest inexplicably setting one of your locations on the moon?[32] Because it is RIDICULOUSLY FREEING. All of my thinking, as the Dude once said, was really uptight. Getting E.M.P.I.R.E. onto the moon did something in my head, opened up a range of possibility that I'd never connected with before.

As the album continues, and you start to see more and more...I dunno, New Wave flourishes...creeping through, know that, somehow, it all came from putting a fucking base on the moon[33].

•

Now is a good time to tell you to go watch Gerry Anderson's U.F.O.[34]

•

Sasa Lisi. Sasa Lisi, Sasa Lisi, Sasa Lisi. Everything I can do to put her in a different costume form scene to scene, I do. I go into ridiculous detail describing her clothes—I think I'm apologizing to her for keeping her offstage so long. Literally, if I had the time and energy and didn't think Fábio would kill me, I'd inexplicably change her outfit every time we changed camera angles.

I love the zero-g effect Fábio gives her hair inside the bubble on the last panel of page 5[35].

•

SASA LISI: THE GIRL FROM M.O.T.T.[36]

---

29   All true. Bing it.

30   There was some kind of grammatical apocalypse here that I've corrected. Sue me.

31   I had some not long ago and they remain totally Worth It.

32   Totally true. And totally the best part about this ridiculous job. And an important rule I learned for writing CASANOVA: stop worrying so goddamn much and trust you'll land safely.

33   This is the most process-wonk thing I think that's been said here so far, and the thing I can really see starting to change in my work around this time. I stopped *giving a shit about why there were rules* and started instead to focus on *giving a shit about making the story better*. I'd start chopping boring scenes out, tiresome bits; I'd start making fun of the clichés as a way to get through them (because, as we learned last time, *the genre demands it*); I'd stop thinking about A-B-C and start wondering why not C-A-B, if C-A-B made the journey more engaging.

I think about this shit too much.

34   There is never a *bad* time to watch Gerry Anderson's U.F.O.

35   This remains true. Sasa remains my favorite character in a lot of ways.

36   The closest to figuring out what that stands for – Monkey Otter Tater-Tot – gets blown out of the water by M. Chabon in CASANOVA: ACEDIA #1.

See what I mean by "New Wave flourishes?" Is that panel diagetic, or metadiagetic, or mimetic, or...or what? What the hell is that image? What does it mean?

I dunno. I don't spend too much time thinking about it. The more I write CASANOVA, the more it becomes like automatic writing. Who is Sasa Lisi? She's the Girl from M.O.T.T. If she was a movie poster, she'd look like this.[37]

(Also: Paco Rabanne sneaks back in the book via Sasa's skirt.)

Oh! There's a reason why Seychelle recognizes Sasa right off. If you think it through, you'll figure it out before we explain it.[38]

I dunno if SISTER FISTER will actually appear. I dunno if Sister Fister is a real character. As she purports to be a "kung-fu voodoo queen," I'd say it's a safe bet she'll go from punchline to a character sooner rather than later.[39]

•

"It's gonna take you people YEARS to recover from all the damage," is from the Mountain Goats song, "Up the Wolves." It was playing as I wrote the scene. Literally, as I typed "SASA:" and tabbed over three times, John Darnielle sang the lyric and I transcribed it[40].

"Visions come to prepared spirits."[41]

That's not a lyric, but it doesn't seem to make it any less true.

•

I'm starting to see things in the work that aren't actually there. It occurs to me that the cow joke is in a Liz Phair song called "California," off the record JUVENLIA. Then on WHIP-SMART there's a song called "Crater Lake."

Wholly unintentional, but if you were looking for obtuse references in the work and you saw Liz Phair, I couldn't argue that it wasn't, in fact, there.[42]

•

I love the easy physical intimacy Fábio infuses the Kaito/Ruby scene. The casual nudity and comfort, the décor of the space, their body language—the way she tussles his hair!—all of it. I love them loving each other, I totally by that they're a couple, and I love the breadth it gives the two of them. And that's all on Fábio—I'm not patting my own back—I'm saying I'm falling in love with the way Fábio shows Kaito and Ruby falling in love[43].

You know what it reminds me of? Pope's THE BALLAD OF DR. RICHARDSON.

(Am I imagining that familiar design on the pillowcase?)

"Be Ready and Be Brave." I need to send Darnielle a check I think.

•

Ooooph, man, then it goes and gets wordy.

There's a famous rule of thumb that I ignore as often as I obey that says you should aim for about 210 words a page, every page. I think it was Mort Weisinger's rule, and I heard about it from Warren Ellis, who got from Alan Moore. Then you figure no more than 35 words a panel. And then try to keep it to, like, 27 words a balloon, mac, or else it'll look too big[44].

Page 9 pisses on that rule, points at is, laughs, takes its picture, send that picture to the rule's mom, posts a phonecam quicktime of the pissing onto YouTube, and then sets up a CafePress "Pissin' on the Rules" t-shirt and thong emporium.

But hey: we had a lot of pipe to put down. And in a book that's refused to explain itself to YOU, the reader, I had finally gotten to a scene where two characters needed to explain themselves to one another.

It's funny: as I write this, I've put CASANOVA #11 to bed (mostly) and have cranked out several more Marvel scripts and have, in the last few weeks, for whatever reason, become more and more obsessed with the Weisinger Algebra. If I had to write this page NOW,

---

37   Exactly the kind of thing I was thinking about. It was revolutionary to me, to my work. And if I'm being honest the beginning of the end of my Marvel career having a bloom on it. Because after a while you (I) spin against the way those kinds of stories drive, and the people that read them sometimes don't dig that they way you dig that. And that's totally fair and deserved when you (I) try to make these vehicles move in ways they're not meant to move. You buy a ticket for an airplane, you don't want a ride on a boat. Y'know?

38   CASANOVA: ACEDIA #1. Sort of.

39   Not yet.

40   This isn't new to the way I work; I've always grabbed snatches of things out of the air and integrated it into my stuff. Whether that's a preference for collage, growing up in the era of sampling, art school damage or what, I don't know. What's new, however, is how doing stuff like this, referencing work I dig, spreads out from my work like radial waves from an antennae that get picked up by the people I so admire and adore. Like Darnielle, whose first novel, WOLF IN WHITE VAN, is completely great.

41   Ever hear about the Benzene ring?

42   Oh this is grasping at straws. I'm not sure that I buy into cryptomnesia.

43   See CASANOVA: ACEDIA #3.

44   This rule, like a posted speed limit, is really an advisory that no one ever pays attention to, except when they do. When they don't you can tell. When they do you can't, even when they break the rule. How is that possible? And yet.

here, tonight, it would be wildly different. But tonight? Tonight I say fuck you, Mort Weisinger. I might be a hack but you're dead so you can suck it.[45]

"A time traveller that loves to step on butterflies," is, of course, a reference to Bradbury's "A Sound of Thunder."

•

Sasa's arms need no explanation[46].

•

Kubark, in the helicopter, signs the backwards parts of "Open Eyes" from The Apples in Stereo's NEW MAGNETIC WONDER, only he's singing them forwards. Angain, it was what was on when I wrote the panel, so I dug around for what Robert Schneider was singing.

•

I saw a picture of X.S.M. Island once, but I don't remember where it came form and I don't remember what it was. But is say in my CASANOVA V2 file for, like, a year, waiting for this issue to come along.

Yes, I know what they're building.

No, Kubark and Zeph do not.

Yes, you'll find out by the end of the arc.

•

I love the Lara Croft: Camp Counselor outfit Fábio had Zeph in at the end of the book. And Doctor Benday's insistence that everybody eat[47] is somehow more fun when it comes out of that weird little science hobbit. I love the way Fábio draws Zeph so taken aback by Doc Benday's genuine enthusiasm and decorum at meeting her. She's a lady that's not often been treated like a lady in her life.

As evidenced by Newman Xeno creeping back into it. Even when he's not around, he's around. To me, he's like a choking black cloud of death and doubt, the kind of anxiety you can bottle up and show into the back of your psychic fridge for a little while, but, ultimately, one that can't be ignored forever. Sooner or later, everybody has to deal with their own Xenos.

You, me, and Zephyr Quinn included[48].

MF
KCMO
7 AUG 07

GULA 1, Issue 1[49] (Icon Comics, 2011)

BRYAN LEE O'MALLEY[50] made a comic this one time called SCOTT PILGRIM'S PRECIOUS LITTLE LIFE, which begat SCOTT PILGRIM VS. THE WORLD which begat SCOTT PILGRIM & THE INFINITE SADNESS which begat SCOOT PILGRIM GETS IT TOGETHER which begat SCOTT PILGRIM VS. THE UNIVERSE which begat SCOTT PILGRIM's FINEST HOUR which begat a major fucking motion picture and the most fun I had in a theater since INGLORIOUS BASTERDS—Edgar Wright's SCOTT PILGRIM VS. THE WORLD—which begat a 20-story Michael Cera on the side of a goddamn hotel at San Diego this past summer. Surreal doesn't begin to describe it[51].

Mal and I started taking stabs at making comics around the same time; we both had our first graphic novels published in 2003 (his, LOST AT SEA, mine LAST OF THE INDEPENDENTS). When I think of my classmates, as it were, I think of Mal. And now I think of Mal and am awed by this journey his singular vision and focus took him on and could not be more pleased for him. I love it when my friends become successful, and when they earn it, it's even sweeter[52].

That the two comics that most dominated the San Diego Comicfuck Orgy of Death and Hollywood Entertainment this past summer were

---

45   Now go read Stephen Sondheim's FINISHING THE HAT and come crawling back, Past-Matt, you supercilious asshole, you dumby, you vamping little prick.

46   Eh.

47   *Gula.* Gluttony.

48   This is me, telling me to *shake it off.* As well as tipping my hand towards the end of V3, but whatever. Nobody knows what I'm ever talking about anyway.

49   Because LUXURIA #1 was long, a short story was added to the first issue of reprints to bring the page count to 32; the subsequent 16-page issues were collected two-at-a-time and reprinted at Icon. Now, because symmetry?, GULA would collect two-at-a-time until it's extra-sized finale issue which, when *it* first appeared, contained a new short story. It's here at the end and teases AVARITIA. This is the very definition of "trivia."

50   Continuing on in the Icon reprints of GULA were interviews with other cartoonists, writers, and/or people making work I admire. They were usually friends, too, which helps.

51   More obfuscation: I came home from that convention and my father was in the hospital with a collapsed lung. And lung cancer. And then my mom got breast cancer. And then Aunt Polly got cancer. And then Kel's dad got cancer.

52   The longer I stay in comics the more I recognize this in myself as a rare trait in the industry, except in people that manage, somehow, to stay in the industry for a long time. I know correlation isn't necessarily indicative of causality but, hey, there you go.

two independent black and white comics that were ordered, on their initial release, in numbers that matched my SAT score[53] delights me to no end.

This started as kind of now-that-the-dust-has-settled-how-are-you email chain; then there was a break as the SCOTT DVD release ramped up again. That's okay, though. This tends to be rather how we communicate, when we communicate. There's been very little editorial revision inflicted here. If it gets jumbled or confusing or in-jokey or referential…well, it's CASANOVA, what the hell do you expect?

•

Bryan Lee O'Malley: For your column, by the way, what kinds of things would you want to talk about?

I'm sure I could find a way to pontificate. I just don't know where I'm at right now, culturally.

Six years of work, bigger and bigger and bigger and then boom, the movie's tanked and that's all she wrote. What a weird world.

Matt Fraction: We could talk about anything for the column, really. It doesn't HAVE to be about your SP experience at all—in fact, unless we came up with some really interesting angle on it, I'd really rather avoid it. Like, I'd want to come at it obliquely. I'd want to ask questions about how these last six years treated you but nothing terribly SP-specific. Processy shit.

Basically, the impetus to do these backup pieces came from getting my life threatened on the internet, finally, and the anonymous superhero that wrote in to tell me nobody wanted to hear about hipsters having miscarriages[54]. That was kind of my breaking point.

Instead of talking about the book or what *I* thought or was thinking—about my process AT ALL—I just wanted to recede entirely. Then a couple high school pals died[55] and I decided I wanted to talk to people I knew because of comics, because of my work, because of work itself, because of CASANOVA, whatever—about the stuff they capital-L love, people I met because I got the fuck out of my death trap hometown through my work and now have this amazing professional life, all things considered. So I wanted to try and put stuff out there that might inspire—arrogant as that sounds—whomever it is will one day do the next CASANOVA or SCOTT PILGRIM or whatever. I want to make something like Morrison's run on DOOM PATROL; something where, like, if you're 14 or 15 years old and suddenly there's this thing you like reading and it's full of references to OTHER cool things, you go out and start digging.

The first issue I just rattled off stuff I loved that fed into CASANOVA—DIABOLIK and all that stuff. Then me and Michael Chabon talked about superspies. Me and Mike Doughty talked about getting sober and how it influences writing. Me and Chaykin did a kind of evaluation of AMERICAN FLAGG! I'm trying to talk to John Darnielle but we can't quite seem to get our act together.

Shit, we could talk about Radiohead, for all I care. Or Tezuka, whatever.

Mal: I haven't had my life threatened. I've been trolled a bit since the movie raised my (SP's) profile, but just snarky assholes who are nerds but not the right kind of nerd, nerds who don't get it or see it as pandering or see it as kids' stuff or see it as "gay" or whatever. I've stayed away from the mainstream and I guess I've avoided having my life threatened, so that's nice[56].

And yeah, you know, I was so stoked on THE INVISIBLES around the time I first started thinking about Pilgrim. I came to Morrison late, but of course I branched out and read the PKD and the science and the Gnostic texts and everything. And now I see kids doing the same with Pilgrim, but only leads to dead ends like Nintendo games.

I worry that all I'm good for is examining the content of my own brain, like I can't make new neural connections or something.

OH WELL.

MF: Don't sell yourself short on tracing the postmodern cultural resonance of THE CLASH AT DEMONHahfuck I can't even go through with the sentence.

I remember buying NAKED LUNCH because of DOOM PATROL on a…9th grade field trip to Washington DC. And JUNKY. Jesus CHRIST I bought JUNKY and NAKED LUNCH on a school field trip, Jesus Christ. I used to hide that I was reading INVISIBLES from my comics friends as it had such a patina of…deliberate obtuse-ness and…like, educational shame or whatever. Like, INVISIBLES was the comic that always looked a little bit like homework.

Um…the letter columns there, and in INVISIBLES a few years after that were completely indispensable if you were, like, the weird kid in rural NC and knew you wanted to get the fuck out.

I still have my copy of WHEN RABBIT HOWLS[57] from that time. Dunno when or where I sold the Burroughs but they're long gone…

Mal: Yeah, being the one Asian kid in bleak Northern Ontario probably didn't hurt my chances of identifying strongly with the

---

53   Hint: less than 1000.

54   Yeah, well. There you go.

55   Oh yeah. There was that, too. Goodnight, Jay. Goodnight, Ry.

56   I actually forgot about that until I read this. Guy threatened to kill me at a convention. Made videos showing how he was going to smuggle the weapons in his backpack. Because of course it's a backpack.

57   An early precedent for what I wanted abstractly to do with the CASANOVA backmatter: Morrison, in his letter columns, would talk about all the Stuff he was reading or watching and how it was influencing what he was making. And in those days when The Internet meant paying thirty dollars a month for a 14.4K connection to a corporate-curated BBS, that kind of stuff was gold.

Uncanny X-Men when I was ten. Outsider stories have always been my thing, so I'm not sure how I ended up doing this ultimate insider story and being embraced by nerd culture. I guess they're all outsiders too.

It's just, like, since the movie started or...even...I don't even know. I think the last two Pilgrim books and the movie just blurred into this giant mass that devoured my life from late 2008 to now. Two years of my mind being turned to mush.

So like I don't want to harp on that but my mush-mind has nothing else in it. I got nothing. Culture is opaque to me. I watched Kanye West be the only remotely realistic or talented or human thing on the MTV VMAs the other day, for whatever reason. I have a copy of KING CITY #11 in front of me. I started reading the Franzen, really only because my UK publisher publishes it over there and gave me a giant hardcover copy. It's good so far. It's about humans.

What did I like when I was younger? What went in? I made this big list earlier this year, all the COMICS that went in. I'm just gonna copy and paste it:

TRANSFORMERS #19 at the drug store when I was 7 years old -> Marvel -> X-MEN -> X-FORCE -> Image -> GEN 13 -> high school -> ugh, comics -> (but I was still drawing them, secretly, all by myself) -> staring at BONE #19 on the shelf for 3 weeks and eventually buying it because I felt bad about handling it so many times -> BONE, CEREBUS, REPLACEMENT GOD -> SAILOR MOON on YTV -> anime -> RANMA 1/2 -> RANMA 1/2 manga -> like every other manga I could find in the late '90s -> I FEEL SICK -> SETH, IT'S A GOOD LIFE IF YOU DON'T WEAKEN, because it was set in Southwestern Ontario -> HICKSVILLE[58] -> Bendis & stuff -> Paul Pope, HEAVY LIQUID -> tracking down every other Paul Pope book that ever existed -> Jamie Hewlett, TANK GIRL reprints that came out around the same time -> THE INVISIBLES! -> Grant Morrison -> PARADISE KISS -> mange boom -> manga in French that I couldn't get in English yet, like NANA -> older manga -> Tezuka manga -> everything.

We can also talk about this: over the last five years, my musical taste has completely swung in a different direction. I was all into soulful honesty and acoustic guitars and now all I listen to is plastic European pop, female singers with uni-names like Annie, Robyn. And, like, Das Racist. What happened to me? Or is it our culture? I mean, I thought the same thing watching the VMAs: the only indie rock I heard was in Honda and Converse commercials. Plastic pop and glitzy hip-hop is where we're at as a culture, musically.

MF: I hit a patch where MK12 was going on, on one hand, and my nights were full of trying to write comics, on the other, and I just completely burned out. I didn't want to do, write, make, shoot, or say anything anymore. I stopped listening to music and writing and doing anything at all that involved any kind of art in any way, actively or passively.

So I got invited to speak at a design conference in Memphis, to do the MK12 dog and pony show, and the keynote was this guy named Marc English. Marc did this thing, this "design shamanism" sort of spoken-word slide thing. It was, I swear to god, life-changing. He traced, basically, his entire life concurrent with his understanding and development as a designer. Really amazing. Anyway, so I got home from that and did something like that for myself where I re-watched, re-read, or re-listened to any piece of art or media that I'd ever loved. And somewhere in the middle of ALPHAVILLE, I started to write again.

I was noticing the other day that my music crushes burn out way faster these days: I was obsessed with the new M.I.A. for a few days; the new Teddybears or Pendulum or whatever. I don't remember the last time I compulsively listened to a guitar record. I told you the other day that, like, I just don't get Arcade Fire, for example. Maybe last fall when the Beatles remasters came out. Or now I'm going through a Springsteen thing. But then, like, I'll listen to a shit-ton of drag/spook house stuff that's all like the Conet Project with a beat and space out while a baseball game is on. Kel can't listen to music that has lyrics when she writes. Maybe I can't listen to music that has feeling when I write anymore, I dunno.

That said, "Born to Run" sounds amazing in these Dr. Dre headphones[59].

Mal: I do this thing where I make a mixtape for the book. The mixtape comes first. Scott Pilgrim vol. 1 had a mix, and I tried to recapture it with a new mix for each subsequent volume but never as successfully. This new thing I'm working on has a mix that I started compiling in 2005. Still tinkering. I dunno, it feels ridiculous but I really like having the mixed to set the mood when I'm making notes and writing. It's not like I listen to it on repeat, but once in a while I'll pop it on to get my head in the right space.

This was Hope's bday weekend and I'm hung over as shit and it's horrible.

MF: ROBOTECH streaming on Netflix. Nothing ever gets written again. Hats off to Roy (Focker).

Mal: I know, I'm waiting for the day I start up that shit. Game over man, game over.

(TIME PASSES)

OK, so, it's been a while since we talked—six weeks?

I assume we're both listening to the Kanye record now. It came out. I think it's great. I joke on Twitter about how I can't relate to anyone except Kanye West anymore, but it's only half-joking. My life is pretty ridiculous, more ridiculous than an indie cartoonist's like is even supposed to get. 30,000 followers on Twitter is a lot of voices to have screeching in your head. So, I mean, I get a lot out of the Kanye record.

I haven't gotten the Springsteen thing, the Promise box set. I guess it should go on my Xmas list.

---

58 So good. So, so good.

59 I can hardly listen to anything while I work anymore, not even a ballgame. I think it's because my time is at such a premium I'm worried literally any distraction will derail the whole thing.

This Fall has been weird. You can imagine. It's the comedown from six years of this one thing, the END OF AN ERA if you want to get pretentious.

In the weeks since we last spoke I did a bunch of press for the DVD release of SCOTT PILGRIM VS. THE WORLD (it's very available in almost all stores, that's a plug for your readers) and came home and got a new puppy and then Thanksgiving and now I'm exhausted. I don't want to go anywhere or do anything. I'm trying to write new stuff, but, honestly, I'm mostly just fucking around on Twitter and buying books and movies and pretending to do research.

I'm tired. I'm cranky. I had to go to ComicCon and then get over myself and then pretend I'm a movie star and then get over myself again and it's all taxing and nobody every really wants to talk about it. I mean, I don't even want to talk about it. I sound like an asshole talking about it. So there, that's all I'm going to say about it. It had its ups and downs, I feel positive about the whole thing, but I'm also pretty tired of it and fortunately the main part of my job is rolling around my house thinking of ideas and then turning them into comics. That sounds really great right now. Really great.

I kind of wish I had more vices that I could disappear into, but I don't smoke, I hardly drink. My vice is procrastination, and everyone keeps telling me I deserve a break, which isn't helping.

MF: I—I don't think I told you my Kanye stories—but I worked with the dude on a video. I, uh, turned him into a supervillian in INVINCIBLE IRON MAN later. He is a piece of fucking work. It's all hilarious now but it was lousy to have to live through.

Anyway, so I checked out the new record because of that "douchebag" song; it seemed remarkably self-aware for the dude. The whole record is...like a wildly ornate car-crash. There's literally nothing that made me a fan from THE COLLEGE DROPOUT here. Instead it's... like a countdown to a rich guy's inevitable overdose...and, uh, I've caught myself gawking. I'm not proud.

You want to know what the dictionary definition of "First World Problems" is? "Self-imposed exile in Oahu."

What does that guy have to say about anything these days? When you've got Das Racist, OFWGKTA, and Curren$y fucking tearing shit up...who gives a fuck that you got Nicki Minaj to pretend to be British? What I dig about FANTASY is the coke-and-pussy opulence and decadence and...and that it feels like, uh, like STATION TO STATION. Like that moment of cracking up captured and put to tape. That record's a fucking warning.

The Springsteen documentary is remarkable. There's something kind of...y'know, there's that COMPLEX piece now, where they tried to do the, like, oral history of the making of the new Kanye record, as though it were hip hop's White Album or something, yeah? So read that, and then watch the Springsteen documentary. They tell the same story of an artist struggling to both accept the fact that he wants GREATNESS and the fact that that means he has to deliver GREATNESS...and the other is about a jerkoff millionaire like Kanye West.

Did you draw or write or commit ANYTHING to the page that wasn't SCOTT over the last two-three years? How monofocused have you been? And what does that do to your head?

Mal: I like the STATION TO STATION comparison, actually, and that's kind of my favorite Bowie album, so...I guess I just like slow-motion wrecks? I still romanticize the debauched decadence of a rock star tailspin? I do think he has great ideas, or at least is able to shape other people's great ideas into something kind of amazing. I can't apologize for liking him but I can completely understand hating him. That's the problem with having perspective.

So to answer you question: no. Wait—yes. I can't remember the question. The answer is: I have been working on Scott Pilgrim since I can remember. I did book 4, then I moved to NC and was immigrating and trying to have a life, then book 5, then the movie happened, and book 6 during that, then I moved to LA, and then the big promo whirlwind devoured the past six months. No other work, no development, no time for love Dr. Jones. Just writing it, drawing it, selling it. I have had my fill, I am sick of it.

And now all day on the internet I hear, "You should do more Scott Pilgrim," and, "When are you going to continue Scott Pilgrim?" and, "I'll like whatever you do, but I really hope you do more Pilgrim," or even just the baseline assumption that I'm going to be doing more Pilgrim, like what else would I do? And that can be discouraging. All the chatter can be discouraging, but the chatter is a way of life now. I'm still figuring out how to navigate it.

I mean, the problems of my work are totally first world problems. I have fans and they would like me to continue producing work they enjoy waaahhhhhhh.

The new experience I'm having is that, well, as you might have guessed, Pilgrim is, um, I mean, I've been "writing what I know," so to speak, which is being in a relationship, playing video games, being in a band, and retreating into an elaborate fantasy world (lol). Now I'm trying to write about something else, someone else, new places, things I haven't specifically lived through. New protagonists in new situations that I can't just pluck out of thin air. Pilgrim had the automatic verisimilitude of taking place in my city and in my own recognizable milieu, and if I want to do new things I have to create verisimilitude the hard way, by doing RESEARCH and shit, UGH.

Now I'm the guy sitting on the back porch in December in Los Angeles, it's 11 AM and I'm in the shade because the sun is a little too hot. I'm the guy with the good life in California trying to dream up less-good lives in other, colder places. It's a cliché, but it's where I want to be.

MF: I can't wait for you to blow it[60].

---

60   He didn't; Mal's follow-up to the Scott Pilgrim cycle, called SECONDS, came out in 2014 and is in every way remarkable. More mature, more confident, more complex, more ambitious, and more satisfying, artistically, I think, for it all. Fuck you, Mal.

GULA 3, Issue 10 (Image Comics, 2007)

Hiyah, earthmen,

You know how Jon Bon Jovi has seen a million faces, and he's rocked 'em all? Well I've attended a million film schools, and I dropped out of 'em all. Well, three, but you get what I'm talking about, right[61]?

Anyway at one of them there was an absolutely extraordinary private film archive owned by a guy named Raymond J. Regis. Ray had everything, man, every movie you could ever want to see, several million you needed to see but never even heard of, and all of 'em in their pristine, preferred format of actual, honest-to-god celluloid. This was seeing Shakespeare as it was meant to be played, truly.

The school would show two, three of 'em a night in a small theater they build just for Ray and his outrageously excellent collection. Attendance was mandatory, most nights.

It was kind of like drowning in film. It was kind of like Heaven.

There were more than a few world-rocking movies Ray showed that, as an 18-year-old, managed to, well, rock my world. Charles Burnett's KILLER OF SHEEP comes to mind immediately. PINOCCHIO, on film, through an industrial grade sound-system. Ray's Technicolor master print of STAR WARS (one of only five in existence). The 70mm JAWS print that came from the UK. The night he showed the print of Lang's METROPOLIS, but insisting with his crooked Bahhhhstan giggle that it HAD to be the reissue with the Giorgio Moroder soundtrack. AFTER THE FOX. THE FORTUNE COOKIE. A gorgeous print of THE SEARCHERS. Or NORTH BY NORTHWEST and PSYCHO—I recall Ray had almost all of Hitchcock's works on film. THE THIRD MAN. Or THE MANCHURIAN CANDIDATE, which we all had seen, but had never wondered if Janet Leigh was activating Sinatra's programming during that weird scene between the two of 'em on the train—a notion that Ray couldn't WAIT to suggest to us after the screening, some time well after midnight.

Christ, I could go ON about Ray until after midnight[62].

Anyway. One night he loaded up a shorts program, one of which was Paul Bartel's THE SECRET CINEMA (1968). In it, a sweet but dimwitted girl (whom I recall as looking like Ellen Greene—a sweet bleach-blonde with raccoon eyes and a cute overbite that made her trembling chin look even more tremble-y) secretly being filmed by everyone in her life, all of whom were conspiring to drive her insane. It was cute. It was funny. It captured the sights and backdrops of the New York film scene in 1968 in beautiful 16mm photography. For whatever reason, it reverberated with me. I only saw it once but I can remember at least a couple dozen shots from the thing with perfect clarity.

Bartel would make DEATH RACE 2000 and EATING RAOUL and later remake the short as an episode of AMAZING STORIES.

The thing that his film had that no other Reality TV show or show/movie ABOUT reality TV had was that it was relentlessly and utterly cruel. The Secret Cinema existed to destroy lives, to anger, debase, and humiliate. The Secret Cinema was just mean.

Something about its malicious evil stuck with me. Nightmare of nightmares—I'm not paranoid that I'm being watched, I'm paranoid that I'm being laughed at...

He was "Mister Toppogrosso" in the film. But since he would be the therapist here, I made him 'Doctor.'

•

"Asa Nisi Masa.[63]" Any Fellini fans in the house? In 8 ½, "Asa Nisi Masa" is the spell-chant-drone that young Guido and his—what, sister, cousin, who was that little girl?—chanted at night, by the light of the fire, while staring at a painted portrait. The words made the picture move, y'see, its eyes pointing to hidden treasure as the phrase, the egg-latin mangling of the word 'anima,' points to the core of what 8 ½ is all about. Jung, of whom Fellini was a fan, says the anima is one's unconscious and true self, and the feminine inner personality.

And to Fellini, and his alter-ego, the blocked director Guido, they were the magic words that made pictures move.

•

Fellini, during the shooting of 8 ½, apparently taped a sign beneath his viewfinder that read REMEMBER: THIS IS A COMEDY[64].

On my computer is a Post-It that reads DON'T SUCK.

•

"Open your head and let the pictures come." The Stones.

•

"I want to shoot this guy so bad my dick is hard," was, I believe, a line from NEW JACK CITY. I think Ice-T said it. It always made me laugh. I love that Ice-T[65] plays cops now. There's a whole generation that knows him as a cop and not the O.G. Cop Killer that wasn't

---

61 Wrong.

62 I think about Ray often. One of *Those Teachers*, y'know?

63 I'm stealing the idea of getting this tattooed over my heart. Fuck it.

64 I should get that too, right under it.

65 I do an amazing Ice-T impression. And I met him once. Ask me some time to tell you my story about meeting Ice.

to Get Buck Naked and Fuck.

Awesome.

•

I didn't make up what KUBARK was. Is. Whatever. Here's an excerpt.

> Intense pain is quite likely to produce false confessions, concocted as a means of escaping from distress. A time-consuming delay results, while investigation is conducted and the admissions are proven untrue. During this respite the interrogate can pull himself together. He may even use the time to think up new, more complex "admissions" that take still longer to disprove. KUBARK is especially vulnerable to such tactics because the interrogation is conducted for the sake of information and not for police purposes.

Your tax dollars at work. Fun stuff.

•

The Lamb recipe: serving near night-blooming jasmine is ESSENTIAL. Do NOT waste your time on insult the Benday family recipe if you cannot enjoy the meal in precisely this manner[66].

In all seriousness, I think the inexplicable Sasa Lisi movie poster or whatever it was got me thinking about other stuff we could try.

Also: I love Fábio's little Chef Benday illo there in the corner.

•

I overwrote the shit out of the second panel of page eight, with Zeph on the couch with her arms folded. And Fábio adds one detail that actually nails what I was going for—her shoes being off, feet arched.

Fucking brilliant.

•

Flip-flopping Hera and Zeus[67]: In the pre-release hype leading up to the release of a Marvel book I write called THE ORDER, where these superhero-types are spiritually modeled after the pantheon of Greek gods, I flipped Hera and Zeus or Hera and Apollo, I don't remember which. But I flipped them. I was tired, I was sick, I'm pretty stupid to begin with and I just—I dunno, it was a human thing to do, I figured. Oops, a slip-up, we're all human, CLEARLY I didn't mis-recall the sec of these two god-figures, let's move on.

AND YET.

I decided to go a'lookin' on the internet to see how the pre-release hype was being received, as it was a new book with new characters and nobody had any idea what to make of it, and found a few places where I was getting hammered for swapping the names. Or rather, not for swapping the names but rather just misspeaking. It was clearly a brainfart moment and yet, thanks internet!, I/the book was not given the benefit of that particular doubt.

Anyway later when I wrote the scene I wanted to exorcise that one a little bit.

•

I love Toppogrosso's little fez. LOVE. IT. Fábio, what do YOU have to say about all this?

> The first time I read the name Toppogrosso, I immediately imagined Porco Rosso, a Miyazaky character who's kind of fat and has a pig nose on a kind of human face. I considered making Toppogrosso the villain with the pig face, since all is fair in the Casanova universe, but I later decided to go to a different direction and went after Ugarte, the strange big eyed friend of Rick on Casablanca, who looked like a sick pervert, only fatter. Way fatter. His posse, the secret cinema society thingie, always in black tie and masks, were cool to do as well, and it's strange how, at the same time I was drawing the same book again, and it felt good. It felt right.
>
> I love creating cool worlds, backgrounds, rooms, building and stuff like that. Exploring a little more of XSM Island was cool in that sense, not to mention the giant structure being built on page 8. I love when the whole "turn the page for a big review" works the way it worked there and shows the potential of comics. I have this impression that this second arc of Casanova has a lot more "big revealing panels" than the first arc, and I'm enjoying the different energy created by this kind of storytelling.
>
> Finally, the sex. Look at all this sex. I can't help but think Matt was about to have a baby (which he was) and was thinking about sex all the time by the time he wrote all these scenes (which probably is the case as well). Seriously, it was a challenge to draw the erotic content of this issue and keep it interesting as a story, making people get into the story and not distracted by all the nakedness. I hope I succeeded, even if the artist part of me made a real effort to make the reader drool over Zeph. It worked for me, maybe it will work for you.

•

And now we're back to ASA NISI MASA, tattooed on Zeph's breast.

---

66   I've never actually tried this.

67   I have to admit that, rereading this now, I'm amazed I went this far to try and lay down cover fire over the twist.

I once knew a guy. A writer. Incredibly pretentious. Wire-thin, tremendous hair. He had it tattooed across his heart. It was the coolest thing, man—the absolute BEST tattoo[68] on absolutely the WORST guy EVER.

Man, I hated that guy so much.

Anyway. It sounds dumb, but every time—every single time—I've been on a short, whether it's a video or a commercial or a short or a whatever-the-hell—I've written ASA NISI MASA somewhere on my skin. A hand, an arm, somewhere, anywhere. A little mantra to go to, a quiet little prayer that makes the pictures move. It's the closest thing to magic words I know.

One of the best producers I ever worked with is named Rosali. She saw the scribble on my hand and asked me what it meant. I told her. Sasa Lisi's name comes from the same word-game with Rosali's name that turned Anima into "Asa Nisi Masa." It'd be "Roso Sasa Lisi." Anyway. That's where 'Sasa Lisi' came from.

You knew why I love Fellini? His movies feel like my dreams feel.

•

Man, there sure is a lot of sex in this issue[69]. That's okay, though—the violence kicks in next time.

•

Oh yeah—one of those things I totally lied about[70].

•

Oh yeah oh yeah! My son was born on 9/9/07. His name is Henry Leo. Mother and son are doing just fine.

When I was researching this stuff to put these notes together, I read that Ray Regis passed away in June.

So goodnight, Ray. And good morning, Henry. May god be between you and all the empty spaces you walk.

Fraction
KC MO
18 Sept 07

GULA 4, Issue 11 (Image Comics, 2007)

Hiyah, earthmen,

Sometimes CASANOVA tried to kill me. This was, by far, the hardest script I've ever written, CASANOVA or otherwise[71]. It took forever, even once it was broken, and even then I fucked something up and had to get Fábio to redraw a panel at the last moment.

This is the halfway point in GULA, our second album, and by now it should be pretty apparent that it's a different piece of work than LUXURIA was—shit, I'd hope so; who wants to read the same comic book forever? Who expects a comic to remain the same forever[72][73]? I mean, this album would've been a single issue in LUXURIA. It's a different beast, with different concerns and objectives, different tools and different agendas. Hell, it's even turned into an ensemble book, for the love of god. So like I said. Different.

GULA means "gluttony" if you're into themes and motifs and shit. And this issue marks the turning point in that thematic obsession of ours/mine between gluttonous sex to gluttonous violence (there's a food preoccupation going on, too, if that's your thing. Lot's of eating and drinking, y'know?). Starting off this issue, I knew that here was where that shift occurred, at the halfway point—another thematic obsession being symmetries, twins, dualities, binary states, halves…

Anyway. Starting off, I knew that here was where the boobs go away and the blood starts to flow.

And I knew it was the Modesty Blaise issue.

And I knew the basic story—the kids infiltrate a casino, Zeph seduces the Boss, they misdirect their murder scheme by looking like clumsy thieves; all hell breaks loose, and the Lil' Rascals clue Sasa in on the moon. All of it, I had.

But I didn't have anything. No soul, no air in its lungs, no life. Bloodless, dumb, dim, nothing. I was stuck.

I hate you CASANOVA.

---

68   "Remember what Godard said: 'It's not where you take things from, it's where you take them to.'" - Jim Jarmusch.

69   Gluttony, gluttony. Everybody always eating, drinking, screwing, killing. What happens when you replace fight scenes with other moments of conspicuous and violent consumption?

70   Ahem.

71   CASANOVA is always the hardest thing to write. This one was special, though. Pulling this one off, formally, let me finally know I was a lifer, that me and comics were a special kind of thing that I wasn't going to be able to shake.

72   You'd be amazed.

73   Probably not.

When I get absolutely stuck it means something's not in the mix, and whatever it is I'm working on isn't ready to cook. Something's missing, and it's always odd. It's never, like, a major plot point or anything like that, it's always a small, seemingly inconsequential detail that nobody but me notices or cares about[74]. To take the first issue of CASANOVA for example, once upon a time I had the whole thing beaten out to a pancake in my head; I had whole scenes ready that landed in the issue line for line but I couldn't actually WRITE a line of it. It wasn't until the first page fell in my head, with the dumb little CITIZEN KANE riff (I mean, come ON), that I could start writing.

Other times it's a turn of phrase, an angle, a shot, a transition; a structural game to play, or a layout to work from, a grid to mutilate... it's never ever a broad essential. It's the hood ornament, not the engine. And yet, on some level, the hood ornament is always the essential Thing at the heart of it all, somehow—it's always the core to me.

I try to find it by dicking around a lot and working really hard at trying not to work. It never seems to happen like that, but I have too much of a Protestant work ethic to let myself actually physically leave the space in which I write[75].

So this time, seeking the hood ornament, I started to obsess on the number 11, since it's our 11th issue and everything. See? Clever. I started researching the number: Apollo 11. The Tarot cards for Strength and Justice, each of which can be the 11th card, depending on who you ask. The mythology behind those cards. Sodium, silver, copper, and gold. M-theory. Himalia, the 11th moon of Jupiter. Hendecagons and Aquarius and the Wild Duck Cluster of stars. Solar cycles. Armistice Day.

These are the desperate and ridiculous straws I grasped at, convinced that I would spark to what the issue was Really About, that the structure would sit up and sing suddenly, that I was, in fact, a real writer, just like Alan Moore, and I was full of bright, big, important, and horribly clever ideas rife with intelligence and wit that would spill off of every panel of every page.

Yeah. Right.

So I kept waiting, hoping to god that Fábio would fall behind on the production of #10 and buy me more time.

Because apparently CASANOVA isn't easy to draw, either.

I don't know what makes Casanova such a hard comic to draw. I saw Bá doing it, and it took him so long, and I kept thinking "he's such a wuss, I'm doing two pages a day and he can't finish his 16 pages in one month." His pages, to me, always turned out awesome, getting better all the time, so I left out of the equation the possibility he didn't like the story (which, for me, and for us, makes us poorer artists when it does happen), so the reason for all this time he spent on each page got to be somewhere else. At first, Bá and I discussed the possibility that doing every page with four rolls of panels, and keep the page interesting and the flow natural, was the big problem, but since Bá managed, that problem shouldn't be that big after all, Once Matt started writing the second arc, and he changed his eight panel grid to a six panel grid, we figured, and Matt through about it as well, that it would be easier to draw.

It isn't. It's hard and, even when it's simple, it's not.

A new theory blossoms now.

It's the amount of information in each issue that makes it so hard to draw. The attempt in telling a satisfying piece of fiction each issue, and to fill it with as much information as humanly possible, makes Casanova a hard comic book to draw. I'm sure it's also a hard comic book to write, and possibly for the same reasons. Everything I draw is there for a reason, trying to obey a certain invisible "Casanova logic rule," and for each rule I drew there are a thousand more I'm thinking and researching that are not even on the page. The strange aspect of the collaboration with Matt is the stuff I know about the book that Matt doesn't, and vice-versa. I have no idea what's the big picture, or where the story is headed, and matt has no idea where I take my visual ideas from, or how the world I draw "works." If it's not on the page of the script, it's a secret to me, and if I don't draw on the page, it's a secret to him. This web of secrets creates this mystery mood that surrounds this comic, a mood that fit it well, but makes it hard to draw.

How much research did I make, and how many sketches, for Kubark's rocket car? And to appear small on two panels and dark from the inside in one? How many pictures of Casinos, and of more interesting looking buildings than a Casino actually does look like, did I see in order to create the outside of the Casino, which we could barely see? Creating Suki Boutique was actually easy, liked the first version I did, and I was sad to see her go, even if I already knew I created her for only one issue's worth of life (we never know about these things, actually, as Matt can bring her back again moment as some sort of "Ruby Boutique," or "Suki Berserko"). Maybe I think too much, and maybe that's a problem Bá and I share, and maybe Casanova isn't really as hard as we think if we don't think about it so much. But, hey, when you teach me how not to thing, I'll teach you how to draw.

At least, this issue I got to draw two naked chicks in bed, and one of them was poisoned only to die in the arms of the other. Hard to draw, but totally worth it.

I think, on page one, panel one, Doc Benday's line is clearly me trying to blow off Imminent Dad steam. I don't think that's him talking to Kubark going off his mission; I think that's me, a few days before my son was born[76].

---

74   Boy does this remain true. It's like being able to sense a void. Weird. And never wrong.

75   Better at this now. You know what'll destroy your writerly sense of preciousness? Having kids. They say in certain rooms one should endeavor to "keep it in the 'I'," meaning, don't say you need this and you should that, but rather, I needed this; I did that. This is an instance where I'd bet it's a universal truth and so dabbling in "your" feels acceptable.

76   I do this a lot. Especially in CASANOVA. I always tell people it's autobiographical except for the boobs and explosions and that's really true. Nobody gets it but me and nobody has to but, I swear, this book might as well be a teenage diary for how painfully confessional it gets.

I love the Benday's relationship with one another. I love writing it, when the chance presents itself. I love the dynamic that comes when the sickest minds in the book are, somehow, really great as a father and a son. And it pushes the greater leitmotifs of the book further along, I guess.

And the second panel, I just love. Zeph with the mask on her head makes me think of an Alex Raymond drawing, somehow, and I dream of a world where Fábio and I tell FLASH GORDON stories.

And then I realize we have CASANOVA[77], and I can't wait to see how he handles #12.

•

Hand down, bar none, one of my favorite Bond gags of all time is in GOLDFINGER, where Connery comes out of the water in the wetsuit, plants the bombs, then unzips to reveal a tuxedo underneath. That's the essence of Bond, to me.

I also think that's be the greatest Halloween costume[78].

•

The open bubble on page 3 was Konot's suggestion, a way to tie the silence to Zeph's funeral scene in issue 1; as the book goes along and I fall deeper into my Nouvelle Vague compulsions, little things like this appear to me more and more. This issue is the most BAND OF OUTSIDERS-y one yet, too, as we'll see[79].

And, hey, check out that snake eyes there. That's more me pretending to be Alan Moore.

•

Zeph exposing herself is, short of having the kids fight in front of a giant sign that reads PETER O'CONNELL, the biggest MODESTY BLAISE gag in the issue. Modesty would do that, y'see. And so hypnotic were her breasts that her male foes would be nigh incapacitated, as they are here, while Modesty killed or kicked them[80].

So anyway when Suki arrives and declares she invented the gag, you're pretty clear where we're standing, right?

If Winston Heath, in CASANOVA #2, was a kind of James Bond as Col. Kurtz, then here Suki as Modesty fills the same kind of role, replacing wanton sex with a...same-but-different sort of gluttony, I suppose[81].

I love Moon's design of her, though. You could put a crown on that head and Suki would carry it just right.

•

About sex: Fábio thinks this issue is, in his own words, "horny Matt writing through KS' pregnancy," which, I dunno, maybe it is, maybe it isn't, and maybe protesting at all is protesting too much[82].

That said, I absolutely love his figure-work, stagecraft, and acting when Suki and Zeph are in bed together. The whole scene I just love.

I bring it up, though, to talk about sex in comics for a second. There's not much it, is there?

There's barely even sexuality—prurience, at best, seems to be the coin of the realm. As always there's LOVE AND ROCKETS; and Alan Moore[83] never shied away from it...I dunno. It's an important part of life; why not comics? (There's the obvious answer, but it starts a thousand more arguments than it solves: in the American comics industry, 33-year-olds that still enjoy the entertainments of 13-year-olds and behave accordingly. I mean, I GET that part, but it's just been beaten to DEATH, hasn't it?)

(Also, in a genre work like CASANOVA, it'd be disingenuous to behave otherwise or to not include sex; it's be counter to the mission statement to treat sex and sexuality as the fuel for Bondian boy-fantasies[84] and nothing more.)

I remember reading Chaykin's AMERICAN FLAGG! for the first time, and there's a scene in #7 where Flagg sleeps with Dr. Weis and, in the process of stripping her down to the eternally-glorious standard-issue Chaykin Girl lingerie, Flagg—a Jew—finds that Weis is wearing a swastika. Even though the Nazis are galled the Gotterdammercrats (!! Chaykin !!), Ruben's filled with anger and self-loathing; even though he's filled with anger and self-loathing, he sleeps with her anyway and hates himself even more later[85].

---

77   This has happened time and time and time and time again. People will ask me *if you could do any book what would it be* and the answer is always CASANOVA.

78   Oh shit! I should totally do this.

79   Everybody doing comics should do a comic like this where you can just see what happens when you break the rules and make stuff up and try the wrong way to do things just to see what happens. I've learned more from what doesn't work in CASANOVA, I swear. It's freeing. It's freedom. Find a stage and put on whatever kind of show you like.

80   I regret this now. Not the reference, not the riff, but its inclusion at all. Just ignorant.

81   Hey that's not bad.

82   I also knew stuff about CASANOVA: ACEDIA that he didn't.

83   That's a weird... that's weird. I wouldn't make that connection now. I forgive a lot of Moore because I love his formalism and craftsmanship.

84   I don't think I articulated this well here. My favorite Bond is ON HER MAJESTY'S SECRET SERVICE – Lazenby and Rigg, directed by Peter Hunt. In the end – spoilers – Bond gets married and you totally get why he married her of all the Bond girls. Because she wasn't a goddamn thing like the other Bond girls – and was great for it. So somewhere in CASANOVA there's the thought of, what if instead of just misogyny and spank-fuel sex, sexuality, and sexual relationships were given the same weight and importance as the lasers, moon bases, and cool cars... why not write Bond in love? Eva is the coolest thing about Diabolik, right?

85   I literally, last NIGHT, talked to a book club about another comic of mine called SEX CRIMINALS and cited this exact thing.

It was a complicated barrage of signs and signifiers to parse when I first read it. And, admittedly, I read it too young to understand it, if not reading to be reading it entirely, but still. There was the sex part—that I understood; that I liked. Hot lady! With a big ass! In lingerie! Got it!—there was the political commentary—that I kind of got; if nothing else, I got it at a base Jews-good, Nazis-bad level—and then there was self-loathing, which, being a…maybe 12, maybe 13 year old at the time?…I didn't understand at all.

Because, y'know. The interplay of sex and self-loathing is a pretty adult thing to parse, especially when sex is quickly becoming all you think about, when you're not thinking about comics. It's beyond the ken of children; you won't find that adult conflagration of emotion and hormones looking up Lightning Lass' skirt, y'know?

To this day I think it's an incredibly adult—and really funny—scene. What stuck—and sticks—with me was the complication Chaykin folded into it. You could have sex, and you could even have sex with a Chaykin girl, but somehow, you'd hate yourself the next day. It made me feel guilty for finding the prurience in how hot Weis was, you know?

Whenever I think of the kind of sex I want to see in comics, I think of that; or I think of Maggie—Perla—being handed money out of an open hotel room door in CHESTER SQUARE. I think of Maggie and Casey in 100 ROOMS, and Casey wondering if he'd just raped a girl he'd kidnapped or, maybe, found a new girlfriend. I think of Maggie and Hopey, or the whole of Palomar.

I guess what I'm saying is, I think sex in comics should be more than the window over Power Girl's tits[86].

And here, where the sex stops and the violence starts, it seemed like we had to take one last stab at it. And be gluttonous. And try to find something real inside of it. I dunno that it works—not for me to say—but goddamn, the intent was more than just to create a comic with more spank fuel. God knows there are enough of those.

Fábio's interpretation is way funnier, though, so go nuts.

•

Page seven, panel three: the blue ringing inside of the glass; the bubbles.

You can make fun of me all you like, Fábio Moon you glorious goddamn genius.

•

Amiel Boutique. CASANOVA V4. Stay tuned.

•

Aces and Tens—twenty-one, or eleven, depending on your way of thinking. Aces and Eights—dead man's hand. See?[87] Not all of that card research went into the crap file.

•

And again, I love the body language in Suki's death scene, the tenderness of the figures. I find nothing prurient or provocative about it at all. I think it's really kind of lovely.

I'm not bringing that up because I don't think YOU see it, too, dear reader, or that you need to be reminded of Fábio's talents. I bring it up because, goddamn, I love comics. I write things down and send it to a brilliantly talented guy who takes what I wrote, the thing I saw in my head, and absolutely makes it something real and wonderful and unexpected. If that alchemy isn't magic, I don't know what is[88].

•

Suki and the title cards. I'm a big fan of skipping scenes where you lay plot-pipe altogether[89] and just moving the story along. See, I know you are smart, savvy, sexy, and savage as far as readers go, and you'll trust all will be revealed. But there are so many layers and levels of secrets that I didn't think we could do it this time. I found myself having to write a scene where characters got each other up to speed and dreading it.

So, like I said earlier, I just dove head-on into Nouvelle Vague-style anarchy. Fuck it: fill the panels with the questions the readers—and the cast—are asking. Make fun of it all, celebrate it all, break rules and see what happens[90].

As the mystery Suki is investigating ties into the mysteries and confusion at the very root of the book, why not go for broke?

In the writing scene, I realized I needed to have Zeph telling us the page she poisoned Suki on when she confessed. So I went back and put it in. Would that she were saying it in the diagetic! Soon, surely. That's a ridiculous confection and masturbatory indulgence I doubt I'll be able to resist. Maybe Sasa will embrace the fourth wall, I dunno.

•

---

86   Between CASANOVA, SATELLITE SAM, and SEX CRIMINALS, one could argue I've staked a claim.

87   Man this is reading really defensive to me now. I suppose because I was feeling Really Defensive when I wrote it but, Jesus, it just radiates off the page.

88   Someone somewhere should write something about the great acting illustrators in comics. Writing near-impossible-to-draw interior moments, actorly moments, remains the biggest thing from writing for film I can't seem to shake.

89   This has just continued. If I'm bored writing it, I'd be bored reading it, so cut it out and move the fuck on…

90   I feel like Barney after Fred takes what he just said and says it himself and takes credit for it. Or like a dicky LOOPER.

KAA-FWOOM: with all this talking and fucking, a body could almost forget how agile and epic Moon is when shit starts exploding. The smoke, the fire, the energy of these last few panels—get ready for next issue, cats and kittens. It's called "Fuck Shit Up[91]" and it takes place on the moon. When I told the twins how it ends, they both gasped.

●

Oh! The hood ornament. I figured out the title for the issue. Once I had that, all was revealed[92].

Matt Fraction,
KC MO 2007

GULA, Issue 2 (Icon Comics, 2011)

DUSTIN HARBIN, who not only letters this book by hand, but is an amazingly talented cartoonist (www.dharbin.com!), used to work in the same comic shop as I did, Heroes Aren't Hard to Find, in Charlotte, NC.

It seems like we've been talking about comics ever since we were 20.

●

Matt Fraction: So you always had the best handwriting of anyone I ever met. And I remember, when we were working together at Charlotte, NC's premiere comic store HEROES AREN'T HARD TO FIND, as I taught you everything you know about being a Retail Superman, that, one day, when I was making comics and not just selling them, I'd bring you along with me, and give you the chance to share your exquisite lettermakingsmanshippery with the world. And now here you are! Dustin, I just wanted to take this opportunity to say YOU ARE WELCOME.

Dustin Harbin: Yes, well, thank you, I'm sure. Although I remember this a little differently? I remember how you would follow me around, as adorable and loyal as any puppy, asking questions about comics, correct use of dashes and hyphens in writing, girls, you name it. Shelton and I would nod knowingly to each other. "The little scamp is really coming along," we'd say, watching you toil away building a website for a shockingly low hourly wage. I always thought of you more as a "Retail Firestorm" or "Retail Booster Gold" to my Retail Superman.

MF: I remember the day I first taught you, a lowly high school drop-out, how to use a semi-colon properly; I shall remember it until my last. We turned that comic book store into a regular PYGMALION-a-thon, and you, dearest Dharb, were as plucky and spirited an Eliza Doolittle as I could ever dream of finding.

Now that I've so thoughtfully molded you in my image, and you've begun making comics on your own, do you find that your time on the other side of the glass counter, that your time working in the direct market—and all "joking" aside, you're one of the guys that understands running a comics shop is more than sitting on a stool and reading your precious BOOSTER GOLD but aggressively, constantly, and largely thanklessly trying to grow your customer base—has informed your work, work habits, release strategy…at all?

DH: Ugh I keep typing and retyping answers, but they all come out NEGATIVE! Sorry to be slowing down.

MF: It's okay—we can bring it back around.

DH: Okay. I'm just trying to keep it…well, less negative. Besides the fact that too much grousing makes for dull reading. I feel some responsibility to you not to get too shitty about comics in general. You're like the fucking Denny O'Neil[93] of Marvel now, so any swipe at you, which is not what I mean and I'd prefer not to leave space for that in there. Does that make sense? I'm super down on comics as an industry lately, so it's hard to pick through ideas without coming back to that.

MF: It's okay; I promise. I don't take it personally.

Should we discuss something else? Some piece of work we both love.

DH: Now, I trust you. I just want you to know where I'm coming (and not coming) from—I trust you to steer the interview wherever you want it to go.

MF: No, wait, y'know what? Let's talk about something we love. You just did that big piece with Tom Spurgeon and this would just be

---

91 One night in art school some drinking was done by some associates and a game was invented called "Fuck Shit Up." On a drunken rampage, while I slogged away on the crashing-all-the-fucking-time Avid, they proceeded to destroy a lot of stuff in and around the studio, culminating in hosing the place down with a fire extinguisher. The next morning they were out with hangovers and I played dumb as our department chair speculated on what happened to everything and why it was all coated in this "weird alien dust." IT WAS MAYO AND TIMMY, PATRICK. IT WAS MAYO AND TIMMY.

92 A-ha!

93 I'm still not sure if Dusty meant this as an insult or not.

dancing around that shit again.

Or we just skip it. I dunno. What do you think? What do you want to talk about?

Is there anything you actually love about retailing?

DH: Haha I'm almost done with my answer now. Don't let's let it blow up too much. Since it's for print, we can always edit it later for sizes. Forget my nervousness!

MF: No, it's okay. I like this bit. You should read the me-and-O'Malley thing. It's very…this-ish.[94]

DH: Hm, that's a trick one, even for an experienced ex-Eliza-Doolittle-cosplayer like me—although if I were you I'd put a semi-colon between "GOLC" and "but" above.

If there's anything working in a comics shop—and one of the great shops of North America at that—has taught me, it's that you have to be bananas to run a comics shot. Shelton (Drum) certainly is—I've worked with that dude through some highs and lows, whoa Nellie, and he is nothing if not slavishly devoted to comics. I think most people who run comics shops, good or bad, have that hell-or-high-water approach to things. In Shelton's case, it makes his shop one of the best in the country, and HeroesCon one of the best-regarded comics conventions around.

But oo-wee, you run into people. One of the weird things about comics is that ANYone can join—honestly, I'm lettering a book for Marvel Comics because you like my handwriting, right? Mark Bagley did a Marvel Try-Out book and ended up doing AMAZING SPIDER-MAN within what? A year or two? Kate Beaton just started making comics one day a few—like 3? 4?—years ago, and now she's in the New Yorker and agents are calling and she doesn't have to pay for lunch if she doesn't want to. If you have talent and even a little moxie you can make a career in comics. But by the same token that open door lets a lot of mediocrity in. It's always a danger. Some of the worst people I've met in comics have been retailers, it's a field that demands single-minded purpose and a willingness to either do what you're doing because you love doing it, or to squeeze every penny from every person, product, and prospect until the Lincoln-head weeps. And occasionally, tragically, both.

MF: Well, you'd be fucking stupid, because starting a sentence with "But" is fucking stupid god dammit stupid Dharbin.

Sometimes I feel like—whatever little victories I achieve—that it's like winning the award for Tallest Guy in Your Whole House. Sometimes you feel like the bar is so low that as long as your script doesn't arrive with feces smeared across the title page, it's at least a B.

There's something weirdly freeing about eating it, in comics, though; you just do better next time, or give up coming at all and turn into a fat stupid hack. It's a thing that Wacker says—that every 30 days the book has to come out. Being forced to deliver on a deadline, even when you can't quite make it work…it's a brutal, awful, crippling, terrifying lesson to learn that makes me want to run for the shelter and safety of just making fun comics all the time. Another thing Wacker says—he's full of wisdom, that guy—is the worst day in comics is Wednesday. And it is. It's the day all the mistakes are made permanent and forever. I hate Wednesdays now. I can't look at my own work, is how bad it gets. It's like how they say you have your whole life to make your first record, and about two years to make your second…

I had to go back and reread CASANOVA before starting to write v3 and all I came away with was that it wasn't as good as I'd hope it was. It was crushing.

I've said this like a billion times, but there's a part in ED WOOD where he's trying to get a meeting with a producer and says he's the guy that made GLEN OR GLENDA? and the producer says, "That was the worst film I've ever seen," and Ed takes, like, half a second, shakes it off, and says, "Well, I'll do better next time," and rolls on with his pitch, indefatigable. I cling to that scene like a comfy angora sweater. It doesn't always work but it's all I've got.

Um…Christ what a bummer this is. I hate you, Dharbin.

Is there anything you miss about retailing? I genuinely miss ground-zero evangelizing books I love. As much of a grind as it can be, as awful or as sad-making or whatever, I do sincerely miss the days of being able to put a book that needed support into people's hands and watching it take root and go. I remember a long weekend when you and I, like, tripled PREACHER'S subscription numbers or, like, moving more copies of BERLIN than Michel Vrana had to send us…racing to put out new Pope books or whatever. I miss feeling like I was helping. Now I feel entirely removed from the equation?

DH: That's ridiculous, Matt. You write X-Men and Iron Man now, for God's sake. If there's anyone in a position of "helping," it's you, dummy[95]. Yes, the Preacher thing! That was when we started the "Heroes Preferred Club" for Preacher #18, right? The one with the lighter on the cover, the John Wayne "Eff Communism" story inside? If I remember right, any customer that bought that book got a free membership in the club, hand-written by one of us on a slip of receipt paper, and an extra 1% discount off. BARGAIN$$Z$$

Do you remember recording the Heroes Hotline? That's what I miss about retailing—I think you hit it on the head. Back in the 90s, when we'd cheerfully sell comics all day and then work till the wee hours pricing stock for HeroesCon, those are some of my favorite memories of those years. A few years later when I was up late organizing the show, it seemed to matter more somehow, all the fun of goofing around at the comics show had work off a bit. But yeah, there was nothing better than loaning my set of THBs to someone

---

94   This is actually very much like what conversations – all of my conversations – with Dusty are like.

95   Again, I remain unsure as to how this should be taken.

so they could turn on to them, since dumb ole Pope would never reprint that stuff. Or talking about the latest INVISIBLES letter column. "Whoa, Grant Morrison is totally a magician is he serious?!?"

I guess it's easy to forget that comics are COMICS, while they don't have to be escapist, most of the time they are, and that's a thing that comics is really, really good at.

Anyway.

You're totally on the beam about the do-better-next-time thing. It's the same with my little diary comics, they're mostly terrible, when I go back through them it's like listening to my own Most Boring Hits mix-tape. But there's something really freeing about getting to a certain point with them and just FINISHING, just pushing it out the door and getting on to the next thing. A certain amount of obsession can be useful, but past a point of being able to improve something, it's just energy you could be spending on the next good thing. Plus, while my comics are still mostly boring, when I do actual comics about things now, it's like I've been running with weights, suddenly I have 300 little comics under my belt that I didn't have this time last year. Cheers to progress, for sure.

MF: It's different now, though; I don't put books in readers' hands anymore unless I'm at a show. It's hard to articulate, but it's different. My customer is ultimately the retailer these days...at least it feels like it, sometimes. Like, the worst X-Men book in the world is always going to sell more than the best CASANOVA book in the world, whether it's me, Grant Morrison, or Whatever K. Whoeverington writing it. The direct market is designed to sell BATMAN. Of course there are exceptions but they're just that; it's...I dunno, like I said. Hard to articulate. Also I'm dumb.

It was interesting to me that you withheld some bad strips from the DIARY COMICS collection that Koyama Press put out and tweaked some of the others. I write SORRY in every copy of MANTOOTH that comes my way. That urge, that embarrassment-by-youth thing. As shitty a thing as those reworked STAR WARS movies were, I get it now. Harlan Ellison, when I met him, hand-corrected the typos in the book I got him to sign for my mom. As we talked, he just, like, took his pen and flipped to four different pages and made little tweaks.

Is that why Pope never put out a THB collection?[96]

So, so, okay, tell me about the decision to leave the if-artistically-unsatisfying-at-least-reliably-paying world of Comics Retail for the Broke-Ass-Realities of Cartooning. When we were together—"together"—it was a sprout in the dirt, a thing you were more protective of and embarrassed by than anything else. Then suddenly nine years later there was a website and you were clearly moving in the direction of Maker rather than Vendor. Tell me about, uh, what the fuck is wrong with you that made you think that was a good lifestyle choice. As you, a boner-fide Retail Superman, had to know just how difficult a road you'd chosen.

DH: Oh man, you're right, I DID know what a dumb decision it was! But I am an optimist, despite what I'm sure sounds like deep negativity.

But first: I think you do yourself a disservice by thinking of the retailer as your customer. The retailer, even a retailer a savvy and high-quality as Shelton, is just a middleman. Your audience is always the customer. You're just serving them in a different way. Think of it like this: where you are now, writing big-name books and event comics and also more personal stuff like CASANOVA, you're in the position of bringing people along, influencing the pond you're in with your ripples, and essentially writing whatever kinds of comics you want. It's true that selling comics directly to someone, especially an enthusiastic someone, is a different experience; and I've seen you selling your own books at shows and it's pretty heartwarming to watch how you Retail Superman them yourself, even with your own books.

But now you're a Maker, right? We are Makers, we are supposed to Make things, we're supposed to chuck our stones into the pond and smack our ripples up against everyone else's ripples and see what happens. You're still delivering art into the hands of an audience, you've just climbed up higher on the chain. I can imagine how you might feel more removed, though, especially at a big publisher where it's not like you're interacting one on one with most of your readers. But you're still talking to them, and they're still listening—that's the important part, I think. Imagine Young Matt and Young Dharb selling copies of CASANOVA to people back in 1997, y'know? Is that not the coolest imagining ever?

I did NOT withhold any strips from DIARY COMICS! They're all in there, even the very worst of them (most of the first half). I even included a couple of blank panels from the very earliest ones. Nor did I tweak anything, except in a couple of places just for the print collection—mainly formatting or figuring out how to render color lines in black and white to the best effect. I understand the impulse to go back and self-edit endlessly, but I try to avoid it wherever I can. Don't you think that stuff just kind of gets plunked out there in the art stream and becomes its own thing? I feel like maybe it's a waste of energy to go back and retouch things later—to use your Star Wars example, think of all the time Lucas spent fiddling with his great accomplishment, essentially hiding his inability to even make anything that good again. I mean, those prequels, am I right? That last Indiana Jones movie? Fiddling with Star Wars was like George Lucas buying a penis pump.

As for leaving Heroes, it was mainly just an idea of semantics. I wanted—and still want, although I'm more sanguine now about the economic difficulty of living without a weekly paycheck—to BE a cartoonist, not a part-timer, not a by-nighter. I think it's a quality thing—like, when I was working for HeroesCon and doing comics on the side, I think they were judged really positively because I was a hobbyist, you know? And as soon as that was MY CAREER, I was forced to start thinking about them in a more serious way, both in terms of how my stuff was developing and how they fit into the larger landscape of an eventual body of work. Basically I wanted to move from apprentice up to journeyman level. Don't you feel like your writing—and approach to writing, maybe?—changed when you quit working in animation and advertising and started JUST BEING A WRITER?

MF: Well, yes and no but it's way more yes than I realized before I started. On something like CASANOVA? It's down to retailers way more than readers. It's a sad fact but it's true. There's an autopilot to the way so much of the DM orders that it doesn't matter once you get outside of the top fifty or sixty books. My audience is always the customer, yes, and that's why I do the shows I do—shaking hands

96   I would still bet anything the answer to this is "Yes."

and signing my name a few times seems the least I can do—but my customer is oftentimes ill-served, ill-informed, and under-serviced by their vendors.

Bendis, for example. I've seen this happen more than once. Some kid comes up to him at a show, says I'm a huge fan, he says, "Awesome! Thanks! New POWERS out next week (or whatever)" and the kid says, "What's POWERS?"

There were DM stores that wouldn't order CASANOVA in its other form, but are ordering it now. Surely the raised profile of all involved doesn't hurt, but neither does the Marvel listing[97], nor the color…

Also the attendant irony of discussing the perils of tweaking the work of the past in a reprint book that tweaks the work of the past does not escape me.

And…and I didn't just, like, leave animation, I knocked the table over, set the room on fire and went running out with my middle finger in the air. Not my proudest or most mature moments but I burned the bridge while I was still on it. So, y'know, when I BECAME A WRITER I had a pregnant wife and exactly 1 and 1/2 books at Marvel, earning the New Kid rate, the short term by MAKE THIS WORK and…and I got super lucky and worked super hard and here we are. My approach changed because I had a mortgage and a baby on the way.[98]

It occurs to me more and more each day we've planted our flag in a field that is, at the moment, withering. It's grim out there. Do you find yourself discouraged? Are you able to parse "monetary security" (whatever that means to you) and "the work?"

DH: Well, I have the benefit of being able to do things that aren't making my own comics, but are related in a way that improves me overall—for instance, lettering CASANOVA has made me a way better letterer, and buttressed me financially a little bit, insofar as being able to depend on a certain amount of money per issue. And doing the odd illustration job is similar, it's practice, and it helps pay the bills.

I think you're right and wrong about the "withering" landscape, though—if anything, I think comics is in a sort of a pupal stage, and then—wait, is pupal after larval?—anyway, it's about to change into something else again.

I just read all these end-of-year posts, where everyone is asked what the new shape of comics will be, and everyone is saying "comics on the iPad" and so forth. But who knows what the landscape will look like in 2010, no one would have guessed the shape it is now. I think we're in a stage where we're wrestling with the nostalgist idea that comics has always been mired in—with the direct market being the physical avatar of that dysfunctional self-chaining to the past—and the necessity to adapt to what might be an exponentially larger marketplace, more sophisticated readership, and attention from things like…movie studios, people with money, shifty people and honest people with the resources to actually Make Things Happen.

So I think comics is in for some enormous changes in the next few years, and right now we have weird amalgams like motion comics and $3 digital versions of $3 print comics. People are just trying to stuff right now. But I feel like, if anything, comics is a much much MUCH more fertile playground than it was when you and I were clerks together. I mean, that PREACHER #18 is hard to even read now, but back then it was like "whoa, this guy is on a whole other level." Now people get raped in superhero books; it's a whole new world! I find the direct market, meaning the distribution and content-creation mode comics has followed more or less since the mid-70s, enormously frustrating and discouraging. But that's just the track the machine is moving on right now, you know? I feel pretty optimistic about comics in general, it's ballooning pretty fast these days and it feels like there's ample room for pretty much everything.

MF: It's funny, my first day at HEROES was the day that the Heroes World kerfuffle kicked off the implosion. I've never NOT been in comics as it's appeared to be spiraling down one toilet or the other…

So where do you want to go with your work[99]? Are you going to keep producing DIARY COMICS collections annually after they appear on the web? Are you looking to do any fiction? To work with any writers or to stay a one-man band? Tell me, Dharb, about a world where everything is beautiful and nothing hurts and you can set your own course in comics.

DH: I'm ending Diary Comics as a daily thing, once I finish up with 2010 strips (I'm about 2 months behind "real time"). Although I'll probably keep doing them when the mood hits, or when something interesting happens (rare). I am doing a couple of further print collections of them, but as self-made minicomics, although funded by the uber-amazing Anne Koyama of Koyama Press. She is really just the bee's knees.

You know what's funny is that my girlfriend was making fun of me before the end of the year, pointing out that all the stuff I put in my New Year's resolution comics never gets done. So on her advice, I wrote out a list of goals and a rough schedule for them for the year; which, weirdly, I've never ever done before. I read in a recent interview with your wife Kelly Sue that you guys do a similar thing[100]? Although way larger in scope and time period.

Anyway, by the end of the year, I want to have done a couple more color collections of my comics, at least 2 more DIARY collections, stuff like that. But I'm definitely going to try and collaborate some this year, which I've never done before. A couple with me as writer, a couple with another writer and me drawing. I'm kind of a control freak, so it'll be a learning experience for sure.

---

97   To a point.

98   This remains true. The end of my writerly preciousness happened when I removed all other safety nets in my life between me and being a writer. Now obviously I had at least a long enough shot at making it happen to have a shot to take at all (if that makes sense) but still. This remains the piece of advice I wish I could go back in time and give myself: if I wanted to write I should've started writing sooner.

99   A curious coincidence: Dustin lettered Mal's SECONDS.

100   We have, literally, every six months, a kind of State of the Union meeting where we talk about our careers, family lives, and marriage. We make short-term and long-term goals and check in on past ones. It is a fascinating (to us) document of who we are and who we become.

But I think if I had my real, pure-tee druthers, the high point of a future career in comics for me would be at least one, long, satisfying, dense, and most importantly REALLY GOOD adventure story. Something Bone-ish, something that kids who are smarter than their parents think will pick up and enjoy[101]. Or find on their parents' bookshelf and read in secret. Whichever. But I'm still a baby in comics-career terms, I think the future shape of my career is as much in flux as that amorphous, poorly described picture of our current stage in comics' history. The answer is hard to pin down; that baby might not have been ensperminated yet. Enspermatized? Jizzled?

I'd like to hear your answer to the same question, Matt. I'm maybe more aware than some people, mainly due to how excitedly I've watched your fortunes rise in comics, of just how short a time you've actually been doing this professionally. I mean, it's nuts—if I'm a baby, career-wise, you're like the teenage prodigy taking AP Calculus at the college up the street. What does YOUR ideal comics world look like? And don't shirt your place in it, that's what I'm extra-interested in. What does Future Fraction of 2016 see out the hard-light window of his flying space-car?

MF: As of this writing, since 2004, I've made enough money on my independent/creator-owned/non-superhero work to buy an iPhone. My notion had long been to chase after a kind of Steven Soderbergh-kind of model, where I could work in the mainstream doing work I enjoy in ways I enjoy so as to be able to afford to do more idiosyncratic—which is really just code for not superhero—work, and hope the fortunes of the former trickle down to the latter. Um...not so much.[102]

I sort of don't know what else TO do; to make a living in mainstream comics and to have not caught any hint of lightening in the bottle of my independent, non-maintenance work, this kind of paradigm is the only thing that makes sense. I love the superhero stuff; genuinely and sincerely, and I always have—you can testify to that—so there's no holding-my-nose that goes along with the Marvel part of the equation. You can see guys that DO only type with one hand as the other tries desperately to keep the stink of greasy kids' stuff from offending them but that ain't me now and it never will be...in fact I like it even MORE now that I've got kids. I like comics. I like superhero comics. It's all a joy to do.[103]

That said it's not the only kind of comic I want to write, so...so hopefully as my career builds—if my career continues to build—I'll keep trying to crack the market with other stuff, hoping an elevated profile in the mainstream will grow my all-around audience. The good news is it seems to be working; the Icon CASANOVA moves more than the Image CASANOVA ever did and so far it's all been reprints.

I don't know...ANYTHING. About ANYTHING. And I started trying to do this because I realized precisely that, sitting in that shitty little apartment in KC, banding away on "critique" pieces about comics so full of assumption and hyperbole as to still embarrass me, ten years later...So now here I am, the kind of guy I used to make fun of because I wanted to do what I do so bad I didn't know how to get it, and I find it just as mystifying. The only thing I know how to do is write the kind of books I want to read and hope to god my taste are commercial. Get my collaborators paid, work hard, think about everything, don't turn into a fucking hack, don't punch up, don't punch down, and keep thinking big. That's...uh, that's as deep as it gets, I'm afraid.

I want to write less and get paid more. I don't really know how to do it.

DH: You know, I was about to say, "Well, you write less and make more now, don't you?" meaning compared to when MANTOOTH and FIVE FISTS were your main claims to fame, but of course you write more now, don't you? Haha, you are a workaholic in your bones, you poor sap; your carpal tunnels must be filled with pure coffee.

I think one thing comics is really REALLY good at is providing a place for hardworking people who love what they do. I'll admit, when I hear people asking about how to "break in" to comics, I'm always slightly mystified that it's a question. And even more mystified that editors rub their chins all, "Hmmm, pull a chair, young bucks, where to begin?" Even before I was really thinking about cartooning myself, it never seemed especially tough—I don't think I know a single motivated person with a little talent and patience who hasn't cobbled out a place for themselves. Like, I can't think of ANYone I know who tried to "break in" to comics and failed, you know? It's a medium that rewards practice, for sure. I am enjoying slowly getting better, although my pace is way way behind yours. But you're a bigger thinking than I am anyway. I like that shitty apartment[104]!

MF: I've been running as hard and as fast as I can to get as far away from that shitty apartment as is possible.

GULA 5, Issue 12 (Image Comics, 2008)

Hiyah, earthmen,

This issue was wrapped up[105] thirty some hours before my son was born.

Let me back up[106]:

We found out about a year ago this time that we were pregnant. We'd been trying again, of course, using these little pee strips to

---

101   I would love to read this, Dharb, if you ever get around to making it. Check out his recent book BEHOLD! THE DINOSAURS! from Nobrow Press.

102   This has now changed. The market has changed. Comics have changed. And my profile has changed.

103   And it was, until it wasn't, and then it was time for a break. And I was lucky enough to find a changed market, elevated profile, and new world waiting for me when I got there. Dumb luck and hard work, dumb luck and hard work.

104   It was demolished in 2002.

105   The script, I meant.

106   I am amazed, looking back, that I wrote this. Tugging on Superman's cape, as it were.

check ovulation. After a year and some change of trying to chart and graph and take temperatures and everything else, someone recommended these things that you dunk in a cup of pee. If it, I dunno, turns red or something it means you're ovulating and should maybe try making a baby.

Try as I might, I never ovulated, but one day Kelly Sue did, so we totally did it. And the day after, to make extra sure. And then a month later the pregnancy test showed two line, a plus, an asterisk, seven gold stars, and some flitter shot out of it, letting us know that indeed my seed had found purchase[107]. We used the entire box of pregnancy tests, eventually, just to make sure.

That, then, was late January. Having gone through the drill once before, I think both my wife and I set about being secretly expectant in a different way. More reserved, sure; more nervous. We'd already seen the end of the movie and weren't eager to revisit it. To be honest, that I spoke about our miscarriage here, in these pages, and that so many of you reached out to me, and so many of you had tried again and were successful was a huge comfort, inspirational, even; for all the bitching I do about writing these pages, I don't know what I'd have done without you[108].

As I think back on it now, I remember it almost feeling conspiratorial, as though that inexplicable and inconceivable chemical reaction cascading along inside of her was a bank heist on the make, a Rube Goldberg blueprint rife with causes and effects, a conspiracy we'd hatch one day once we'd gotten the Cubans on board.

I was clawing myself out of the Holiday Sickness that dropped my ass into the ER and trying to get moving again, to get working again, to get living again. I was trying to come back from all the stuff. I got sick again and couldn't shake it; I couldn't speak and couldn't stop coughing. Life wasn't getting any easier.

I'd try to sleep, palming Kel's belly beneath my hand. I didn't know how to pray; that was as close as I could get.

And then one day he started to swim[109].

I went crazy with work. I'd never been so busy or worked so hard in my entire life. Some of this was hunter-gatherer shit, I think. I took on as much as I could handle, working ridiculous hours to get pages done, to get the house ready, to stay a moving target.

Unless something was on fire, I stopped replying to email entirely. As I write this my inbox, with mail still unanswered from last December, is up over 400 messages. Did you write me? Did I not write you back?? Sorry. I kind of lost my mind. I stopped hanging out, I stopped doing stuff. Or at least I cut way back. It FEELS like I stopped hanging out and stopped doing stuff. All I could think about was cranking out pages, getting more books in the can, building up bank, preparing for the kid. Because kids are expensive, and I'm a dumbass, and the depth of my parenting strategy was, "Save up money."

The end of the first trimester, when we could finally start telling people, and the beginning of the second trimester, when the minnow became a goldfish, was when Kel really began to change shape. That came with a death in the family, the start of baseball, and the feeling that we were gonna go the distance. Passing our last-time milestone was the biggest deal to me; after we'd gotten past where we were last time when we miscarried, I exhaled. Something about that array of days, that span of time…that's what spooked me. After we lapped it, I felt like the little fish was going to just keep getting bigger.

I kept writing. The Cubs started losing. We tore down our collapsing garage and rebuilt it. This brought down the backyard fence and replaced it with a tangle of snow fence, which is an orange plastic sheet with holes in it, like the rings that bind a six-pack together dressed up to hunt deer. I brought in a stray dog, then promptly left Kelly Sue to care for it while I fucked off to California to research a Marvel project. The dog could easily leap the snow fence, so he was forever getting away, forcing Kel to chase after him. She wanted to kill the dog; I begged a reprieve until I got back. He ended up sticking around.

We tore up and replaced the kitchen. If you're thinking about doing a stem-to-stern tear-out and rebuild of YOUR kitchen, might I recommend you do it late in your wife's second trimester of pregnancy?

We painted the house and had bits of repair work done to it, fixing joists and all that shit[110]. Comic conventions, legal shit, friend shit, everybody's got their something. The Cubs stopped losing.

Still, through it all, I kept writing like a maniac, doing my best to get ahead so when the baby came I could slow down and enjoy it some.

I bring it up because, when I think back to the three trimesters of my son's incubation, the first one is marked by death and plague and nervousness that ached like a grinding jaw, the second was constant flux, everything upending and reinventing. We found out it would be a boy. This was good news, as we had the boy's name picked and adored; the girl's name had led to a Cold War détente from which we saw no escape. So thank god it was a boy. We started taking classes then; we started hunting for a doula and building the nursery and everything else. Everything was changing, everything. I wasn't frightened, or nervous, or panicked. I was just doing my best to keep my eye on that ball. Every morning you wake up and every morning she's a little bit bigger. Every morning was a reminder of everything left to do.

And then, finally, the third trimester. When I think back on it, it's an array of boxes on a piece of typing paper I taped on my window.

---

107 RAISING ARIZONA.

108 This is true, and something I failed to bring up earlier: the outreach that continues still from readers touched (or punched, or stabbed, or hurt) by miscarriage. It was the first… it was the first time I realized that there was something beyond… well, that readers like you, dear reader, could be more to me, and each other, than *just readers*.

109 This was true – and fantastic. A pregnancy that would've been rife with tension and worry (we'd have been That Couple that rented their own sonogram machine I bet) wasn't hardly at all. Because all we had to do was talk to the wee man while he cooked and he'd start to wiggle.

110 All of this was done with the money I got from selling my stake in the animation and design company. So my Origin In Comics has a little bit of a cheat – I had saved a lot when I made the leap and was able to afford the time I needed to build a career in the mainstream. I'm writing this here not to confess or to suggest that be *your* strategy but rather to remind myself: in my self-aggrandizing story of leaving one career for the other I forget sometimes that leaving that one career *paid out*.

I made a map of the books I needed to do before the birth. It was basically seven books a month for three months. As I finished one, a big satisfying black X got drawn up. And in that battle of inches my summer whiled away. A few more days, a week, two weeks; another book done, another X drawn. What started off being an encouraging prison-cell hatch mark calendar very quickly became a ticking clock. Every book I'd wrap up was another book closer to Baby Time.

CASANOVA 11 was a monster, logistically. Not as bad as 13—more about that next time—but it was a beast, even by CASANOVA standards. That's the price you pay for being so awfully certain you need to be so awfully clever all the time, I suspect. Anyway it took forever. A big gain from that, though, was that it was kind of an end and a beginning; I was free from that crap for a little while and I knew that what came next was 12, and that 12 was…well, just Zeph fucking shit up. Hence the title. As precious and considered and airless as 11 was, in contrast, this issue had to be visceral and fast and swooping and splattered. The writing went quick; I think it was even faster than CASANOVA #5.

When I told the twins in San Diego about this issue, they both gasped[111]. I tell that story a lot because that gasp delighted me. You get inside your head so much—or rather, I get inside my head so much, that you can forget sometimes an audience is going to encounter the work at all. I don't often go looking for reviews, especially since taking on Marvel work, but I do sometimes, in moment of egomaniacal weakness, and as wonderful and thoughtful and well-written as some of the CASANOVA reviews have been, nothing's topped that honest gasp of theirs. With CASANOVA, where it's so much in my head all the time…I guess I tell that story so much because the twins have become my ideal audience. If I can get them, then I fell like I've done my job and when I told them poor old Cornelius was gonna get decapitated, as a moment in the story, it totally worked and goddamn wasn't that nice, wasn't it nice to get our of your head for a second and see someone react so purely.

Because more than anything else by this point in September I was running on exhaustion and writing almost entirely on instinct. When I started the script, I started by just writing physical actions and building panels up around them[112]; in my original plans, there would've been grunts and sound effects in the murder scenes. I left it all dialogue-less as a placeholder, and then went back and reread it and realized that it worked better, it was a better CASANOVA gag if the airlock breaches sucked the sound out. Happy accident, and hey, no grunts and groans and screams and sound effects to write. Just pure action, no thinking, all automatic.

Konot added the little hatchmarks to the balloons. I loved 'em.

As the writing happened—I think over six days, soup to nuts—as Zeph killed her way to Cornelius, as I killed my way through the last of my days as a not-dad, I remember hoping the boy stayed put just a little longer as I had two or three scripts still to finish. We were three weeks away yet, that seemed like a likely possibility; as Kelly Sue started to really, REALLY get uncomfortable, It seemed more and more unlikely. It was at the very end that it got bad; when she woke up as her water broke ("Or I just wet the bed," she announced) it was a relief. Even though the bags weren't 100% packed because we[113] unpacked and were repacking; even though all the boxed weren't on the paper and all the scripts weren't in bed; even though any number of things we wanted done weren't done, the long grey smear of these last eight months, with all their adrenaline and anxiousness and panic and worry and wonder, were finally fucking over.

And that was fine with us. We drove to the hospital, along the rehearsed route, skating down the highway as the sun came up. It was a lovely morning; I remember we commented on it to one another while taking bets as to whether or not labor had actually started.

It had.

Try as we might for natural birth—or try as Kel might, really; I didn't really have much to do with the outcome—it wasn't in the cards. 12 hours of back labor led to an epidural; a few more hours there and we'd started to de-dilate. Redilate? I don't know what you call it, but she started to swell closed, basically. The little man had nowhere to go.

The doctor called for an emergency C-section; a couple hours after that—I think? Time gets weird there in the middle—Henry Leo Fritchman was born, at 9:40 at night, 7 pounds, 11 ounces[114]. Healthy, happy, and without an eye in the middle of his forehead. Hello son.

I think back on that first night, and I think about holding him as we both nodded off. I think about looking over to his mother, smiling and shaking off the drug haze, watching us. I remember falling in love with the little man, and watching Kel fall in love with him. And I remember thinking that, finally, oh, god, finally, if just for that one night, I could finally stop.

When he woke up needing changing—and it had only been a few hours, two, three, four—I felt like I had been asleep for two weeks.

Thanks, son. I needed that.

Matt Fraction,
23 Jan 08

PS: Sorry for the lack of Fábio in this section this month; he was late and leapt straight from 12 to 13 and didn't want to contribute to the backmatter this month. Believe me, I miss it more than you do.

---

111   This remains a collaborative high point for me.

112   Kind of think this is the way to go all the time now, personally, but what do I know? Somewhere along the line I stopped trying to out-write an artist's hand.

113   I. Not "we." I unpacked 'em. Stupid fuck.

114   In between the writing of this and today I had a catastrophic data loss and about twelve years of my digital life vanished, including this little bit of information. So, uh, nice work on that overshare, past-me. Future-you says "Thanks."

GULA 6, Issue 13 (Image Comics, 2008)

Hiyah, earthmen,

This is the first CASANOVA postgame I've done since wrapping the[115] second volume. Add to that I've wrapped up a big IRON FIST storyline and another Marvel book of mine called THE ORDER in the last week and I'm all kind so of melancholy. Or wait a second and I'll be feeling completely weightless, freed up from all these massive things[116].

And, hey, baseball's coming back to life so it can't be all bad.

We open with a setting that calls back to the page from Vol. 1 that Bá told me was his favorite in the whole run—Cornelius in the ruins of his family retreat, staring at a family photo. So I wanted to see how Fábio would handle the same setting. Is that weird? I dunno. There's a part of me that almost can't remember what Bá's pages were like anymore. Between the eye-searing blue and Fábio just owning everything he touches, CASANOVA is a different book to me now. So I admit on some level I wanted to pit brother against brother and see what shook out.

The first time I remember finding out about superguns, and about Gerald Bull in particular, was after reading Ellis and Cassaday's PLANETARY #18, which was called "The Gun Club." Bull was a real guy, who really was hired to build a supergun—dubbed "Project Babylon" by Saddam Hussein, clearly as unimpressed by mediocre names like "Desert Storm" and "Enduring Freedom" as the rest of us were—ostensibly to lob stuff into orbit. Then he started noodling around with missiles and that was that: the Mossad did, as stated, assassinate him. Although it could've been the Iranian VEVAK that did it, as both Iran and Israel would have good motive for wanting the program shut down. But it was Mossad.

So the supergun, and the Island, were two parts of the storyline that had come together long before anything else in GULA, phantom bits of ideas waiting for narrative to come along.

I came along to thinking about the flashbacks with a sick kind of dread in the pit of my stomach. Because—I don't know, because it was going back to fun times for the cart, because it was bringing Cass back and really, for a book called CASANOVA, I really feel like we've moved beyond the guy. Bringing back stuff from LUXURIA in the middle of all this darkness was really hard for me to get through. This script lingered for a long time, undone.

Part of that was aided by Fábio off doing a paying gig, so there was no time pressure to complete the script. I told myself I was waiting for him, or that the paying work needed priority. Also I just don't like to be that far ahead. It cuts me off, I lose urgency, and I feel like I'm just waiting around. I know it infuriates the twins but I really prefer to only be jusssst a little bit ahead of them[117].

These were all excuses I used to not write this script, when really I knew it was because I didn't want to write the funeral stuff and the flashbacks. It might have been a bit of dirty pool to lop off Cornelius' head last issue only to bring him right back, but that was only to emphasize that Ruby Seychelle wasn't coming back. Only the robots stay dead in CASANOVA, I don't know.

I've gotten pretty obsessed with symmetry this volume, when I figured out it was about sex and violence, pivoting around the monstrous issue 11. There's a lot of reasons that sort of psychic division fits with this volume I don't want to ramble on about, so saying that we're now mired in the violent half of things should, I hope, suffice. Taking it a step further, it was in CASANOVA #6, once again the second-to-last issue in LUXURIA[118], where we added a second color to the mix. One upping the trick here seemed, well, symmetrical. And that was good enough for me.

Doing it LUXURIA green is just the kind of clever crap that amuses me so, even if it adds a ridiculous expense to the price of the eventual collection.

The funny thing about writing the flashbacks was how white-hat good guy Cass came out as, what a sweetheart he became. This volume just seems so much heavier than LUXURIA, and having Cass blow in saying these sweet and wonderful and hopefully very honest and true things to these depressed and brutalized people that love and miss him very much somehow didn't make it any lighter.

Another opportunity, too, to force Fábio to restage and recreate Gabriel's imagery[119]. Fábio told me they played around with having Bá actually do those scenes but rejected it because Bá is in fact now a big time rich and famous comicker who has no need or use for the likes of us. True story: Bá won't even return his brother's phone calls these days. It's a heartbreaking story, dead reader. Avert your eyes! Avert!

The first flashback is from a scene in CASANOVA #2. When I first wrote it, I was still very much learning how CASANOVA moved, and it was way, way longer than appeared on page. Eventually it got whittled down to the two or three panels that saw print, and I was left wondering where the fuck my scene went. Apparently it was here all along.

The second flashback is from CASANOVA #7, and was one of those editorial omissions that depends on the reader filling in some gaps. I love those edits, I love treating our readers like co-conspirators. But you lose weird, fun bits sometimes like this, where you just want to see what happens when these three guys are stuck on a boat, arguing.

Also I miss writing the awful Buck McShane.

Kaito hits the sauce as he and Seychelle have an argument straight out of GREAT MAMBO CHICKEN AND THE TRANSHUMAN CONDITION. I was, oh, gosh, sixteen maybe seventeen, when I came across this book, a portrait of weird science just ahead of the 21st

---

115 "Writing of"

116 This remains a thing that happens when I finish books. Or finish my time on books rather. Like the end of school, like the end of high school or college or something.

117 And ACEDIA is being written "plot style" so – three issues in for Fábio and I've yet to make the words come out of anyone's mouth.

118 RIDICULOUS. We were paying to print all of the colors but choosing to only print two. OY.

119 A kind of motif now.

Century. There's a whole bit about the future of consciousness there, about transcribing your brain to digital, replicable data. It was the first place I can recall encountering that particular stab at immortality and it's vexed me ever since. There are people that swear that this is a perfectly viable way to achieve immortality (assuming such tech were possible, available, etc). And then there's me convinced, much like poor drunk Kaito, that while we may be replicated we can never truly be duplicated. IN fact it kind of terrified me...like imagining some specific kind of mouth torture, or suddenly thinking about a papercut between your toes, I suck air in sharply and wince at the thought. I can feel my intrinsic me-ness never making it to the digital backup.

Anyway. In a book where numerous characters have back up brains and digital copies I wanted at least ONE person to say, holy crap, this is a nightmare, we cannot be copied, for we are unique in subjective ways never to be repeated.

And here is the start of Kaito's long way down[120].

The third flashback uses a gimmick I think I abuse, quite frankly, as its transition point, where I use a repeated phrase or cluster of words as a kind of call-and-response transitional link into a new scene[121]. I know I did it because I needed a way into the dead robot's flashback and had to break the rules of good and orderly narrative fracture. Oh well. I really noticed the gimmick in this issue which has made me sort of hang it up across the board on my other work. At least a little bit. I figure, shit, if I'm sick of it, any right-minded reader must be running for the fire exits...

The empty words at a funeral are slowly turning into a CASANOVA leitmotif. And I love how Fábio presents Kaito here, the last vestiges of that sweet boy from inside the robot gone.

Oh, this is maybe a funny story. Originally I wanted to make Kaito the Kefong character from my pal Joe Casey's lamented book THE INTIMATES. I was just gonna plunk the guy into MY book and plug along. Joe thought it was hilarious and insisted I do it. But then I realized that, ho ho clever gets your ass ha ha sued.

But yeah. Kefong[122].

Our last flashback is from CASANOVA #7 and breaks off from the rest of the flashbacks in that...well, it actually takes place in between CASANOVA #7 and CASANOVA #8. The reason for that has to remain obscure for the time being, but it's a specific choice.

This was another chance to see Cass being sweet, to see Kaito as a sweet kid, and to just have people sit and drink and talk and, again, I couldn't resist. As much as it bummed me out to do, letting just a hint of light in was a relief in the end.

When I was doing the proofreading pass on this issue, I noticed the weird deformity Fábio added to Sasa's leg on page 14. I said something to him like, ew, gross, I only just now caught that. He said, pssh, you never look at the art.

I had to agree, it gets in the way of all my precious text. So, here: here's some of Fábio's precious text for a change.

> I could go into the references I used to create the big spaceship I created in this issue, or how it was to draw flashback scenes from Casanova "green years." I could talk about drawing characters who are now dead, or missing, and I could talk again why 16 pages take so long to draw. This is easy, and I can do it anytime. Instead, I want to talk about this issue's script. When I read the script for issue 13, I told Matt it was the best script I had ever read. It was. It is. And I start wondering why.

> The more "one mission per issue" formula of the beginning of the Casanova saga was great to give the story enormous speed and rhythm, and to show how much you can tell in just 16 pages. Also, I think, it showed how much story you can tell by cutting the fat and all the explaining comics seem to use these days. There's a lot of information that the reader doesn't need to enjoy the story, and all this information got cut out. This is a great "tool" Matt uses as the writer, and one that he's getting better and better at. But writers do think about these informations they don't show, sometimes writing it in the script for the artist (who will suffer trying to show everything without showing it) to know as well, sometimes just putting on the "backstory" notebook.

> Issue 13 dove into the "backstory" notebook to build a new layer to the characters and their relationships, taking the reader alopng for the ride. You see, the flashbacks are "filling the gaps" from moments we already saw in earlier issues, moments we as readers remember in a similar fashion the characters remember them, and because of that we feel part of the story, and we join the character to mourn the loss of a loved one. We feel included in the story, and it doesn't feel forced. All the memories show Casanova, our main character (which I finally got to draw again), but through his eyes we see all our ensemble cast with a new light, a new layer. Casanova makes each character feel unique, and human, and special.

> That's how Matt makes us feel as well with this script.

> That's beautiful writing, Matt, and I applaud you.

•

He's right. I am a stone cold genius and a master of comic bookery. All hail me.

In all seriousness I have no idea how to follow such a wonderfully kind thing to say, so let's wrap this up.

Only one more to go. The wolves allll come home. Get the party hats ready.

Fraction
KC MO
03/04/08

---

120   See CASANOVA: AVARITIA.

121   Eh, I still do this. It's either a thing good enough for David Lean so it's good enough for me, or I'm a hack and I can see my own fingerprints and hate it. Back and forth, back and forth, no rest for the wicked.

122   Oh, shit – I completely forgot about that until just now.

GULA, Issue 3 (Icon Comics, 2011)

About a year ago, in a Marvel editorial summit, Steve Wacker[123] asked me if I'd be willing to contribute something to a near-WHAT THE—? kind of parody book he as putting together, spoofing the return of Steve Rogers, called WHO WON'T WIELD THE SHIELD. I said yes but it was couched will all kinds of outs for myself in case no idea ever came to me or I got too busy. A soft yes, I suppose you'd say. Anyway, later that day he turned to me and, having just finished editing comics legend Brendan McCarthy's Spider-Man and Dr. Strange book FEVER, suggested teaming the two of us up.

I wrote the script that night, in one frantic blast, listening to James Brown's LOVE POWER PEACE: LIVE AT THE OLYMPIA, PARIS, 1971 over and over. It was one of the greatest and weirdest joys of my career[124].

I can't adequately express to you how much I love McCarthy's work. I could barely articulate it to him. I am eternally grateful to Steve for connecting us, and to Brendan for letting me pick at his brain for a bit while gushing all over the guy.

●

Matt Fraction: At the last signing I did, a guy brought a copy of your book SWIMINI PURPOSE[125] by—just to show it off. To prove it existed, to prove that he had one. I offered him everything I had on me for it, but he wouldn't budge.

I keep trying to talk about your work, as I have encountered and experienced it, in a way that doesn't make you sound either DEAD or like some weird European party drug. And I keep failing. You are WONDERFUL and MYSTERIOUS and, at least over here, EXOTIC and all-too-RARE. Never moreso than with STRANGE DAYS, a kind of anthology series you were a part of, splitting art duties with Brett Ewins, and written by Peter Milligan. Finding this book, getting to read it for the first time, was one of those revelatory, shearing-off-the-skull-cap kind of moments for me. I have a feeling that STRANGE DAYS is to comics what Brian Eno said the first Velvet Underground record was to music: only bought by a few thousand, but it inspired every single one of 'em to start bands of their own...without STRANGE DAYS there's no Vertigo, for example...

Anyway, it's been a great year to be a fan of your stuff, as you've been seemingly exploding with comics work and new ideas for comics, but before I get to that, what can you tell me about how STRANGE DAYS came together?

Brendan McCarthy: Strange Days was published by Eclipse Comics way back in the mid 80s.

I had gone to California from the UK for the first time a few years before. I was trying to sell a movie pitch I'd cooked up with Pete Milligan called Freakwave, a "Mad Max goes surfing" concept that I'd come up with whist traveling around Australia. Mad Max 2: The Road Warrior[126] had totally blown me away and I had gotten into the surfing culture and put the two themes together...(the Waterworld[127] movie came much later.)

Anyway, I had no luck selling a movie in LA, but I met Dave Stevens (creator of The Rocketeer)...He saw my work and put in a call for me to Eclipse Comics and raved about my stuff to them. They were one of the major companies of the day. So they commissioned a Freakwave comic, eight pages as part of an anthology series called Vanguard. The fan reaction was strong, so Eclipse asked if we'd like to continue Freakwave in its own limited series comic and see how it went. I talked it over with Pete Milligan and we decided to create a new series with three stories in every issue, as we had so many good ideas for new characters. With London artist Brett Ewins on board to complete the trio, we came up with the title Strange Days.

We were an early part of that new British comic invasion—and other than Alan Moore doing Swamp Thing, we were the first Brits to get out own American creator-owned series. Love and Rockets was in its early days...The Dark Knight Returns was just coming out, and Judge Dredd was hitting the USA...There was a lot of buzz around the comics scene and I was looking to shake things up a bit; the Freakwave strip mutated into a bizarre Lewis Carroll type of story about giant floating headships (inspired by the film Zardoz) and the surreal adventures of Captain Cracking and his Merry Meringues. It was kind of "abstract comics"...It almost wrote itself, a real fusion of me and Pete's art school methodology and influences.

My other strip was me trying to be bit more commercial. A new kind of superhero: Paradax! was the first of the fuck-you media-brat type heroes. It led to a million wannabes, most notably Zenith. Pete's X-Statix was a group version. You can even trace a line through to Kick-Ass[128]. It was miles away from all the boring shit that was going on at the time. It was a break with the older type of heroes.

Sandwiched in between all this was Johnny Nemo. Brett and Pete created a futuristic, hard-boiled detective who was the nastiest PI in all of comics! And it was very funny too.

But the main thing about Strange Days was the big fucking swaggering attitude[129]: punk and sci-fi and drugs and sex—anything we wanted, when we wanted it—and a few weird one-pagers thrown into the mix for the hell of it! Now that's what I call a comic!

---

123   Now a part of Marvel Animation out on the west coast and the east coast publishing world is worse off for it. Steve's one of the good ones.

124   That feeling, that all-too-rare, all-too-quick-to-fade feeling is better than drugs. It's better than anything. Those times when I feel like a conduit, like a vessel. It's all automatic. It's the best. I chase it every day.

125   While SWIMINI remains rare, Dark Horse published THE BEST OF MILLIGAN AND McCARTHY in 2013 and it is worth ten times its cost.

126   Brendan has subsequently worked on MAD MAX: FURY ROAD.

127   The first of many times Mr. McC was... well, let's call it *ahead of his time.*

128   STRANGE DAYS and MARVELMAN/MIRACLEMAN, both out of print and unavailable for so long, both cast shadows long and dark that fall over comics to this day.

129   It remains a blast of energy, anarchy, and excitement. Comics own *nouvelle vague.*

MF: Yeah! Yeah, that's completely is—STRANGE DAYS has that punk swagger like REPO MAN and VIDEODROME, those early years of LOVE & ROCKETS or Ryu Murakami books...something atmospheric about it that makes it so compulsively readable and amazingly cool. And effortlessly so. I don't know what or how it could be replicated or duplicated. Even today it's a wholly singular thing and I love it so much it drives me crazy. I'd smoke it if I could.

How did you guys work together? I know when you and I did DOCTOR AMERICA it was "Marvel Style[130]"—were you working that way, even then? Tell me something about Pete, I guess, and how you two met and collaborated. I feel he's so unsung for so much of his overall body of work; the stuff the two of you did together are really roadmaps for the western industry's "alternative" model throughout the nineties.

BMcC: Pete has been one of the best writers in comics. In the short period when he worked mainly with me and Brett, he was at his greatest: Freakwave, Paradax!, Mirkin the Mystic, Johnny Nemo, Bad Company, Skin, Skreemer, and Rogan Gosh were a fantastic run of incredibly ballsy, original and funny strips, with wildly different styles and voices in the writing[131].

How it usually worked was, I would start with an idea for a character and the style or attitude that the strip should take. We'd then sit around, often in a bar, and throw it all about and have a bit of fun with it all and when we felt we had something good, Pete would bugger off and write a brilliant script and I would then draw it...But if I thought of a new good scene or whatever, I'd call Pete and we'd char come more an often change the thing as we were working on it. It was all very loose and easygoing, not too much ego going on in those days[132].

I realize now that the creative relationship we had was rare, as most writers tend to be somewhat dictatorial and want you just to illustrate their mighty script and don't you dare change a word, etc. I think that if writers loosen up a bit and share the creative authorship, then you can get a bit more of that "Lennon-McCartney" synergy happening. You can that going a bit with Casanova, I feel.

For me and Pete it was a certain time of our lives, when we were just starting out, both fresh out of art college, so we really had no idea of what we were doing. We were just relying on artistic instinct, really. We were so ignorant about the production of comics that Pete, as the writer, would actually do the lettering, as we assumed it was his job to sort all that part of it out. He'd turn up with a load of word balloons in his pockets and we'd glue them onto the artwork—before getting too drunk!

MF: Okay, that's amazing. How was it received, in its day? And what other comics were you guys looking at, thinking about, considering? I'm curious to know what the scene was like, then.

BMcC: Strange Days was pretty much ignored by the comics establishment[133], as we weren't interested in playing the game. And it didn't fit into the Fantagraphics' indie culture[134] and it was too fucked up for the mainstream. It was kind of pre-Vertigo...It's hard to explain—maybe it was too British or something. It was its own thing. But I can tell you that some of today's key star writers and artists certainly were "inspired" by it, most notably Grant Morrison and Jamie Hewlett.

We were more like an art or rock group, but as comic creators. That's how we saw ourselves, anyway...Still, it's all water off a duck's arse, isn't it?

In terms of influences, you had Brett Ewins' "big bastard with a gun," Dredd type in Johnny Nemo, mixed with Pete's hilarious Mickey Spillane pastiche scripts. The British gangster film The Long Good Friday was a big influence there. I was more into Mad Max, Infantino, Liberatore, Moebius, Ditko, Yellow Submarine, art school things like Surrealism, Max Ernst and Dada. Pete was bringing a lot of literary stuff to the books, particularly James Joyce. It all got mixed up together into an anarchic, punk-rock soup. There was a "group think" at work too, which gave the comic its cohesion.

If you're coming from musical influences like the Velvets, Beatles, Bowie, Roxy Music, etc., it produces a different narrative style than from aping noir film clichés—which is where Watchman and Dark Knight were coming from. We were the opposite of "grim and gritty." Our psychedelic occult strip Mirkin the Mystic later became a big influence on Alan Moore.

Strange Days was radical in its day...But now, I'm a "hipster apostate"...These days Hipsterism is a totally safe position, it's just commodified critique designed to bestow a neutered cultural superiority on some "ironic" smart-asses. It's become a "savvy understanding" of no consequence.

MF: I get the art school group-think thing—I was in art school, then film school, then animation, and a group of pals and I went into business because—well there were lots of reasons—but mostly because we all knew what we could accomplish together was something more remarkable that we'd either do alone or for some other fucking company somewhere else. Art school is like being in the army for sensitive moody young men or something...

It's funny, how you talk about rejecting the grim/grittiness of it all; to me you're one of the very few guys that have an idiom, or at

---

130   Also known as "plot style," this is a method and format of creating a comic script less like a screenplay and more like a piece of prose, with plot description rather than called panel shots for the artist to create. Often with no dialogue or sketchy dialogue (or, alternately, all dialogue, like a stage play, and only a vague notion of stage direction), this technique – which I've adopted almost exclusively since the writing of the above – cedes a lot of the visual control of a story back to the artist and creates, in my experience, far more visually compelling pieces of work.

131   I keep trying to find fault with this? To take pause at the ego reflected here? But... but I don't think he's wrong. Milligan's done amazing work since but that all of the above were happening *at the same time*...

132   This remains the best way to make comics. Have collaborators, have partners, have co-conspirators, not employees...

133   I find this shocking until I think about equivalent works in other media going unheralded and unsung in its day only to be appraised as a masterpiece later.

134   Again, kind of shocking. I wish Spurgeon's history-of-Fantagraphics book had come out.

least a body of work, directly traceable to the Silver Age in all its wackadoo purity and pre-psychadelic wonder. There's something so effortlessly surreal, something so Magritte-esque about Kanigher, Schaffenberger, Broome, and Fox, and Infantino that transcends all that teenage posturing and HARD MAN bullshit…anyway there's a straight line from that kind of stuff directly to you, I think, that somehow avoids all the Big Talk of later eras. And whereas so much of that wave of comics dates very badly in terms of its fashion and vide and attitude, STRANGE DAYS—and everything you've done since, really—remains as inventive and fresh as ever.

So as a hipster apostate[135]—which, if you've not gotten put on to business cards, you should think about it—tell me about where your head is at with regards to comics now. You've done film and television and animation and, like the Velvets, like Roxy, you've inspired waves of people to follow in your footsteps (oftentimes with precise cadences)…still comics draw you back to them.

BMcC: Lately, I find most comics difficult to read, in that I can glaze over pretty quickly. There are the obvious bits of genius here and there, but the more comics ape movie tropes, the less they interest me. Storytelling in comics and the subject matter have become very "filmic" as Hollywood has turned its spotlight on our humble art form. Don't get me wrong, I'm happy for Hollywood to turn something of mine into a monstrous cash cow. But I just don't enjoy deploying film clichés in my own work to achieve that. When you've worked on lots of films, the moves are easy to spot. That's when I start looking for something more original.

I want to take people places they haven't been to before[136]. Comics at their best have, to me, always been about ideas, imagination and interesting, different stories. The movement to online reading may be a great game changer as all sorts of digital techniques can enhance the experience. I want to get Apple to fund a "flash"/comic hybrid, sort of one of those "motion comics" but actually done right[137]…I'm curious—when does a comic stop being a comic and evolve into another art form?

Also, comics are all about striking characters. That's what I'm always attracted to initially. And the art. The art has to be good, otherwise I can't read 'em, not matter how good the writing is.

MF: I hear about the budgets on some of these motion comic things and I want to put my head through a wall—for the amount of money some folks are spending on these things I could make an actual animated film, designed from the ground up to work as a comic or as a piece of film from its inception rather than one or the other poorly retrofitted…

What's your process like, when you make you own comics? How do you start and how do you get to where you're going? And just from a practical standpoint, are you all-digital these days?

BMcC: I'm semi-digital in that I like to draw with a pencil and pen on paper. It keeps an organic (or warm "analog") feel to the art[138]. Then I scan it in, semi-colored, and add digital color and effects… I like being able to "mix" the images to give sequences a different production feel that matches the mood of where the story is. Also I look at lots of random magazines to try and get a more "magazine" flavor to the strip. Magazines look totally different to comics, but you still read words, look at pictures and turn pages.

I hugely admire artists that can keep the exact same tone throughout a comic, like the "easy" brushiness of Joe Kubert or the slicker Kirby/Royer stuff. But I'm not one of them. I like things to change a lot, so that the first time you read the story, you don't know what's coming over the next page turn. I like a high degree of novelty—lots of idea and visual surprises. Within the commercial constraints of Marvel, I had a lot of fun with Spider-Man: Fever, taking the reader into some unusual places. There are psychological spaces in, say, David Lynch's Twin Peaks that you don't experience anywhere else, but it's played within a TV soap structure. I prefer a looser feel to narrative, as everything tends to be getting too honed, in that "tasteful" post-HBO style. Let comics be comics. Let a bit of anarchy back in[139].

If you source comics out of music rather than film, you can come up with more original story structures. That short strip we both did for Marvel last year was an interesting experiment. It felt like a Talking Heads song video rather than a short film; it played its cuts at different beats and with differently presented imagery ways…I'm drying for mainstream comics to open up a bit again and stop servicing Hollywood. Let's see an Iron Man done like Frank Miller's Ronin, for example. I'd certainly be taking a look.

I usually start a new piece from a doodle, one that contains a puzzling concept contained in a character scribble. Then I let it brew…it can take years, but eventually other things coalesce around the central idea and soon a story comes.

MF: Do you think you'll ever be done with comics? Do you think you'll ever walk away from the medium completely, never to return? What is it about these insane, frustrating, amazing things that keep us around?

BMcC: I think comics are embedded deep in my DNA. They were the medium that excited me the most as a boy. Later on, TV and film started to enthrall me and I eventually worked in those industries for about 20 years, after a decade creating comics in England in the 80s. That was the most exciting time to be in comics since the Sixties, when Alan Moore and all the British invasion gang were doing their great works. But as it fizzled out, I was looking elsewhere; I grew tired of sitting in a room on my own at an art desk, drawing but not really living. Working in films for me travelling all around the globe and having adventures, meeting all sorts of different people. I loved working on Mad Max 4 in Australia—it was a really great thrill to create the next story in his ongoing saga. I adored the Mad Max trilogy, particularly the second one.

---

135   This is such a cop-out. I should've pushed on this.

136   McC's work has always had this vibe to it. Comics as psychic transportation.

137   The cultural gulf between the art and the money has never been so wide, so prevalent, or so profound than when hundreds of thousands of dollars, MILLIONS of dollars, were flushed down the toilet to create .99-app versions of comics that looked like the SPIDER-MAN cartoon from 1967.

138   Interestingly enough (to me) I work in a notebook with a pen or pencil as long as possible before typing for precisely the same reason: there's *warmth*.

139   Again, McC is ahead of his time and I'm frustrated I didn't chase it down and talk about it more. But then again I didn't get it.

After I left comics, I was there in the very early days of computer animation, creating the visuals for the first long form CGI, the animated Reboot TV series. That was well before Pixar and Dreamworks had gotten going, so it really was a totally new world. Maybe having worked so much in film, I tend to look for something different in comics these days.

I spent five frustrating years living in Hollywood attempting to get my own projects up and running. It didn't happen, and that felt like too long a time to be not getting "voice" out there. The place is crammed with smart, brilliant geniuses, time-wasters, bullshitters, and the mentally ill, and you can often "nearly" get something happening only for it to fall apart for a myriad of reasons. Over and over again. And the endless meetings! Meetings and meetings that lead nowhere. So comics seemed like a good opportunity to create something new that would actually be seen.

Coincidentally, at that time DC Comics offered me the final issue of their Solo series and said pretty much, "Do what you like—it's going to be canceled anyway[140]!" That was an offer you don't get every day by a major comics company, so I jumped into it and had a lot of fun. I think it's one of the most unusual and interesting comics ever put out there!

After Spider-Man: Fever, lots of new ideas started to come, so if it's possible to get something worthwhile into print, I'll be doing it. I'm currently developing a new series with ace British writer Al Ewing called The Zaucer of Zilk, which we should have a home for soon. The only downside to comics is the pitiful money… You get spoiled working in film and TV. But the creative freedom in comics helps to make up for it. Creators like Mark Millar have cracked a successful formula and good luck to him, he's a canny lad. If Alan and Grant are comics' magickians, then Mark is comics' alchemist—able to turn paper comics into movie gold!

I have a bunch of new comics projects I'd like to get out into the market, so I assume I will be doing them for as long as the interest is out there. With comics, it is still possible to create stories that can't be told in any other medium and that's why I like them still.

GULA 7, Issue 14 (Image Comics, 2008)[141]

1. Paper Planes[142] – M.I.A. from KALA (3:24)
One night, pretty much out of nowhere, this track came on and in one weird and gleaming second the entirety of CASANOVA #14 was in my head. Every beat, every frame, every line, all of it. The book was done; I needed to type it.

2. Young Folks – Peter Bjorn and John, from WRITER'S BLOCK (4:39)
Hadn't heard this song since summer when Jim McCann at Marvel played it during the winter editorial retreat. The whistle stuck in my head for the week of Christmas when I wrapped the book, sick again like I was in spring. A warning: HURRY UP.

3. You Only Live Once – The Strokes, from FIRST IMPRESSIONS OF EARTH (3:05)
As we got closer to babytime, I went back and listened to The Strokes. I never really gave this record a shot and was really surprised by how much I liked it. Anyway. This, and maybe Frank Sinatra's "The Coffee Song" were in my head when Henry came.

4. The Beat That My Heart Skipped – Dan Le Sac vs. Scroobius Pip (3:48)
The song of the summer. I listened to this obsessively, like a lunatic looking for secret transmissions. Thing is, I can't find or don't' have a clean, studio-produced MP3 so I had to rip this from YouTube. Will streaming audio flange replace radio static?

5. Ashes to Ashes – David Bowie, from SCARY MONSTERS (AND SUPER CREEPS) (4:28)
I would give my right arm for a phrase like "pictures of Jap girls in synthesis," which became some kind of mantra for me back in June. This whole album is the unofficial soundtrack for GULA. Just between us girls, HUNKY DORY was the jam for LUXURIA.

6. 7 Stars – The Apples in Stereo, from NEW MAGNETIC WONDER (3:47)
Summer: lost in Robert Schneider's pop symphonies, walking the dogs in blast furnace heat, thinking about baseball and CASANOVA. When I figured out the Big Secret in 14, the Apples were on. It was Friday; me and Kel went for sushi. I was distracted[143].

7. Woke Up New – The Mountain Goats, from GET LONELY (2:57)
I typed all of CASANOVA #8 from my notes in a singe day, on Kel's grandparents' porch. Inside her grandmother was dying. I felt like I didn't belong there, in those most private of moments. So I wrote. Hard.

8. Evil Will Prevail – The Flaming Lips, from CLOUDS TASTE METALLIC (3:46)
We'd lost the baby. I had left my job. Everything was shaped like a question mark and felt like a stomach ache. I saved Zeph's life; things started to get a little better. Evil might prevail. I didn't care anymore.

9. Six Days – DJ Shadow, from THE PRIVATE PRESS (5:02)
The sound of a noose tightening. This issue, CASANOVA #6, was the hardest one to write. So many pieces to arrange just so, so much bad news on its way. I started to apologize to the characters. Then I started grinding them into dust.

10. River Deep, Mountain High – Ike and Tina Turner, from RIVER DEEP, MOUNTAIN HIGH (3:39)
The ultimate wall of sound epic. Someone once said, it's the sound of god punching the earth, and the earth punching back. Or someone should've said it, anyway. What's the comic book equivalent of this song, I wondered. Ta-da, CASANOVA.

---

140   These are the ten most beautiful words in comics.

141   Working backwards, these songs sum up the fourteen moments in time during which these first fourteen issues of CASANOVA were created, running backwards from the finale of GULA to the start of LUXURIA. People have made YouTube and Spotify mixes of this…!

142   This was before That Movie, before the trailer oversaturation, before throngs of white kids dancing in clubs would pantomime pow-pow-pow-pow with finger-guns in the air. None of this is the fault of the artist. All of this is stated to preserve my own ego and sense of cool and individuality. What bullshit.

143   I RUINED A DINNER because I wouldn't push pause on the idea. That was the end of my belief in the writer's saw about the work just *taking over*. Bullshit. You're being rude, antisocial, anxious, or receding from social obligations. Don't talk about writing like your ideas are malevolent spirits. You just *don't want to do shit and like being alone*, jackass.

11. To Catch a Thief – Lovage, from MUSIC TO MAKE LOVE TO YOUR OLD LADY BY (3:17)
This was a fun issue to write. The method had given itself up finally and I could start having fun. Smashing ideas together and finding a spine. I called it DÉTOURNEMENT for a reason. It wasn't a title—it was a promise.

12. She Will Only Bring You Happiness – McLusky, from THE DIFFERENCE BETWEEN ME AND YOU IS THAT I'M NOT ON FIRE (3:28)
On the road to Big Sur, daydreaming about islands out of reach from the world, of writing the story as we drove, and of murdering my friends to see if I could get away with it. Those rocks go all the way down, y'know?

13. Taxman – The Beatles, from REVOLVER (2:39)
Spent a Christmas gnashing this weird milky mint gum, obsessing over REVOLVER + RUBBER SOUL. All the themes rolled out in CASANOVA #2: creations killing their creators, fathers and sons, sex, pop, secrets. Cass even says: Let me tell you how it will be.

14. Execution Day – The New Pornographers, from MASS ROMANTIC (3:00)
CASANOVA came to me on an elliptical trainer, the New Pornos in my ears. The first time I ever saw him—really, really saw his, the first time I got him—was over the ending of this song. He walked towards me and stared. Hi Cass[144].

Fraction
KCMO
22 April 08

GULA, Issue 4 (Icon Comics, 2011)

God am I glad this is over.

The last part of GULA, contained herein, was finished nearly two years ago.

The short story was written not quite nine months ago.

For those of you that never read the one-color edition of CASANOVA, this kind of ramble is pretty much what the backmatter used to be like. Since this is the last time there'll be backmatter I'm going retro. As it were.

•

Tangentially, I need to apologize to the brilliant Rian Hughes; we'd started an interview piece using his new book CULT-URE, a breathtaking and vital piece about the meaning of design in this day and age, as a centerpiece. Then I realized this was a short-piece, in terms of backmatter (26pp story + 8pp backup = shorter than usual) and we'd already blown through the word count and barely GOT to CULT-URE.

So Rian, my apologies for the wasted time, and do yourself a favor—get a copy of CULT-URE. It is a tremendous piece of work as inspiring as it is informative. Seek it out.

And I need to apologize to you, gentle readerfolk, who may have been dutifully awaiting an interview with John Darnielle of The Mountain Goats ever since our first Icon issue. John and I tried several times to get it up and going, but he was wrapping up a tour and then writing and recording ALL ETERNALS DECK, which should be available by the time you read this, and I was distracted by god only knows what, and we never quite pulled it off. Trust me, between an interview about the enduring allure of cavemen fiction or ALL ETERNALS DECK, you're gonna want ALL ETERNALS DECK. Get the vinyl, too. The packaging is remarkable.

•

Anyway. Here we are at the end of GULA, at long last.

Yes, a collection will follow soon. July. No, there has never been a collection before. No, I don't know why Amazon says there's one. No, I don't know how to get that unlisted from Amazon.

•

I knew before I started writing it where and how it would end; I saw in my head the image of the bullet ripping through Zeph and crows exploding out of her and wrote all of GULA towards that. When I got there, though, I froze up and burned through my lead time, watching Fábio crank through more pages and more pages, not writing a thing.

One night, stuck, I was driving around and M.I.A.'s song "Paper Planes" came on, and in a flash—no other word for it—the whole issue fell into my head. I literally knew in a single instant what fell on every single page. The entire outline just magically appeared, as if I was trying to recall my phone number. All I had to do was type it all out. I think it took me two, three days, to do that—it was a matter of endurance more than anything else.

It was the first time I'd experienced something like that. Every the song titles—I wasn't sure what the songs would be straight off—across the tops of the pages. All of it just magically appeared. Poof! Fucking magic. The net result is that it's totally validating my belief that starting off into space like a dumbstruck moron totally counts as "writing."

You hear stuff about writers going crazy, about the magical thinking that creeps its way into your process. You hear about Alan Moore digging a cave under his house and worshipping a snake god and Grant Morrison being Grant Morrison and you start to wonder if one day somebody's gonna have to feed you applesauce from a fork with a cork stuck on the end.

---

144 A real accounting here would have Roxy Music's "Casanova" as a zero track.

I've woken up from dreams saying names that ended up being real people whose work has inspired me; I've had conversations with characters. One time in a dream a guy walked up to me like opening shot of LAWRENCE OF ARABIA and told me his name and I woke up and knew what his story was all about. I talked to Thor and Odin all night one night and Thor told me he needed his "Doom Ring" back. I dug up something called a dohmring (I think that's how it's spelled; I'm on a plane and can't dig up the reference right now) that Thor had—it was a kind of ringed court with an altar stone in the middle for rendering punishment—that I surely read about and forgot and remembered in the dream. Odin told me he liked the sound "Wotan" more but could never admit it to his fellow gods. I've had crows circle overhead while talking about Odin that were loud the guy on the phone with me wanted to know if I was okay. I've been able to catnap and force-dream my way through a story block. I've misheard song lyrics as dialogue that turned into some pivotal bit of scene work; I've had slabs of images occur to me and wait in my head until they found a home. And then there are the countless ways CASANOVA has predicted events in my life with a degree so eerie I'm tempted to just have Cass win the lottery and fuck off to Maui until he dies peacefully in his sleep at the age of 135.

I've never, ever, ever just "remembered" how to write the story I was supposed to write as if reciting the alphabet.

Anyway so I wrote it like that.

•

Then I added the songs.

It seemed like, since "Paper Planes" was what unlocked the book for me, I should at least pay a little tribute to the majesty of rock.

Music was, at least it was then, a crucial part of my writing process. I tend towards silence these days. Each chapter break counts backwards to the first issue; I had to find the line between songs that actually WERE in the mix while writing those particular issues for the sake of…I dunno, verisimilitude and the like. Sometimes it's not THE song of that particular timeframe or issue in question as a previous song would've made it redundant.

Just a bit of goofy lagniappe for you, if you care about such things. I saw someone on YouTube had made the mix stream-able but I don't know if it's out there still.

Visually, I always like how old Silver Age DC comics had "chapters" with titles—Ed and I did something similar in UNCANNY X-MEN #500—so I wanted to recall that, reclaim that, fiddle with it some. Not sure if it works but it's too late now.

•

YES: I changed the last line.

As scripted, the last few panels read like this:

> 28.5
> FIXED POV ON SASA. Smiling.
>
>   SASA (small)   Yes.
>
> 28.6
> ON CASANOVA: not sure what to make of that either way
>
>   NO DIALOGUE

As drawn, though, I thought it read…off. At least off from my intention somewhat. I know all art is subjective and stuff, but subjectively, it didn't hit right for me and, objectively, it's my fucking book and if we're adding color, then I can tweak the last line so the closing beat hits right. Or rather hits more right.

I hate—let me amend that—I capital-H Hate asking the boys to redraw anything in CASANOVA[145]. I figure it's a collaboration and they process what I give 'em and produce what they produce, and I sure as shit won't ever out-write them. So I let it lie, but it's bugged me ever since. Even if the note hits right with everybody else in the world, it drove me nuts just a little bit. Since this is the version that'll finally be collected, I tweaked it and can now sleep the sleep of the just.

•

The short:

We are the Dead.

•

I literally cannot express to you how glad I am not to do this anymore.

When CASANOVA started, it was very much due to the graciousness and kindness of Warren Ellis, who had created what was know as the "slimline" format of book—16 pages plus 8 of backmatter in which the author—Warren, in FELL—would create value-add text stuff to encourage the readers to check out the periodical format rather than tradewait.

CASANOVA was invited to be the second book of a nascent line—hence the "line" part of "slimline"—and to adopt the same format. Which I did and was immediately uncomfortable with.

---

145   This remains true. I will do anything to avoid asking for redraws.

I felt like I'd entered into a contract, though; that I'd agreed to produce a certain thing and needed, then, to produce it, no matter how miserable it was making me. That I'd agreed (to no one but myself, make no mistake; I'm the idiot that kept doing it) to be rigorously honest in whatever I wrote and would thusly continue on now, no matter how miserable it continued to make me.

I regretted it almost immediately.

I come from an art school culture; as I learned how to make work I learned how to talk about it. It's not that part that I hate, it's that by its very nature, talking about your work the way I did—or about your life—makes the work less special. Or your life.

I wanted to make something that appealed to process nerds like me; I hated laying it all so bare for whomever to react to however they chose. I was stuck. I had stuck myself. I was fulfilling a promise to nobody but me, but I'd do it, because I always suck at follow-through, goddammit, and surely this was building character.

I love DVD commentaries but I have the option of turning them off or not listening to them; I suppose someone could simply elect not to read these things, but back then they were about a third of the issue—how could they not? Best of intentions and all that and, as I said, it's my wheelhouse, it's where I come from, I LOVE talking that nerdy process trivia stuff but, Christ, am I glad this is the last of it.

At the very best, this stuff never made me feel like anything less than a whore. Even in the Icon edition, where I wanted to do these evangelical interview sorta pieces...my ego is too dense and too massive to not bend all light towards it, I suppose.

Anyway, that's why it's going away.

•

That said...

What if we did a letter column in CASANOVA III?

Not 100% on it yet—but I'm thinking it over real hard. I think back to the letters in INVISIBLES and HATE and EIGHTBALL and think it's a shame we lost them. To me, a letter column is as different from a blog/tweet/net conversation as a letter is from an email. So...so maybe we try that. Maybe.

If you've got something to say no blog or tweet can contain, drop a line to casanovaquinn@gmail.com. Tell me something funny, something beautiful, something weird or sad. Teach me stuff. Draw me something. Tell your fellow casanovanauts what you part of the world looks like.

If you send it, you're giving me permission to print it.

If we do it. I dunno yet.

•

I just finished going through the black and whites of the first issue of CASANOVA III: AVARITA. Its palette selected, I'll start seeing the colors soon from Cris.

There's something appropriate about CASANOVA existing in four different time periods—2008, 2010, 2011, and "September"—all of them collapsing in on one another as I write this, the last of whatever these things are.

God am I glad this is finally starting[146].

Fraction
28,000 miles over South Dakota the pilot just said
17 Mar 11

146 God am I glad this is finally ending.

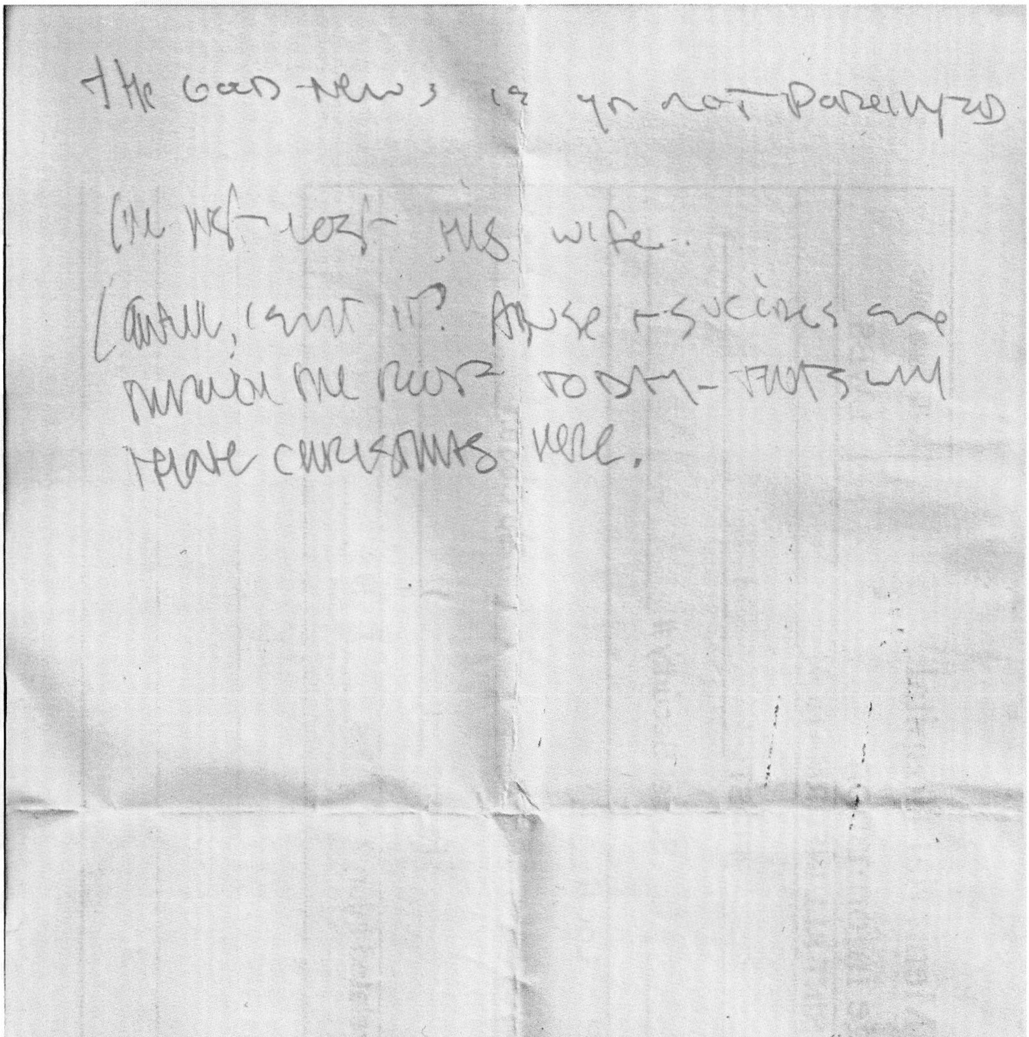

The good news is you're not paralyzed

(He just lost his wife...

Cancer, isn't it? Abuse & suicides are through the roof today - that's why I hate Christmas here.

FIRST WORDS

On Christmas Day, 2006, I was admitted to an emergency room at Fawcett Memorial Hospital in New Port Richey, Florida. During my triage, the above was said to me more or less as it would later be said to Casanova on the the second page of the first chapter. I grabbed another intake form and transcribed as quick as I could and that was the start of the writing of CASANOVA: GULA.

It was, as they say, all true.

James Brown died that day, too; it was on the TV. What kind of god takes James Brown on Christmas?

-Matt Fraction

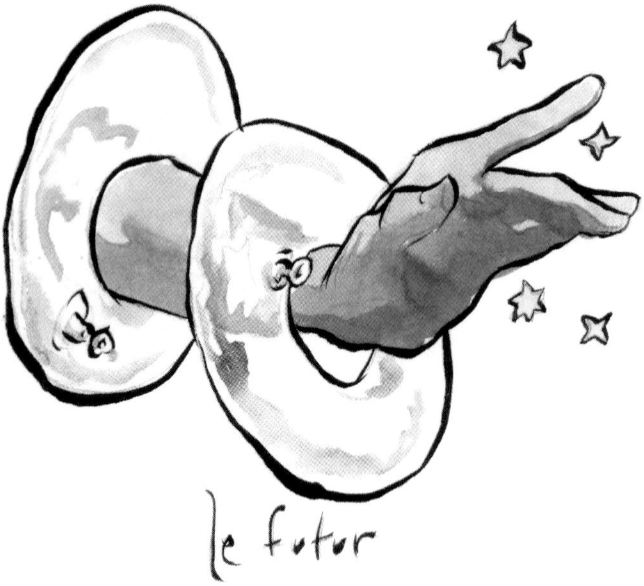
le futur

COVERS

"What will they think of all of this in the future?" comes to mind specially when I think of covers. Maybe it was all those years in Fine-Arts school, surrounded by painters, sculptors and photographers, where you had to look at somebody's work and you could see there was a line of thought that was always there, unifying the work, or maybe it was just a design-based decision to make a nice collection on somebody's bookshelf, but covers have to work together.

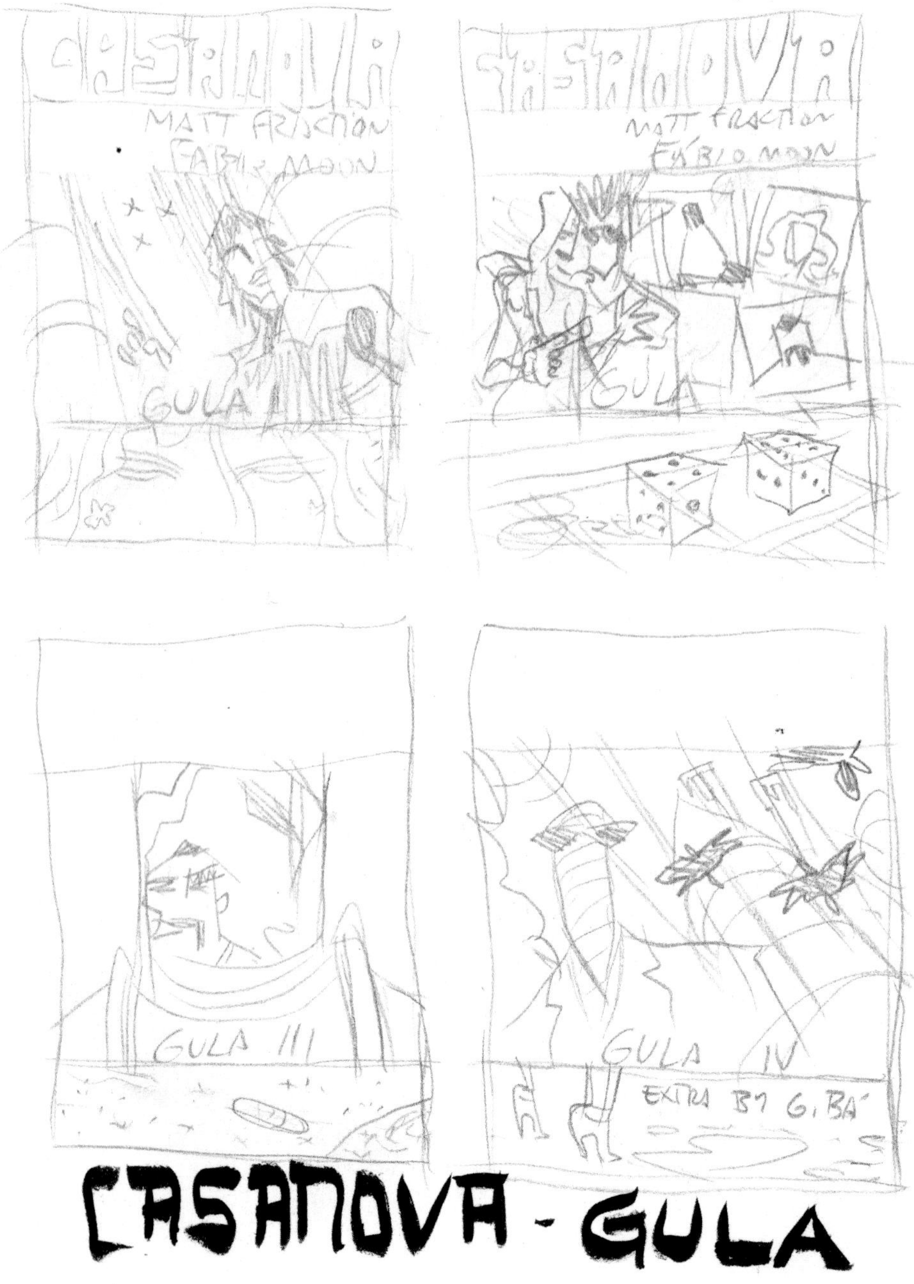
MATT FRACTION
FABIO MOON
GULA
GULA III
GULA IV
EXTRA BY G. BA
CASANOVA - GULA

"In the future", when they bump into any of the covers from this series, they'll go "Ah, that was a Casanova cover." Bá did four amazing covers for the LUXURIA story arc and set the model the covers would follow. My job, still trying to maintain the unity of the collection, was to keep the covers interesting and dynamic instead of repetitive.

The best sensation you get when you're creating a cover is when you do the sketch and you see it working right there on those simple scribbles. I was lucky to be able to do the covers after the entire story was done, so I could do all four sketches at the same time and watch them, together on my notebook, working as a series, telling the same visual story, which starts with our hero, Casanova Quinn, and in the ends reinforces the impact of our villain, Newman Xeno.

The cover of the Icon collection, aside from having the same design as Bá's LUXURIA cover, had the advantage of having a sexy hot Sasa Lisi in it, because nothing sells more books than a sexy hot alien from the future.

Fábio Moon

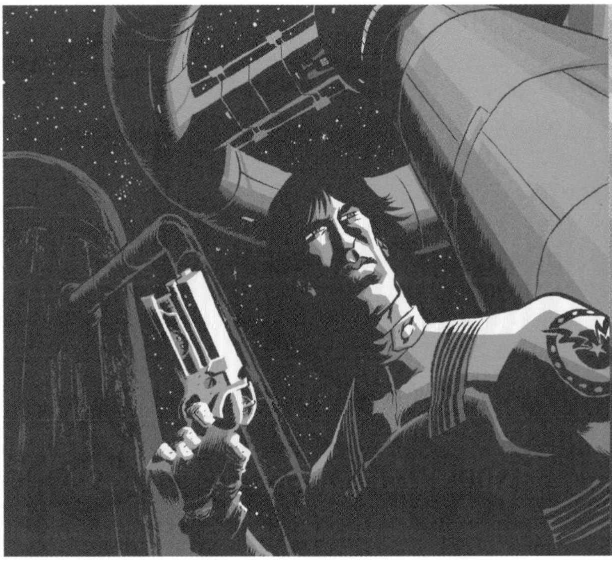

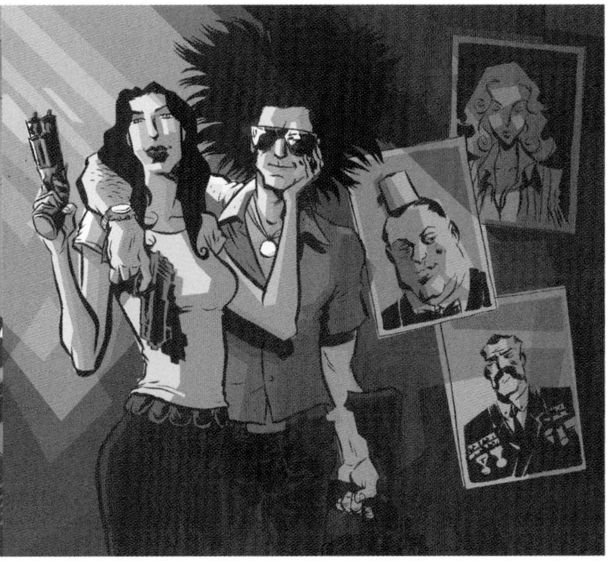

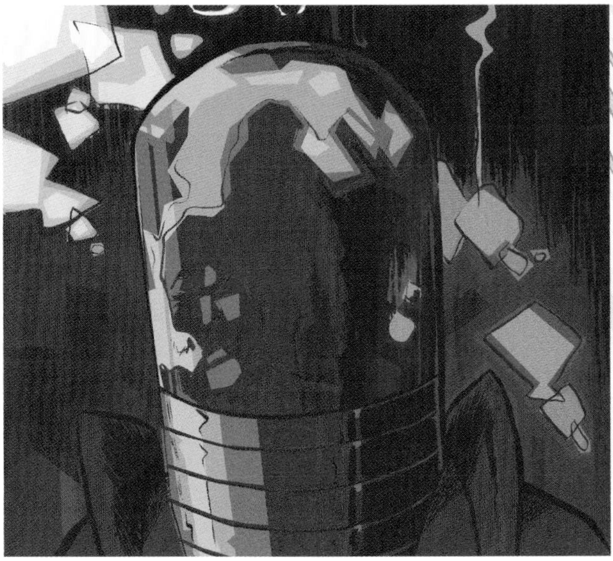

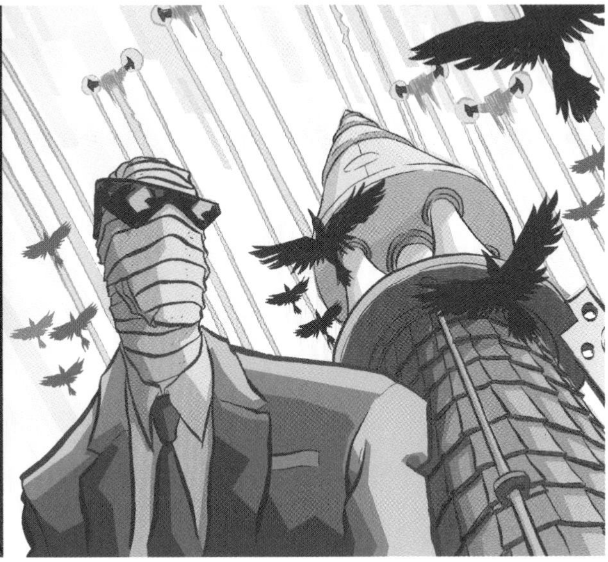

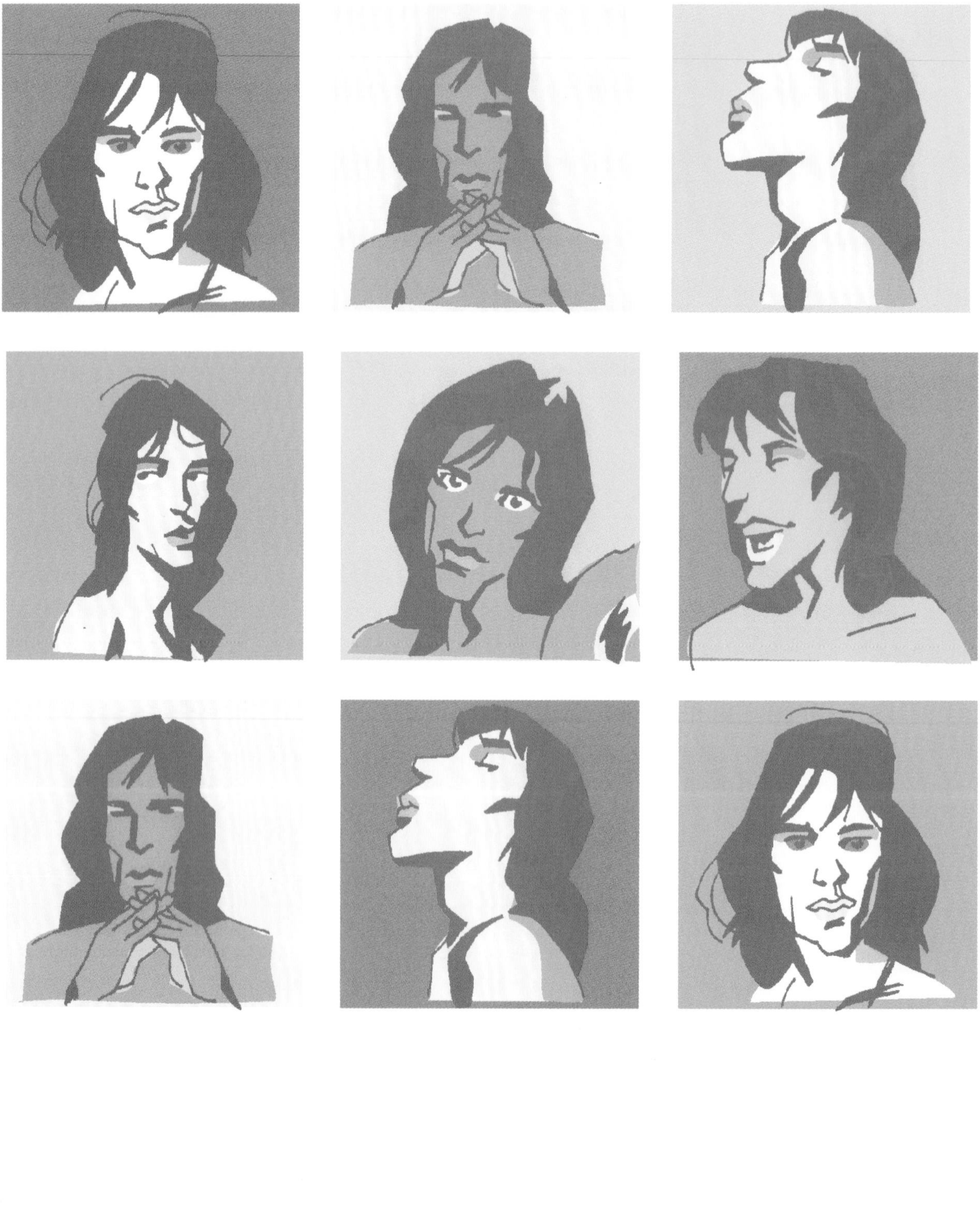

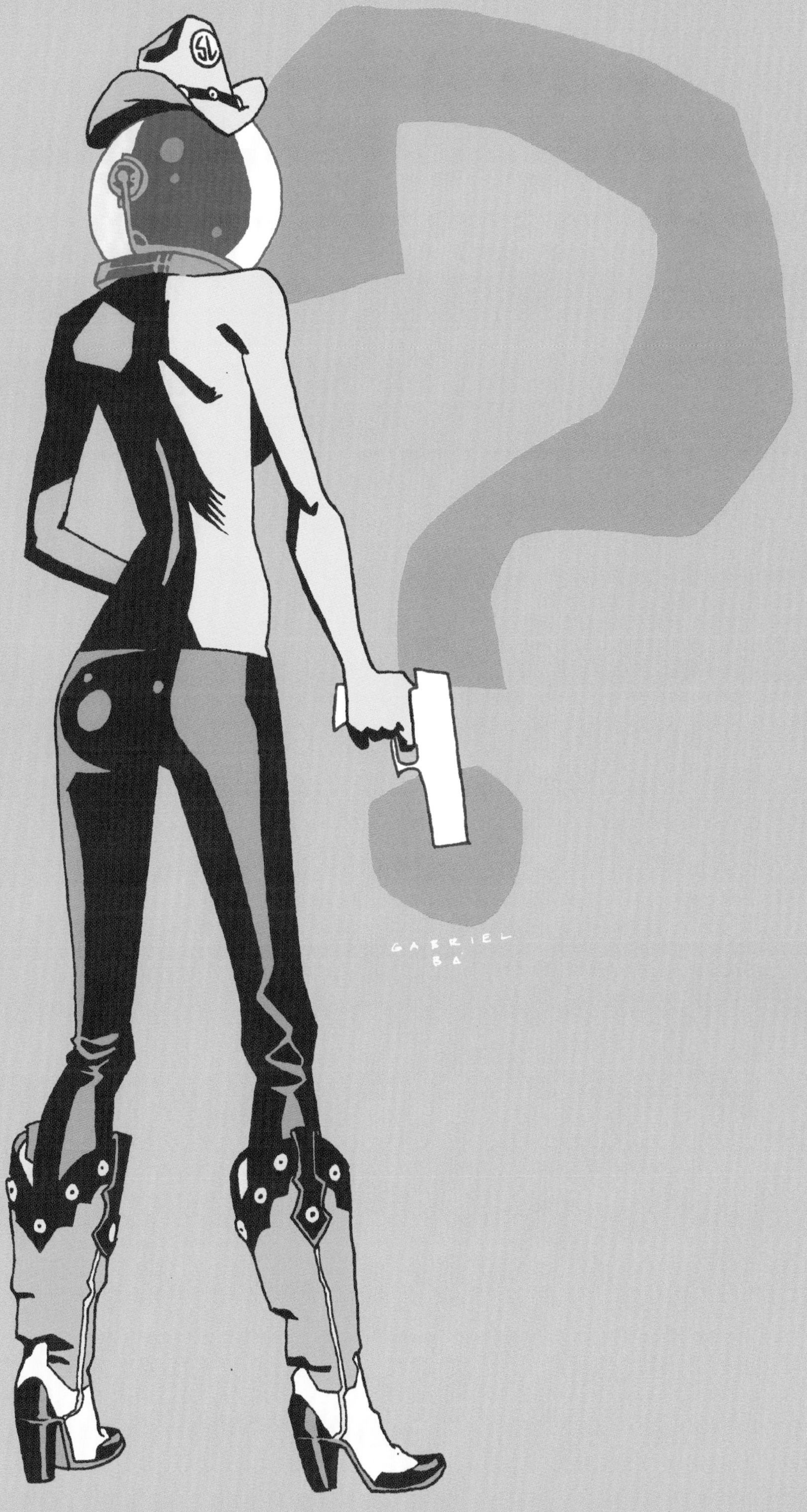
GABRIEL BÁ

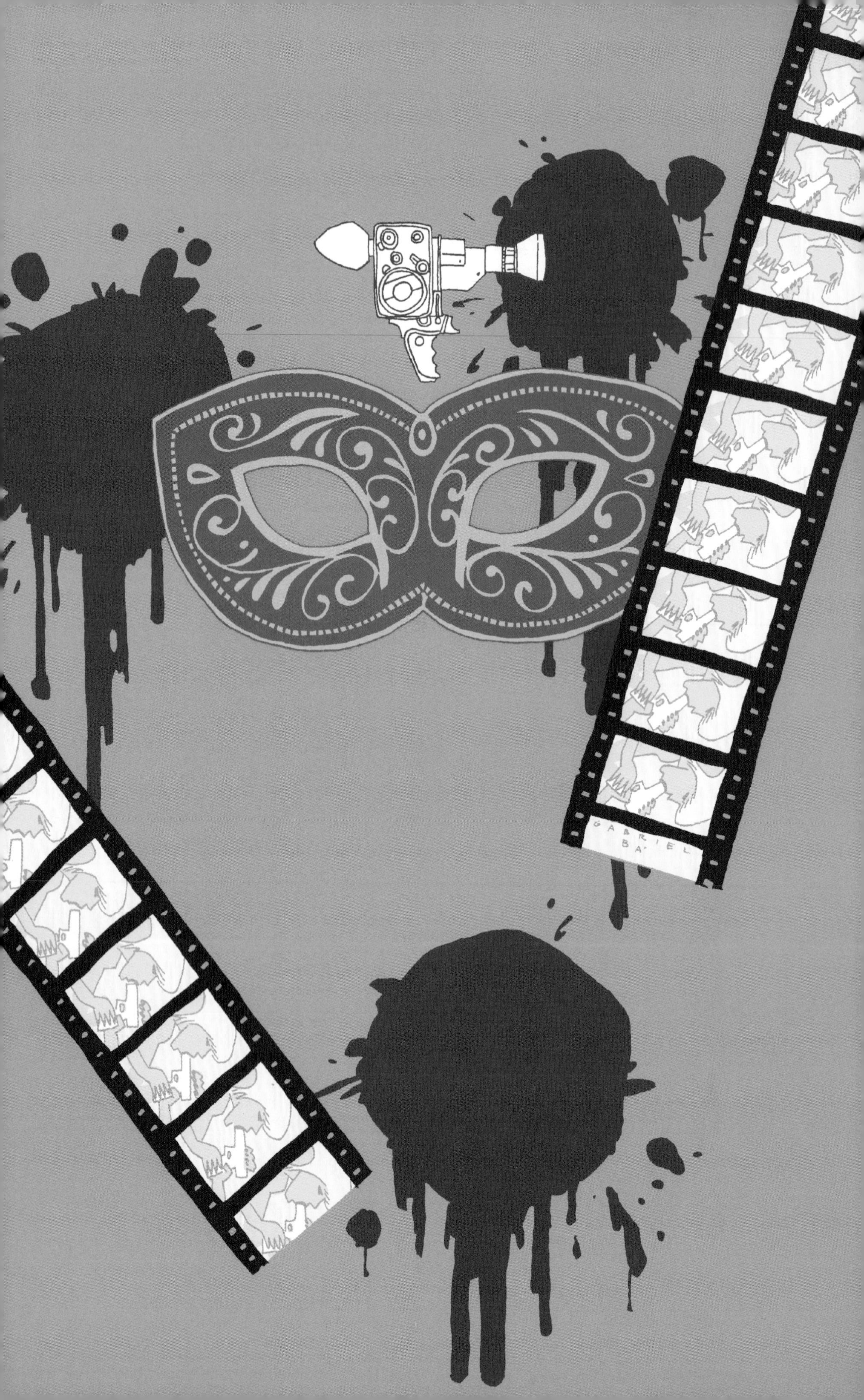
GABRIEL BÁ

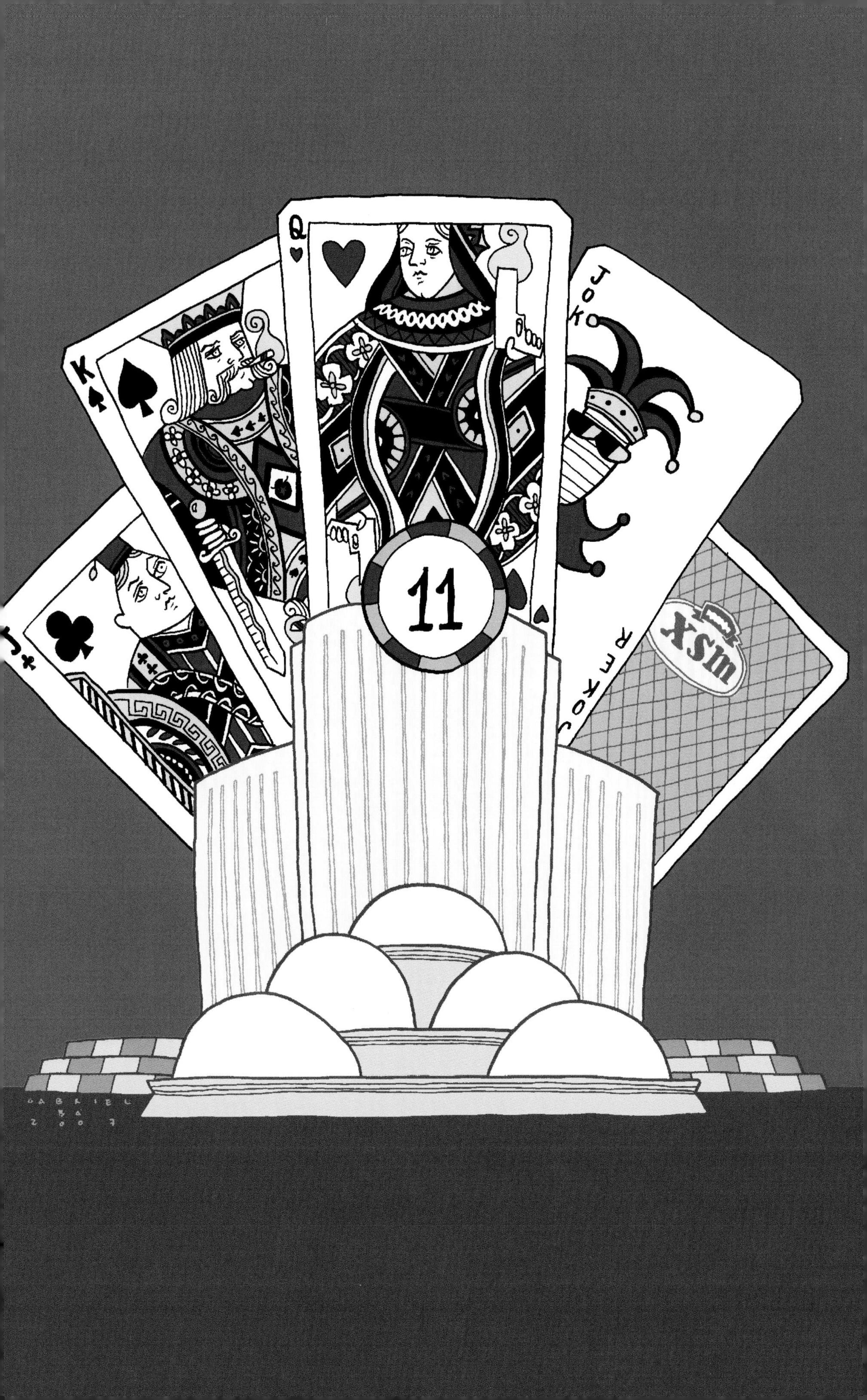
11
GABRIEL BA 2007

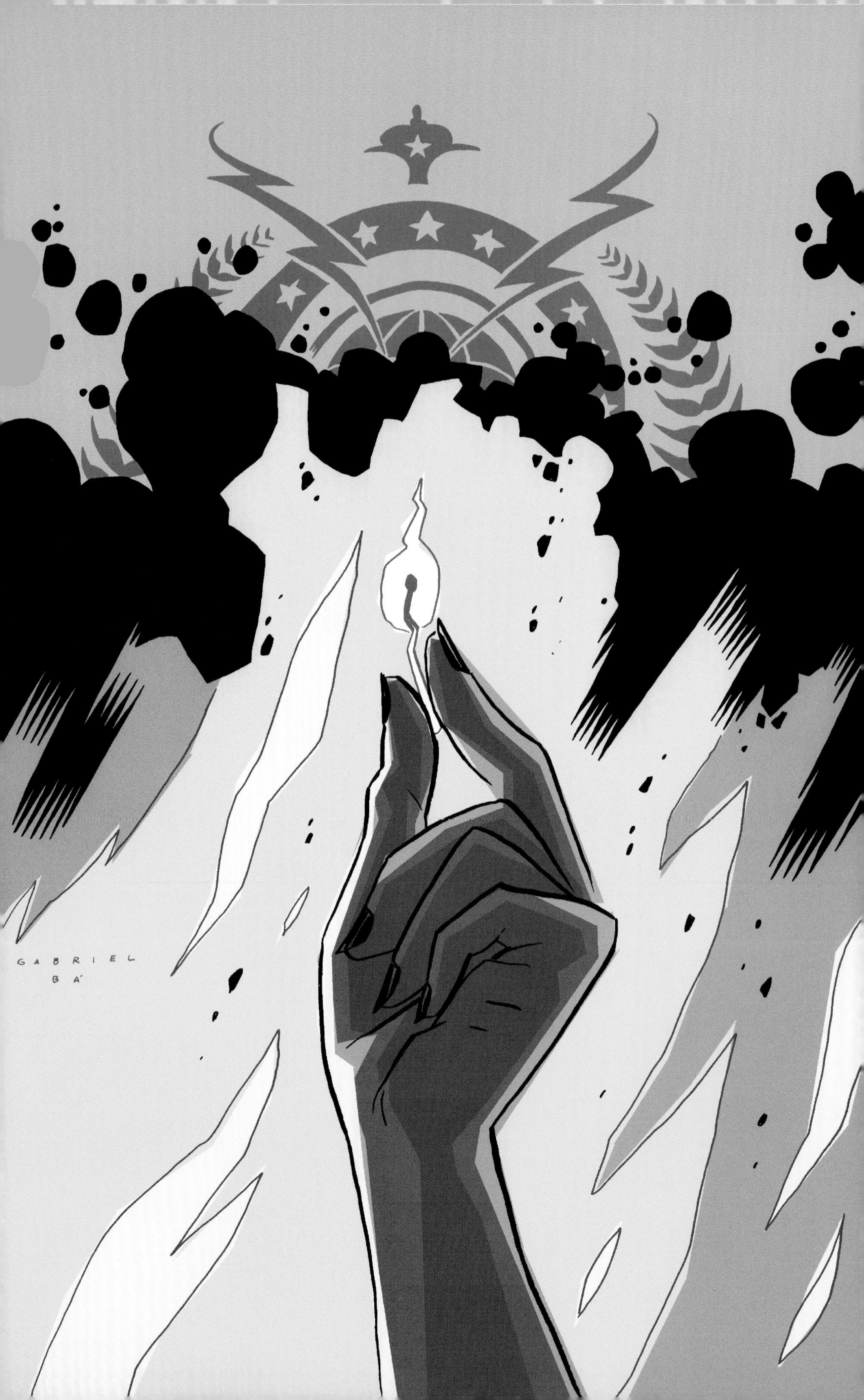
GABRIEL
BÁ

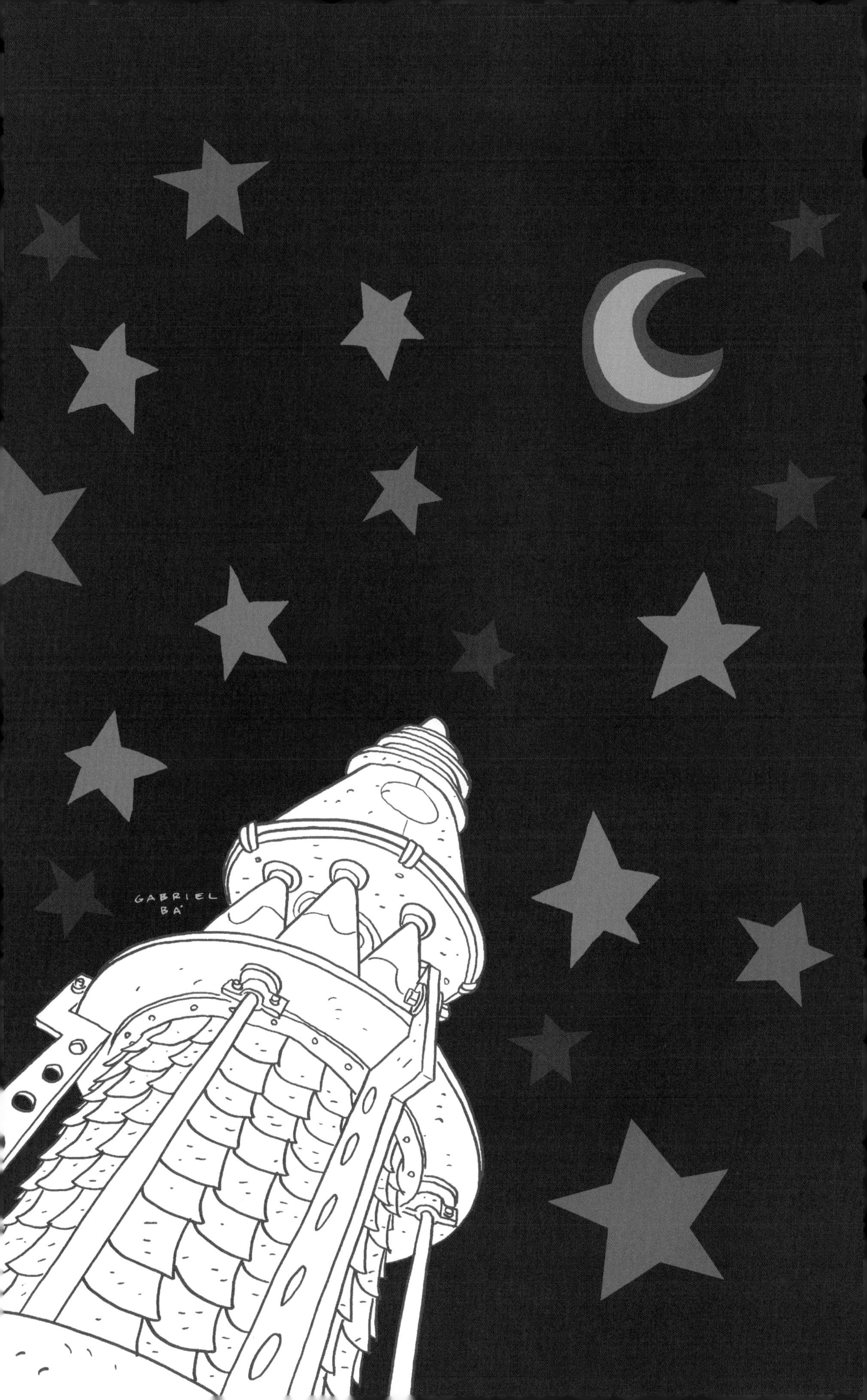
GABRIEL
BÁ

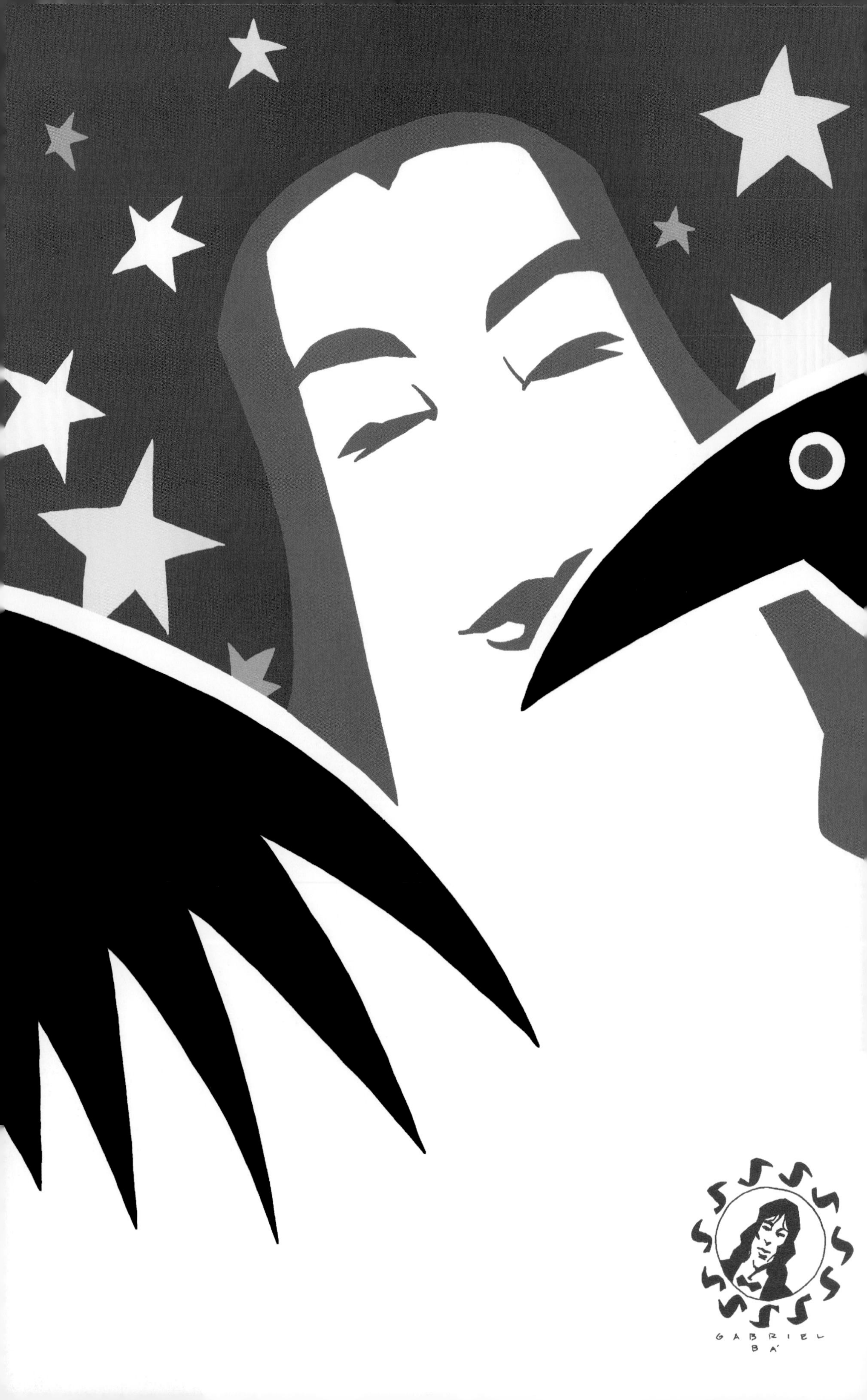
GABRIEL
BÁ

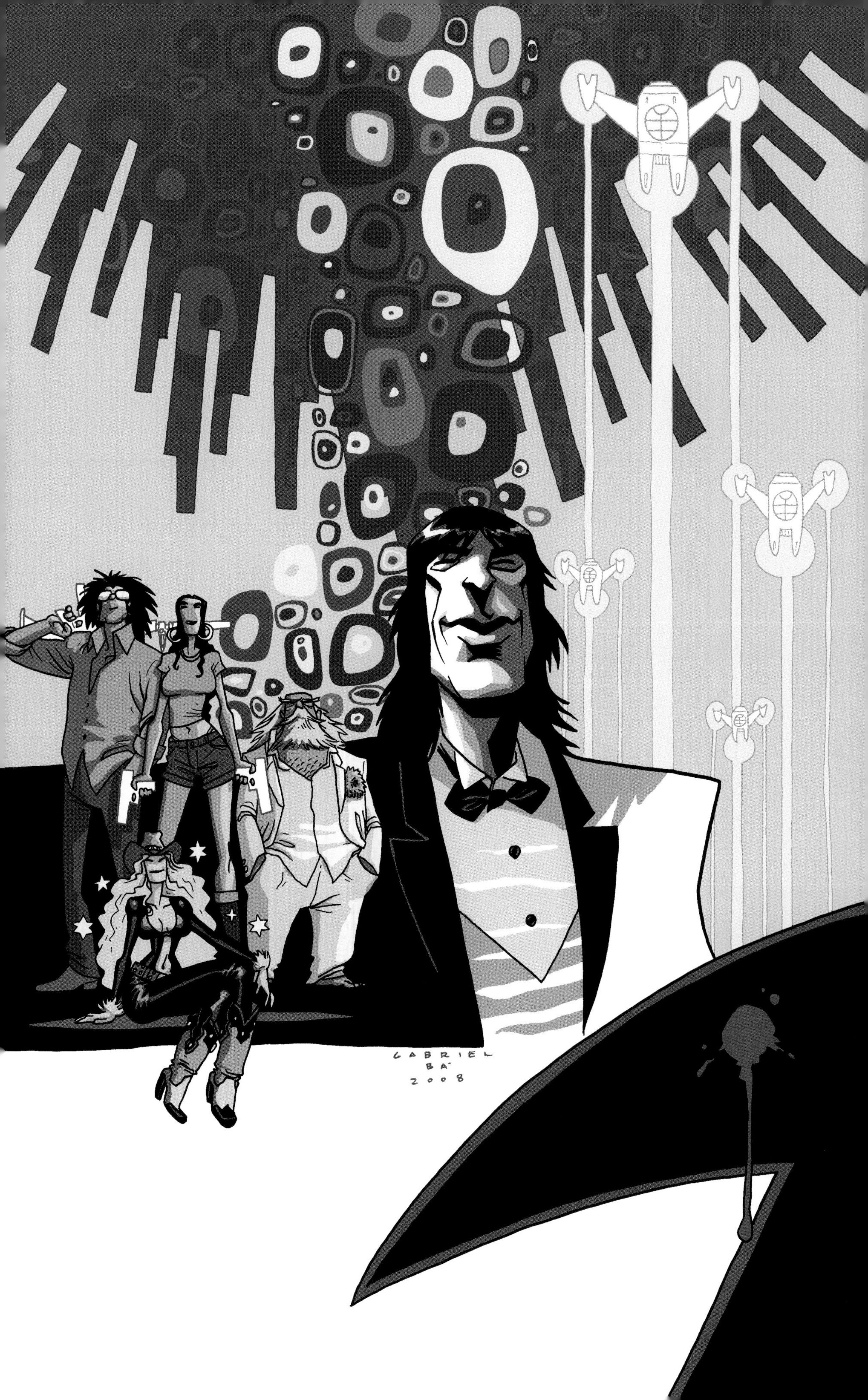
GABRIEL
BÁ
2008

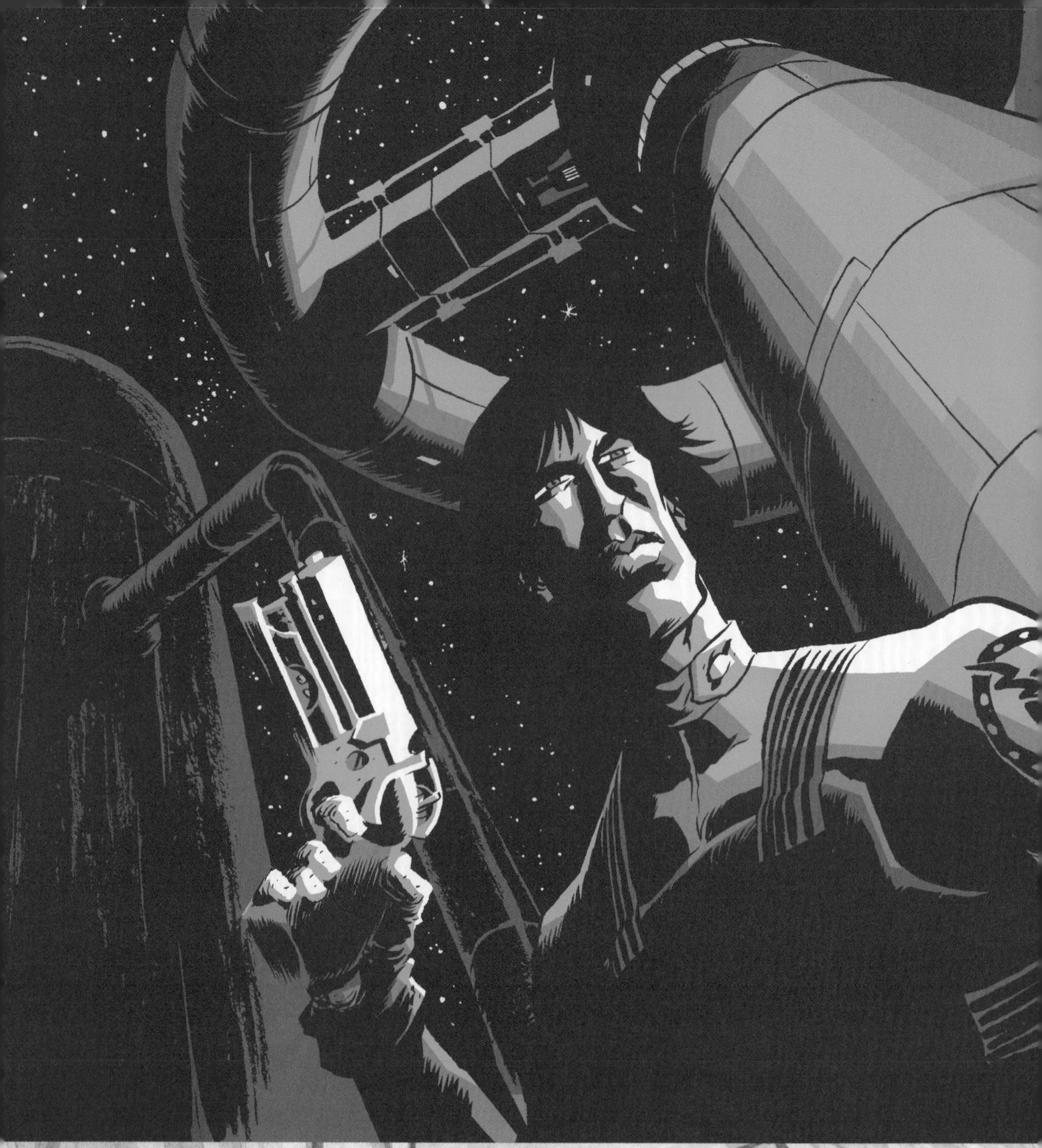

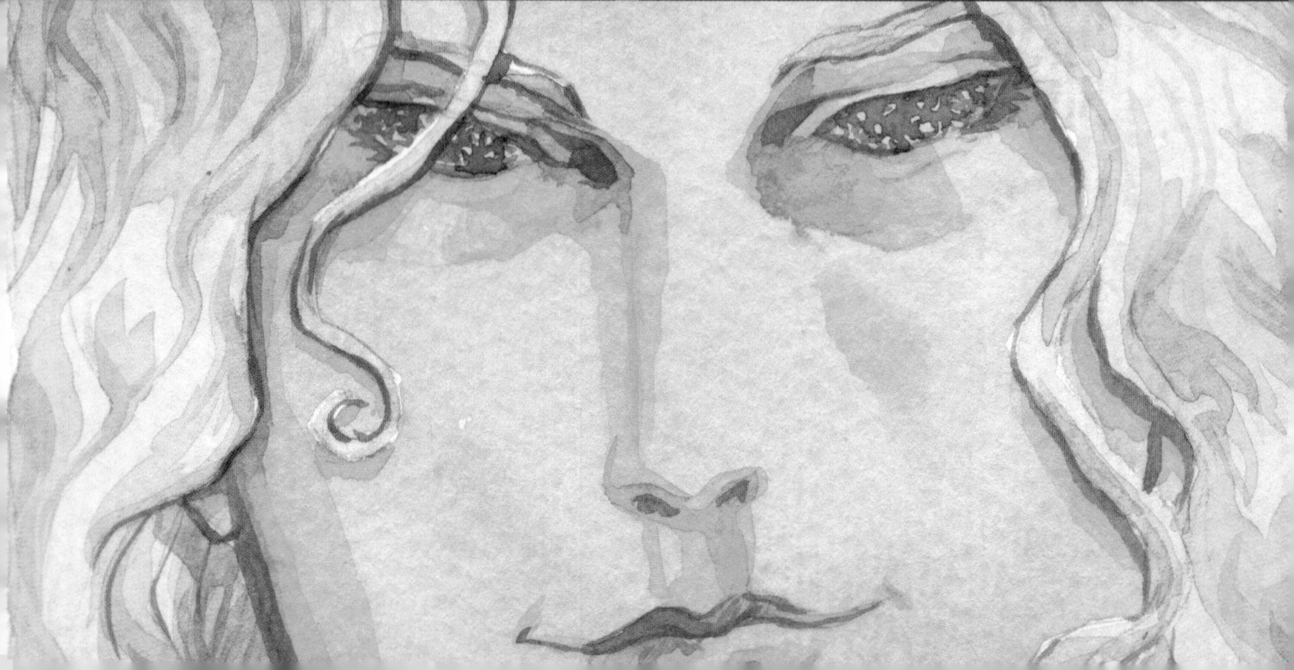

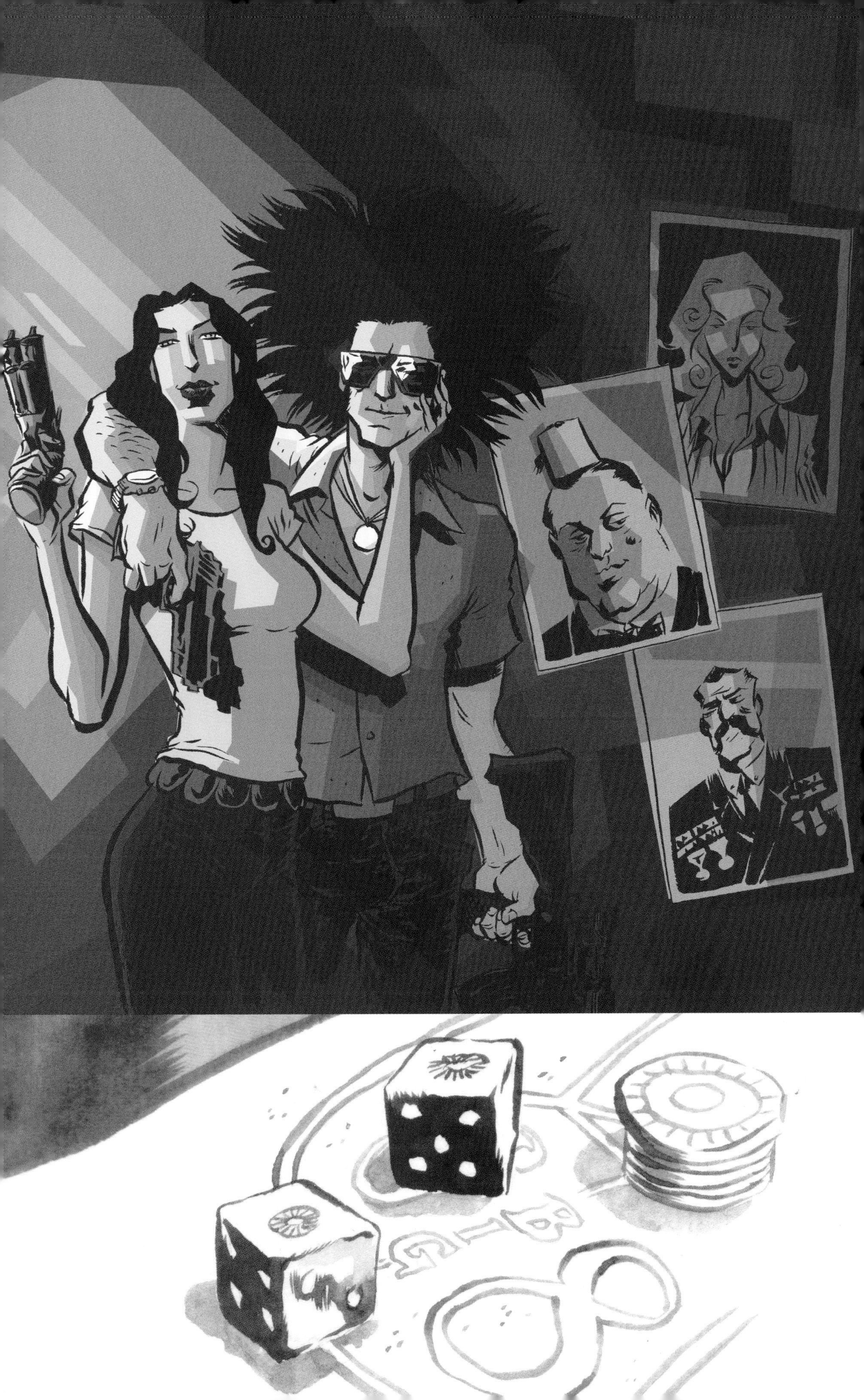

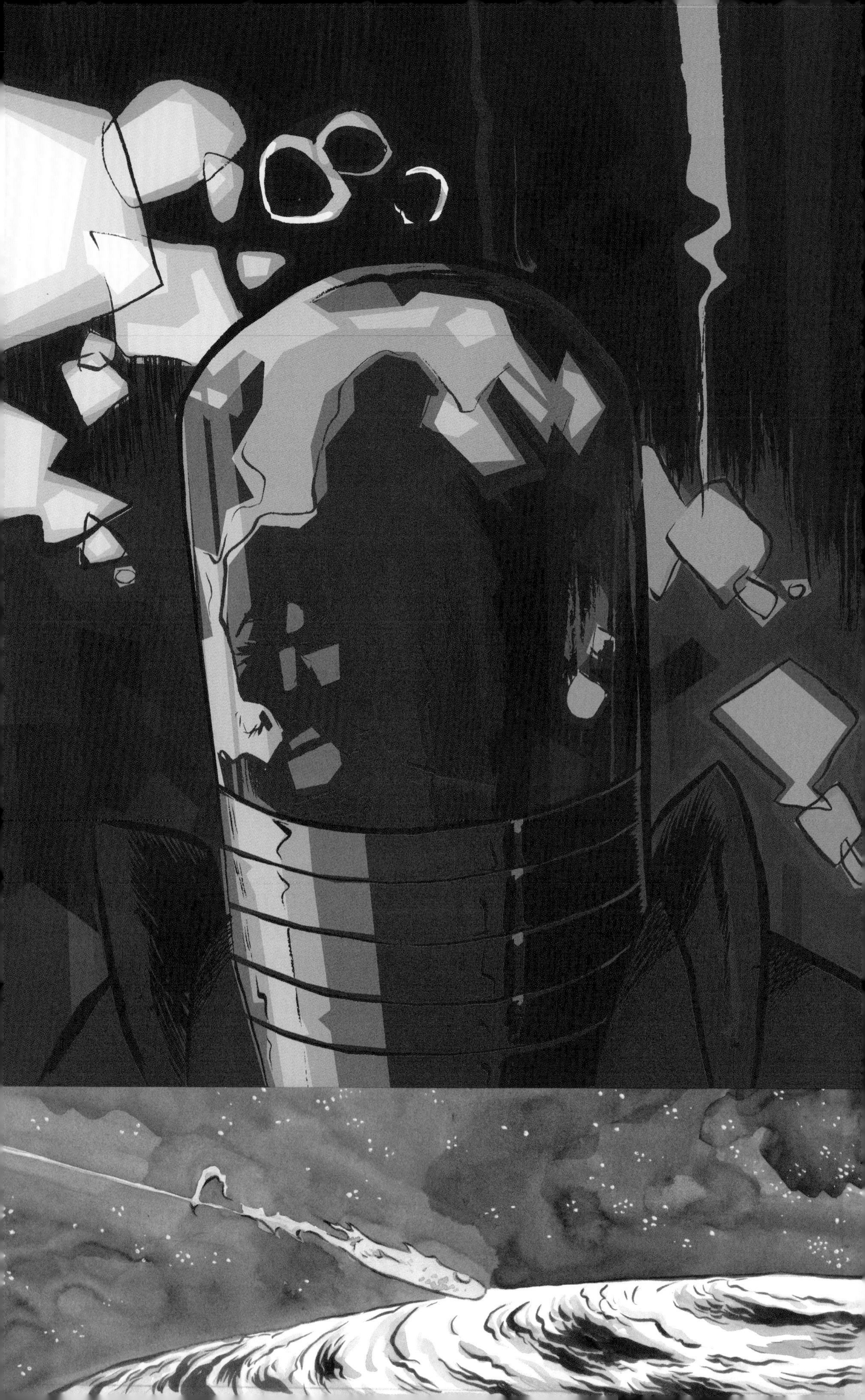

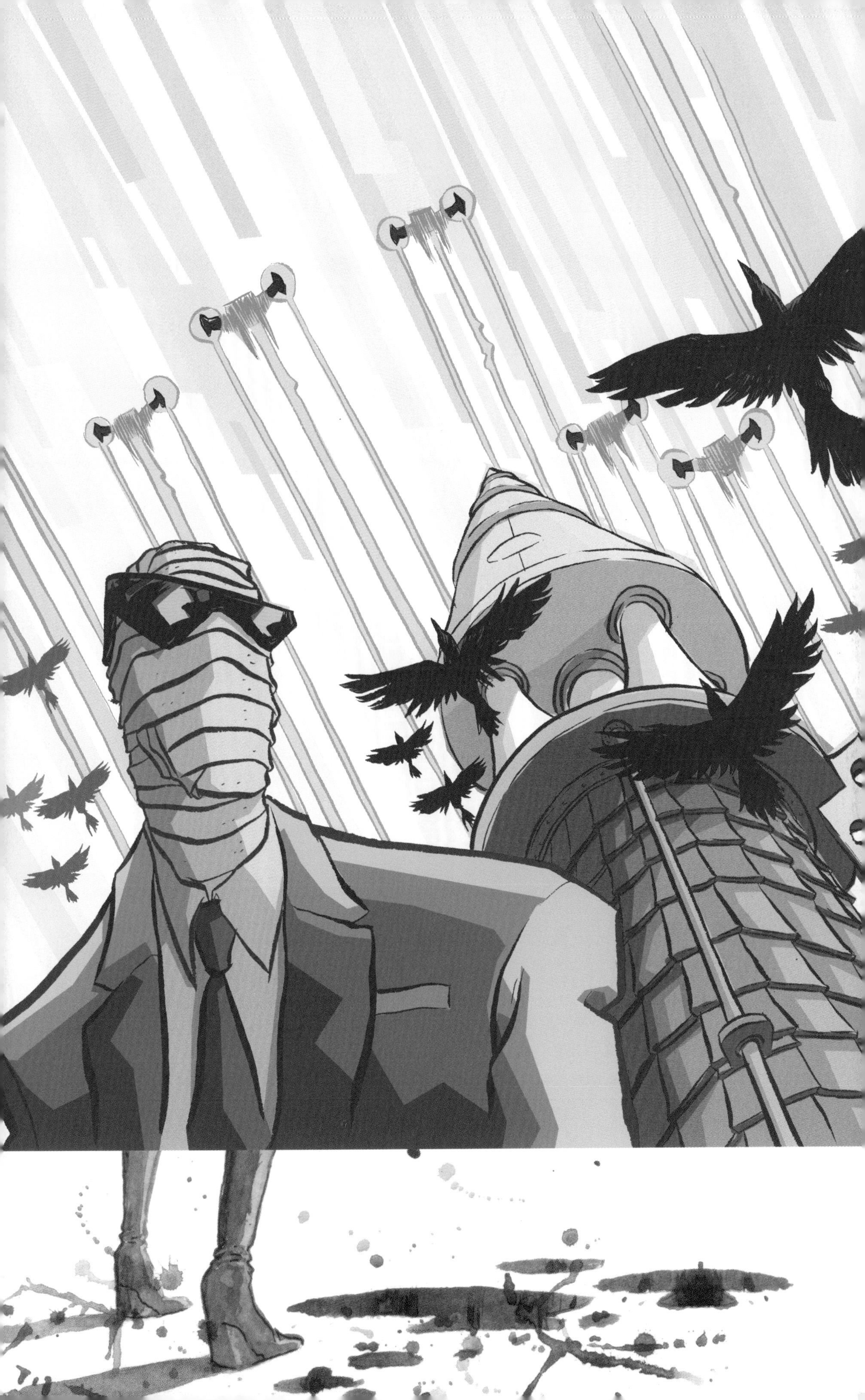

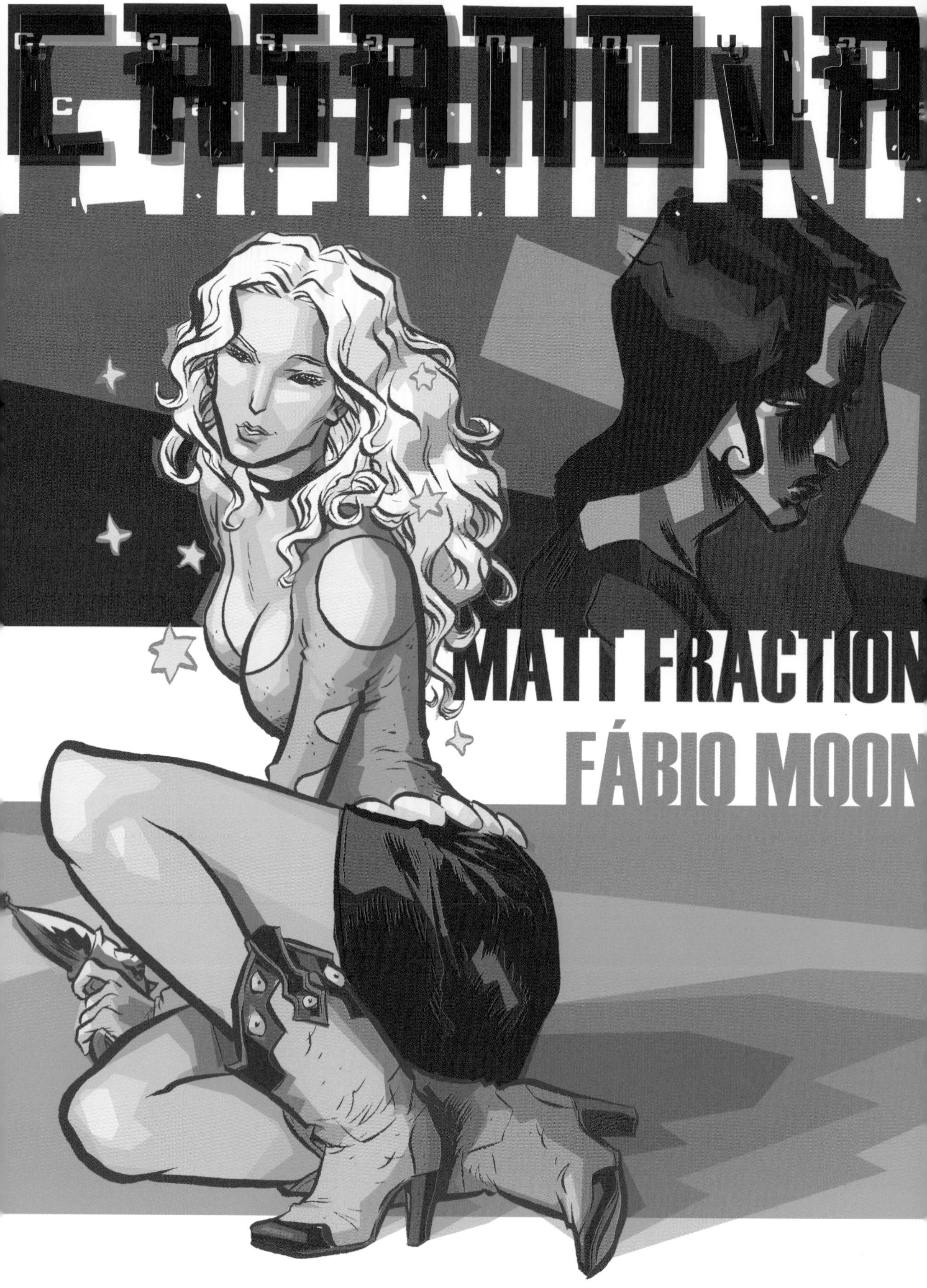
CASANOVA
MATT FRACTION
FÁBIO MOON

GULA

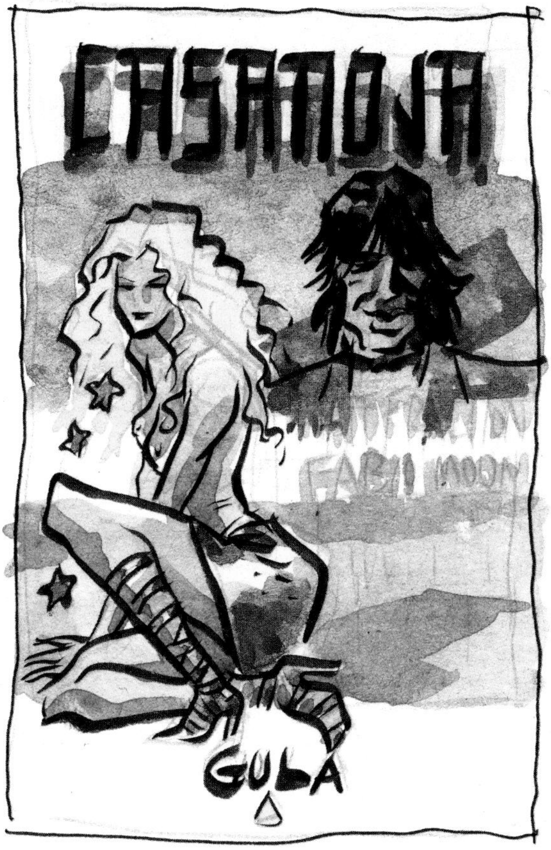
CASANOVA
GULA

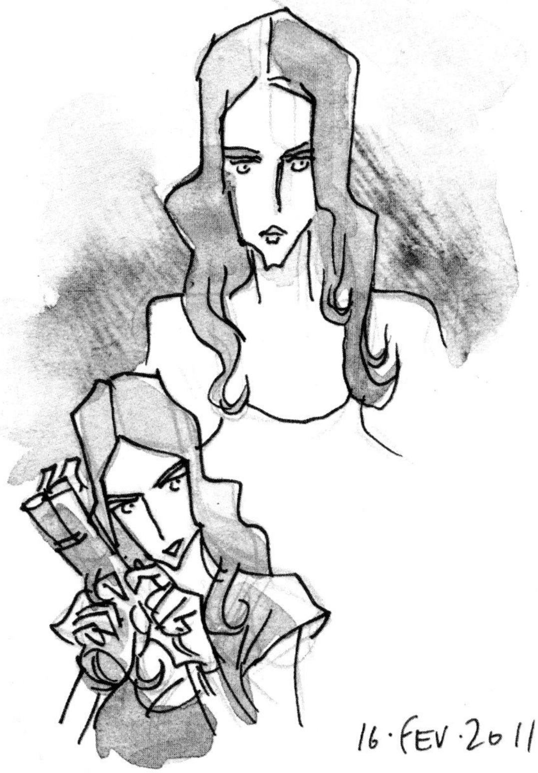
16·FEV·2011

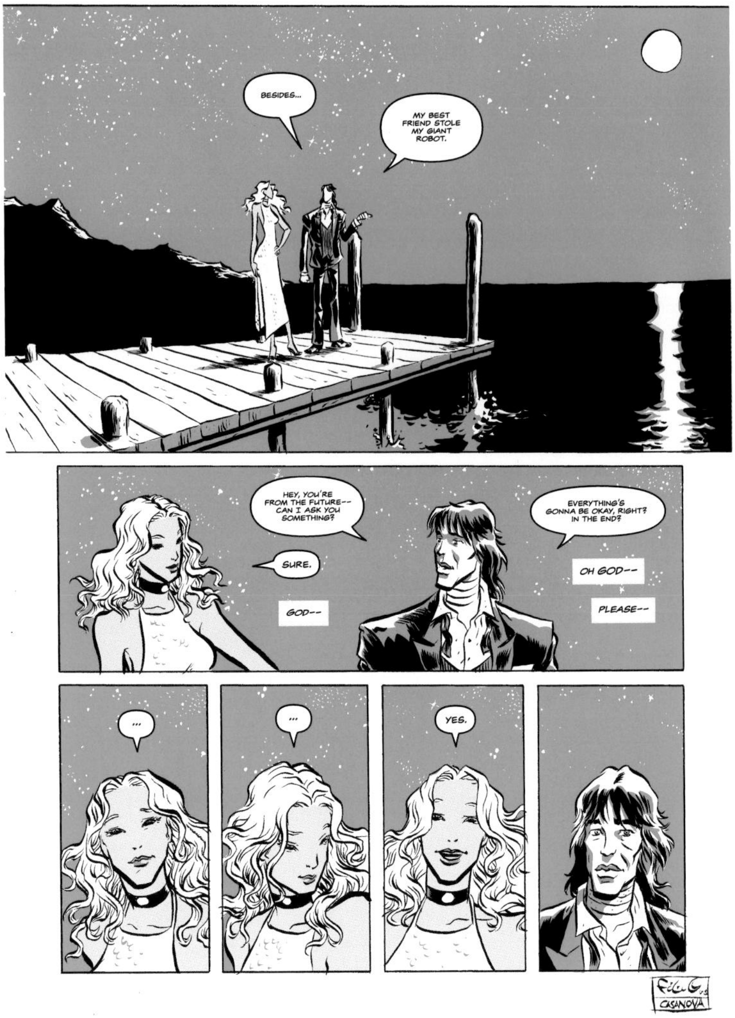
BESIDES...
MY BEST FRIEND STOLE MY GIANT ROBOT.
HEY, YOU'RE FROM THE FUTURE-- CAN I ASK YOU SOMETHING?
SURE.
GOD--
EVERYTHING'S GONNA BE OKAY, RIGHT? IN THE END?
OH GOD--
PLEASE--
...
...
YES.

The original ending to issue 14 (Image Comics), which was later changed for Gula issue 4 (Icon).

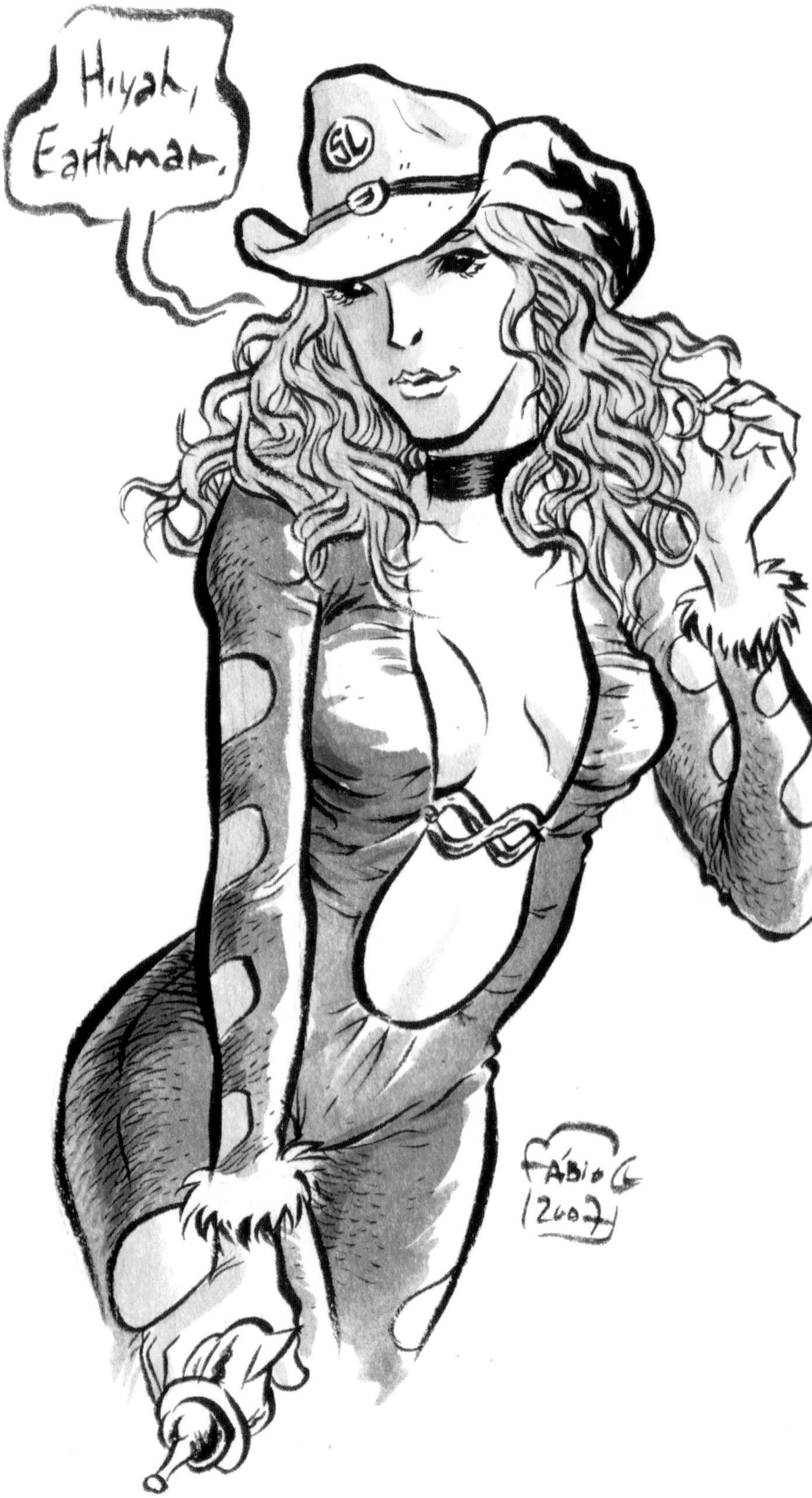
Hiyah, Earthman.

SASA LISI

This was my first drawing of Sasa Lisi, back in 2007 when I first got the script of this story. On the next page, the image and the initial sketch I did for the cover of this collection. Smaller, a loose watercolor sketch I did just for fun. Without a doubt, she's still my favorite character in the book because in her are all of this story's qualities: it's sexy and weird, it seems to come from a strange place you're not familiar with and, as you know more, it only gets sexier and weirder. She comes from another planet, and from the future no less, but still she could have come from Europe. From one of the many sexy erotic French bandes dessinées or Italian fumetti that inspired an entire generation of artists, to be more precise.

One of the greatest advantages of collaborating on a project is the unintentional mix of influences that end up inspiring the work. Matt's Sasa is Barbarella, both the comic book and the movie versions, mixed with all those cosmic Jim Starlin comics, and then mine was a super-model from fashion week, and she was my Druuna and she was my Leia.

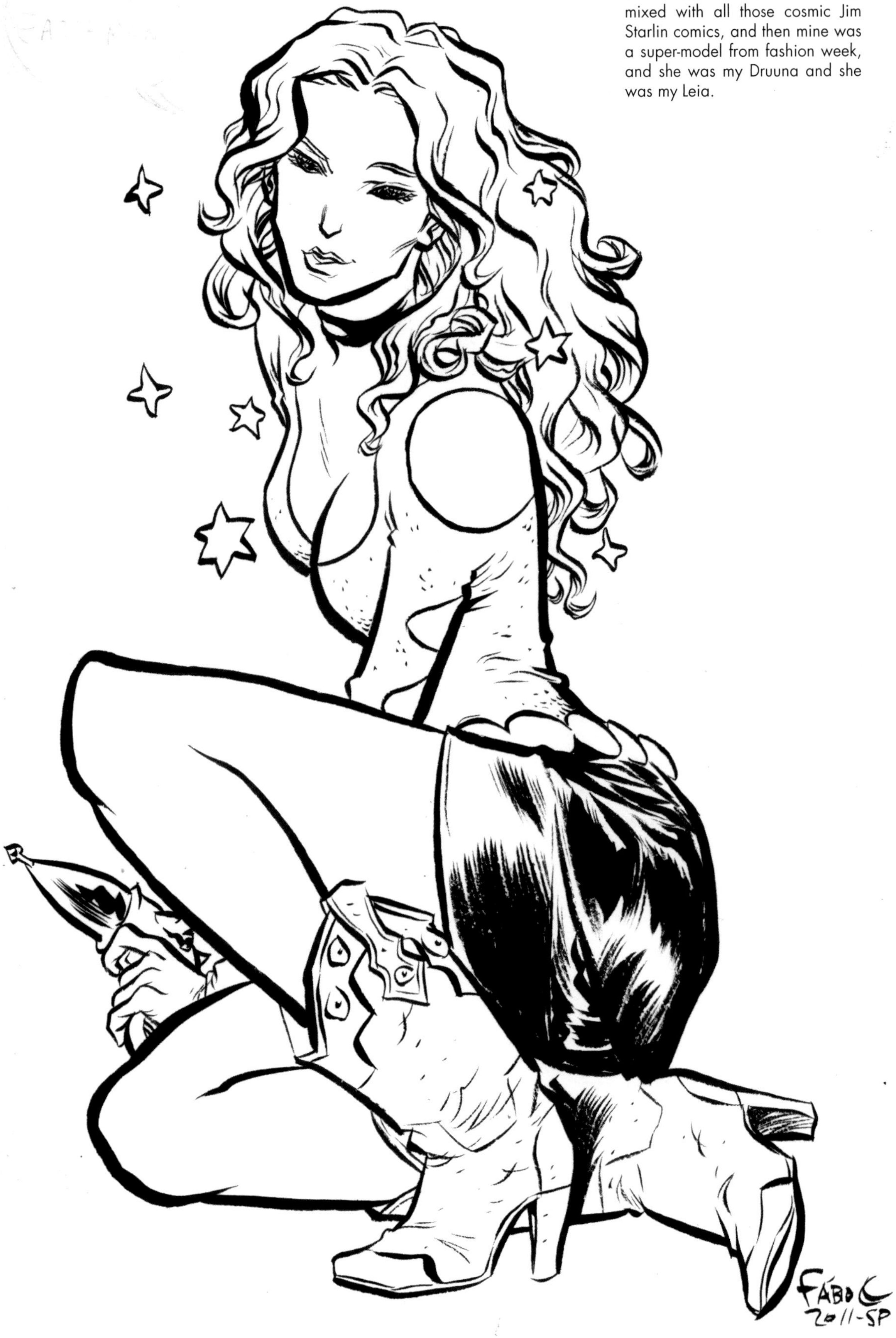
2011-SP

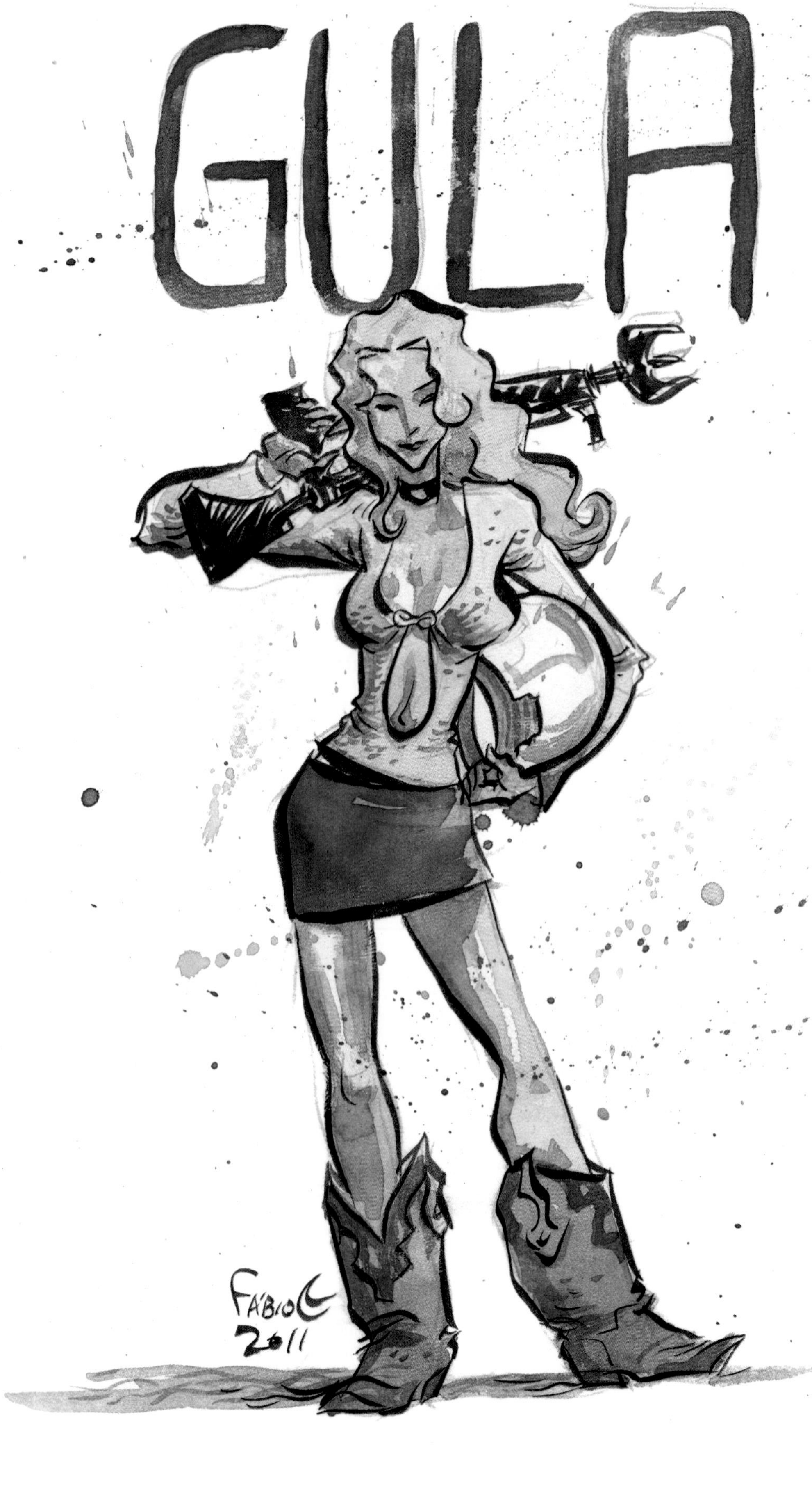
GULA
FÁBIO
2011

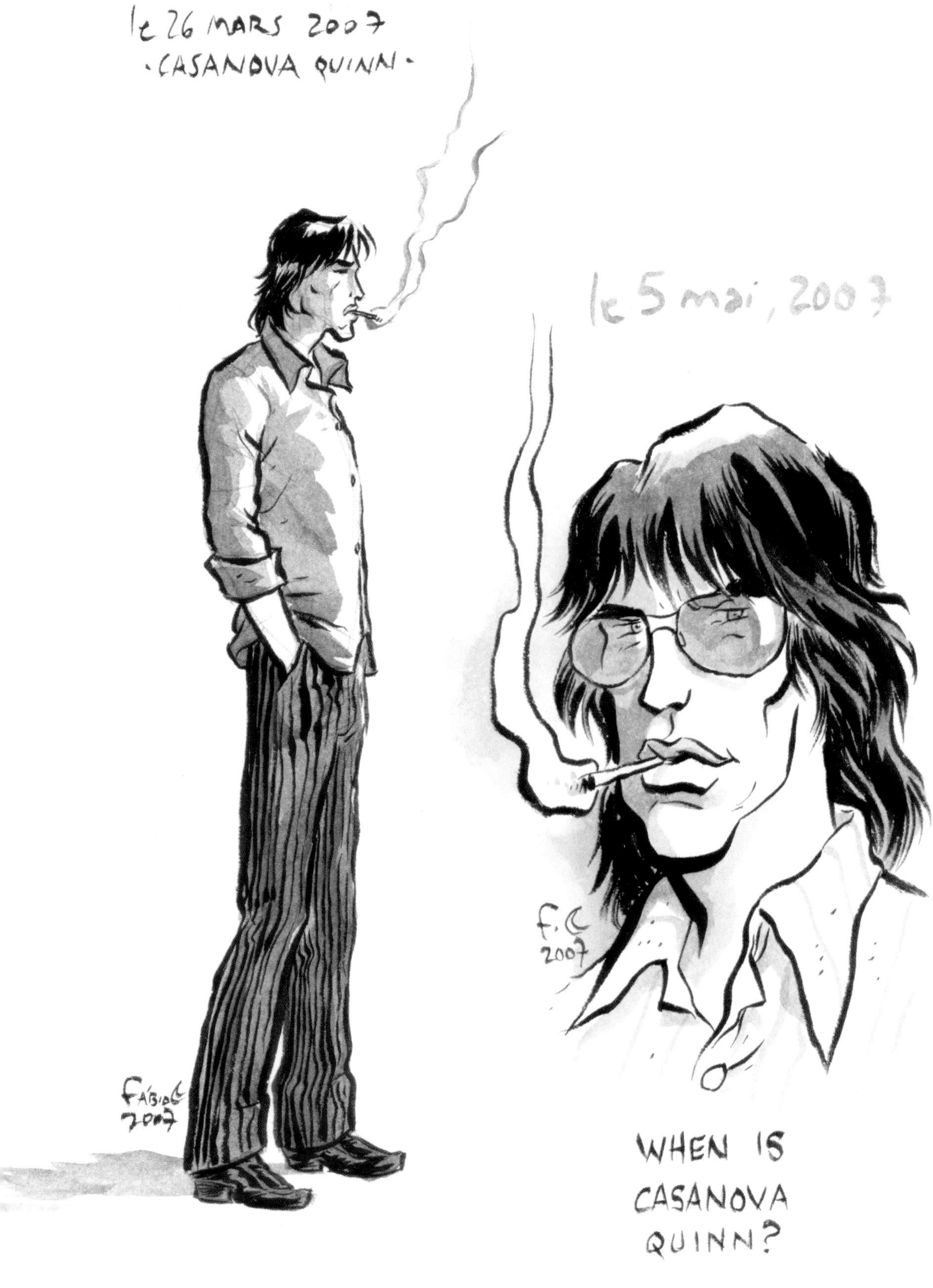
le 26 MARS 2007
·CASANOVA QUINN·
le 5 mai, 2007
FÁBIO C
2007
F.C
2007
WHEN IS
CASANOVA
QUINN?

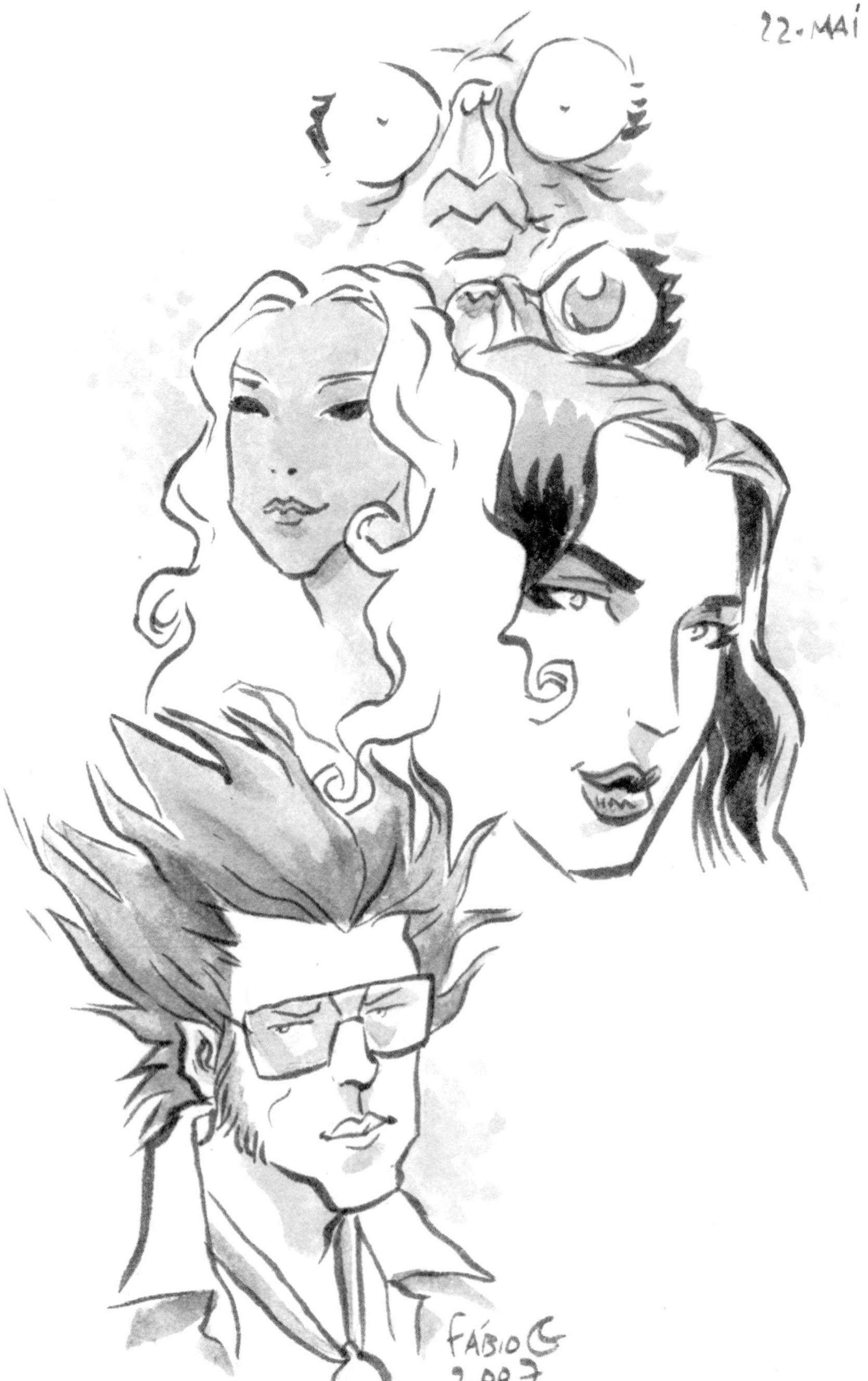
22-MAI
FÁBIO
2007

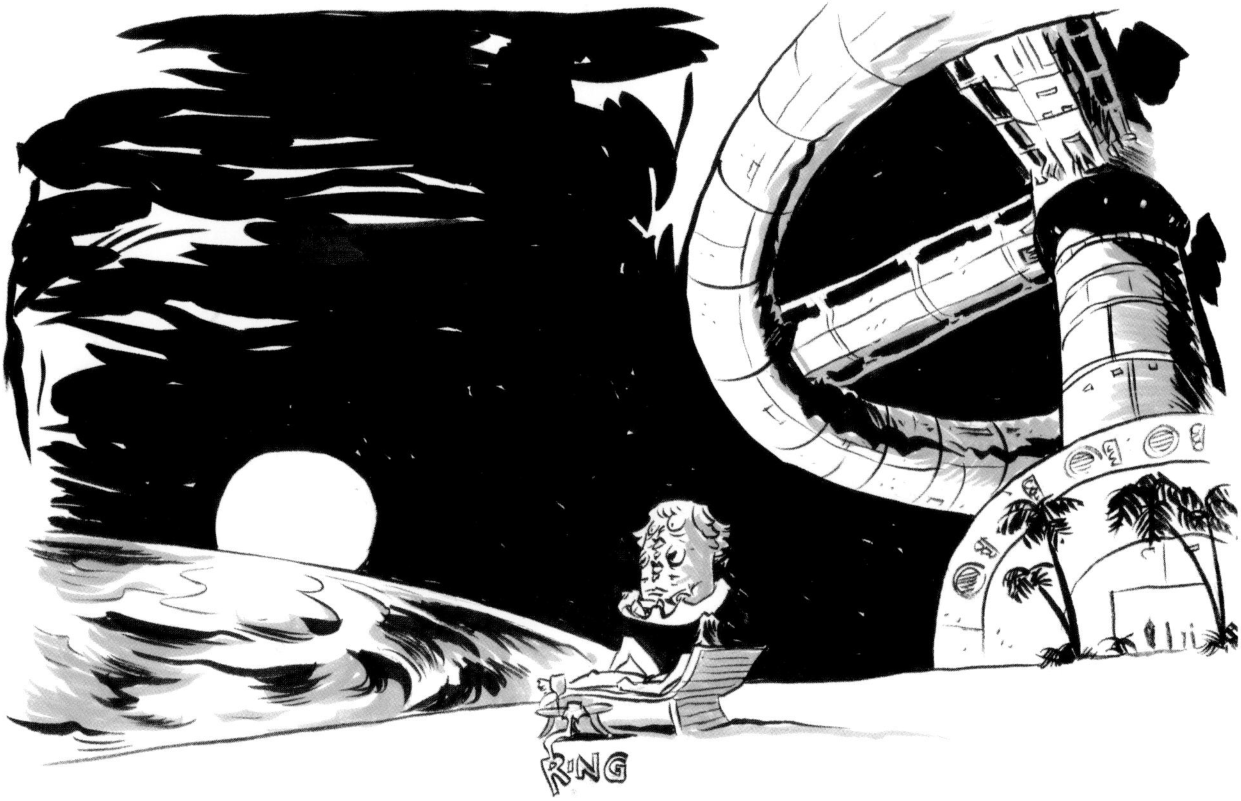
RING

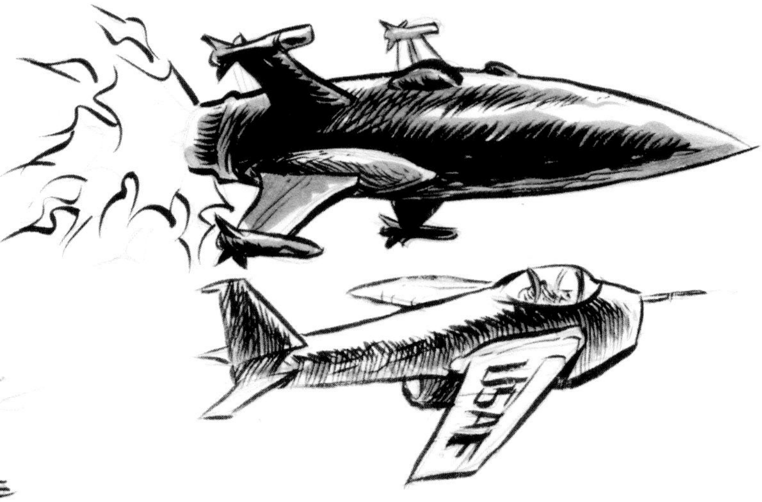
USAF

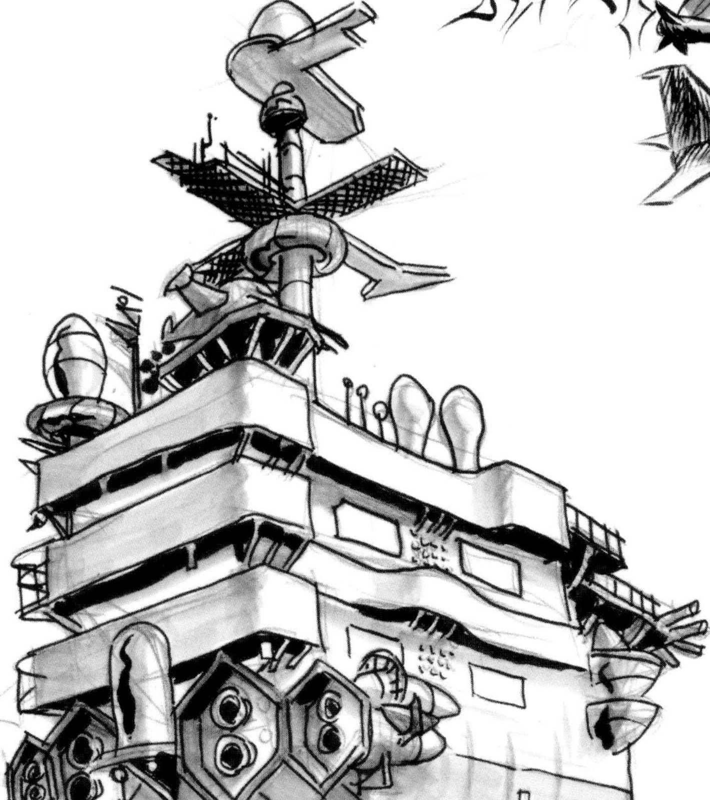

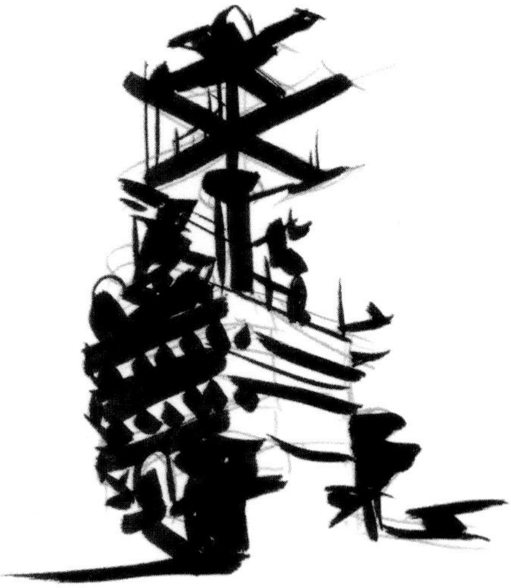

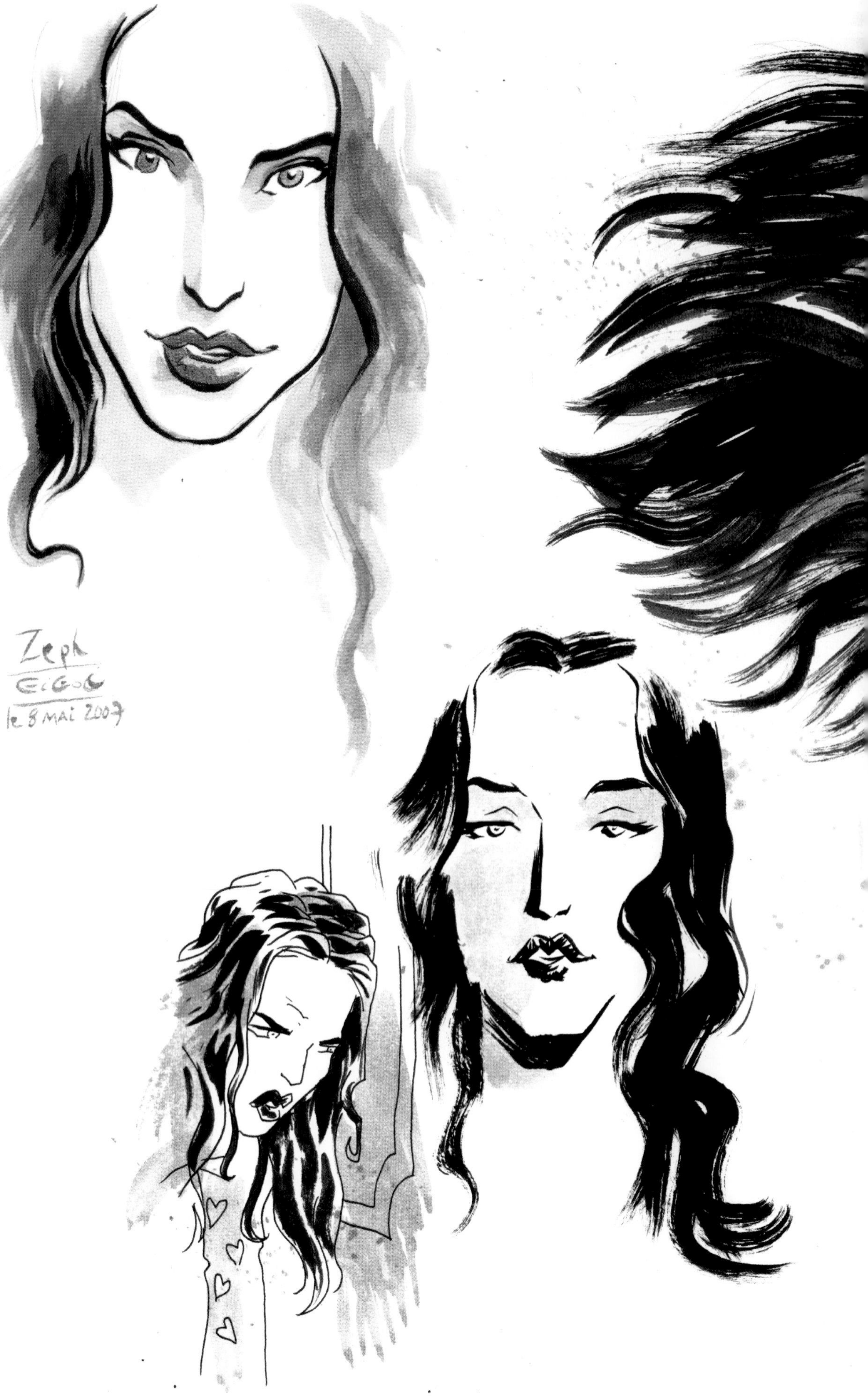
Zeph
le 8 MAI 2007

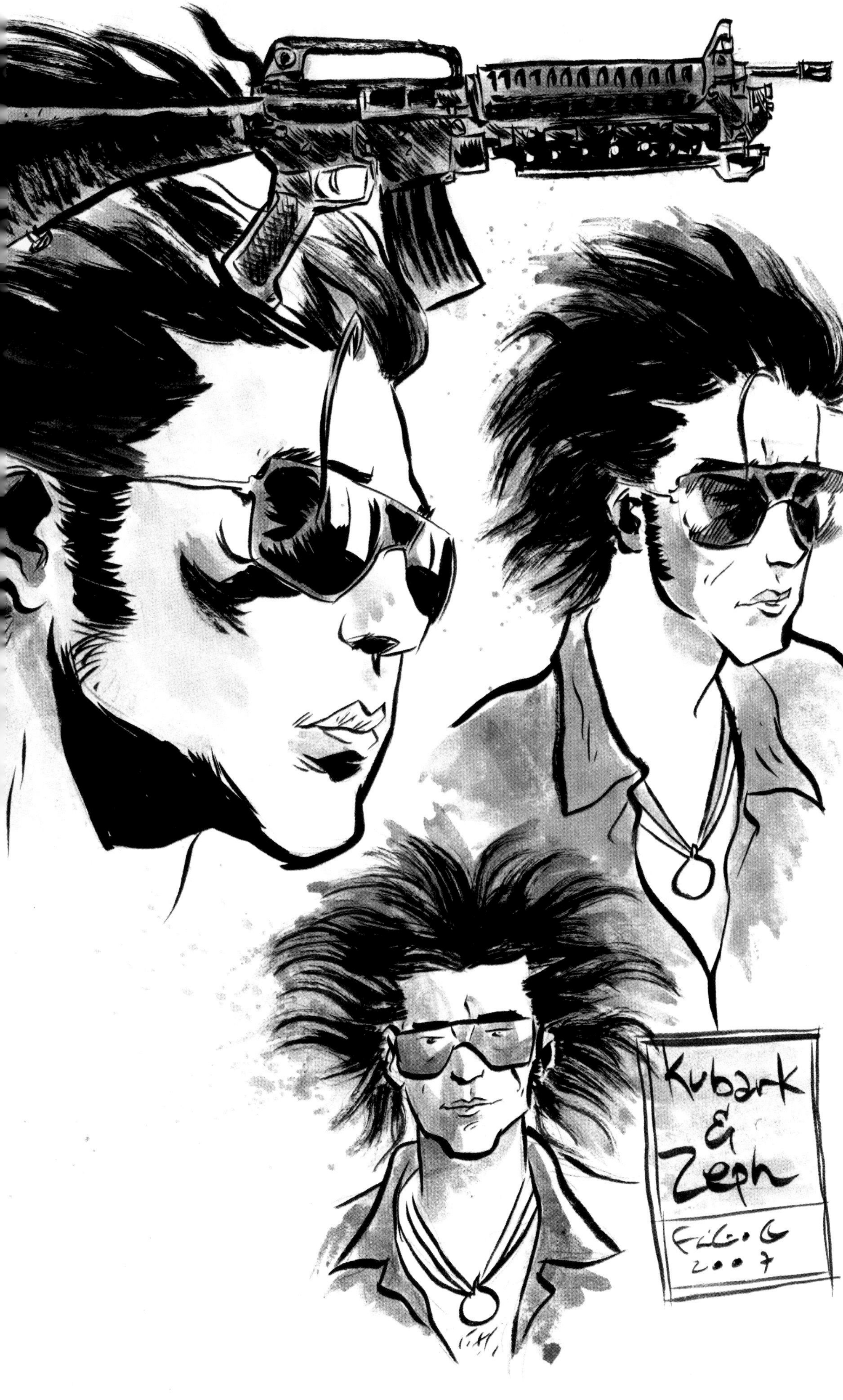
Kubark & Zeph
2007

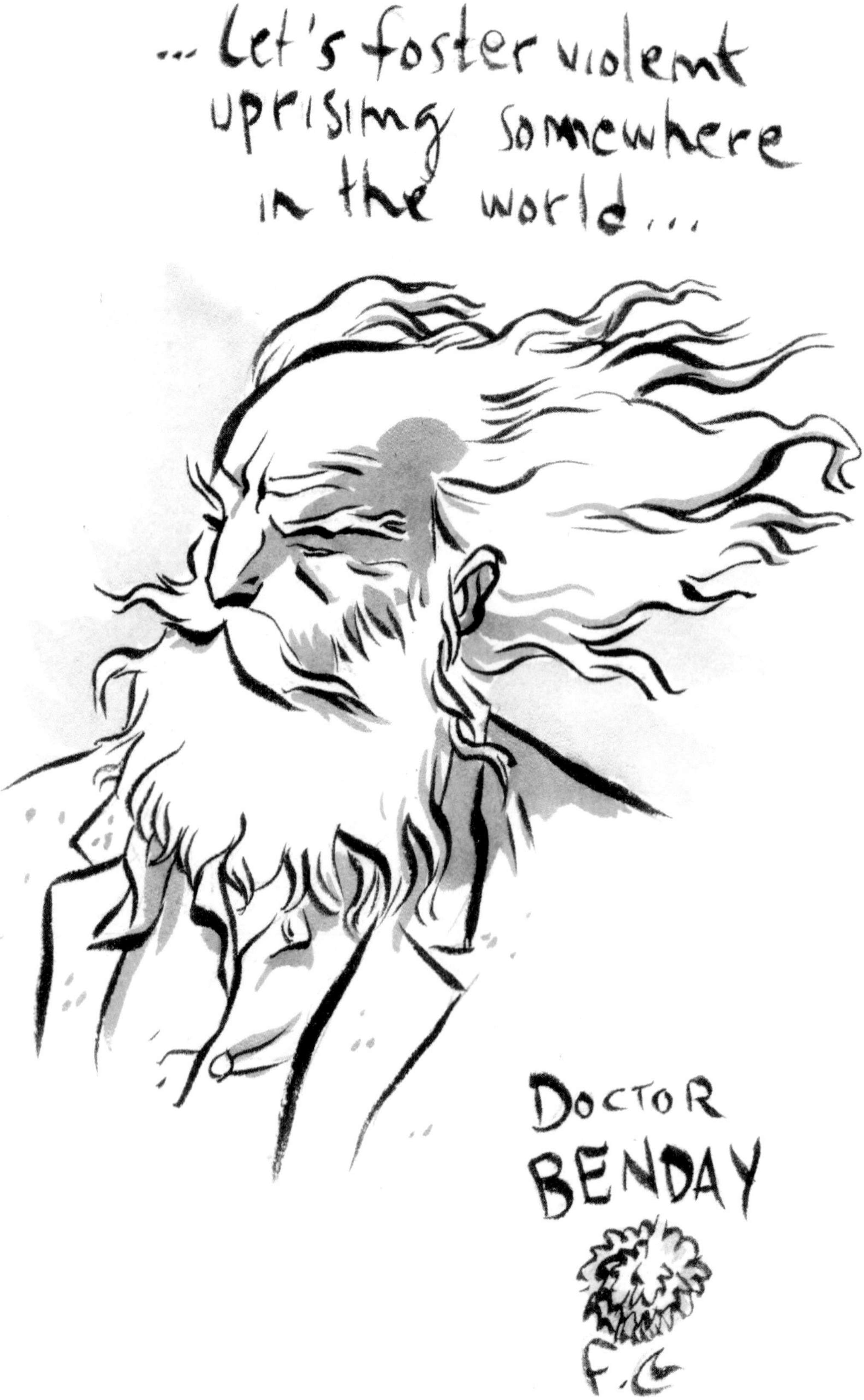

... let's foster violent uprising somewhere in the world ...
DOCTOR BENDAY
F.C
2007

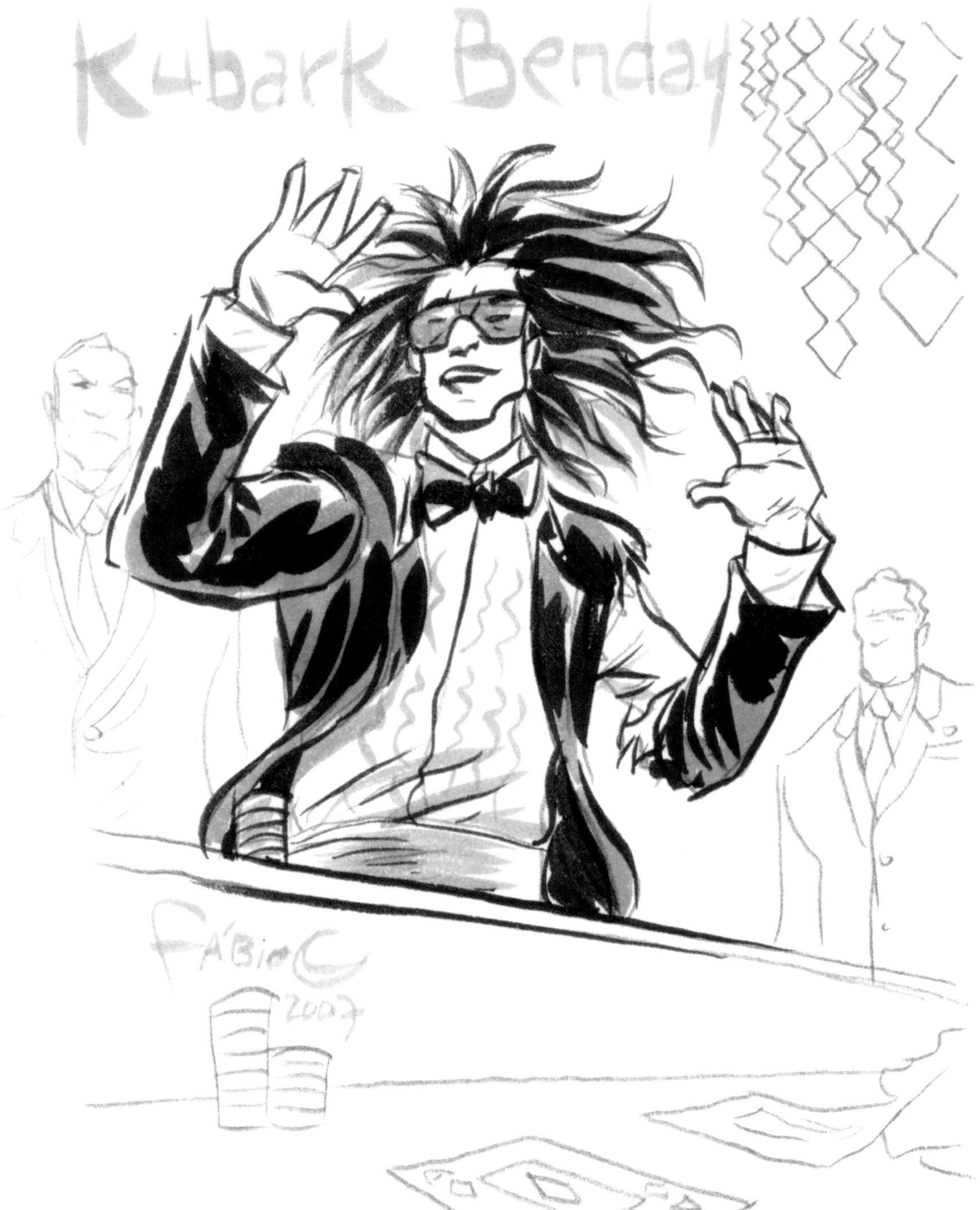
Kubark Benday
FÁBIO C
2007

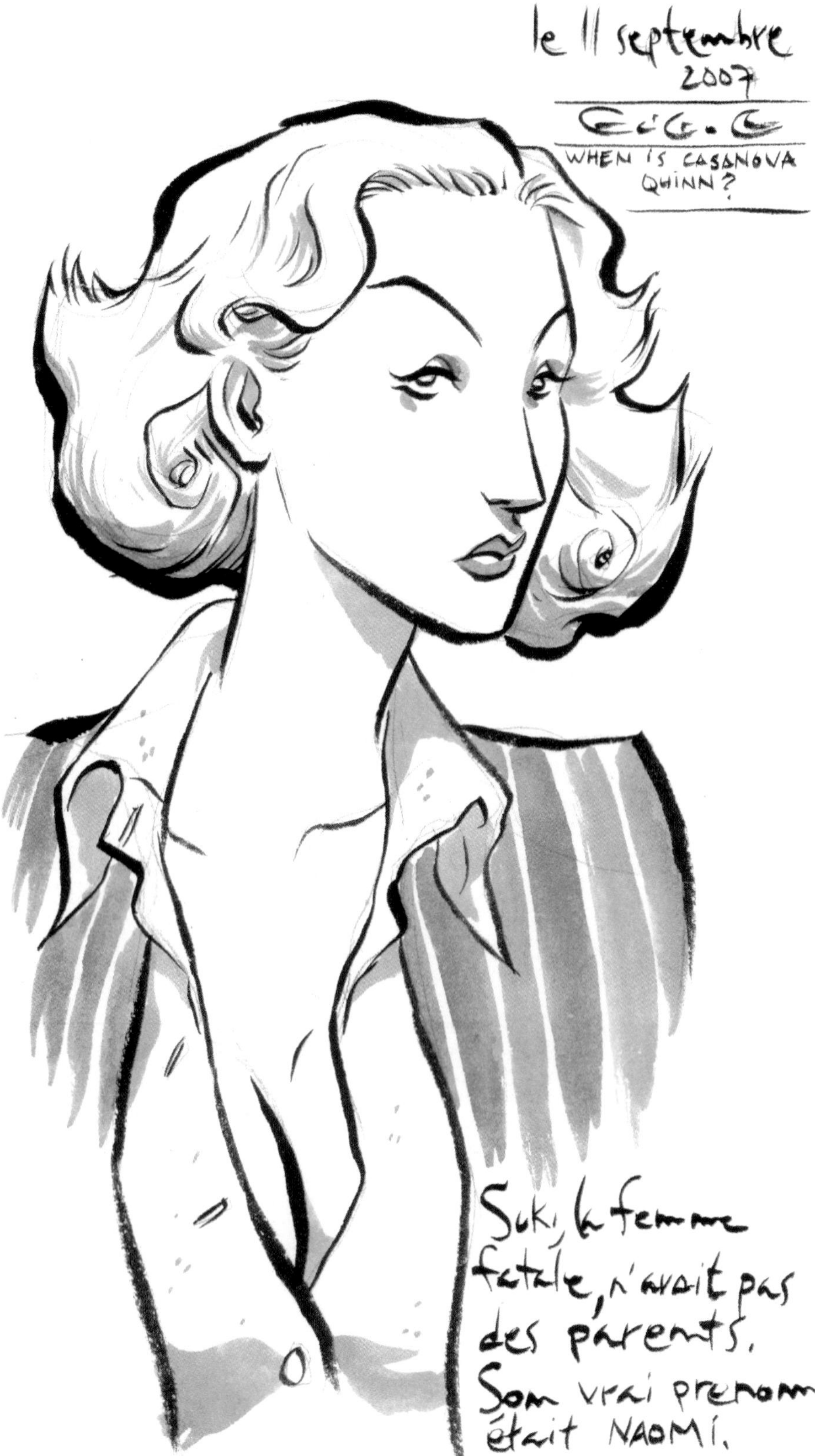
le 11 septembre
2007
WHEN IS CASANOVA
QUINN?
Suki, la femme
fatale, n'avait pas
des parents.
Son vrai prenom
était NAOMI.

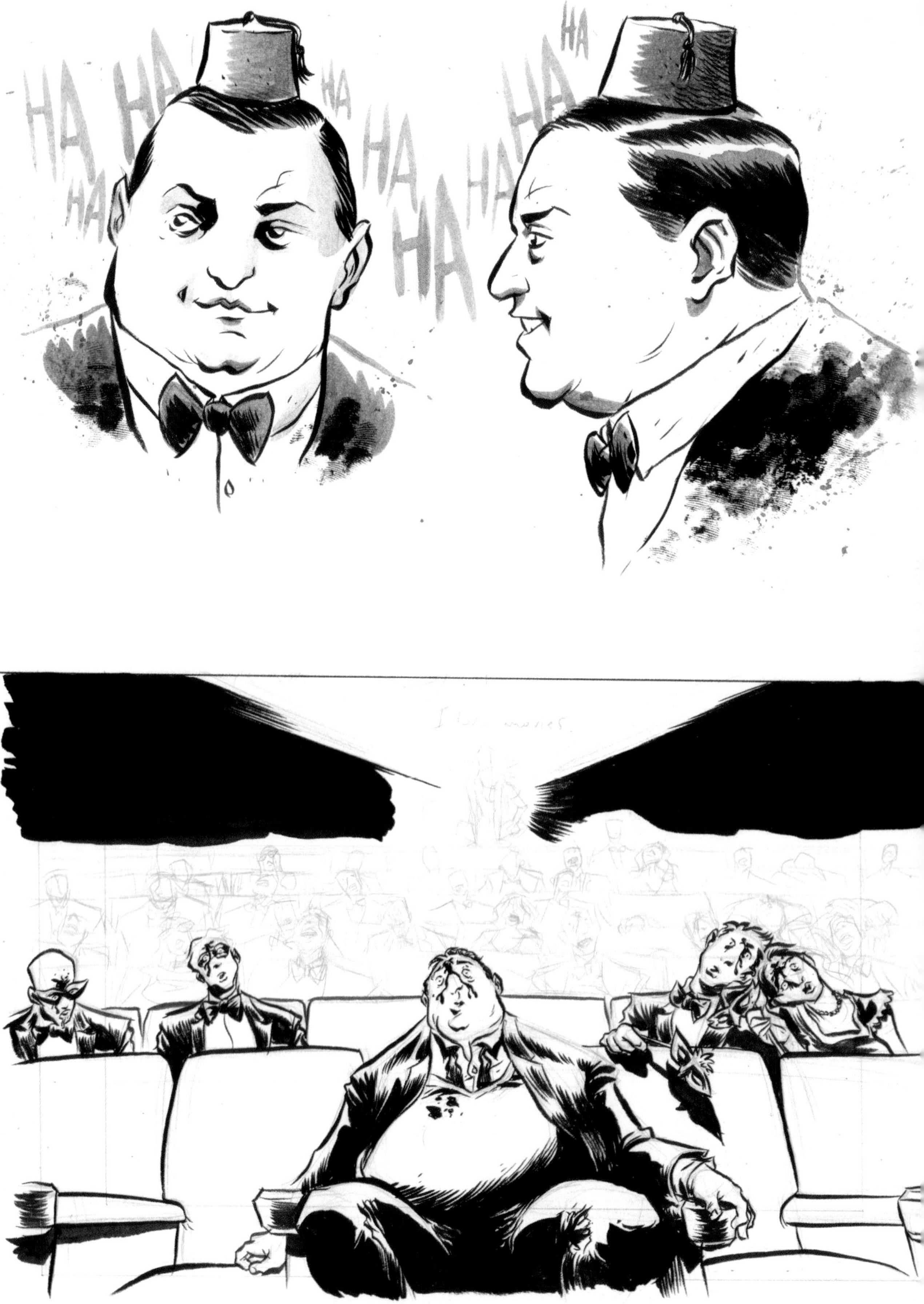
HA
HA
HA
HA
HA
HA
HA
HA
HA
HA

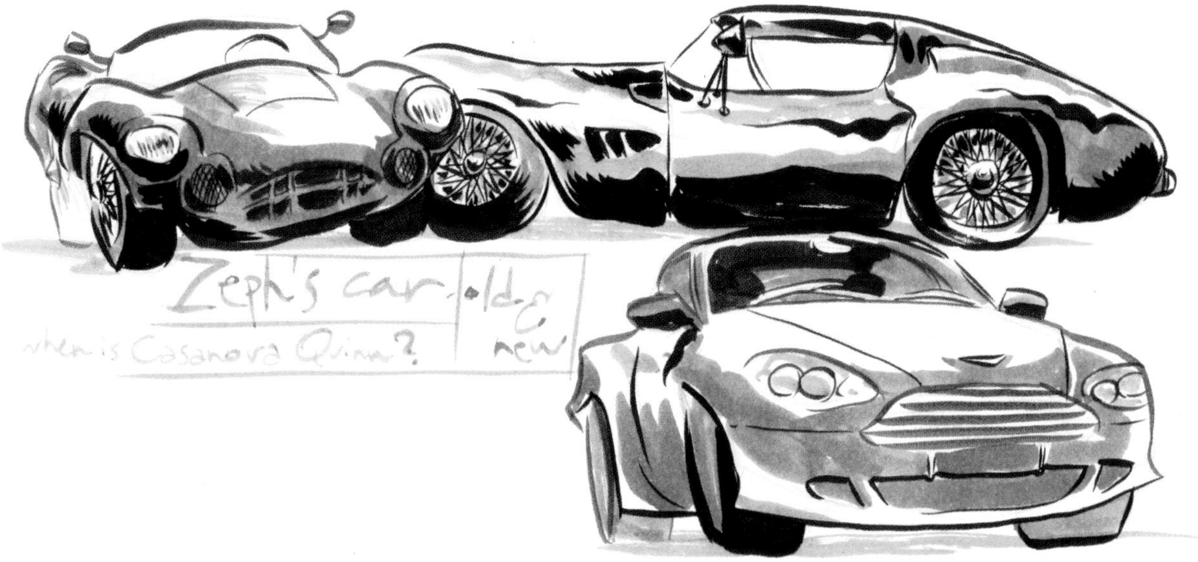
Zeph's car
old & new
when is Casanova Quinn?

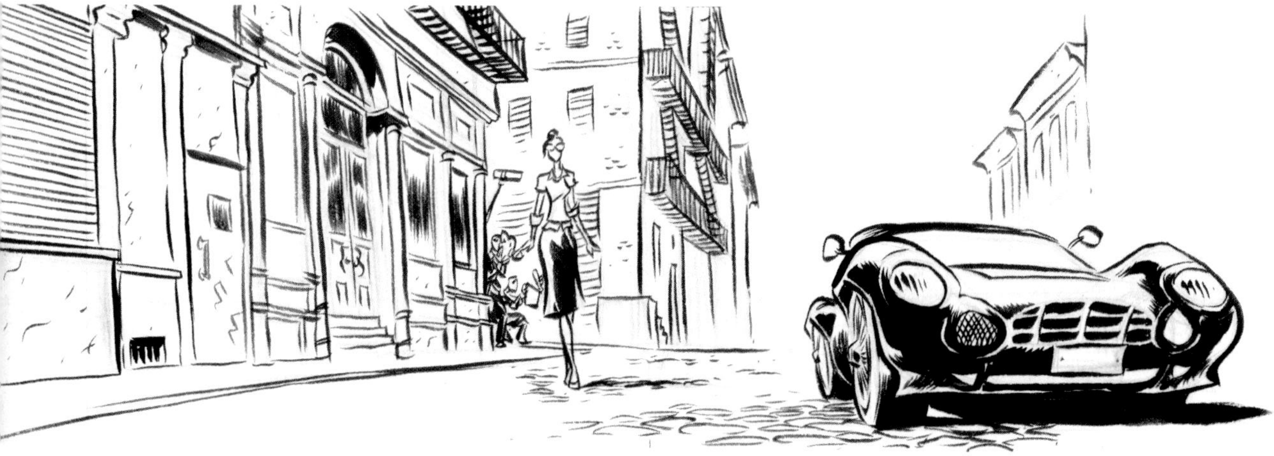

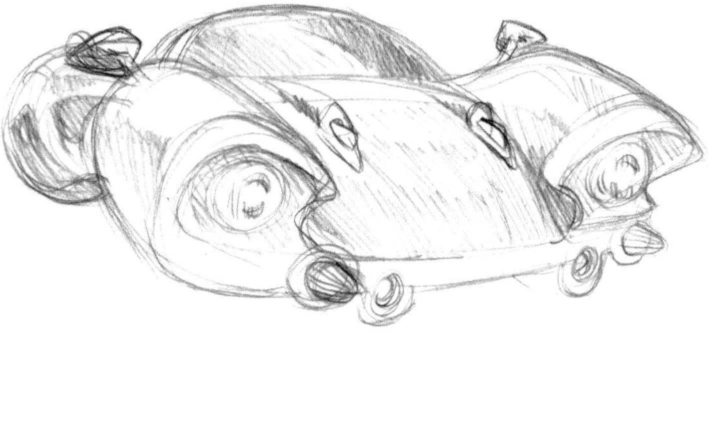

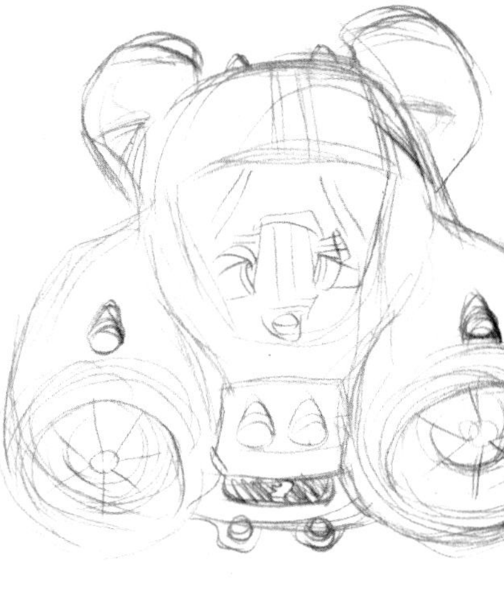

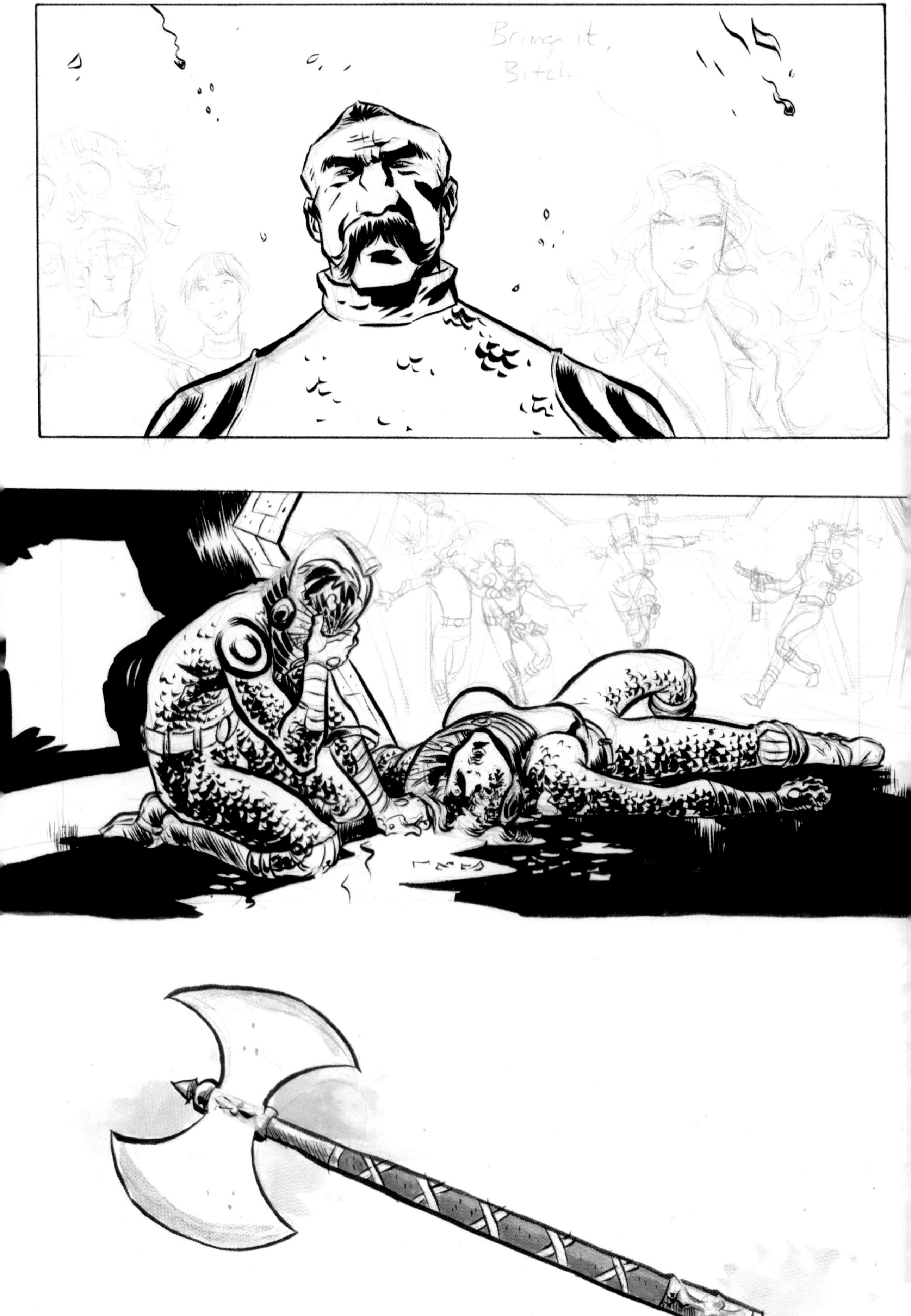
Bring it, Bitch.

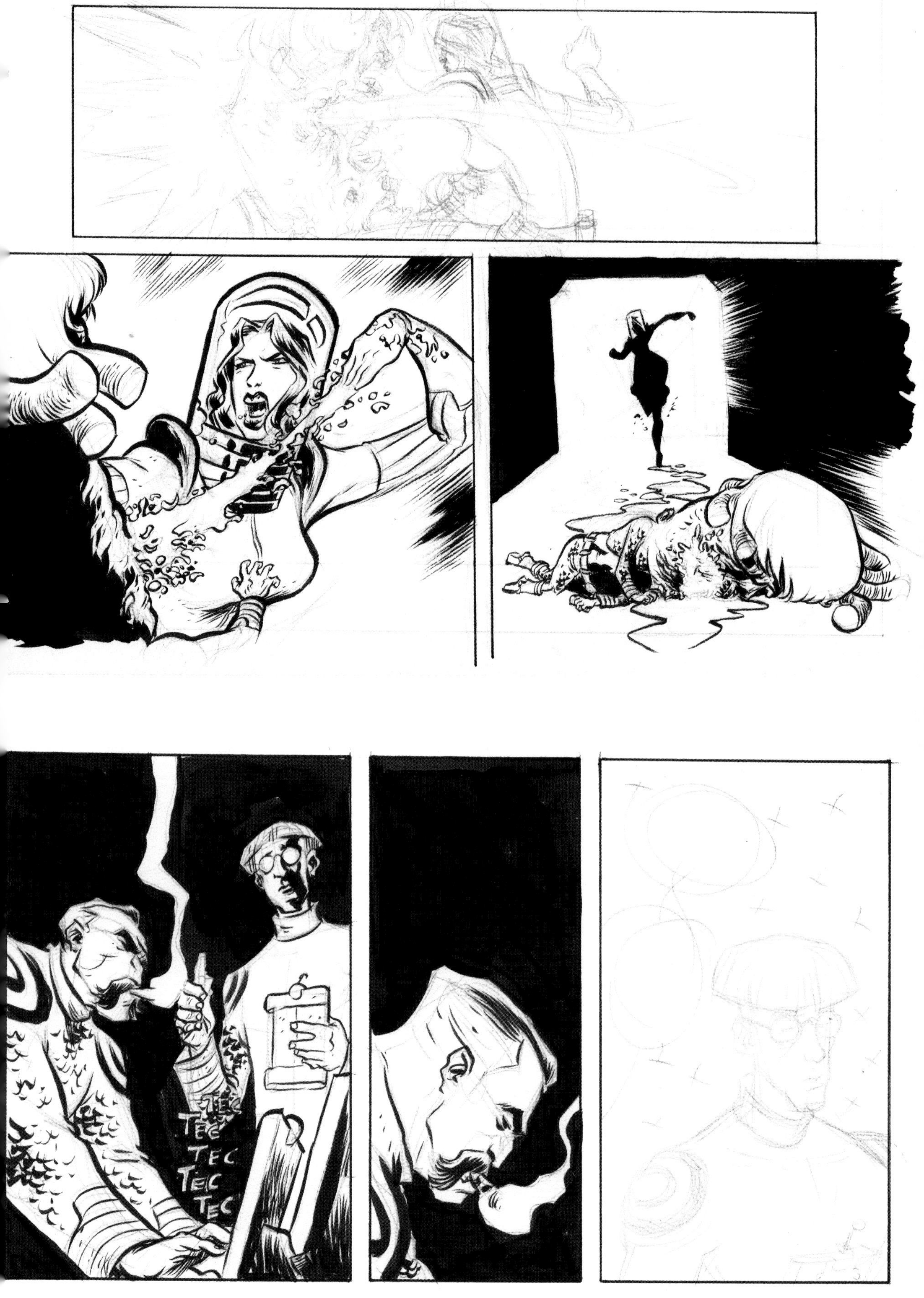
TEC
TEC
TEC
TEC
TEC

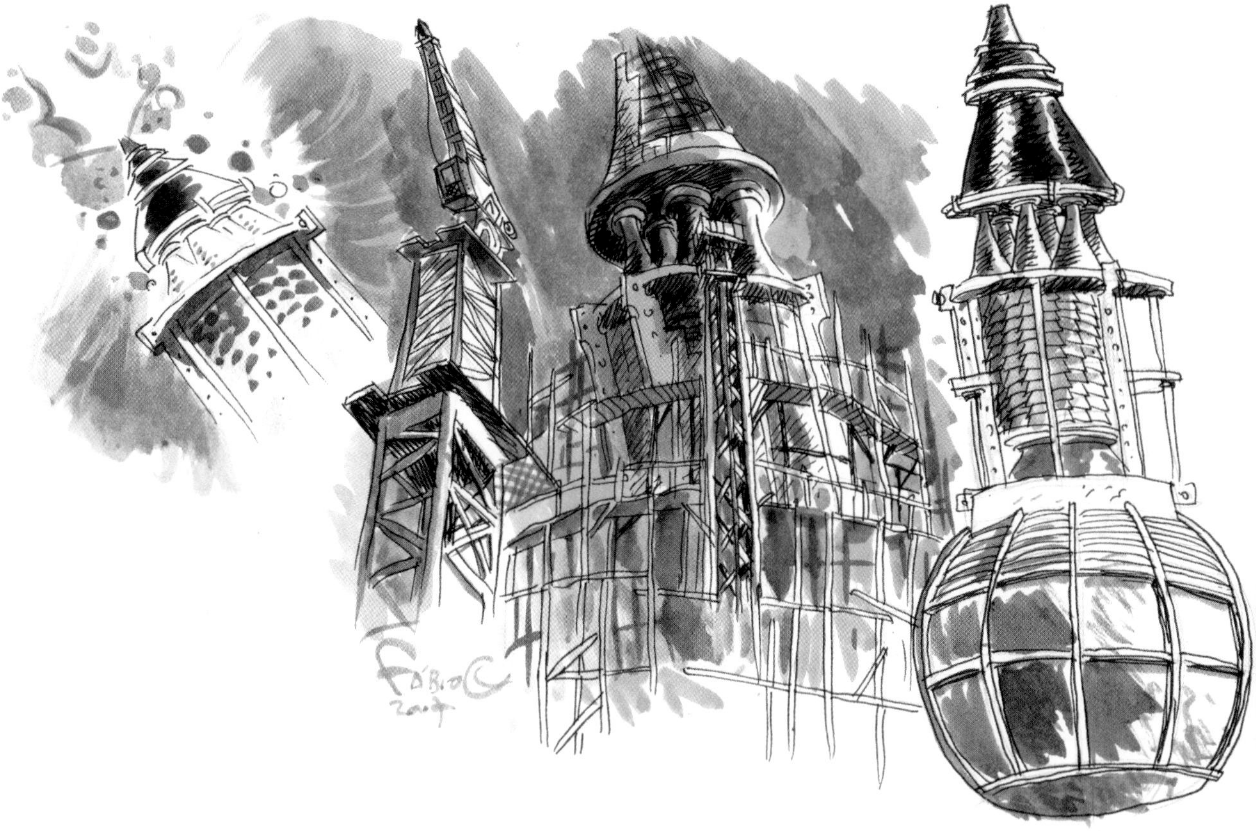

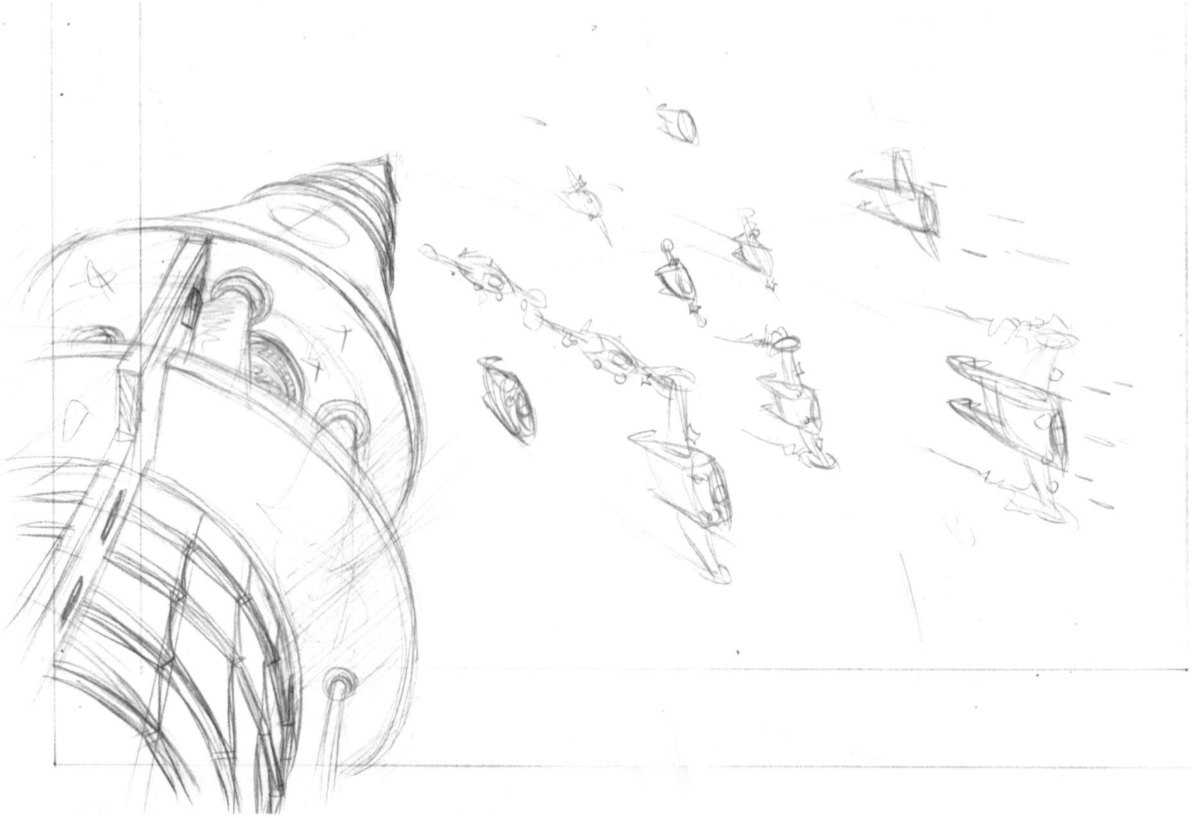

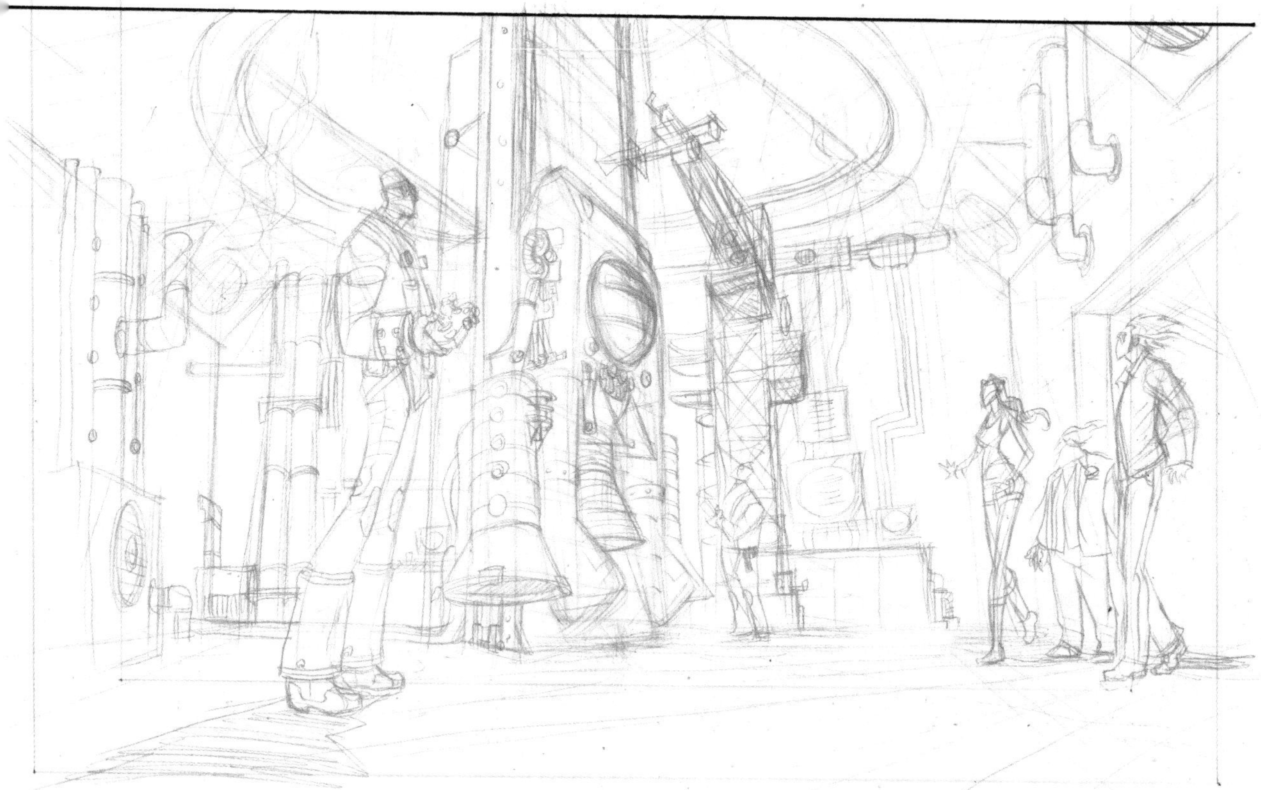

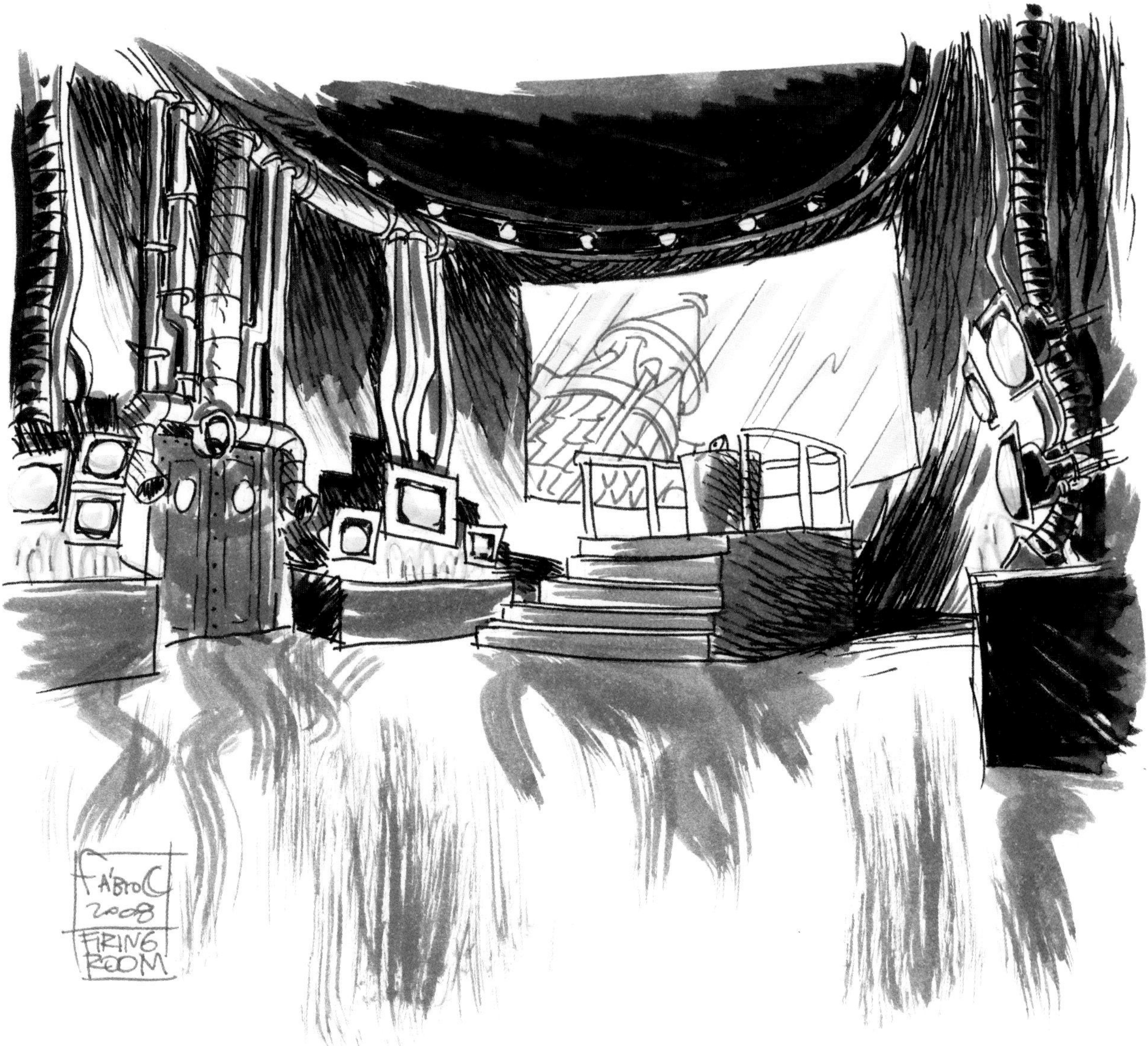
FÁBIO C
2008
FIRING ROOM

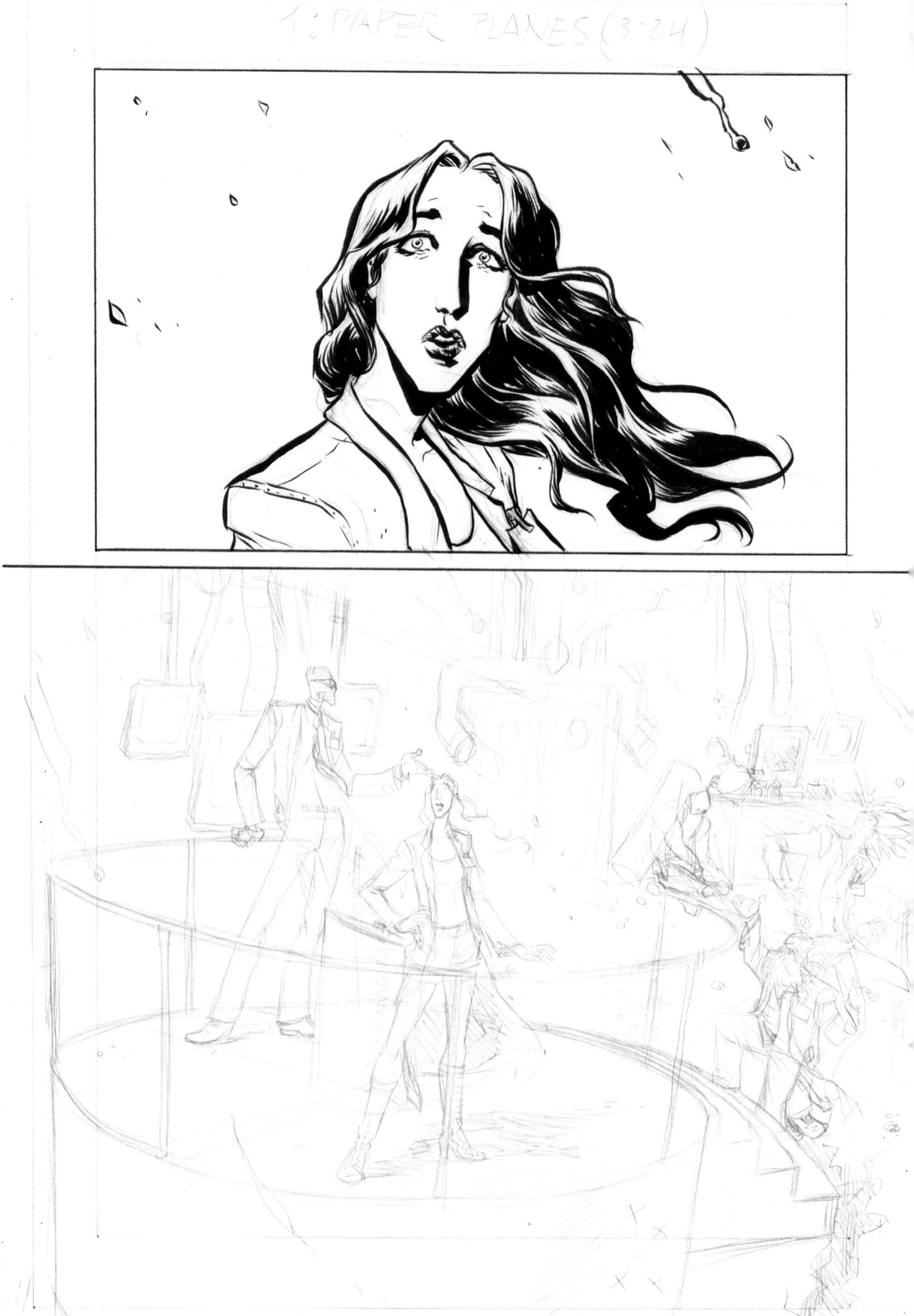
1: PAPER PLANES (3·24)

TEAM CASANOVA HONOR ROLL

Alejandro ARBONA Editor, CASANOVA: LUXURIA, GULA, AVARITIA (Icon Comics reprints and collections, 2010-2012)

Érico ASSIS Translation: CASANOVA: LUXURIA, GULA (Panini Comics, Brazil edition, 2012, 2014)

Estudio FENIX Design Group, CASANOVA: LUJURIA (Panini Comics Spain edition, 2011)

Drew GILL Designer, CASANOVA: LUXURIA (Image Comics collections, 2008, 2014)

Jennifer GRÜNWALD Designer, LUXURIA, GULA, AVARITIA (Icon Comics reprints and collections, 2010-2012), spare Russian bits, salvage and recovery

Gina KAUFMANN French bits and obscenities, CASANOVA: LUXURIA (Image Comics edition, 2006-2007)

Sean KONOT Letterer, CASANOVA: LUXURIA (Image Comics edition, 2006-2007)

Laurenn McCUBBIN Designer, CASANOVA: LUXURIA issues, hardcover & softcover (Image Comics edition)

Willem MEERLOO Designer, CASANOVA: LUXURIA (Urban Comics France edition, 2012)

Harris MILLER III Team CASANOVA representation, 2007-2013

Ben RADATZ E.M.P.I.R.E., W.A.S.T.E., and X.S.M. logo design (2006)

Marco RICOMPENSA Supervision, CASANOVA: LUXURIA, GULA, AVARITIA (Panini Comics Italy editions, 2011-2013)

Benjamin RIVIÉRE Translation, CASANOVA: LUXURIA (Urban Comics France edition, 2012)

Raúl SASTRE Translation, CASANOVA: LUJURIA (Panini Comics Spain edition, 2011)

Rosie SHARPE Backmatter transcription, general bedlam (2014)

Andrea TOSCANI Translation, CASANOVA: LUXURIA, GULA, AVARITIA (Panini Comics Italy editions, 2011-2013)

Lucia TRUCCONE Letterer, LUXURIA, GULA, AVARITIA (Panini Comics Italy editions, 2011-2013)

Steve WACKER Senior Editor, LUXURIA, GULA, AVARITIA (Icon Comics reprints and collections, 2010-2012)

Eric STEPHENSON Patron Saint

Warren ELLIS Patron Sinner

Matt Fraction writes comic books out in the woods and lives with his wife, the writer Kelly Sue Deconnick, his two children, a dog, a cat, a bearded dragon, and a yard full of coyotes and stags. Surely there is a metaphor there. He won the first-ever PEN USA Literary Award for Graphic Novels; he, or comics he's a part of, have won Eisners, Harveys, and Eagles, which are like the Oscars, Emmys, and Golden Globes of comic books and all seem about as likely. He's a *New York Times*-best-selling donkus of comics like *Sex Criminals* (winner of the 2014 Will Eisner Award for Best New Series, the 2014 Harvey Award for Best New Series, and named *TIME Magazine*'s Best Comic of 2013), *Satellite Sam*, *ODY-C*, *Hawkeye* (winner of the 2014 Will Eisner Award for Best Single Issue), *The Invincible Iron Man*, *The Mighty Thor*, *The Uncanny X-Men*, *Fantastic Four*, And, Oh, Lordy, So Many More. Also, for *Sex Criminals*, he was awarded a free nipple piercing.

Fábio Moon is Gabriel Bá's Eisner Award-winning evil twin whose world domination plans include creating great comics, be it with great authors like Joss Whedon and Mike Mignola (and Matt, of course), or be it with his twin brother Bá doing their weird twinnery in such books as *Daytripper* and *De:TALES*. He lives in São Paulo, likes his coffee black, strong, with no sugar, and divides his days at times thinking he works too much, and at times thinking he could do more. He shaves more often than not—his twin has claimed the bearded look for himself—but sometimes he rebels and looks like a hobo. In another dimension, he works wearing a suit and tie every day, but in ours he's still looking for a portal between the two, dressed as a regular cartoonist.

PA-ZOW!